The Birthday Party Business

How to Make A Living as A Children's Entertainer

Bruce Fife • Hal Diamond • Steve Kissell
Robin Vogel • Mary Lostak • Bob Conrad • Marcela Murad

PICCADILLY BOOKS, LTD
COLORADO SPRINGS, COLORADO

Cover design by Michael Donahue
Photos of storyteller on cover and page 14 by Tom Kimmell

Piccadilly Books, Ltd.
P.O. Box 25203
Colorado Springs, CO 80936

International sales and inquires contact:
 EPS
 20 Park Drive
 Romford Essex RM1 4LH, UK
or
 EPS
 P.O. Box 1344
 Studio City, CA 91614, USA

Library of Congress Cataloging-in-Publication Data

The birthday party business / Bruce Fife . . . [et al.].
        p.   cm.
   Includes bibliographical references and index.
   ISBN 0-941599-27-2
   1. Children's parties--Planning. 2. Birthdays--Planning.
3. Home-based businesses. I. Fife, Bruce, 1952- .
GV1205.B57 1998
793.2'1'068--dc21   97-45200

Simultaneously Published in Australia, UK, and USA
Printed in the United States of America

This book is dedicated to all those
who are young at heart

TABLE OF CONTENTS

Introduction

DARE TO DREAM

Take a moment and imagine yourself standing before a small group of wide-eyed children all seated attentively before you. With anxious anticipation they cling to every word you say, obey every command you make, and have the time of their lives. As if by magic, you've captured their imaginations and are hurling them into a world of make-believe. You create lovable balloon animals, perform feats of stupefying magic, spin tales of wonder and excitement, and transform puppets into living creatures. Your youthful audience is spellbound. To them you are a star—a celebrity.

After you have delighted them with your skill and humor, they clamor for more. They don't want to see you leave. Some give you a hug and say, "I love you." The birthday child is overjoyed. Parents are grateful to you for entertaining the children and making the party a success. All the kids had a good time. You had a good time. Everybody is happy and, perhaps best of all, you get paid for doing it!

The vision over, you may think, "Sure it looks fun, but it's only a dream. I can't entertain kids. I don't know how to do any of those things. And besides, getting paid to doing something that's fun is just a dream."

We say, "Not so! You can make this image a reality, and this book will show you how."

You don't need to be a polished magician or seasoned entertainer to enjoy the benefits of becoming a birthday party entertainer and owning your own birthday party business. Young mothers, college students, retirees, engineers, police officers, and others enjoy the benefits of operating their own birthday party businesses. Many do it part-time on weekends and after work. Others have found it more enjoyable and more profitable than other ways of making a living and do it full-time.

A birthday party business affords many benefits. You can operate the business out of your home so there is little overhead expense, it requires very little start-up capital, you work when and where you choose, and you have no boss but yourself so you manage your time as you please. Being a birthday party entertainer allows you to step back in time and reexperience the fun and joy of your own childhood. You also make children happy. The attention and praise received from children provides a psychological lift that is highly rewarding. Experience the thrill yourself of bringing laughter and smiles to children's faces only once, and you'll be hooked!

For those who have already discovered the thrill and excitement of making kids laugh and are considering a career or avocation as a children's entertainer, birthday parties provide the ideal starting point. Most children's entertainers learn their craft doing birthday parties.

The birthday party business can be very lucrative compared with other types of work. A fee of $100 an hour is typical, but pricing will vary with location, economic climate, and services offered. If you offer entertainment with party decorations and catering, the price can triple.

This book describes how to set up and successfully operate a birthday party business. It covers party planning, catering, decorations, and entertainment. Emphasis is placed on entertainment, as this is the primary function of most birthday party businesses. Some businesses may specialize in catering and decorations, while others will focus only on providing entertainment, and some will do both.

In this book you will learn everything you need to know to share in the joy of operating a successful birthday party business. Topics include the basics of setting up a business, designing a wardrobe, character development, party services and entertainment, handling children, finding and keeping clients, finances and record keeping, advertising and publicity, games and activities, and the art of entertaining using storytelling, magic, clowning, face painting, puppetry, ballooning, and other skills.

One of the objectives of this book is to teach the reader not just how to perform certain skills, but how to be entertaining. There is a difference between doing magic, for example, and entertaining with magic. Anybody can read a book on magic and mechanically go through the motions of the trick and repeat the canned patter. But this is not entertainment! When kids laugh and have a good time, that's entertainment. You don't need a lot of skill in magic or balloon modeling to be successful. The ability to entertain kids is largely within you. All you have to do is let it out. Satisfy that urge to show off and have fun with kids. Let go of adult inhibitions and be silly.

Kids like silliness, they like fun activities, and they like to laugh.

Since entertainment is the backbone of most birthday party businesses, this book starts out by discussing this important topic. General information on the art of entertaining children, as well as making this business a success is covered first, then specifics using different types of entertaining tools, such as storytelling, magic, balloons, etc. are discussed in depth in subsequent chapters. The final chapters discuss in detail business and marketing aspects.

Seven authors, all experienced birthday party entertainers, contributed their thoughts and experience in creating this unique book. The editor and compiler, Bruce Fife, participated in the writing of almost every chapter but made significant contributions in Chapters 1-5, 7, 8, and 10-14. The following authors contributed primarily to the chapters indicated: Hal Diamond, Chapters 2, 3, 5, 13, and 14; Steve Kissell, Chapters 2, 8, and 13; Robin Vogel, Chapter 4; Mary Lostak, Chapters 3 and 11; Bob Conrad, Chapter 6; and Marcela Murad, Chapter 9.

The opinions expressed in this book are those of the authors, all of whom have had many years experience in the birthday party business. The advice they give works, but it is by no means the only approach. Other party businesses may operate a little differently and be just as successful. This book presents to the reader ideas and guidelines that do work. Use them as your guide, network with others in the business, read trade journals, see what works best for you, and develop your own methods and procedures.

Chapter 1

THE BIRTHDAY PARTY ENTERTAINER

In this chapter we will explore what it is to be a birthday party entertainer. You will learn how to develop a unique and memorable stage character and how to create entertaining children's shows.

CREATING A CHARACTER

One of the first things you must do before jumping into the birthday party business is to decide what type of character you will portray and what skills and props you will use. Will you be a magician? In that case you will need to obtain magic tricks and learn how to use them. Or perhaps you will be a puppeteer? If so, what type of puppets will you use—hand puppets, mouth puppets, finger puppets? Will you use ventriloquism or will your puppet communicate in other ways? Will you be a balloon worker and make balloon animals and toys? Or perhaps you will be a storyteller, face painter, clown, juggler, bubble blower, or some combination of these? A clown can be both a magician and a balloon worker, or even a storyteller and face painter. A puppeteer can use puppets, storytelling, and even magic. You don't have to stick to any one skill. Combining skills offers greater variety and more options for entertainment.

Choose at least one skill you enjoy doing. You don't need to be an expert in this skill, but you should practice enough to feel confident. If you want to learn more skills, you can add them later.

Whatever skills you use, you will need to develop a distinct character to accompany them. For children's audiences comedy is most effective. If you choose to learn magic, for example, will you present a comedy magic show? You have the choice to become either a comic magician or a clown magician. You can present a comedy magic act as either a comic magician or as a clown magician. What's the difference? The character. A magician dresses seriously and conveys the image of the traditional magician, even though he uses funny stories, tells jokes, and may even make a mistake now and then. The other is primarily a clown, pretending to be a skilled magician. The clown is a buffoon and not a skilled, intelligent master of the magical arts. His character is more light-hearted and whimsical. He may perform some impressive feats of magic, but most of the time he appears confused or frustrated, because he hasn't quite mastered the techniques of the art—or so it seems.

Character Development

What type of character will you portray? As an entertainer, you play a part. The character you play must be consistent and identifiable, the character should have recognizable characteristics that are constant throughout your show. Your character may be silly, skillful, clumsy, absent-minded, bashful, boastful, a showoff, unlucky, clever, playful, intelligent, sophisticated, jolly, cranky,

9

high-strung, dumb, a practical joker, etc. You will have to determine the characteristics of your own character. Although you may be able to easily define some of your character's most prominent features, the fine details will make themselves apparent over time as your performance skills improve and your character develops.

It is helpful for you to define your stage character's major characteristics. Once you have them defined and feel comfortable with them, make a concentrated effort to remain in character throughout your performance. For example, don't be boastful one minute and then shy the next, simply because you want to use a shy joke—it won't work, at least not very well, and you will only confuse the audience. The audience is trying to understand your character's personality so that they can better understand and enjoy your show. Once they know you and get an idea of how you act and react, they can enjoy your jokes more fully or freely. If you confuse them by changing your character traits, they will not respond as well because they are confused. Once a character is defined, the audience can anticipate reactions and responses so when you do something, they understand why you did it.

Your character may be able to do magic, juggle, etc. so you are not restricted in the skills you choose to use. But if your character is clumsy, then when you do those things, you must mess up. You may work some wonderful magic tricks, or do some great juggling, but it must appear to be by accident because your character is clumsy and, therefore, does not have the real skill to perform these things. You might pretend to attempt these skills, claiming you have had (or are taking) lessons but mess up on everything—using skill but done so as to look clumsy.

For heaven's sake, don't be a clumsy character and then all of a sudden possess great skill—unless it fits a routine, for example, like you eat a skill pill. Have the pill wear off and during an important trick, suddenly turn clumsy again at the most critical part of the exhibition.

Don't use a character who uses humor you don't necessarily enjoy. If you don't like slapstick, for example, then don't do it. The more you enjoy your character, the better will be your portrayal. Be willing to modify your character or parts of your character if audiences don't respond well to it.

Some people are lucky enough to quickly discover a character that they are comfortable with. Others struggle for a while until they find what is right for them. You don't know what type of character to portray? In that case just be yourself. Let the child inside of you come out. Let your character be yourself. Concentrate on exaggerating your own unique qualities, add dramatics, have fun, play with the kids, and you will be off to a good start.

Character development is dynamic. Nothing is written in stone to make you keep the first character you come up with. Just as you learn and grow, so should your character. As you work with your character, you will gradually learn more about how the character thinks and reacts to various situations.

It doesn't matter what you do, so long as you entertain. You can simply act silly, tell jokes, have the kids participate in amusing activities, and be every bit as entertaining as a professional magician who enchants the audience with clever magic and comedy. The type of vehicle (skill) you use is not that important. What is important is entertainment.

Your Stage Name

As a birthday party entertainer, you will need to develop at least one clearly defined character whom you portray throughout the party. Whether you plan to do magic or tell stories or whatever, you need to present your entertainment with your character in mind. This character must have a name. An ad reading "Fred Smith the birthday party entertainer" will be much less attractive to a potential customer than one which reads "Mr. Bubbles—Balloon Master." Which one would you hire to entertain at your party—Fred or Mr. Bubbles? The name conveys meaning—it's fun, exciting.

Choose a name to fit your style and character. If you plan on being a clown, choose a clownish name like Blimpo, Zippy, or Chuckels.

If you are a magician, choose a fitting name such as Mr. Wonder, Dr. Amazing, or Waldo the Wizard.

Choose a name that describes your character. If you

are a clown, don't choose just any silly sounding name, choose a name that fits your character—a name that means something to you. A clown who specializes in blowing bubbles or working with balloons might be called Bubbles.

An important point about creating a character is becoming somebody. Ronald McDonald is somebody. Barney the Dinosaur is somebody. Kermit the Frog is somebody. The worst mistake you can make in the children's entertainment business is to become a generic entertainer. You don't want to be just a clown or just a magician no different that any other clown or magician. Personalize your character. The first step in doing that is to choose a unique performing name. Rascal the Clown, Mysto the Magician, Professor Bubbles the Balloonologist. In some cases you can use your own real name or some version of it. But if you do, then you need to identify your particular skill such as Fernando the Magician or Professor Drake—Storyteller. If you work with puppets, you can incorporate the name of your puppet, Sandra and Chelsea, or if you have several puppets, Sandra and Friends, or Sandra's Puppet Theater.

Whichever name you choose, it must be as unique as you can make it. Avoid commonly used names. There are dozens of clowns with the names of Buttons or Rainbow. The World Clown Association has over thirty members who use Happy as part of their name. Names that sound too common or are used frequently become generic. The public will not remember them nor will they identify those who use them as anything more than generic entertainers.

On the other hand, if your name is memorable, you are different, you are somebody, you are a professional, you are someone parents want for their child's party. Take time to choose a stage name that will set you apart from all other children's entertainers.

Use your name. Print it on business cards, stationery, advertising, and even on your props. Answer your business phone using your stage name. Use your stage name at the party and make sure the kids know who you are. You are not just a clown. You are Mobelli the Clown. Examples of some names currently used by clowns and other party entertainers are Pretzel, Kooky, Merry Pockets, Hiccup, Giggles, Fashoo, Petunia, Twinkles, Macaroni, Strudels, Cream Puff, and Mottsorelli. Some play off their own names like Chuckles (Chuck), Jimbo (Jim), Ricky (Rick), Merry Lee (Marilee).

> Why does a cow wear a bell?
> *Because its horn doesn't work.*

Consider adding words or a title like Avnar the Eccentric, Kookie Dee Klown, Lucinda the Story Princess, Hank the Yarnspinner, Professor Potbelly, Mr. Fantastic, Kaptain Kornball, or Ms. Millie.

If you were a kid and you had the choice of having Ronald McDonald coming to you party or some unnamed clown, who would you choose? Ronald, because he is a celebrity. In order to be a celebrity, you must have a name. The fact that you have a name sets you apart.

If the kids at the party loved you and go home and say they want a clown at their party—if you didn't impress upon them your name and unique character, they will allow mom to call up any clown. Kids will believe that all clowns are the same. And many people tend to believe all clowns, magicians, etc. are the same and of similar talents.

Make your name easy to remember and relate to your character. Name recognition is important. All great entertainers have a name. Names which are difficult to read or pronounce are little better than generic names because people won't be able to say them and therefore won't. They will tell their friends a "clown" entertained them rather than Bosco. Gaetane Letourneau (this is an actual name) may be unique but it's not particularly memorable to kids or parents.

Wardrobe Selection

The clothes people wear and how they wear them are extensions of their personalities. Each piece of clothing you wear tells others something about yourself. For example, what would you deduce about the personality and lifestyle of someone wearing dirty, wrinkled clothing, who has unkempt hair, desperately needs a shave, and is carrying a half empty bottle of vodka? Or, what would you say about a person wearing a spotless three-piece business suit and gold cufflinks, who smokes a cigar and carries a copy of *The Wall Street Journal* under his arm? How about a person in greasy overalls, oil stained hands, a wrench sticking out of his back pocket, and a cap with the words "World's Greatest Lover" written on it? We all can and do make judgments about people by their appearance.

The clothes entertainers wear are extensions of their stage personalities. Because we make assumptions about people by the clothes they wear, actors, including children's entertainers, wear clothes that help them to impersonate the characters they portray. Traditionally the bad guys always wear black hats and clothes, while the good guys wear white. White suggests purity and goodness, while black depicts deception and criminality. Black is also associated with knowledge and seriousness. Professors and judges wear black robes signifying their professional status. Magicians usually ware black because it conveys an atmosphere of mystery and knowledge. Bright, cheery colors are associated with bright, cheery personalities; that is why clown costumes are usually very colorful.

Wardrobe selection should be done after you have defined your stage character. The outfit you choose must support your stage personality and the skills you perform, and be professional looking. An outfit designed by you, using your own choice of colors and prints, becomes your trademark. Such an outfit would fit your character and be unique.

What you wear helps to identify your stage character and distinguishes you as somebody special. You should take care in choosing your performing outfit. For heaven's sake, don't wear street clothes! When someone hires a birthday party entertainer, they expect a professional and not someone who looks like they just walked in off the street. Your costume helps to create the atmosphere for your show. If you walk in wearing street clothes, what type of impression do you think that will make? It won't be favorable (parents will pass judgment on your ability based on the clothes you wear). The kids won't be impressed. The atmosphere of fantasy and make-believe will not be created. Some birthday party workers may feel it isn't necessary to dress up for the type of work they do; perhaps they do storytelling or just supervise games. If your appearance isn't distinctive, how are the children going to remember you? How are you going to get them excited when you step through the front door? How are you going to instill curiosity in them and get their attention? How are you going to appear different than any other parent at the party? Why would the kids want to listen to you? Wearing some type of distinctive outfit will get their attention.

If you come dressed in a clown suit, you are telling the kids who you are and what to expect—they know you will be silly and fun. If your show revolves around a theme, such as animals, you might wear a colorful jumpsuit like a zookeeper, or an African big game hunter's outfit, or some other animal related costume. Dressed this way, you could present a puppet show (using animal puppets), tell a story (featuring animals), do magic (with tricks including live animals or puppets), or do games (with an animal theme).

No matter what type of presentation you do at a party, come dressed for the part. If you dress like a magician, do magic. If you dress like a clown, clown around. If you dress like a storyteller, tell a story. If you showed up to a party looking like a magician, but

Dean "Cuz'n Cal" Cooke wearing distinctive costume and makeup.

presented a juggling act, the kids expecting you to perform magic would be disappointed and confused. A face painter who dresses as a clown, but tells no jokes and doesn't act silly, likewise, will be a disappointment. Don't wear a costume just to wear a costume. Wear a costume that matches your performing character and skills.

The best costumes are color coordinated and pleasing to look at. They are not a hodge-podge of old second-hand rejects. Your appearance tells customers how professional you are. Make them sharp and neat looking. Most birthday party entertainers use bright, cheery colors and designs which are not obtainable in second-hand shops. A good costume is a product of a carefully selected arrangement of style, patterns, and colors.

Visit fabric stores to see what is available. Some carry patterns for making costumes. Patterns not specifically designed for children's entertainers can be modified slightly by a tailor to make a pleasing, unique stage costume. Costume shops and several enterprising individuals sell custom made costumes. Periodicals such as *The New Calliope* and *Clowning Around*, published by two clown associations, carry ads from costume makers. These publications contain a wealth of information about performing for children. The addresses for these associations can be found in the appendix.

A custom made wardrobe is the most suitable. Costume stores sell only a few outfits. These are usually good but generalized, mass produced, and designed for the average person to wear at costume parties and plays, not for anyone doing professional work. They might work well with your party character, but nothing is as eye catching and memorable as an original outfit.

Costumes often reflect a certain time period, national origin, profession, or lifestyle. Most children's entertainers rely on their wardrobe as a character aid to identify their roles to the audience.

Red Skelton, one of America's best known comedians, played the part of several different characters ranging from country bumpkin to a mischievous little child. Each character required a completely different wardrobe. His character Clem Kadiddlehopper wore an old plaid suit that was far too small, giving him a naive country boy appearance. As Freddy the Freeloader, Skelton dressed as a down-and-out, but happy, tramp in an old tattered and wrinkled business suit. The Mean Widdle Kid wore shorts, knee-high socks, tie, and jacket, depicting a spoiled rich kid.

Every piece of clothing conveys meaning. The addition of just a hat can change the perception of your character. A person in a business suit wearing a derby would look like an English businessman. Change the derby to a cowboy hat and you get a Texas oil tycoon. Even the way the clothes are worn reveals something about the person. The same man in a wrinkled and soiled business suit, with his shirt-tail hanging out, and messy hair conveys a different character than if he were wearing a clean and pressed suit with his hair neatly trimmed and combed.

Tweedle Dum or Tweedle Dee? Morris Costumes

Larry Mahan as Mr. Sonshine.

Use accessory articles of clothing to help define the personality portrayed. These include ties, suspenders, hats, gloves, handkerchiefs, boutonnieres, eyeglasses, beards, belts, umbrellas, canes, and the like. Even the hair style is important. Add color to your outfit and perhaps even exaggerate style and fit. A policeman is recognized by his dark blue uniform. Add a billy club, a bobby's helmet, and perhaps large black bulbous shoes, and you have turned him into a silly Keystone Kop character.

A scientist is considered intelligent and highly analytical, yet often absent-minded and eccentric. He is recognized by his lab coat and white hair, styled like Albert Einstein's. His life is dedicated to making new scientific discoveries. The goofy scientist can emphasize these traits and create a lot of funny material with his "new discoveries," like his anti-gravity balloon that keeps falling to the ground.

The key in choosing your wardrobe is to select something that fits your character and the skills you do. If all you do is supervise games, a colorful jumpsuit or fancy sweatsuit may be appropriate. If you tell stories, wear something that relates to the story. If the stories are folktales, dress as a hillbilly, or an old-timer (grandfather with cane, wire-rimmed eyeglasses, pocket watch, overalls, etc.). If you tell fairy tales, dress as a fairy godmother, princess, or traveling minstrel of the Renaissance. For mysteries, dress as a detective or reporter. Use your imagination. Perhaps just the addition of something simple such as a hat, scarf, or other adornment is all you need to set you apart and make you special.

Magicians traditionally wear tuxedos or black business suits. For children you can snazz up an otherwise drab-looking outfit a bit by adding a little color, such as a red flower in the lapel, or you may use color in your cummerbund, shirt, tie, or handkerchief. A magician can assume other identities other than the traditional, formally dressed conjurer. He may appear as a genie, wizard, gypsy, mystic, sorcerer's apprentice, or even a clown, the wardrobe reflecting the character. The wizard, for instance, may wear a long, dark blue robe, decorated with stars and moons.

Let the clothes tell who you are. A clown magician may wear a tuxedo, but to reveal his cheery, silly nature,

Storyteller Molly Harris spins an action-packed tale.

his clothes should be illfitted or mismatched. The farther the clown's clothes are from the black formal wear of the serious magician, the more whimsical or apparently incompetent the character portrayed. A magician who tells funny stories and does funny magic tricks should look like a magician, but add a little color to his wardrobe. He should be professional looking, yet not too stuffy or serious. A clown who does serious magic with lots of jokes and silly antics would have much more color. A clown who only thinks he is a magician, but always goofs up the tricks (on purpose) should have the most outlandish costume and makeup design. Even the makeup worn depicts the character. A pretty whiteface clown is considered more intelligent and skilled than a lowly hobo or a colorful auguste. The auguste clown has multiple colors and the most exaggerated facial features.

In general, the more slapstick or silly your stage character, the more bizarre your makeup and wardrobe. If you wear a highly exaggerated costume, the audience will expect a character just as exaggerated.

Clowns have been favorite children's party entertainers. The makeup and wardrobe of the European auguste and character clowns are popular. Unlike the traditional circus-type clown with heavy makeup and outlandish clothes, the European auguste looks more like an average everyday person. Makeup is more subtle and the costume less flamboyant, yet still easily recognizable as a clown or silly person. Character clowns range in appearance from the traditional circus look to that of the European auguste. The character clown's costume and makeup is styled to imitate a particular person like W.C. Fields or Charlie Chaplin, or a profession like a policeman or nurse. The most popular character clown is the tramp. A character clown can depict a jester, country bumpkin, wacky professor, eccentric artist, old sea captain, or any other profession. Any of these characters could be used to present a children's show in clowning, magic, storytelling, balloons, or whatever.

Keep in mind to choose a character that is you, one you would enjoy portraying and having fun with. Incorporate whatever skills necessary to present a children's show. Most children's shows revolve around some type of skill (e.g. magic, balloons, puppetry, etc.). But you can do other things as your form of entertainment. Participation games, stories, music, and other activities can be very successful. Or you may use a little of everything: perform a little magic, work with a puppet or two, do some silly gags, give out balloon animals, and tell short stories and jokes. As long as what you do is fast-paced and entertaining, it will work.

Diane "Tookels" Jolly and Junior.

Grooming

Don't wear dirty, worn-out clothes, even if you portray a hobo or country bumpkin. All costumes must be washed clean, ironed, and fresh smelling. You're supposed to look like a bum, not be one. Patches and tears should be real, but worn as part of the costume. Keep in mind that you are a children's entertainer. As such you are a fantasy to them, much like a cartoon, comic book, or television character. Your clothes should help create a joyful make-believe world, and not bring in realism from the streets.

Pay attention to your appearance and personal hygiene. Be cleanly shaven, well manicured, put on deodorant, brush your teeth, and use mouth wash if necessary. It is a bit embarrassing for you to bend down to the birthday child, smile, and say "Happy birthday Sarah," only to have Sarah immediately respond by grabbing her nose and say, "peww-wee, your breath stinks!" Style and/or cut your hair, trim nose hair, and do whatever it takes to look your best. Wear makeup to accent facial features. Even if you are not a clown, a little eye shadow or blush brightens your face, helping to create the fantasy you are trying to create.

Wash and iron your outfit frequently. If you are busy, you may want to invest in two or more sets of clothes. After doing a couple of shows back-to-back, your outfit

may need washing, especially in hot climates, when perspiration is a problem. A backup outfit would be beneficial.

DEVELOPING AN ACT

You've learned some skills and have defined your stage character; now you are ready to put an act together. The key to developing a successful show is entertainment. This may sound obvious, but many new party entertainers don't understand how to be entertaining. Kids today have grown up watching television. The shows they watch are filled with fast-paced humor, blazing color, trick photography, and mood-enhancing music to provide super-charged entertainment. To some extent your show must compete with what they have become accustomed to as entertainment. In this section you will learn how to be entertaining and how to create an effective act.

The Magic of Entertainment

The biggest mistake you can make when developing an act for children is to believe that simply showing off your skills will entertain them. Watching a juggler toss and catch balls can be entertaining for half a minute or so, but if that's all he does, it gets boring real fast. Showing a cute hand puppet to the kids will get them excited, but if all the puppet does is wave "hello" and say "hi, what's your name?" the kids will soon lose interest. If a magician performs one trick after another, he may perform the tricks flawlessly, but if he doesn't talk to his audience and entertain them while he is doing the tricks, his show will fall flat on its face. The same is true with face painting, making balloon animals, or performing any other skill. Simply demonstrating your skills is *not* entertainment. The magic of entertainment comes with the *way* you present your skills.

Some years ago a father approached me and said, "I'm really impressed with your show. How do you do it?"

I looked at him inquisitively. "How do I do what?"

"How do you get kids to laugh at your tricks? Whenever I try some of those same stunts, my kids look at me as if I'm dumb. But when you do it, they can't stop laughing. What's your secret?"

What is my secret? What is it that makes a simple trick, such as pretending to remove your thumb, hilariously funny when one person does it, but a bore when performed by another? This so-called secret is simply the creative use of a buildup or story to accompany the trick. Tricks and stunts by themselves may be interesting, but have limited entertainment value. Silly stunts, that even kids can do, appear corny unless accompanied by a creative funny story that transforms the trick into a humorous event.

Magic tricks, for example, lose much of their real magic, the magic of entertainment, if they are not accompanied by jokes or stories or some other clever patter (talk). Tricks and stunts become lifeless by themselves. For older audiences or in dramatic magic presentations, other techniques besides the stories and jokes are used to attract and retain the audience's attention. Children, however, demand more action or verbal accompaniment, particularly in the form of jokes and gags to be entertained.

To be effective, each action must have its own accompanying patter or story. In magic for example, since most shows are composed of several different tricks or routines, a central theme or storyline is needed to relate one trick to the next. Each trick should flow into the next. A single story can incorporate several tricks, jokes, and participation activities.

Shows can be composed of independent little skits or routines connected to each other by a single plot or storyline. The following short magic routine (borrowed from the book *Creative Clowning*) provides a good example of using patter and a centralized theme with magic. The magic skills needed are minimal, relying on silly stuff that anyone can do.

My Magic Pencil

For this routine an ordinary pencil is used. The magician must wear long loose-fitting sleeves so that the pencil can slide in and out easily.

"I have here a very unusual pencil. This is no ordinary pencil but a special magic pencil. It looks ordinary, and in fact, is indistinguishable from the type you use at school. But this pencil possesses magical power—yes, magical power. To prove it to you, I will take a piece of paper and with this pencil I will be able to write down things about one of you that I could not possible know. Let me have a volunteer. You young lady, have you ever seen me before? Say no."

"No," she says.

He continues. "Good. Would you give me a hand with this magic trick?"

"Yes," she replies.

"This girl does not know me and I do not know her. I could not possibly know anything about her, including her name. But with the power of this magic pencil I will be able to write down on this paper things about her such

as her name and age. Let me show you. . . . I will write your name."

He writes a name on the slip of paper. "Your name, according to this magic pencil, is Paul Harvey,"

"No," she says.

"No? . . . It's not?" He looks curiously at the name on the paper. "Hmm . . . that is a strange name for a little girl. Let me try again."

He writes another name on the paper. "Okay, I've got it now. Your name is Petunia Bellyhose—No? . . . What about Sarah Jane Figwiggle?"

"No."

"Judith Finkelstine?"

"No."

"Well, what the heck is your name?"

"Susan," she says, or whatever her name is.

"Susan! . . . What kind of a name is that? . . . Oh well, let me try something else. I will write your age."

He writes something on the paper. "According to my magic pencil you age is . . ." He looks at the paper, acts surprised, looks at the girl, then back at the paper and back at the girl again. Making a funny, inquisitive face, he asks, "Are you 28 years old?"

"No."

"Hmm . . . maybe I've got the figures backwards. How about 82? No, that can't be right . . . Maybe this isn't my magic pencil after all." He thanks the helper and sends her back to her seat.

With a doubtful expression, he examines each side of the pencil. "Let me try something else. I'll put it in this hand, like this." (See illustration below.) "Bringing it behind my back, I'll do some magic."

He brings his hands around in front of him, palms down. The right hand is cramped to make it look as if the pencil is in that hand. "Which hand is it in?"

The kids will all choose the correct hand. The clown turns both hands over and looks surprised. "Hmm . . . it was supposed to disappear. I must have done something wrong . . . oh I know, I didn't say the magic word. Let me try it again, this time using the magic word."

He keeps the pencil in the same hand and puts both hands behind his back. While his hands are out of sight, he slips the pencil up the sleeve of the other arm. He says the magic words, "Liver pudding . . . what did you expect me to say, abracadabra or something ridiculous like that?" Bringing his hands out in front and raising them so that the pencil doesn't fall out, he holds the backs of his hand to the audience at about chin level. The hand which originally held the pencil is bent slightly, still pretending to hold it. "Which hand is it in now?"

Everyone will think it's in the crimped hand. "Nope," he says and shows them the empty hand. The kids will say it's in the other hand, but that is shown to be empty too.

"Ha ha, it's gone. See, I knew it was my magic pencil." Some of the kids might think it was stuck behind the magician's back, but to prove that it isn't, he turns around. "See, it's not behind my back either." As his back is turned he palms a coin out of his pocket.

"I will now make the pencil reappear." Holding the empty hand out in front, palms down, fingers crimped slightly, he says the magic words, "Liver pudding on a stick, the pencil will now reappear quick." He turns his hand palm side up, but it's empty. Nothing happened; no pencil. He tries it a second time. Still nothing happens. He looks puzzled.

"Hmm . . . what's wrong? . . . Oh, I see," he says. Reaching over with the other hand, which secretly holds the coin, he grabs something from behind a child's ear. "How silly of me. Those magic words always make the pencil appear from behind somebody's ear."

Pulling his hand away he says, "Here it is." But instead of the pencil he's holding a coin.

"Hey . . . this isn't my pencil! . . . That's all right, I needed the money anyway." He sticks the coin into his pocket. Reaching over, he gently grabs the child's ear and looks in "Got any more in there?"

Slowly a giant sneeze begins to build up in the magician's nose with exaggerated accompanying facial expressions. "Ah . . . ah . . ah . . AAAH!" Turning toward the kids he makes as if he is going to give them an unwanted shower. The sneeze builds to its final climax as the kids squirm, "AAAAAAH!. . ." ending in a comical and almost inaudible "hew."

With a smile on his face he says, "Scared ya, didn't I?"

Wiggling his nose to relieve a tickle he continues, "Let's see where could that pencil have gone?" The pencil is secretly allowed to slide out of the sleeve and into the magician's hand Suddenly he begins to build up another big sneeze. "Ah . . . AAAH . . . CHOOOO!"

Just before sneezing he clasps his hands to his nose, concealing the pencil. As he sneezes he opens both hands wide and gives the pencil a little flick so it flies out as if it were the cause of the magician's ticklish nose. "Why there's my magic pencil. That's the problem with making things disappear,—you never know where they'll wind up."

Analyzing the Routine

This routine can be broken down into its basic elements by eliminating the dialogue. What we have left are four elementary magic tricks. The first was a psychic demonstration, trying to guess the girl's name and age. The second was vanishing the pencil, followed by the appearance of a coin, and finally the reappearance of the pencil.

Each of these tricks could have been done seriously without comic patter, but they would have made a terrible magic show. With clever dialogue, tied together by a central theme, these simple tricks produce a funny comedy magic routine.

The theme on which the dialogue was built was the magician trying to prove that he really had a magic pencil, but none of his tricks did what he wanted them to do. Children enjoy it when an adult makes an error, such as forgetting a name, mispronouncing a word, or when a magic trick appears to go wrong. Telling the audience that you're going to do one thing and then doing something else, often to your displeasure and embarrassment (or so it seems), is delightfully funny.

What Makes an Act?

Many novices and even some working children's entertainers do not understand what constitutes an act. They may have what they call an act, but it is really just a series of unrelated jokes or activities. A balloon worker, for example, making balloon animals for 30 minutes or a face painter painting body tattoos and face designs is not an act. These are activities. This is not to say that activities cannot be entertaining, but they are not acts. Likewise, a magician doing a series of tricks one after another without a unifying theme is not an act. It is merely a demonstration of tricks, again only an activity. This is true of any skill. Even puppeteers and clowns tell jokes, do gags, and short sketches, with no unifying theme between each of the separate bits, then their efforts are really only a walk-around or strolling activity (like what is done at malls, company picnics, and parades). There is nothing wrong with doing walk-arounds and other activities, but they are not acts and should not be promoted as such.

The word "act" is often used to mean show. You will hear these terms used interchangeably. A children's variety show (entertainment by a magician, clown, puppeteer, etc.) should consist of a series of segments or routines all related to a central theme which lead logically from one to the other. The show should have a beginning, a middle, and an end, just like a story. You in fact, are telling a story with a series of gags, sketches, and tricks.

Unlike activities such as making balloon animals, acts are built around a central theme and require some degree of memorization and rehearsing. Your entire show, including your dialogue, should be preplanned and defined. This doesn't mean you can't ad-lib, but a show isn't made up entirely from ad-libs or the random recitation of jokes.

A balloon worker can present a short show centered around balloons, filling in the rest of the time with group activities and balloon figure tying. A five-minute group participation warm-up (as described on pages 44-45) followed by a ten-minute show, would constitute the main presentation. The rest of the time could be filled with making balloon animals for the kids. This could make an effective 30-minute party event.

In some cases parents will be primarily interested in activities such as making balloon animals, face painting, or games. A formal show is not necessary, but you would be expected to interact with the kids like you would when doing a walk-around by telling jokes, doing gags, and otherwise being the life of the party. This is okay, so long as you don't pass it off as a show.

Putting an Act Together

The thought of creating an entire 45-minute act may seem insurmountable for a novice birthday party worker. Where do you get the material to fill all this time? What will you do? How should it be presented? What props will be needed? What type of story will keep children entertained for this length of time?

When putting your act together, it is easier not to think of it as a 45-minute act, but as a series of smaller

How does a cat keep his breath fresh?
With mousewash.

Avner the Eccentric.

routines that may only last five or ten minutes each. Focus on developing a short routine that could be presented independently. Working on a short routine is not as big a challenge.

To start, center your routine around a single theme. Decide what skills and props you are going to use. Will it be a juggling routine with balls and clubs, or will it be a magic routine with color-changing scarves and a tricky magic wand? Once you have narrowed down these parameters, creating a short routine is relatively simple. Use you natural creativity and sense of humor to develop a dialogue or story to accompany the presentation of your skill. Many books are available with sample routines and dialogues to spark your imagination. Use them as resources and stepping stones to give you ideas in creating your own routines. In the appendix I have listed several resources for ideas for birthday party entertainers.

Once you have a routine finished, practice it, become familiar with it, and modify it as new ideas emerge. As you practice, your creative juices will be flowing and jokes and ideas will come to you. Experiment, be silly, and above all, have fun. If you enjoy the routine, chances are kids will too. After you make one routine, start working on another, and another until you have enough for a full show.

As an example, a typical birthday party show may consist of: (1) an opening warm-up with audience participation; (2) introductory magic routine (like "My Magic Pencil" routine presented above); (3) puppet routine with the birthday child; (4) magic routine with audience volunteers; (5) closing trick and awarding of party favors (balloon animals, personalized giveaways, etc.). Each segment may constitute a mini-story with its own theme with a beginning, middle, and end; it will tie in with or complement the general theme. The length of the entire show is determined by the length of each segment or routine and the number of segments used. If you need to lengthen or shorten your show, you can either add or remove a segment.

Each segment, although funny and basically complete in itself, builds upon the next. Although each of the segments can be a strong individual piece, they often aren't strong enough to be presented by themselves and need the others to make up an entire act.

Keep in mind as you create each routine to tie them together with one central theme. If in your first routine you present yourself as a clever, but absent-minded magician, don't all of a sudden become a skillful master of magic in the next. You must continue with the absent-minded theme throughout your show, even if you use different skills. Your second routine, for example, may show you as an absent-minded balloonologist. Be consistent. Each routine builds on the next.

Look back at the sample routine "My Magic Pencil." It has a simple plot with a beginning, a middle, and an end. The beginning is the magician introducing the magic pencil and claiming it has magical powers; the middle is trying to get the pencil to do something magical and still be under the magician's control; the end is the magician accidentally having the pencil reappear.

This routine can be presented as one segment of a larger show. The performer would move from this segment to the next with a connecting statement or joke. For example, the magician may say, "See, I told you this pencil is magic, but I have a pet rabbit (puppet) I would like to introduce to you that is more tricky than this pencil . . . ."

Here we move from a magic routine to a puppet routine, quite a difference! In the puppet routine we can keep the theme of the unskillful magician or magician's apprentice. One way to do this is by having your character be a less than skillful puppeteer/ventriloquist (obviously moving his lips and not fooling the kids at all), or by the puppet being smarter or more skillful than the character is, or even by bringing back the magic pencil and have it "accidentally" appear in the puppet routine. The pencil

Ed: My dog has no nose.
Fred: How does he smell?
Ed: Awful.

can act like a running gag and somehow appear in each succeeding segment of the show. A good finish would be to hand out as party favors "magic" pencils with your name and phone number on them. (Kids will love these special pencils because they had so much fun with you and your magic pencil. They will go around trying their own magic tricks and even showing them to their brothers, sisters, and parents.) This is just one example, but there are any number of tie-ins you could make to associate one segment of your show to the next.

The sequence in which you place the individual segments or routines is very important. The first bit or routine you perform will be your introduction. During this time you will identify your stage character and personality. The kids will know who you are and what you are like and how you will react to situations. They get to know you and feel comfortable with you. Audiences (children or adults) cannot fully enjoy a show until they understand the players (or entertainers). This is because their minds are working trying to figure out who the players are and how they fit in. Since you only have a few minutes, your personality must be made clear to them as soon as possible, preferably within the first couple of minutes. Often this can be done before the show (or prepared material) begins during meet-and-greet or warm-up activities.

Your first routine should be your second strongest routine. You want to start off with a bang to get everyone's attention and draw the audience into your world of entertainment. If you don't get the children excited when you start, they will still be distracted by preshow activities and conversation.

Your strongest routine, material which leaves the greatest impression or gets the biggest laughs should be presented last. You want to build up excitement and laughter throughout the show and end with a bang. Leave the audience wanting more. This will produce a positive impression and a desire to see you again. If you ended with your worst routine, people would get bored and be glad you finished. Even though your earlier material was well received, afterwards the audience will remember how they felt when you finished. If they felt bored, they will consider your act too long and dull, but if it ended while they were enjoying themselves, they will judge the entire show as entertaining.

In general, the routines between the first and the last should go from the weakest and work to the strongest. All the routines should be good solid entertainment, but the first and the last should be your best. The first routine gets the audience's attention and lets them know the show will be fun. The next routine is the weakest, with each succeeding routine getting better, building up to the grand finale. You wouldn't want to put the strongest material first or before any other material as everything else would be a letdown.

ELEMENTS OF A GOOD CHILDREN'S SHOW

What makes a good birthday party show? The following are some of the major elements of a successful birthday party show. Incorporate these into your routines as you build your act.

Look the Part

To build excitement, wear a costume and portray a character—sweep the children into your world of fantasy and make-believe by your appearance.

Keep them Busy

Keep the children busy thinking and laughing. If their minds are absorbed in what you are doing, they don't have time to get bored or to cause trouble. Don't allow any dead time. Fill each minute with something.

Keep them Guessing

Arouse their curiosity. Make your stories and routines interesting so the kids will want to know what is going to happen next. Don't tell them what to expect or what you are about to do; let them find out when it happens. Don't tell them what you're going to do next—show them. Tell them only enough to build your story. Telling an audience, "I am now going to make this scarf turn from blue to red" is boring. Instead say, "Watch what happens when I pull this scarf through my fist." Not knowing what to expect will arouse curiosity and greater interest.

Audience Participation

Use audience participation activities. Kids have lots of energy and love to participate. Let them.

Make it Short but Sweet

Limit your show to about 30 minutes. Energized kids have short attention spans and get restless quickly. Also,

the anticipation of cake, ice cream, and other goodies can become distractions.

Focus on Humor

Build your show around comedy; the more comedy the better. Use the humor that is you and that you enjoy doing most. Your personality makes the show, not your skills or props.

Physical Comedy

Incorporate physical and visual comedy into your routines. Children love slapstick, sight gags, and visual humor. While jokes and verbal humor can go over their heads, physical comedy is easily understood and enjoyed. The younger the kids, the more they enjoy physical humor.

Be a Good Actor

Use facial and vocal expressions freely and exaggerate them. Play your part to the hilt. Vocal fluctuations add variety and make you more interesting. A public speaker, for example, who delivers a speech in a monotone, can bore you to death. The same speech delivered with emphasis and vocal variations, will be immensely more interesting.

Body Language

Use body language to emphasize your words and thoughts. Move and speak with your whole body—hands, arms, legs, head, torso, and face. Don't move just for the sake of moving, make gestures natural, yet slightly more exaggerated or animated than you do in normal conversation. Motion helps keep the audience's eyes fixed on the speaker. It adds subtle action and thus keeps the audience's attention.

Body language can also enhance your humor. For instance, if you accidentally get hit on the head, a simple "Ouch" may get a few chuckles, but a louder reaction with goofy faces, and staggering body motions are funnier and will produce hearty laugher.

Show Enthusiasm

Smile. Have fun! If you have fun, you will perform with enthusiasm and the children will have fun. Show the audience that you are excited and they will pick up on it and become excited too.

Play to the Laughter

Focus your eyes and attention on those who are enjoying your show the most and who are responding positively to you. Play to them and give it your best. Their smiles, laughter, and responses will inspire and encourage you to do your best. As a result, *everyone* will enjoy your performance more, especially you. If you focus on children who act bored or are unresponsive, you will find yourself getting discouraged and your performance will suffer.

Be Original

Don't copy another performer's act. The material you use must fit your own personality and style. You can find ready-made routines in books and with magic tricks that you buy in the store. In most cases these will not work well for you exactly as they are written. They don't fit your style of presentation. Many other entertainers and hobbyists have purchased and performed the same routines that accompany magic tricks, so that a child is likely to yell, "I've seen that trick before," "I know how that works," or may even blurt out the ending to a joke or gag, spoiling the whole routine. Use printed routines as idea generators and create your own routines. Routines you create will fit your style of performing best, and be more successful for you. It is unethical to steal or copy another performer's material. People will look down on you and the person whose material you stole will be displeased. If you liked someone else's material and feel it would be just right for you, use it as a guideline, change some elements of the routine, and make it your own.

Keep Current

Use names, objects, places, people, and events that are familiar with kids. Often I hear adults tell jokes that relate to situations that occurred in the past which the kids do not understand. The jokes may have been funny to one generation of kids but not the next. Keep up with popular movies, television shows, and cartoons. Know the characters and make reference to them where appropriate. Show the kids you are familiar with their world, and they will relate to you and enjoy your presentation more.

Personalize Your Act

Give the birthday child special recognition. Use the name of the birthday child, his or her friend's name, teachers, and parents in your show. Make them the characters, if you can, in your routines. Use local places as the setting, such as the neighborhood school or park. This gives your show a customized appearance that kids and parents appreciate and enjoy.

You may even incorporate into your act some of your guest of honor's favorite hobbies or activities. If the birthday child likes the Ninja Turtles, use them if possible. If the child loves sports, use sports stories or props. Often props or stories can be altered slightly to conform to the birthday child's interests. For a child who likes baseball, for example, a juggler could juggle baseballs instead of rubber balls or standard juggling clubs and call them little fat baseball bats.

Practice Makes Perfect

Practice your routines, jokes, and gags until you have them memorized and you feel comfortable with them. If you perform a skill, practice until you can perform it without error. The better prepared you are, the more comfortable you will feel and the more confidence you will have. Consequently, you will concentrate more on your presentation than on trying to remember what comes next, allowing you to do a better job.

Strive for Improvement

Keep trying to improve your show and your skills. As new ideas and jokes come along, add them where appropriate. Experiment with new routines and jokes. Drop material that doesn't work well and try something else. Try a new short routine with the rest of your show. If the new routine is favorably received, add it to your show, or use it to build a new show. If the routine is not successful, modify it or dump it and try again. A few minutes of mediocre material will not ruin an otherwise enjoyable show, so don't be afraid to experiment.

WHERE TO FIND MATERIAL

If you have a creative imagination, as most birthday party workers do, you will have the talent to dream up entertaining skits and routines for your birthday party show. Watch other children's entertainers and see how they present themselves and work with kids. What type of material gets them the best response? Keep a journal and record the things you learn and observe. A journal can provide a wealth of information, jokes, and ideas as you gather material for your own shows.

Be careful never to copy or plagiarize another performer's act word for word. No performer can become a success by copying other's material. Many do borrow jokes and ideas, and that's okay, as long as they change them to fit their own style and personality. In this way the joke becomes personalized.

This book will provide you with a lot of ideas, short stories, and gags to help you in creating your own unique show. There are lots of books with skits and routines you can use—clown skits, juggling skits, magic tricks and routines, puppet dialogues, etc.

Use joke and riddle books. Memorize several of your favorite lines. Incorporate them into your routines. You don't need to tell them exactly as they were written; change them to fit your show and your personality.

There is plenty of material to give you ideas. I have included many of these resources in the appendix of this book for your reference. You can find some of these books in the library. Bookstores may have a few, but the best place to look for these resources is in magic shops or mail order dealers. Except perhaps when you first start out, you will rarely use any of the routines written in books verbatim. The real advantage of these sources is to provide you with ideas that can be adapted to your own performing character. A skit described in a book can become very effective and original when it is tailored to fit your personality and performance style.

I highly recommend that you subscribe to some of the periodicals published by the organizations listed in the appendix. They can provide you with ideas and new material which you can adapt for your own use. They also offer invaluable instruction from experienced professionals to make your shows better.

Watch and read as much as you can. Gather ideas and record them in your journal. Take your props and start practicing or "playing around" with them and ideas will come.

Another source of material will come from your shows—as you present them. While most of the things you say and do should be preplanned and rehearsed, you are free to ad-lib whenever applicable. Ad-lib humor is spontaneous and often highly effective. Make note of those comments that bring good responses and incorporate them into subsequent shows. The children themselves can be excellent sources of material. Children have amazingly creative minds and while doing your show, some wisecracks from the audience may be hysterical. Make note of these comments; maybe you can use them yourself in future shows.

Keep a journal of all the jokes and gags you find amusing and that might possibly fit your character. Build up this file of material and refer to it as you create new shows and routines.

CREATING YOUR OWN SHOW

Use all the material you have gathered, past experience, and your natural creative genius, and put together your own show. Use all the ideas presented in this chapter to guide you.

You are encouraged to study all the chapters in this book even if you don't think they would apply to you.

If you plan on doing only magic, you will still gain a great deal of performing tips in the chapters on storytelling, clowning, and ballooning, as well as the others. Important performance techniques of story delivery are contained in the storytelling chapter and instruction on physical comedy and movement are found in the clowning chapter. Any children's entertainer will benefit from the information in these other chapters. The information in these chapters should be incorporated into your show in order to make your presentation as enjoyable as possible.

Sit down and write out your script word for word. Include every joke and a description of every trick or gag you use. Your journal should be a valuable resource for you at this time. Some people at first don't see how they can create funny routines. It's not as hard as you may think. Once you start working on a routine, perhaps taking a routine from another source and changing it to fit your style, your natural sense of humor and creativity will come out freely.

After writing everything down, perform the routine. Some things won't work as you envisioned and you will have to modify or discard material. While rehearsing, your sense of fun will be sharpened and you will discover new jokes and better ways to present yourself. As you practice, you will become more familiar with your material, timing and delivery will improve, and new ideas will surface.

Continue to practice your material until it is memorized and automatic. Use a mirror and analyze your facial expressions, body movements, and the handling of props. Use a cassette recorder and tape yourself. You will be surprised how you actually sound to others. Tape your first live show and play it back later. The audience could be from your own kids and their friends or a free show given at a neighbor's party. Analyze how you said things and how you could make your delivery better. What jokes were received well and which ones weren't? Modify, adapt, and improve both your material and your presentation. As you become more familiar and automatic with your show and more at ease working with kids, you will improve. In time, you will have a complete show prepared that you will be proud of.

What sound do two porcupines make when they kiss?
"Ouch!" _____

Why shouldn't you tell a pig a secret?
Because it squeals too much.

Chapter 2

WORKING THE PARTY

One of the great pleasures of being a birthday party entertainer is the opportunity to be the center of attention for groups of laughing, smiling kids, enchanted by your presence. For most entertainers this joyful reception produces a psychological high that is truly thrilling. Self-esteem and pride are by-products of performing and two of the prime motivators for getting into this business.

Birthday parties provide an ideal way for beginning entertainers to experience the thrill of being in the spotlight. The small audiences and informal atmosphere relieve many beginners of the apprehensions and fears that might accompany more grandiose performances. Many family entertainers begin their careers as birthday party entertainers. It is here that they learn to perfect their performing skills, learn how to handle an audience, and test material, while gaining practical experience. As a birthday party entertainer, you learn how kids react and how to control them. You learn what kids like and don't like, improving both your entertaining skills and your show.

Working at birthday parties also introduces you to the business aspects of the entertainment field—how to sell yourself, talk to potential clients, and keep records and time schedules. It builds your reputation, giving you exposure and opening the door to activities other than birthday parties. As a so-called family entertainer, you will undoubtedly receive offers to work at office parties, picnics, ranches, fairs, and other types of family and children's gatherings.

Some entertainers enjoy working parties so much, that is all they do, and they make a decent living at it. You can expect to make anywhere from about $50 to $300 for each party. The prices depend on the area of the country, the type of show, and your degree of skill. Obviously a puppeteer who does ventriloquism, juggles, and performs magic, will demand a higher fee than a clown who just tells jokes and hands out balloons.

When you first start out, you may be hesitant or unsure of yourself and your material. You might want to give your first couple of shows for free just to see what it's like and to get some experience.

The first party is always the hardest. If you have a friend who has a child with an approaching birthday, offer to entertain for free. Your friend will probably love the idea of getting free entertainment, and you'll get some valuable experience without the pressure of having to give a polished performance.

PREPARING YOUR SHOW

Most entertainers will spend a total of between 30 and 60 minutes at a client's house. The show portion of the party will take up from 20 to 40 minutes. The remaining time is filled in with greeting the kids, passing out giveaways, playing games, and other activities.

When you start performing for a fee, you technically become a professional. As a professional entertainer you are expected not only to look the part, but to act the part. To give a performance worthy of the title "entertainer" and earn the fee you are paid, you should present a well-planned, rehearsed, and tested show.

Some entertainers view birthday parties as an easy way to make money without having to do much work. They go to their parties with little preparation, tell a few canned jokes, show a few tricks, and generally goof-off with the kids, acting almost as one of the guests. Sometimes the ill-prepared entertainer feels he can get by with old worn-out tricks and jokes the kids have heard and seen a dozen times before. This type of entertainer is often disappointing to the children as well as the parents.

An entertainer is hired to entertain and, if he fails to do that, he has not honestly earned his wages. A good birthday entertainer should have a well-planned and prepared show, and should present it with enthusiasm. This is the standard for professional entertainment, and what parents usually expect.

For the beginner, having a well-prepared show will eliminate those butterflies that many novices experience. I recall how nervous (and excited) I was the first few times I went "on stage." I worried about how well I would be received and whether my presence would help make the party a success. Once I started into my rehearsed material and began to get a few laughs, I forgot about these apprehensions and hammed up my act to the fullest, making the show fun for the guests and satisfying for me.

Practice your show to perfection. Be able to perform all your tricks, stunts, or movements flawlessly and coordinate your patter for greatest effect. Kids can be unmercifully honest; if they see how you did a magic trick, they will be quick to tell you. Likewise, if your jokes aren't funny, they will let you know, either by word or by action. It's a tad bit discouraging when in the middle of a show one of the kids says "Let's do something else."

Audience response, even if negative, is valuable to you. The feedback you receive gives an indication of what the kids like and don't like. Your shows should continue to evolve: add new jokes, cut material which doesn't prove effective, and improve timing. As you gain more experience with a new show and make modifications, it will become a polished performance.

Once you are comfortable and confident with one show and get a good response, you can start working out a second, and even a third one. As your business increases, you will want to have the second show ready. Use it for repeat customers or for parties of kids who had been guests at one of your previous shows. A happy party guest telling his mother what a wonderful time he had is excellent advertising and results in many additional bookings. The child is likely to have many of the same friends who attended the first party, so you need something new for them. Kids love to get attention, and will shout out your punch lines and make other comments such as "I've seen that before," often spoiling the surprise of your tricks and jokes. Having a second show helps to eliminate this problem.

Most of your requests for parties will come from parents of children ages four to nine. As kids get older, parents feel that their children are outgrowing children's entertainers such as clowns and puppeteers. Family entertainers billed as jugglers, magicians, and such tend to pick up more of the older kids' parties because they are not restricted to the children's entertainment image, even though the material presented could be basically the same. For clowns and such, teenage and adult parties are rare. However, a family entertainer has a greater chance of being asked to do parties for these older groups.

On some occasions you will be asked to entertain for children four years old or less. Children this age are too young to appreciate magic, juggling, and other traditional skills. Shows that may be a big success with a group of seven-year-olds may be a miserable flop with a bunch of two-year-olds.

If you're asked to entertain at a party of preschoolers, in most cases your prepared show will not go over well. Some entertainers explain to parents that their shows are designed for older children, and will not accept such jobs.

Even though very young children will not appreciate many of the things a birthday party entertainer ordinarily does, you can still entertain them. I would suggest that if you get booked for such a party, you leave your regular show at home and do something else. I find that telling stories, using hand puppets, and playing games with the kids, while acting silly, work best. The parents can go into another room and relax while you "play" with the kids. (For more information on working with preschoolers, see Chapter 3.)

BOOKING THE PARTY
The Telephone

The majority of all birthday party bookings will be transacted over the telephone. What you say and how you say it will determine if you get the booking or not. Your telephone voice is very important. Since people cannot see you in person, your personality and appearance is conveyed

through your voice. The mental image you project will be a big factor in whether you are hired or not.

I once knew a school secretary who kept a mirror on her desk. I thought she was very vain until I noticed how she used it. Each time the phone rang, she would glance in the mirror and smile. She would then pick up the phone while smiling. This allowed her to transfer her positive feelings through the phone to the caller.

You, too, must be in a good frame of mind and have a positive attitude about yourself. You must answer the phone with an energized personality and keep it throughout your entire conversation. I promise you there will be clients who will hire you based solely on your attitude on the phone.

When the Phone Rings You Must be:

Enthusiastic

"That's a great idea."

"I'd like to go to this party."

Who wants to book a humdrum entertainer that sounds like they just rolled out of bed? No one.

Friendly

"I love kids."

"This sounds like a very special party!"

Would you really book some old crab for your darling daughter's birthday? Of course not.

Courteous

"Thank you for calling me."

Use "please" and "thank you," and don't interrupt.

Busy

"I must check my calendar to see if I'm available."

Pause a few moments; it keeps them in suspense and hoping, now more than ever, that they can get you.

Inquisitive

"What day is the party?"

"Who is attending?"

"What are the ages of the children?"

"What room will it be held in?"

The more they say, the more you'll know if you really want to do the party or not.

Attentive

"I'm following you exactly."

Listen to what your caller says. The more you can get the person on the other end of the line to talk about the party, the greater your chances of a booking. Let them talk.

Interested

"Tell me more. This sounds super!"

Different

"And I do a special illusion with the birthday child."

"The show ends with the surprise appearance of Fuzz-Face, the magic rabbit."

"I make each child a colorful balloon birthday hat they can wear during the party and take home as a souvenir."

"I present each guest with a magic book containing one hundred and two tricks they can perform with objects easily found around the home."

Cooperative

"I'm delighted to work with you to make Fred's birthday a really special day!"

Knowing

"I know how exciting birthdays are for children and how much work they are for Mom! Here are a few ideas and suggestions to make the party run smoother and be more fun: A great time to eat the birthday cake and ice cream is directly after the show. You'll have plenty of time to get the food and drinks ready while I entertain the kids."

Active

"My show really gets kids involved. It contains lots of fun audience participation and features some great magic. It's just perfect to captivate those active young minds."

"If it wasn't so much fun, you'd think it was educational."

Businesslike

"Let me double check your name, address, and phone number."

Go over all details twice. Be certain they know anything you require (like keeping the windows closed because your bird might get out!) and when and how they will be paying for your show. They are booking a professional entertainer. Sound that way.

Positive

"Yes," "great," "I agree," "how nice," "wonderful."

We all know birthday horror stories, like the time Marshmallow the bashful birthday bunny bit the birthday boy and he had to be rushed to the doctor for a tetanus shot (and on his birthday too!). But for Pete's sake, don't tell them to the client, even in joking. She'll get cold feet about having some stranger come into her house and wreak havoc. She'll take the kids bowling instead!

Smile!

Trust me, it shows through the phone. People want to book happy, cheerful, pleasant performers. Be one!

Descriptive

"Imagine the cheers, and how important Donnie will feel, when you announce to all his friends at the party that there is going to be a special magic show with a real magician in honor of Donnie's big sixth birthday!"

Paint pictures with words.

Experienced

"I've been performing for over 10 years, and I love kids' parties. I have as much fun as they do."

Truthful

If after talking with the potential client on the phone and it sounds like an event you would really rather not do, say so, but in a nice way. For example, "This sounds like a terrific party for your six-year-old daughter, Esmeralda, and her 20 Girl Scout friends. The idea of a magician is great and my show is wonderful, but I would be less than completely honest with you if I didn't tell you that it's geared more towards boys. I know a magician who specializes in parties for six-year-old girls. I'll be glad to give you his number."

Thankful

"Thank you for calling me. I appreciate your interest and I look forward to performing for your son, Bruno, and his friends. I'll do my best to ensure he has a very happy birthday. Thank you. Have a great day."

Honestly, I've listened to some performers who act like it's a major inconvenience that the client called them.

Sample Conversation

Ninety percent of the time the child's mother will be the one who calls. During this time you must collect all pertinent information and convince the caller to hire you. A typical telephone conversation may sound something like this:

Funny Business, this is Steve speaking.

Yes, I'd like to know about your prices to do a show.

Are you calling about a birthday party?

Yes.

Wonderful, to whom am I speaking?

Mrs. Jenkins.

Mrs. Jenkins, thank you for calling. What is the birthday child's name?

Lisa.

And how old will Lisa be?

Seven.

Oh, that's a fun age and they really enjoy a magical clown show! Mrs. Jenkins, how did you find out about my service?

From an ad in a shoppers' magazine.

Great, you are the (insert number) person who has called me from that ad. What is the date of the birthday party?

Next Saturday.

Well . . . let's see. I do have a two o'clock spot open. I believe that I can fit you in the schedule. Let me tell you about my birthday party program. I can arrive right at 2:00 PM if you want the children to arrive at 1:30 PM—that should take care of any of the folks not able to arrive on time. I can set up in either your living room or den. My comedy magic show usually lasts 45 minutes. The show involves a lot of participation with the children; I also enjoy including the parents and grandparents whenever possible. Since the party is in Lisa's honor, I will make it a special occasion for her and make her the star of the show. She will get a thrill out of it! My performance includes fun magic, juggling, puppetry, and ventriloquism. After the show, I give each child a balloon animal and a puzzle to take home as a souvenir. This way you don't have to worry about the extra expense of buying

A fellow asked me the other day if I wanted to buy a goat hair brush, but I told him *"Naaaaaa!"*

the customary party gifts. Lisa will also receive these, plus another special gift just for her. I'll bring the balloons in a bag and you can pass them out during the show. If you like, I will be happy to provide you with a Polaroid picture of Lisa and me. The total cost for everything is $100. Shall I schedule you for next Saturday?

Well, I'm not sure.

Have I answered all of your questions?

Yes, I think so. I'm just not sure I want to pay that much.

I can understand that. Perhaps you would be interested in my economy show. You get a 30-minute comedy magic show, with balloons, for only $75. Does that fit your budget better?

Yes, that's more reasonable.

Right now I have two o'clock open next Saturday, however, it may be gone in a day or two. Shall I schedule you for the economy show?

Yes, that sounds good.

Telephone Strategy

After securing the booking, you explain all the remaining details, such as when and how you expect to be paid, which room you prefer, what point during the party is best for your arrival, your policy about cancellations, etc.

Keep in mind that you must try to book the show during the first phone call. Your chance of actually being hired greatly diminishes if the caller has to think it over. She may be cruising the *Yellow Pages* or have already spoken to other party entertainers. Note how much information I requested before talking about my fee. I want to know as much as I can and let her know what she will be getting before talking about money. Also, I want the customer to become comfortable with me. I try to do whatever I can to build rapport with the customer.

One of the first questions she will ask is "How much will it cost?" Avoid answering this question until you have explained to her what she will get from you, and has had a chance to get to know you. A simple price quote often scares potential customers away because they don't realize what they are getting. You are more than just a funny person dressed up. You are an entertainer, a performing artist who has planned a spectacular show with gifts and games to make her child's party a memorable experience.

When you speak with a customer on the phone, it's best to take immediate control of the conversation by asking questions. If she asks you for a price, respond by saying something like, "Before I can answer that, I need

---

> What do elephants have that no other animals have?
> *Baby elephants.*

---

some information about your party." Ask for the location, time, and the date. This is really all you need to know to figure the price (and to determine if you are available at that time), but continue with questions such as name and age of the birthday child, number of guests, which room the show will be in, or if it will be outside? Asking these additional questions shows your interest in the child, and the customer feels she will get a custom tailored show. I feel getting the child's name is important. By asking for this information, you are telling the parent that you're interested in the child. It's also helpful to know who the guest of honor is when you enter the party. It shows a lack of respect to arrive and have to ask, "Whose birthday party is this?"

Often the caller will begin the conversation by telling how she found out about you—through a friend, neighbor, or a giveaway with your name on it brought home by a child. Take note of this because it will help you evaluate which promotional materials are bringing you the most business. If the caller doesn't volunteer this information, ask her where she found out about you.

Have an appointment book or calendar and a map ready by the phone. When she tells you the time and date, check your schedule and see if you're available. If you're busy at that time, ask if she has already sent out the invitations (surprisingly many parents will do this before giving you a call). If she has, tell her you're unavailable at that time and refer her to another entertainer, if possible.

If she hasn't sent the invitations, try to have the time changed so that you can attend. Most people will be willing to modify their original plans to accommodate you, so don't be afraid to ask.

If she doesn't have a firm time already planned, suggest a time for her that will work best for you. I find that I can get more business and save time by careful planning. Divide your day into blocks of one and a half or two hours, starting at about 11:00 A.M. If possible, schedule the first party at this time, the next at 12:30, followed by 2:00, 3:30, and 5:00, one right after the other. This will save you the problem of having one show at noon and waiting until 4:00 for the next.

Use the map to locate the area of town in which the caller lives. This will be important in figuring what price you charge. If travel time will be significant, you should charge more to compensate for your time and wear and tear on your car.

Beside the price, another often asked question is "What will you do?" Understandably, mothers want to know what they will be getting for their money.

Your answer should convince her that you're the person she's looking for. You should think about the answer to this question in detail beforehand so that when asked, you can give a brief description that will interest her. Expound on the benefits of your show and how it is unique. Stress the fact that you will give the birthday child special attention. This sales talk should convince her that you are a professional, that you care about providing a special experience for her child, and that she will get her money's worth. Make it sparkle, but be honest.

After asking the caller your questions, showing interest in her child, giving her your sales talk, and calculating what to charge or what party package to offer, you can bring up the price. She now knows what she will get and who you are. By now you should be more of a friend to her rather than simply a voice on the phone.

Information Sheets

You may find it convenient to use what I call an information or booking sheet. These sheets contain a pretyped list of the important questions I ask, such as name, address, and phone number.

I keep a stack of these sheets near the phone. When a potential client calls, I can pull out a sheet and fill it in during our conversation. I can take the sheet to the party so I have all pertinent information at my fingertips. The sheet also serves as a permanent reference that can be filed for later use. The following year, a month or so before the child's birthday, I call the parents and inquire about another party. Even if the person who calls doesn't use my services, I can save the sheet and inquire with them the following year. I then send out a letter reintroducing myself, including a more detailed description of myself and my qualifications, talents, special citations, and recommendations. I also enclose a printed picture. I leave out the price out so the customer will have to call for that information, giving me a chance to talk in person.

Cards are filed by date, not by name. I can either give the parents a personal call or send a letter to let them know I'm available if they decide to have a party and need entertainment.

The front of the information card contains all the specifics on the price charged, location, time, and names. The back can be used for detailed directions to the party or any other bits of information I care to remember. It is a convenient place to note which party I gave, #1 (comedy magic) or #2 (puppets & magic). If I'm booked for a return visit, I know what show I've already given them.

During your questioning, ask where you will be giving your show. Most often the family or living room is used, but the show can be on the porch or in the backyard as well. Depending on the type of show you give, location may be important. Some rooms can become very crowded with 20 wiggly kids stacked inside.

Reconfirm the date and time, and mark it on your calendar. Get directions to the party location if necessary, and make sure the phone number is correct. At times as you are driving to the party, you will find yourself lost. No matter how accurate your map may be, the directions you received may not be accurate, or a street sign may be down. If you find that you're going to be late, give the parents a call. A mother cooped up in a house with 20 screaming, jumping kids may be going out of her mind. She will appreciate your call and won't be angry at you when you finally arrive. In all cases, allow a little extra time to get to the party and give a call if you find you're going to be late.

Since the party will most likely be scheduled several days in advance, it's a good policy to call the day before or on the morning of the party to confirm your engagement and to assure the parents that you will be there as scheduled. Events can alter previously made plans: people get sick, change their minds, or have emergencies. Calling first will let you know if the party is still on as planned; if not, the call will save you a needless trip and preparation.

In addition, I have a laminated calendar of the entire year that allows me at-a-glance availability of dates. Whichever system you choose, make sure that it includes the following information:

Date and time of the party
Name of parent and child
Child's age and date of birth
Address and directions to the site
Work and home phone numbers
How many children invited to the party
How parent found your number
Type of character/show wanted
Mileage
Tolls
Follow-up call information
Theme of the party if any
Age range and special needs of the children

These are a few of the items which will be pertinent to the success of your performance. You may find that additional information is needed. You may also want to send the parent a flyer. This establishes you as a professional and puts something in their hands for future reference. It may also be passed on to another client.

AT THE PARTY

Arrive at the party in full costume. Live up to your image as a professional; never put on pieces of your makeup or costume in front of the kids, or you will destroy the fantasy and appear as just a person dressed up. Give yourself plenty of time in case you're delayed or get lost. Work out all details over the phone so that when you reach the party, you can get right to work.

Schedule your time to arrive at the party a few minutes early. No matter how early you get there, stay in you car until the exact time you are scheduled to show up. Drive around or wait down at the end the block if you have to. Once you drive up to the house you are "on." If you are there before all the guests have arrived, you will be asked to wait. And while you are waiting, you will be expected to keep the other children amused.

Smile and be in character from the moment you are spotted. One of the first things you should do is greet the birthday child and give her that special recognition that she deserves and that parents love.

Ask the hostess (or host) to lead you to the area where you will be performing. Most often the kids will be scattered throughout the house as you enter. Greet the children as they curiously gather around you.

A few short jokes or gags help break the ice and let the kids know they're in for a fun time. Typically you will spend just a few minutes with the greeting, until all the children have gathered. Sometimes the hostess will ask you to wait for a late guest or two. In this case you will

need to have something planned to entertain them before getting into your "prepared" material.

What do you do in cases like this? . . . Anything you feel comfortable with: have the children play some simple games, show them some close-up magic tricks, or show them how to make hats or other things with folded newspaper. Whatever you do should be brief. You shouldn't be expected to wait any longer than about 10 minutes.

Whatever you do, you should be in charge and not become "buddies" with the party guests. If they become too familiar with you, they will feel they can take advantage of your good nature and have fun at your expense by taking your props, smarting off to you, and not following your directions.

Tom Myers, a successful birthday party magician and balloon worker from Austin, Texas, says one of his favorite preshow activities is the slow rocket balloon. He takes the children outside for a few minutes of balloon fun. Inflate a 260 pencil balloon and tie it off. With a fingernail clipper cut a BB sized hold in the end of the balloon opposite the knot, as shown in the illustration below. The size of the hole is very important. Too large and the balloon will fly too fast and deflate too quickly, too small and the balloon won't fly. Push one of your fingers into the balloon where the hole is. Twist the balloon a bit as you push it onto your finger as if you were screwing it on. Release the balloon and it will fly. The twist will allow it to spiral and fly somewhat straight. It will remain airborne for several seconds. The kids will have fun chasing it down. This activity allows the kids to have fun without becoming too familiar with you. You remain in control.

Whether you have another party scheduled or not, tell the hostess that you can wait a few minutes, but no longer because you have other appointments you must

The slow motion rocket balloon.

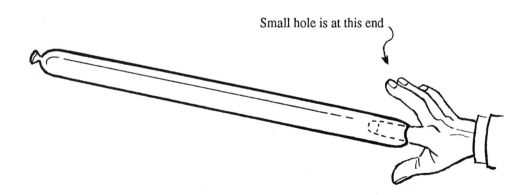

Small hole is at this end

honor. You don't want your 45-minute booking dragging out to 90 minutes; you're not being paid for extra time. Explain to her that you'll be happy to wait a few minutes, but you have a limited amount of time and will have to start the show soon. If you bring this to her attention, usually she will not insist that you wait more than the amount of time you've allowed.

If you explain to the hostess on the phone beforehand that you must stick to the time schedule you have agreed on, you will rarely have problems. She will understand your position and the show will proceed without undue delay.

Controlling the Crowd

When you begin your show, have all the kids come into the room and sit down. Encourage them to remain in their seats and to be still. Kids at birthday parties are wiggly and full of energy, so you need to get their attention and interest from the very start. Show them that you're taking control of the party by having them all participate in a simple opening activity. By having them do this, you are establishing your role as the leader. Use audience participation techniques similar to those discussed in Chapter 3.

Promising to give them a reward for behaving will help encourage them. Tell them that those who sit still and smile will be chosen to be your personal helpers later on. Note that I don't ask them to be quiet, only to be still and smile. It seems contradictory to tell them to be quiet and then try to make them shout with laughter, but when you tell them to smile, you're telling them to behave, yet to feel free to laugh and giggle. Besides, it's hard to talk and smile at the same time.

You can also use a balloon animal as an incentive, promising to give one to all of those who remain in their seats. (Of course you will eventually give one to everybody, but they don't know that.) You might even make an animal and put it aside so that they can see it throughout the show as a constant reminder. You may have to remind them from time to time by pointing to the balloon and asking them to settle down. Never be harsh! You have been invited to come into the home to entertain, not to discipline, and if you follow these steps you should have few problems.

> How could twelve children and two dogs be under an umbrella, and not get wet?
> *When it's not raining.*

At the end of your show, give the balloon to the best behaved child and say, "All of the rest of you have been so good I think I'll give each of you a balloon." Don't leave anyone out, even if they were overly energetic during your show.

The Show

Make it a point of giving the birthday child a special greeting when you first meet, and give him or her some special attention during the show. If you use any volunteers during your show, make sure the guest of honor has a chance to participate. Customize a few jokes, using the birthday child's name; don't make jokes about her, but use her name in a story. Make the party special for the birthday child by acknowledging her in these ways.

You might also consider giving the birthday child a special gift. An ideal gift is an autographed photo of yourself with your name and phone number printed on it. A printed photograph is inexpensive, and serves as a special reminder of your presence at the party. Parents like to see their children get preferential treatment—especially if they're paying for it. They will love you for giving their child this special attention. It makes your show look custom-made and unique. You will also increase your chance for repeat business with her and new business from references.

There are three major parts to most children's birthday parties: the present opening, cake and ice cream eating, and the entertainment or games. As the performer, you will be in charge of the entertainment. Whether or not you include games along with your show is up to you.

My shows lasts about 30 minutes; I spend another 10 or 15 minutes greeting the kids and handing out balloon animals. Altogether I spend approximately 45 minutes at the party, and then leave. Occasionally I will remain another 30 minutes or so, supervising party games (for which I charge extra).

I do not stay for the present opening or cake eating. The food and gift opening are entertainment in themselves and don't need my presence. In fact, the kids become so engrossed in these activities that they don't care if you're there or not.

Some birthday party entertainers do participate in these activities and take on the role of a supervisor. I'd rather avoid this hectic time, with kids struggling over the new toys and eating their share of the goodies. I would rather keep my image as an entertainer and leave the supervisory role to the parents.

Often the hostess will invite you to share in the gift opening and eating. To avoid any problem, let her know while you're on the phone that you will be coming only for the show (and games if that's part of the agreement) and then will leave. You can explain, since you're an authority on the subject, that your presence during those two activities is not needed.

Most parties begin with games or entertainment and end with cake and presents. I suggest that you recommend this schedule to your caller. Arrange to make your entrance at least 15 to 30 minutes after the party is scheduled to begin, so that most, if not all, of the children will be present before you arrive.

I do not recommend opening the gifts before the entertainment because it creates too much of a distraction. You may find yourself frequently interrupted by the noise from some of the toys or from kids fighting over them.

The gift opening is usually the highlight for the birthday child, and ideally should be saved for last. Once the presents are opened, the new owner will be absorbed in the gifts, and other things lose interest.

Some party entertainers like to stay after giving their prepared show to supervise a few games and other activities. Musical games and contests can be loads of fun for the kids and will keep them occupied while mom and dad relax or prepare the refreshments. This extra service will take up another 30 or 45 minutes. I recommend never staying longer than 90 minutes. Leave while they're still having fun and enjoying your presence.

PROPS

Most birthday shows will take place in the living room or family room. I strongly recommend that you avoid any tricks or gags which will make a mess. Spilled milk or flour on the rug will not make a happy hostess, nor will she appreciate cleaning confetti and other scraps of paper off the floor.

If you perform a trick that requires the tearing of paper or some other activity which will create trash, store the debris in your case or prop bag and discard it later.

The props you use should be small, for the most part—no trick guillotines, sword boxes, chain saws, or torches. Shows are usually performed in small (and, at times overcrowded) rooms, so close-up magic tricks and other small props work best. Since the audience is usually small and near the performer, hand held props are easily seen by all.

Most any type of show will require you to carry props. The most convenient way to do this is in a prop bag or case. Any type of portable container which can be closed to keep curiosity seekers out will work. Stack props in the order they are to be taken out. This saves you the time and inconvenience of rummaging through all the props looking for the ones you need. Having pockets or compartments in your prop container is helpful in keeping things organized.

A suitcase table is an ideal way to carry props, especially if you do magic. It converts into a table that can be used in your show, and provides a convenient way to get to your props without digging through piles of gadgets. The contents of the case are kept out of sight, yet are easy to locate. When the show is over, you put the props on the bottom, fold down the top and wheel the case out to your car.

Children are naturally curious creatures. Your prop case will be an enticement to them. If they get the chance, they will be all over it and your props will disappear throughout the room. Store your props out of sight and keep an eye on your prop case at all times.

Birthday party entertainer P. J. Parsons keeps her materials childproof by using a large plastic box that snaps shut. The box she uses is a Rubbermaid product which is available in many stores. These boxes come in bright cheery colors and are strong enough to use as airline luggage. Parsons uses hers to sit or stand on while she is performing. "Many birthday party performers use a bag to carry their shows in," say Parsons, "but a box works much better when it comes to being child-proofed. These boxes can be shut and sat or stood on to keep prying fingers out. Kids may keep poking away at a bag, but once the box is closed, they leave it alone."

PARTY FAVORS

Giving party favors or souvenirs to the guests has become a custom at birthday parties. As the host or hostess, the parents are responsible for providing these gifts to all the kids. When the entertainer takes over this responsibility it not only relieves the parents of this duty, but allows the entertainer to enjoy several benefits. Promising the kids a gift if they behave allows you to keep them under control. Giving a souvenir or a gift to all the kids also makes a good ending to your show. Kids love receiving presents; giving them something will make your show more fun and end it with a bang.

Although giving out presents may cost you a little, it's worth it. Keep the gift inexpensive, and whatever it is, have your name and phone number attached to it somehow. This will remind the kids of the fun they had and will let the parents know who you are and how to contact you if they ever plan a party. A child coming home and telling her parents that a funny clown was at the party is an excellent referral for future parties. The gift provides a way for these parents to know who you are and how to contact you.

What type of gift should you give? The most common gifts are balloon animals, but many other inexpensive gifts would work just as well. Let's look at some of the most popular types.

Balloon Animals

I believe balloons are an ideal gift. They cost only a few cents each, and kids love them! Some children's entertainers have commented that *everybody* gives balloon animals, implying that children get bored with the same type of gift. But how often do kids go to parties—a couple of time a year perhaps? I've never seen a child disappointed at receiving a balloon animal. Most children never get tired of them. My own kids have seen me make hundreds of

the rubbery creatures and have walked away with armloads, only to come rushing back begging for more. They never seem to tire of them, no matter how often they get them.

You don't have to be a skilled balloonologist to make balloon animals, nor do you need to make a different animal for each child. If all you can make is a simple dog (which anyone can learn to do with a few minutes' practice), then give them all dogs. Using different colored balloons will add variety.

Blowing up 25 balloons can wear out even the best set of lungs, especially the hard-to-inflate pencil balloons used in making balloon animals. Few people have the natural lung power to blow these balloons up when they first attempt it. You will have to practice and gradually build up your strength in order to inflate them without complete exhaustion. As a beginner, your lung power may not be up to full strength, but don't be discouraged. You can still inflate 25 balloons at a time by using a small hand held balloon pump (obtainable from magic dealers or wherever balloons are sold).

Some party entertainers feel unprofessional using a pump, but I use one and I don't feel it hurts my presentation at all. The kids still jump with excitement no matter where the air comes from. I can easily fill 25, 30, or more balloons without the slightest strain on my lungs.

If you prefer, you might even consider making up one or two dozen animals in your leisure time before going to the party and handing them out when it's time. Still I feel you should make the first few from scratch (with or without a pump) just so the kids can have the thrill of seeing how you transform an ordinary balloon into a lovable figure.

You don't have to limit yourself just to animals. You can make balloon toys, hats, and games. Even balloon puppets, combined with ventriloquism, can be used with pleasing results.

For more information on balloons, see Chapter 8.

Paper Games and Puzzles

I usually give balloon animals as a gift, but I also like to give a second gift that I can easily print my name and phone number on. A sheet of paper or a small booklet of games, puzzles, or brain teasers works well. This way everyone at the party will know who I am; so will their parents when they take the gifts home. Your expense is the cost of the paper and printing, which amounts to only a few cents each if you buy in large quantities.

You can have an artist make a coloring book taken from pictures of you in costume. This would be an excellent way to promote yourself. A single sheet or a short booklet with dot-to-dot drawings, mazes, crossword puzzles, jokes, and magic tricks can make an excellent gift.

Paper toys can also be made with much of the same success as balloon figures. You can do this yourself, or have everyone make their own as you show them how. Kids always take pride in something they make themselves and will be sure to show it to their parents. Paper hats, airplanes, and puppets are a few easily made items. You may find some intriguing creations and ideas in many of the books available on origami, paper airplanes, and toys. Check with your library or bookstore.

Photographs

A black and white autographed photo of yourself is another excellent gift. Have your name and phone number printed on it and use it as the special gift just for the birthday child, or you can give one to each of the guests.

I like to give the guest of honor a special gift just for her (along with the other gifts). Receiving something that no one else gets will make her feel important and make the parents happy because you give her special attention.

Use a studio photo and look as professional as you can. A studio photo is expensive, but it can serve you for several years.

Handing out actual photographs can be expensive. Rather than using a real photograph, you can have copies of the photo printed for a reasonable price. Have the printer use glossy paper and it will look just like a photo. Don't forget to have your name and phone number printed on it.

The old saying "A picture is worth a thousand words" is true. The children who receive your picture will remember you longer. Parents will be able to see the funny entertainer their child was talking about, giving them a longer lasting impression and increased chance of remembering you when their child has a birthday.

I recommend that you autograph each picture. Autographs give the picture a personal touch and increase the chance the child will get it home and keep it around for a while. I prefer to autograph each picture personally rather than have the signature printed. The autographs can

---

How do you know that carrots are good for the eyes?
Have you ever seen a rabbit wearing eyeglasses?

---

be done beforehand with a simple "Best Wishes, Mysto the Magician."

Toys and Candy

Balloon animals are a favorite giveaway for most party entertainers, but you certainly can use your imagination and try other things. If you do magic, an appropriate gift would be an inexpensive magic trick or puzzle. If you buy them in large quantities at wholesale prices, the cost can be minimal. Whatever you choose, keep the cost low.

Some of the cheapest toys are balloons—not pencil balloons which are used to make animals, but spinners, rockets, and other novelty balloons. They are inflated, then turned lose to fly or spin. They are reusable and kids love them.

Stickers make fun and inexpensive gifts. They come in a wide variety of designs, styles, and shapes and can be pealed and temporarily stuck to clothes or skin. Some of the designs I have seen include animals, clowns, birthday party greetings, sports, food, dinosaurs, musical instruments, and toys. You can even have custom made stickers with your own message or likeness printed on them. This would make a clever promotional gimmick. You can get 100 preprinted stickers for just a few dollars.

Fancy pencils are also enjoyable. You can get them in a variety of designs and with creative, children pleasing eraser heads. Heads can be fuzzy-eyed pom-poms, miniature troll dolls, animals, and sporting equipment erasers.

Stickers and pencils are just a few of the inexpensive toys you can give. Two excellent sources for these and other toys are Oriental Trading Company, P.O. Box 3407, Omaha, NE 68103, and Tipp Novelty Company, 222 N. Sixth Street, Tipp City, OH 45371. They each have mail order catalogs filled with hundreds of items suitable for giveaways. They have yo-yos, puzzles, jump ropes, harmonicas, kazoos, balloons, games, activity books, balls, magic tricks, soap bubbles, glow in the dark buttons and bracelets, and even candy. All of these items are ridiculously inexpensive and can be purchased for a quarter or less. Some of the more expensive items may cost a dollar or more each, but there are more than enough cheap items from which to choose. You can get a dozen wooden paddle ball games for less than $4. That's 33 cents each and you can easily write your name and phone number on the paddle or even draw a picture (or use a custom made rubber stamp) of yourself or your logo. The only catch is that the cheaper items are usually sold in quantities of a dozen or more and you have to pay for shipping, but if you plan to use them as giveaways, you will want to buy in large quantities anyway. With larger orders, the shipping charge becomes relatively insignificant.

Candy and other treats are enjoyable and can make an inexpensive giveaway, but you should check with your hostess before giving this type of gift. Some kids are restricted from certain foods either for health reasons or

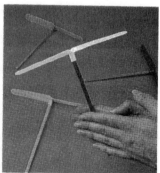
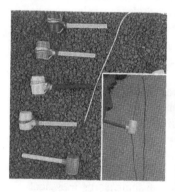

Some of the inexpensive items from Oriental Trading and Tipp Novelty that you can use as giveaways.

simply because the parents don't want to dig candy out of the rug after the party.

Small lollipops and such are easy to carry and are appreciated by the children, but once eaten, they're gone. There's nothing to take home to show mom, and let her know who you are. If you want to give candy, consider combining it with another more permanent gift which has your promotional material printed on it.

Balloons are fun, but don't use them just because everyone else does. Use your imagination and find something different. The more unique the gift, the greater the chance it will be kept by the recipient as a reminder of the fun she had with you.

GETTING PAID

Like other service businesses, birthday party entertainers usually get paid as soon as they have finished their job and just before leaving. You should make this clear to the client on the phone when scheduling the party.

Often the client will be ready with your payment as soon as you finish. You may request this to be so. If you explain beforehand that you need to be paid as soon as you finish, most people will try to accommodate you. You may have to track down your host in the kitchen or some other part of the house and tell her you're ready for payment.

Let the children and parents know when your show will be over. Make an announcement that you have one more thing to do and then you have to go.

Do not leave the home without getting paid! You're just asking for trouble if you do. At times the hostess will be in a frenzy, shoveling out ice cream as rowdy kids eagerly bear down on her. Her hands may be covered with ice cream and cake and obviously frazzled by a group of screaming children. She may play on your sympathy and ask you to wait until after the refreshments have been served or promise to send you payment later after the party is over. Don't let her. You've explained to her on the phone when payment is to be made. Insist that you receive it then, and explain you can't stay because you have an appointment elsewhere. This will help motivate her to pull herself away from the children and complete her part of the arrangement. Be firm, but remain friendly.

The reason you need to get paid immediately after your performance is that you don't want a 45-minute show stretching out to 60 minutes or more. You aren't paid for this extra time and yet you must still be in character with the children. Also, if you leave with only a promise to get paid, it may take weeks to receive it, if you get it at all. Once you are gone, it is too easy for parents to

forget about you or suddenly become short of funds. Payment for services already rendered, especially entertainment, will take a back seat to rent, utilities, and other more vital obligations. If your client decides not to send you your money, there is little you can do about it. You can contact a collection agency, but that may cost you as much as 50 percent of the bill and still is no guarantee you will get paid. Avoid the hassle and headache of trying to collect, and get your money when it is due.

To avoid payment and collection problems, some entertainers use contracts. This is more common with entertainers who work in nonbirthday party settings, such as malls, business promotions, company picnics, and the like. But many entertainers also use them for birthday parties. The contract guarantees that the performer is either notified in advance in case of a cancellation or he will be entitled to full or partial payment. At times parents will change their plans and forget to tell the entertainer or wait until the last minute to inform him that he is no longer needed. In such cases other bookings may have been turned down or rescheduled, compounding the loss. After the booking is confirmed over the phone, a contract is sent to the client, signed, and returned before the date of the party. Contracts don't have to be written in legal terms nor drawn up by a lawyer; any clearly written document will work. The contract should specify what the client is going to receive from you and what you are going to receive from the client. It will include such things as where the performance will be held, how long you will be there, the time and date of the party, the fee, and how payment is to be made. Most contracts include a cancellation clause which entitles you to be given suitable notice if the client backs out. Contracts can contain anything you want them to, depending on your needs.

> Why does a cowboy ride a horse?
> *Because his horse is too heavy to carry.*

Another useful purpose for a contact is to verify the information you took over the phone. You may have written all this down when a client called for a booking, however, when writing the details in a hurry it is easy to record some of the information incorrectly. The client can verify all the information on the contract before returning it.

A contract also serves to show clients you are a professional and serious about your business. If you provide a catering service, especially something that is custom made such as a decorated birthday cake, a contract with a clearly specified cancellation clause is important. Because a contract is a legal document, bounced checks are less likely.

You don't need to pay a lawyer to write a contract. You can have so many clauses full of complicated legal terms that it will intimidate a client and prevent them from signing. Write it yourself, keep it simple, and cover only the main points of concern. To make sure it covers all bases and adequately protects yourself, you may want to pay a lawyer to simply look it over. In this way, it is easier to understand and is more friendly. Once you have written one working contract, you can modify it slightly to fit almost any other client.

A letter of agreement is a contract written in a letter format. A letter is a more friendly appearing document than a formal contract. It can serve as both a confirmation letter and as a contract. Two signed copies should be sent to your client—one for them to sign and return and the other for their records. A sample letter of agreement is shown on the following page.

The example I have provided requests at least half of the payment in advance. You may request full payment in advance as well, which eliminates the hassle of chasing down the hostess after the party to get the rest of your money. You could also offer to accept payment with a credit card and have them give their credit card number and expiration date. If you cater food or decorations, list each item you will supply. You may also request that the room you use be prepared for you by moving chairs out of the way to give you space, and removing breakable objects.

Some entertainers insist on receiving payment in cash in order to avoid bounced checks. This way they avoid the trouble of contacting the parent and requesting payment again along with an additional service fee which the bank will charge you. Not only is this situation an added burden and a needless waste of your time, but some people will delay sending payment, or may not send it at all. When you try to contact the author of a bounced check, you may also find that she has moved.

August 1, 19--

Dear Mrs. Jones:

I want your daughter Stephanie to have the best birthday party possible. I have done hundreds of shows over the years and, as a birthday party specialist, I can tell you she will get personalized, professional attention that will make your party special.

This letter will serve to confirm our understanding regarding Stephanie's party scheduled for ten guests on August 14 at your home. I will provide the entertainment—a comedy magic act and party favors (animal balloons). I will arrive at approximately 11:15 a.m., fifteen minutes after the party guests have arrived, and remain until 12:00 Noon. During this time I will present a 25-minute comedy magic show; the rest of the time will be spent interacting with the children on a more personal level and giving Stephanie special attention.

You can help make this party a special experience by keeping distractions to a minimum. Noise from the radio, television, and conversations should be kept down and confined to a room other than the one in which the party is taking place. Please do not give the children refreshments until after the show. The children participate with me in many activities, and food and drink may end up on the carpet.

The total cost for this service will be $80, one-half payable upon signing this letter of agreement and one-half on the day of the party, prior to my leaving at 12:00 a.m. In the event of a cancellation, you must notify me within 24 hours of the party. Failure to do so will incur a $40 cancellation charge. If notification of cancellation is not received before one hour prior to party time, the full $80 will be assessed.

If this reflects your understanding, please sign below and return one copy of this letter to me along with a $40 deposit. If full payment is made in advance, you may deduct $5 as a prepayment discount for a total cost of only $75.

I look forward to helping to make your daughter Stephanie's birthday a memorable one.

Sincerely,

John Jones, aka Mysto
AGREED:

_____   _____
Customer's Name   Date

P.O. BOX 2345, VICTORIA, BRITISH COLUMBIA V8T 4Y1, (250) 555-990

Sample Letter of Agreement.

Although accepting only cash will eliminate this problem, bounced checks are not common. Paying cash may not always be convenient for the hostess, especially if you charge $100 or more. You will have to decide what you feel is best.

You might want to consider getting merchant credit card status at your bank so your clients can charge it to their accounts. Many people prefer to pay with a Visa, MasterCard, Discover, or American Express card. This method can also be convenient for you. A big advantage you have with credit cards is that when you book a party on the phone, you can get the customer's credit card number and charge the fee in advance. This way you do not have to bother with tracking down the parent after the show. Nor does she have to drop everything to pay you. The party can be disrupted as the hostess takes time to get her purse and make payment, and the performer also must step out of character to transact this part of the business. Some parents would rather make payment out of sight of the children.

With a credit card you can reserve a specific day and time for the customer's party. Although most any booking will reserve the performer's time regardless of the method of payment, the credit card acts like a guarantee or contract and the customer can feel assured that the time is reserved.

Because you have made a firm reservation, it means you may have to turn down other customers who request your services at the same time. Since you are reserving this time, your client would be expected to pay you even if she cancels the party. You may charge her the full price for canceling with less than a 24-hour notice, or charge a reservation or cancellation fee which would be only a fraction of the total amount. Your policy should be clearly stated beforehand so the client is totally aware of it. This prevents clients from canceling just because they change their minds or decide to do something else.

Credit cards are nice in that they help to make your business look more professional. Businesses that can qualify to take credit cards give an appearance of success. Many people prefer the convenience of using credit rather than bother with cash or checks. The fact that you can take payment by credit card is another advantage that might help a potential client decide to use your services over someone else.

To use credit cards you must get credit card merchant status with the bank that services your account, preferably your business account. Talk to the people at your bank and tell them what you want. You will need to fill out an application. If approved, you will be required to purchase an imprinting machine (less than $20) and fill out a merchant agreement which specifies how credit sales work. All banks are different; some will not grant credit card merchant status to home-based workers, others will. Some may require that you be in business a certain number of years first, so if you're just starting a business, receiving credit card payments may be difficult. You may need to shop around. If you don't have a business checking account, get one with a bank who will be willing to let you use credit cards. You don't have to have a business checking account if the bank allows you to use a personal account for business, as some do for individuals who are self-employed. You will just have to see what bankers in your area will do.

With credit card status you can take the customer's account number over the phone and charge the price of the show to them. You fill out a deposit slip which is run through your imprinting machine and deposited in your bank much as you would a check. Your account is automatically credited with the deposit and the credit card company then bills and collects from your customer. The cost for this service runs around three to five percent, depending on the amount you deposit each month and the bank you work with. The more you deposit, the smaller a percentage they take.

Chapter 3

WORKING WITH KIDS

Kids, unlike adults, are in a hurry to get older. Witness the little girl who holds up four fingers and proclaims she is "almost" five, or the boy who boasts that he is six *and a half* years old.

The birthday anticipation and excitement begins weeks before a child's actual birthday. Picking the special day for the party, as well as inviting the "honored" guests, is very important business. Although some people, like relatives must be invited (even Noreen? Yes even Noreen!). Never has the child been given such power to select and rank his friends. The eagerness continues to build the week of the party as the little friends confirm with delight that they will be at the "event of the year."

When the day of the party actually arrives, it is almost too much for one little body to bear. Crepe paper is strung, and banners proclaiming the occasion are hung. Colorful balloons are blown up. Fun! They bounce real high when punched and make a great big wonderful bang when broken. More fun! There might even be a game of sit on the balloons, where the youngsters purposely try to destroy them. Great fun!

The birthday cake arrives with the guest of honor's name on it, and candles (with real fire!) will soon be placed on top of it. How dangerous! How exciting!

True, the birthday boy has to be dressed up, but if you think that's going to stop him from mopping up the floor with his body or wrestling with Noreen, you've got another thought coming. Besides that snazzy bow tie isn't going to last long once the real party gets going.

The table is being set. Guess who got to pick out the paper plates, napkins, and matching paper table cloth. Isn't the drooling Godzilla on the lime green background a real grabber! The kids are really going to have a blast. The guests should be arriving any minute.

The doorbell rings. Yeah! The child is hopping up and down with excitement. He can't control himself. The party is beginning! His guests are coming in; each has a gift. All enter and pay homage to the king (or queen) of the birthday party.

More guests arrive; the excitement builds. More little munchkins in frenzied motion. More presents! Frustration occurs when his royal mother announces that he must wait till after the cake and ice cream to open his presents.

Pretty soon the house is overrun by pint-sized revelers. Mom is lost in the confusion of answering the phone—when she is not answering the door.

Dad and the older boys wisely exited the house to spend the afternoon with Uncle Fred to watch the ball game in peace. (Smart men!)

The dog barks every time the doorbell rings and welcomes each guest with a snarl and a sniff.

Fun!

The record is on the wrong speed.

Fun!

Bang! Suzie broke a balloon.

Fun!

Don't touch the cake.

Fun!

The crepe paper is sagging.

Fun!

The dog just ran out the front door.

Fun!

"Keep your fingers out of the icing on the cake!"

Fun!

No one talks; everybody screams.

Fun!

No one walks; everybody runs.

Fun!

The doorbell rings. Everyone is having too much fun to pay attention. It rings again . . . and again . . . Look! It's the MAGICIAN! Now the real fun is about to begin!

WHAT DO KIDS LIKE?

If you are going to be successful as a birthday party entertainer, you will need to know what kids like. As described above, a birthday party is a lively affair with plenty of distractions and excitement. Your show must interest them enough to persuade them to sit down and remain relatively controlled for 30 minutes or more. For the time you are there, you must be more fun than anything else at the party. If not, their interest will wane and they will start to look for others things to amuse themselves. These other things are usually disruptive and can destroy your presentation and play havoc on your nerves.

If you incorporate into your show the things that kids like, they will be interested, and you will succeed. So what do kids like? Read on.

Comedy for Kids

What do kids like to do most?. . . They like to laugh! The more they can laugh, the more fun they will have. As a birthday party entertainer, if you set your goal to make them laugh, you will be a success. It doesn't matter if you are a clown, magician, or some other type of entertainer, if you can make them laugh, they will enjoy themselves. You will have made the party a memorable event. Whatever skills you use, whether it be storytelling, puppetry, or whatever, you should accompany it with plenty of humor.

Skills in magic, puppetry, juggling and other arts can be used very effectively with children. They like the animation, mystery, and suspense associated with these skills, but the skill alone won't hold their interest for long.

You may be a clever ventriloquist and have wonderful looking puppets, but if you aren't funny, you will not please the kids. If you are going to keep their attention and entertain them for 30 minutes, you must make them laugh. If you are a magician, don't plan on presenting a magic show; you must have a *comedy* magic show. If you are a puppeteer, you must have a comedy presentation or show. Whatever skill you do, make it funny.

Kids like anything that is silly and often corny, especially the younger ones. Simple jokes, one-liners, and planned ad-libs combined with your skills go over big. Children love physical comedy—goofy faces and actions, slapstick, and sight gags. "Accidentally" hitting yourself with a prop, tripping over your own foot, or getting mixed up—anything that is unexpected of a mature level-headed adult is funny.

Kids love to see grown-ups goof up. Whenever the entertainer makes mistakes, kids love it! Getting the children's names wrong, saying something backwards, or having a trick or stunt backfire is great fun for the kids. Kidshow magician, David Ginn, calls this the "Magician-in-Trouble Syndrome." But it can also be called the "Entertainer-in-Trouble Syndrome" and refer to any type of children's entertainer. The entertainer goofs up and the children laugh; he makes a mistake and the children laugh; he compounds the mistake and the children laugh louder.

Combine the humor. When saying something funny, ham it up with silly facial expressions, body movements, and vocal expressions. This will compound the humor of the situation and make your jokes and actions funnier. However, stay in character. A clown can get away with sillier actions than a magician or storyteller can. You must work into your act comedy that fits your character and your personality best. This will take time and practice to develop. Your humor and presentations will evolve with you as you gain experience and hone your skills.

Stories

Children like stories. Stories have the power to transport children into a world of make-believe and to get them interested and involved with you. Jokes and comedy situations can easily be presented through stories. Incorporating stories into your routines will help to make your show a success.

A magician or even a clown may tell a story as he performs a magic trick. The trick becomes part of the story, with the climax being the magical effect at the end. Or he may use situation comedy, typical with comedy magic. He attempts to perform a trick but has forgotten the magic word. Whenever he attempts what he believes to be the correct word, something unexpected happens, all to the delight of the kids. A puppeteer tells a story as the puppets interact with each other, or uses situation comedy where the puppet is supposed to help the puppeteer do something, but causes him problems instead.

Demonstrating your skills, such as a magician performing one trick after another, is not entertaining for children. Adding snappy jokes and one-liners will improve it. But your presentation should be built around stories so that you can incorporate jokes and situation comedy. Stories not only provide you an avenue to tell jokes, but also get the children interested in what you are doing or what is going to happen. They want to know how the story will end. Suspense is created which will help to keep their attention. Stories need not be long, drawn out affairs. Short stories work best in most situations. A dialogue between the puppeteer and puppet is a story. The children are listening in on your conversation, just as they do with television shows. The conversation usually has a theme or topic, which may change throughout the presentation.

Stories provide logical reasons for doing tricks and gags, making them more spontaneous and entertaining. Each trick may involve a micro-story to build suspense and interest, or a group of tricks may be strung together by one story, finishing with the most startling effect or funniest joke.

Active Involvement

As I have described earlier in this chapter, children's parties are high-energy events. Gone are the days when children sat quietly in the parlor and marveled in amazement as some gray-haired man in a wrinkled tuxedo, proclaiming himself as "The nation's foremost magician," pulled cards, coins, and other "adult" items out of the air.

Today's youth are active! They want to become involved. They will become involved whether you like it or not. The astute performer will take advantage of the boundless energy and enthusiasm which is inherent in youth, and harness it to his advantage.

Today's successful birthday party performers fill their routines with opportunities for active involvement from the audience. Whether you are a magician, clown, puppeteer, storyteller, or whatever, you can use the children's natural enthusiastic energy to your advantage by having them actively participate in your show. Having them get involved will make your show more enjoyable and you a big hit.

The skilled performer encourages the children's participation with all the mastery of a symphony conductor who directs all the musicians. And as in music, sometimes that participation will be solo, when just the performer is "on stage," a duet when he has one volunteer up to assist, or a trio when he invites two children to assist him. Of course, the most exciting is when everyone can join in and make a lot of noise for the enjoyment of all.

Begin to orchestrate your audience participation the moment the children enter the room. In the book *Clown Magic*, David Ginn says: "The heart of my kidshow is audience participation. Children are full of energy and excitement. They love to be involved in anything fun. When you interact with audience members and use the audience in your routines, the children become a part of the act and the show becomes more entertaining to them." Ginn is right. If you can actively involve the audience in your act, your show will be more entertaining. Anytime the children raise their hands, answer questions, shout out things, clap their hands, and perform an action you've requested, they are participating. Ways of involving the audience in your shows are discussed in more detail later in this chapter under the headings of "Warm-Ups" and "Audience Participation."

Kids enjoy active participation.

What do you do with a pickle when it is one year old?
Wish it a happy birthday.

Pizzazz

Children like action, fast pace, and color. I call this pizzazz. Your show must move at a good pace. Slow build-ups, silence, long explanations, or drawn-out stories slow down the show, making it less interesting. Children nowadays are conditioned by television to expect non-stop action and laughs. You must keep a steady pace. This is not to say you can't have a quiet moment once in a while, but it should be brief and for a reason.

Colors are eye-catching and attract attention. Use colorful props and clothing. Instead of using drab colored props, give them sparkle, paint them bright colors, and give them pizzazz! Visit a craft store for gold, silver, and other colored glitter. Personalize the props you make. Add color, add glitter, and add your name with fancy lettering.

A costume that is distinct and more colorful than average sets you apart from the person on the street. Wear something distinctive and let your audience know you are the entertainer, not the delivery person.

A person wearing a bright yellow shirt and straw hat, red overalls, and big clown boots, with a dab of makeup on the face, will attract much more attention than a man in a drab-looking business suit. The colorful character will also look more fun, and kids will warm up to him easier. Just his appearance will help create the atmosphere and enjoyment for the kids. Your appearance will create excitement and attract attention and curiosity.

HOW TO CONTROL YOUR AUDIENCE

If you are going to interact with a group of rambunctious, highly energized kids, you will need to be able to control them. At the party they may have been running around wild and be pumped full of adrenaline. Your job will be to settle them down and have them sit peacefully for 30 or more minutes while you command their undivided attention. Sound impossible? It's not.

Having a good show prepared will help keep kids interested and paying attention, but having a good show is not always enough. Kids have lots of excess energy, get excited easily, and do things disruptive just to have fun. Unbridled energy can be very destructive to you and the other kids and spoil your presentation. How do you keep them from poking each other, shouting, running around, or even challenging you, and otherwise distracting others? To maintain some semblance of order, you need to take control and maintain control throughout your visit. In this section you will learn how to do that.

Problem Prevention

No matter how terrific an entertainer you are, if the audience is constantly disrupted by a hyper kid or adult, or someone is determined to challenge (heckle) you, or the room you are performing in is bombarded with noise or is very uncomfortable (outdoors in the heat, or not cool in the home), your performance will be perceived to be sub par. It is very important for you as an entertainer to know what conditions work best for your performance.

In my shows, ideally, I would like to have the guests inside the home, in a room that is large enough for them to sit, either on the floor or in chairs. The room is cool enough for all to be comfortable. The floor is cleared of excess furniture so that everyone can sit together. The television and stereo are off. Toys, especially noisy ones, are put away and the guests are not eating or drinking. If this is a child's birthday, the parents join the children to watch the show, instead of talking to each other.

This would be a perfect set up. Most of the time, you will not find these conditions. I usually arrive about 15 to 20 minutes after the party has started. Children are engaged in various forms of raising the roof. Parents usually are gathered around the buffet or bar, eating, drinking, and talking. The television and stereo are blaring, "It's required you know," and the toddlers are playing demolition derby with their riding toys.

As I enter a party, my mind is working two tracks. One part of me is playing the part of the entertainer, meeting the parents, talking to the birthday child and guests. The other track is assessing the environment. Is the stereo or television on? Are the parents drinking (especially alcoholic beverages)? Any riding toys, or noisy items that need to be removed? How much room is there for me to set up? Will this area become a high traffic zone for late arrivals, or is it in the path to the bathroom or kitchen?

While the parent takes me to the area she has decided is best, I will advise her, very politely of changes that need to be made. "Mrs. So & So, could you please turn off the television? Also, if you could put up the toys, the children will be less distracted. You know, if we move the coffee table, the kids could sit on the floor, and that will leave room for the parents on the furniture. Oh, the children will be getting up and down a lot to assist with the show. You might want to wait to serve that popcorn

and soda until later, so there won't be any spills. Thank you."

Parents are usually happy to cooperate. They want the show to go well, and this will assure them that you have the experience to know what will work.

Before the party you might even ask the parents to help you out. Remind them that you are an entertainer and not a disciplinarian. Your job is to present an enjoyable show. If kids act up, they will not only distract others, but hurt the show. If you have to stop and deal with them, the show will have to be cut short because you only have so much time you can spend (you have other appointments). If you waste time keeping kids in line, they will have less show time. Tell the parents that if there are any hecklers who mouth off during the show, you would appreciate help getting those kids to settle down.

If you can explain some of these things to the parents when you call to confirm your show, it will reduce some of the havoc that you may otherwise experience. It also helps you avoid stepping out of character during the party and becoming the disciplinarian.

Setting the Stage

One of the primary ways of controlling an audience and getting them to respond positively to you is simply by talking to them. Show an interest in them, ask them questions, and tell them to do silly things. Be fun. If they enjoy themselves when they follow your directions, they will listen and obey. You must take charge by talking and keeping their attention. If you have their attention, they will not have time to dream up mischievous pranks to play on others or attempt to become involved in "funnier" things. They will be too busy listening and enjoying your show.

Hugh Turley, a pro from Washington, D.C., says his show starts the moment he walks in the door, and he's right. The hand shaking and friendly comments gently train his audience to answer and participate the way he will want them to do later during the show.

If you don't establish yourself as the one in charge from the beginning, the children will run all over you. Be friendly, but let them know you are in control. They will be willing to do as you direct because they want to see your show. But if you are timid and apprehensive, they will run wild. Take charge by talking to them and telling them what you want them to do. They know that if they are going to enjoy the show, they will need to follow your instructions. If you are too timid or unsure of yourself, they will doubt your ability to entertain them and will attempt to create their own entertainment by ignoring or even intimidating you. Likewise, never be critical, speak down to them, embarrass them, or otherwise display a negative attitude in speech or manner. If you do, you will lose them.

When the kids enter the room, be ready for them. If you come in with them, lead them in. Don't hide in another room or behind your backdrop. Don't expect the mother to act as an MC and give you a lengthy build-up or introduction. Don't expect to glide into the room on a wave of applause. Birthday parties aren't like that.

When the kids enter, be standing in front of your table to help seat the kids on the floor and in the chairs. Use very positive comments.

"Welcome! Come right this way. Step right up."

"Excellent orchestra seats right down here."

"Congratulations on your great birthday, Smedley."

"This is a fine looking group."

"Super balcony seats in the chairs."

"The first row starts here."

"Everybody has good seats."

"Everybody can see."

"Everybody can hear."

"Everybody looks great."

"Everybody is going to have a great time and enjoy the special magic show performed in honor of Smedley's birthday."

After you make sure everyone is comfortably seated, begin the show.

Set Boundaries

One of the first boundaries or guidelines you will want to establish is your performing area. About five feet in front of my performance table, I place a length of gold drapery rope on the floor. This defines my playing area and lets the kids know where the boundary line is. Without this boundary line, the children who are sitting on the floor would slowly creep forward and soon be hugging my ankles. Or they may rush up to me to touch my pet rabbit or feel (or grab) one of my props. If you are a storyteller who doesn't move about much when telling your tales, this may not be a serious matter. If you are a magician, juggler, or any other entertainer who moves around or deals with props, it can cause serious problems. With a magic act, the children may gradually move up into positions which will spoil the effect of the tricks. More importantly, with kids spread out all over the floor, you may step on or trip over one of the little tykes. You need to set a boundary where you can perform in safety.

Set boundaries in a positive way. Start by letting the kids know they are in for a fun time. Tell them that in order for you to create the most fun, you need to lay down a boundary line. Some performers use an imaginary line. The children must stay behind that line so you do not accidentally hurt any of them and so that everyone can see you clearly. This lets them know that as long as they obey you, they will have a good time. They are not being forced to obey. It's their decision. They know that in order for everyone to have the most fun, they must follow your directions. Mary "Sugar Plum" Lostak says, "I usually will remind creepers that I have really big feet, and I don't want to step on any fingers. This hint achieves the results I want." For a clown with big feet, this is an effective approach.

I once heard a magician warn the kids that if they crossed the line, he would turn them into rabbits. Although this is a cute line, it can easily lead to a challenge situation. And of course the magician is going to lose. So, I don't use that line, I just put down my own line—the gold rope.

Another boundary you will want to set is the physical and vocal activity of the children. To avoid confusion, roughhousing, and distraction, the children should remain in their seats and pay attention to you. This can be accomplished in a number of ways. You can offer a surprise or reward after the show to all the children who stay in their seats and behave. This gift can be a balloon animal or other party favor.

You will give all the children a gift whether they behaved or not, but they don't know that. A party is for the enjoyment of all the guests and none of them should

actually be denied the gift. Even if a child was a bit rambunctious, you can compliment and reward him for trying, or for helping out. If he participated in your show, somehow you will have an excuse for giving him the gift with everyone else. You may purposely use him as a volunteer, or have him do something silly during the show to "earn" the gift. Most active children love to participate, and he will be pleased to take part in the show.

You may encourage all the children by saying that you are going to need some helpers during your show and will choose only those who are sitting in their seats and smiling. Most children love the attention of being on stage with the performer. This will motivate them to behave. Notice I didn't say to tell the children to "be quiet," but to smile. They are supposed to be laughing and responding to your questions. You don't want to stifle their positive responses.

Hugh Turley begins his show by telling the kids that he will need lots of helpers. He says that anyone who wants to be chosen to come up and help must do two things. First, they must be sitting down, that means bottoms on the floor. And second, they must raise their hands when he asks for helpers. "And by the way," says Hugh, "did I mention that I pay off all my good helpers with big money?" (*Big money* is an over-sized novelty dollar that can be used as a giveaway.) Hugh waves one in the air and their little bottoms are super glued to the carpet for the rest of the show.

At the end of his show, Hugh mentions that all the kids have been wonderful helpers, both those who have helped on stage and those who have helped from their seats, and he gives everyone big money!

Children want to feel special, especially on their birthdays. Let them know how clever, smart, terrific, and funny they are. This holds true for all the children. If they remember to sit and raise their hands, say "Wow, you kids are really smart, you didn't forget." This will help encourage them to behave.

Stop inappropriate behavior as soon as possible. For children who keep standing say, "Please sit down so the children behind you can see. Thank you."

Remember that children will get excited about your activities and will need to be reminded about what you expect.

Music Calms the Savage Beasties

I always start my show with a pretty three-minute routine using colorful silk scarves accompanied by peppy music. At the end of the music I have fifteen seconds of taped thunderous applause. I bow and bow like crazy. This signals the kids they should applaud too. Kids and adults find the taped applause and my bowing very, very funny.

The music is supplied by a small cassette player that runs on batteries. I have it attached to one of the shelves of my suitcase table. The music is always ready to go at the touch of a button. I don't blast the music. I keep the volume in check. This ensures that the kids will be very quiet and sets a more reserved tempo and sound level for my performance.

Adults Don't Count

Unless the birthday is for adults, forget them. If you were hired to entertain the kids, focus on them. If the kids are amused and involved, the adults will be pleased. Likewise, if you play to the adults in the room and ignore the kids, the little tykes will let you know about it in the most unpleasant ways. They will scream, and I mean scream, nasty true things like, "This is soooo boooring!" and "why do we have to watch this?" Play to the kids.

WARM-UPS

A warm-up is a short comic routine involving the entire audience. Using a participation routine to start off your show has several advantages. For one, it announces to everyone that the show is beginning and to pay attention. It also gives stragglers a few minutes to come in and sit down without them missing any of your prepared material. The warm-up is a good way to spark everyone's interest and prepare them for the good time they are about to have. It helps to set up the performer as the one in charge during the show. The audience gets some time to know you. It also primes the pump, so to speak, by getting the kids laughing and smiling before you start the real show. If the children have been prepared to laugh and enjoy themselves with a fun warm-up, they will more readily take to you and more easily laugh. Without the warm-up the kids will need a few minutes to adjust to you. Once they are comfortable with who you are, they will relax and enjoy the show.

Kidshow magician, David Ginn, confessed in his book, *Comedy Warm-Ups for Children's Shows,* that before he started using warm-ups, some audiences would take as long as ten minutes to "warm up" to him and respond. He said there would be "no applause, no laughs, no nothing." After he began adding warm-up activities to the first few minutes of his shows, the children responded immediately when he began his show.

What does a warm-up consist of? David Ginn gives a good description. "Introduce yourself and let them get to know you a little. Get them to shout, clap their hands, stamp their feet, laugh, and so on. Have a shouting or clapping contest. Things like that." If you keep the children involved in your performance, you will face less problems with behavior. Make the children a part of the show by using them as volunteers.

An old favorite is the hello echo. As you come out on stage say "Hello." Bring your hand up to your ear to signal for the audience to respond. They will give back a half-hearted "Hello." Look disappointed and signal for them to speak louder as you repeat your "Hello" with a little more force.

They will come back with a louder response. Shake your head and signal again for them to yell louder as you holler "HELLO!" They are warming up now and will give you all they've got.

The applause contest is another fun warm-up activity. Split the audience into two halves. Have one side applaud as hard and as loud as they can, then have the other side do the same. Go back and forth a few times, encouraging them to clap louder each time. Finish by having both sides give it all they've got at the same time. When the noise dies down bow humbly and say, "Thank you, thank you, I'm glad you enjoyed my show. Good-bye . . . Oh you mean I haven't done it yet? . . ." Then start into your regular act.

Kids love to shout and a shouting contest is sure to please them. If you want to keep the noise level down you can still enjoy a shouting match, but instead of shouting you can make noises. Try mewing like a cat, naaaing like a goat, making a noise like a caterpillar. What does a caterpillar sound like? It sounds like anything you want it to, such as a low-pitched "Waba-waba."

Without the warm-up many children may still be talking to each other or otherwise be distracted. Audience participation forces them to give you their attention so when you begin with your show, they're ready to follow you into your world of fantasy.

An active warm-up is one of the best ways to get an audience prepared for your show. You have introduced yourself, and by the time the warm-up is over, the kids will know you a little better. Jokes and other comic patter intermingled with the warm-up will increase everyone's enjoyment.

At a birthday party your warm-up should start from the time you first meet the kids. This may be the second you walk through the door. This is a good time for the children to get to know who you are and for you to put them at ease, and prepare them for your show by using some short comedy bits with them. Clowns often call this *walk-arounds*, but can be used by any party entertainer.

In a walk-around, you mingle with the crowd doing simple magic tricks, telling jokes, and doing silly gags.

Funny handshakes are one type of walk-around activity. Children learn from grown-ups that the act of shaking hands is a greeting. By offering your hand to the kids, you are telling them you are a friend. When you do it in a silly way, you tell them you are a funny friend. Let me give you some examples of funny handshakes. Extend your hand to shake a child's hand. As the child reaches for yours, extend your hand past his, grab his elbow, and shake that. Or as he reaches for your hand, miss his hand by gong to the right or left. He will keep trying to grab your hand and you keep pretending to grab his, but keep missing. Or when he extends his hand to meet yours, you switch hands and extend your left hand. At first he will be startled and then extend his left to grab yours, as he does, drop your left and extend your right. Keep this up as long as it amuses the children. You can also pretend the child has super strength and as he grabs your hand act like he is squeezing your hand, drop to one knee in pain, ham it up. This can be very funny. You get the idea; make up some handshakes of your own.

Here is another example of a short walk-around gimmick. Ask some of the kids, "Would you like to see my belly button?" They will be surprised at your question and giggle. Encourage them whether they say yes or no, then open up your coat and show a pinned on button with the words "Belly Button" written on it. This will get a laugh. Then ask them "Do you want to see my other belly button?" They giggle. You then show them another button pinned under the other side of your coat which reads "Other Belly Button." Kids laugh. This is a simple little gag that a small group of kids can enjoy up close.

AUDIENCE PARTICIPATION

Children want to be involved, not merely sit and watch you perform. Find ways to make them part of the show. Bring all of them into the act. In order to have a trick work, have everyone touch their belly buttons, or put a hand on their knee, or hop up and down.

Audience participation is a key element in keeping the attention and interest of a group of kids. It makes the audience feel special and creates a more personal relationship with the performer. The performer becomes

---

What do you get when you cross an owl with a skunk?
An owl that smells bad but doesn't give a hoot.

---

a real person who will be remembered after the party is over.

All good children's shows involve some type of audience participation. A good place to start the audience participation is with a warm-up before the show actually begins. Then continue to use the audience as often as you can throughout the show.

Children love to participate. Any time members take an active role in your show, they are participating. Volunteers that come on stage and help you with a trick or gag are participating. But you can involve members of the audience without having them come up on stage. Whenever they raise their hands, shout responses to your questions, clap their hands, or do some action you've requested, they are participating. You can ask chosen members of the audience questions or to perform an action. You could instruct the entire audience to respond to something. If you are going to perform a magic trick, have everyone shout out the magic word. This can be fun if you use silly sounding words and phrases. At times you may set up the audience so that they will spontaneously correct you when you "accidentally" make a mistake. Getting helpers' names mixed up is one way to invoke a response from the audience. They will be quick to correct you. This type of thing can be very funny, especially if you mix up the names of a boy and a girl. Whenever you have the opportunity, include some type of audience participation.

All for One and One for All

Hearing the whole gang of kids yell together is great fun for everyone. Kids like to yell and are rarely encouraged to do so. You'll learn to love the sound of a large volume of voices following your directions precisely as if the power of the magic depended on it. And in their minds it really does! So get some mass yelling and chanting in your show. It may sound like some primitive ritual at times, but kids get a terrific bang out of it. And so will you because you're truly the leader of the pack.

Charles "Buck" Clayton, one of Baltimore's finest children's entertainers, whips the children into a yelling frenzy during several of his routines. Buck is a master showman and always has kids in the palm of his hand. He features a rollercoaster ride of group participation.

Kids are captivated by Buck's hands and arms because he is very animated. When his hands are raised high in the air and outstretched, he's calling for loud volume, just like a music conductor. A cupped hand to the ear means: I can't hear you, make it louder. When his arms go lower, so does the volume of desired response.

Hands, palm side facing the kids and a slight nod means: Thank you, that's enough response.

Buck, a veteran of hundreds of shows, knows exactly how to end the orchestrated chaos and swiftly move the kids to silence without blowing a whistle or raising a fist. The kids never feel manipulated, just led in the right direction. It's called gentle crowd control and Buck has it. With his fluid arm movements, he looks a little like a traffic cop directing the flow of cars. And that analogy probably isn't too far off, because Buck has been a policeman for several years and supplements his income handsomely doing children's shows.

Mass Appeal and Appealing to the Masses

The type of audience participation activity you do doesn't always need to be something that is vital to the routine. Anything that will involve the kids and can be related to what you are doing will work. For example, when telling a story about a rooster, have the kids shout their best rooster imitation. Whenever you need a rooster's noise, have the kids do it.

The more bizarre and meaningless, the funnier it is for kids. In fact, it's downright hysterical, for kids to see all their friends tapping their noses and yelling, "Purple puppy chow!" (A great incantation from the creative mind of excellent children's performer, David Ginn.)

Here are some ideas that work well with an entire group. Keep in mind, if a couple of the kids don't join in with the rest of the gang, that's okay. Never badger them with, "Someone didn't say the magic word . . . was it Mary?" or Mary may command the center of attention with her "Niagara Falls" act.

Okay kids, get ready to repeat after me:

"My mother made me munch marshmallows with munchkins on the moon."

"Red letter. Yellow letter. (Try saying it three times very quickly.)

"Let's do the countdown. Ten, nine (louder!), eight, seven (louder), six, five, etc.

"Moo like a cow, Mooooo like a slow cow, like a real slow cow, etc.

"Scratch your head and say, itchie, twitchie, itchie, twitchie."

"Wiggle your fingers, wiggle your head, wiggle your tongue and say, Great chunks of chocolate chewing gum." (Repeat fast, and faster.)

"This time just the boys yell."

"This time just the girls yell."

"This time just the boys yell." (They'll be ten times louder this round.)

"Clap your hands every time I wave the wand."

"Rubber baby buggy bumpers." (Say it three times.)

"Give three loud cheers for Debbie on her birthday. Hip hip hooray!"

"Laugh like a chipmunk. Growl like a tiger. Oink like a pig."

"Shiver like it's snowing outside."(I once had a kid who ran to the window to look. Everyone laughed hysterically. It was in August.)

"Count your fingers as fast as you can."

"Whistle like a canary." (Hard for little kids to do.)

"Rub your stomach and pat your head." (It's old, but new to them.)

"Name the colors after me." (Strictly for the little tykes.)

"Look like a monkey."

"Pant like a puppy. Bark like a big dog."

"Laugh like munchkins."

"Snap your fingers." (A big accomplishment for the little kids.)

"Twiddle your thumbs." (Show them how.)

"Say the magic words: happy birthday, Joey!"

"Inka inka dinka do, we send happy birthday wishes to you!"

You'll think up many more "Simon says" type bits as you gain experience performing. Incorporate them into your act wherever possible. In time you'll be able to gauge the age group and makeup of the crowd and know which lines work better with which group.

You'll know you have succeeded when you can say the same thing that busy Virginia magician, Jack Nance says. "At the end of my show," chuckles Jack, "the kids are totally worn out! They've had so much fun laughing, clapping, calling out answers, and helping me with the magic, they're ready to settle down, relax, and have some birthday cake . . . and recharge their batteries!"

Using Volunteers

At times you can select a few of the children to help you up on stage. Kids love this because they get to be the center of attention and an important part of the show. The kids sitting in their seats will also enjoy seeing their buddies take part in the shenanigans on stage and have something to tease them about later.

> What would you call a prehistoric skunk?
> *Ex-stinct.*

If you haven't instructed the kids to stay in their seats when you need a helper, when you ask for volunteers you may be confronted with uncontrollable chaos—kids wildly waving their arms, jumping, and screaming "Choose me!"

Most children relish the thought of going up on stage with the performer. To maintain control and avoid a mad stampede, either warn the kids to stay seated or simply choose a helper without asking for volunteers. By not asking for volunteers, you avoid the frenzied response and you can choose whomever you want without hurting anyone's feelings. However, you may choose someone who is a little shy in front of people.

Avoid, if at all possible, asking any child to come up who appears to be shy or who looks as if he or she may burst into tears while in front of everybody. If you choose a child who doesn't want to come up to help you, don't force him or her, just choose another. A crying child doesn't help any performer, especially if he's trying to be funny.

Many children actually believe you are a real magician and may fear you. They know their fairy tales and remember that the man or woman in the story doing the magic was usually an evil witch or a wizard doing something nasty to someone. Treat them with kindness when you invite them to help. Be very encouraging and positive. If they can't remember the color, or cluck like a chicken, or answer a question you might ask them, be understanding.

Once in a great while, a little boy or girl may start to whimper or cry. Sometimes they do it for no reason at all. I guess the thrill of standing in front of the group and in the presence of a real magician is too much for them. Despite the fact that they are grinding your show to an abrupt halt, and all eyes are focused on you and wondering what you may have done to upset little Mary so much, relax and comfort the little kid.

Tell the group that Mary is a fine little girl and that it's okay not to participate. Above all, act like the caring, good hearted, well meaning individual that you are. Show compassion. Next time choose an older child.

Your volunteers can assist you in a variety of ways, ranging from detailed involvement to passively holding a prop. What your helper does on stage doesn't have to be elaborate or even necessary for you to complete a particular routine. Having your helper hold a sign while you continue with your show, gives you the opportunity to use volunteers without designing special routines for that purpose.

Some of the funniest bits of humor can come from volunteers. Their actions and responses are spontaneous and totally unexpected. Some kids are suited perfectly to

these situations and love to play along with you, adding to the success of the routine.

Have volunteers come up to learn a magic trick or how to juggle scarves (easy to do, especially if you use only one or two juggling scarves), or make balloon animals. These kids will get a kick out of it and can be very amusing.

"I usually will start off my show with some jokes and riddles," says D.C. the Clown of Glendale, California. "I then ask the kids if they have any good jokes. They usually do, and it gives me an opportunity to teach them to be a good audience. When they come up, I remind everyone to laugh and applaud even if they have heard the joke before or if it's not funny. It gets to be a game with the applause and laughter getting louder with each child. They seem to catch on about being a good audience and I usually don't have any trouble." This fun activity serves two valuable purposes, it gets the kids personally involved in the show and teaches them how to become a good audience. The kids love the opportunity of getting the limelight when they tell their jokes.

Try a talent contest. Choose four or five volunteers from the audience and give each one a musical instrument such as a harmonica, whistle, drum, kazoo, or jaw harp. Have each play their instrument. After they have all had a turn, place your hand above each child in turn. The one who receives the most applause is the winner. You can finish by giving out little prizes to each, with some special recognition for the child who won. This contest not only gives you an opportunity to use volunteers, but gets the entire audience involved in choosing the winner.

You can do a variation of this contest by giving each helper a card with a different activity written it, such as sing, dance, whistle, hum. Have each one perform for the group. The kids who are the biggest hams usually end up with the most applause.

Lead or Be Led

I met Walt Hudson several years ago at an east coast magic convention. He has been a Baltimore fixture in the children's market for several decades and is a widely read author and magazine columnist for *The New Tops* magic magazine. He told me this story about a children's performer that I will never forget. It has a moral that we should all remember.

"I saw one children's party," laughed Walt, "where the performer decided to do a fill-in-the-blank using nursery rhymes. It started out okay, but then the kids saw the humor of how really funny this game could be if they put in naughty answers instead of the desired responses. When the entertainer said, 'Mary had a little_____' one kid yelled, 'cow!' Everybody laughed. Another kid screamed, 'a baby!' Even bigger laughs. A third kid, not missing a beat, announced, 'Mary had a little pee-pee!' The responses got worse (or better from the kids' viewpoint). As the performer asked, 'Little Miss Muffet sat on _____' Someone belted out, 'her butt!' And it was pandemonium! Soon everyone had 'choice' answers of their own. I didn't even know kids their age knew words like I was hearing. I won't even tell you what some of them screamed when the entertainer asked, "Little boy blue come blow your_____.' But it wasn't pretty. And the performer kept going!"

What can we learn from this riotous incident? One, plan your audience response items geared for the ages of your audience. That group was too old for nursery rhymes. Second, leave nothing open for their own "creative" responses. Tell them exactly how and when they are to respond. Third, don't be afraid to change tactics midstream if you don't get the response you are expecting. Keep control. If you don't lead them, you will be led . . . And where they can take you can be pretty ugly.

Sucker Tricks:
Audience Participation or Ridicule?

When you interact with people, there is always the possibility of offending someone. As an entertainer, you need to be aware of this. Your job is to entertain and make people happy. Your language and actions should always be clean and inoffensive.

You should never try to get a laugh at the expense of ridiculing or embarrassing anyone. Use your skills to make the audience laugh at you. If anyone is to be the butt of a joke, it should be the performer, never the volunteer or the audience.

Sucker tricks and gags are items that can ridicule and embarrass audience members. There are a variety of sucker effects on the market, all of which lead the audience to believe they know what to expect, only to learn that what they expected isn't so. One such simple gag is the coiled snake in a can. The unsuspecting victim opens a can of peanut brittle expecting to get a treat, but is surprised out of his wits by a snake leaping up into his face. Everyone laughs at the victim's uncontrollable reaction caused by momentary fright. Whether the victim lets it be known or not, this laughter is humiliating. He was suckered into this gag. The joke was on him.

Sucker tricks such as the hip hop rabbits, run rabbit run, the sucker die box, the silk bar, the money bar, fooled and fooled again, and find the queen, are quite enticing. These magic effects all lead the audience to believe they know how the trick is worked, but in the end the magician demonstrates his superiority by proving them wrong. Sucker tricks make somebody the butt of the joke. That somebody is usually the audience or the volunteer. They promise four remarkable things:

First, you will fool your audience.

Second, you will make your youthful audience feel like a bunch of fools for believing that they could have figured out your method for doing a trick.

Third, you will look superior in intelligence, talent, and clever wit because you have successfully put down everyone.

Fourth, a sucker trick promises, not only to shoot the audience's thinking down, but to sting them in the process.

I dislike most presentations of sucker tricks because of all four reasons that make them so appealing to many budding performers.

First, it's not nice to be fooled. Whoever said that it's fun to fool people may have been right, but he should have placed himself on the receiving end. People want to be amazed and entertained, not fooled. Who wants to be the butt of a practical trick where really the magician, and only the magician, has the last laugh? No one, but that's exactly what a sucker trick does.

Second, yes, it's true you will probably successfully mislead your audience into thinking the trick is performed in a different way than what it really is. That's the way sucker tricks are designed, but why have them make a spectacle of themselves screaming, "Turn the rabbits around!" or "it's up your sleeve!" and then be proved wrong. Don't you think that besides being disappointed that they didn't figure out the magician's trick, they will also be a little mad? And a little less apt to volunteer and participate on the next trick? Of course! Ask any kid who has touched the flame on a birthday candle and gotten burnt. It only happens once. They learn real fast.

The third reason I dislike most sucker trick presentations is that I don't have to put my audiences down to feel successful. I am the performer; I have the power to entertain.

Last, I hate the sting inherent in these types of tricks. I love surprises; I hate pain. Yes, it's wild to watch their jaws drop on the floor and the dead silence that greets the climax of the trick. After all, sucker tricks are supposed to stop an audience cold. Most do. They leave me cold too.

Some last thoughts on sucker tricks; it's not the trick that's bad, it's the presentation. I actually saw one magician yell, "Ha! Ha! You guys thought you were so smart. You've got a lot to learn. You'd better pay closer attention." That's like pouring salt on an open wound. All I could do was shake my head and think how really insecure this performer must be.

You can win on a sucker trick if you pretend to be as surprised as the kids with the unexpected climax. You should always end up as the victim of any gag. Likewise, sucker gags like the coiled-snake trick, can still be used, but instead of playing it on the volunteer, you should be the one who opens up the can and be startled by the snake. This way the joke is on you. Everybody laughs.

Trite as it may sound, old as it is, the Golden Rule of treating others as you would like to be treated is still the best measure when it comes to interacting with audience volunteers. Guide the children's participation, encourage their responses, channel that boundless energy that nature gives abundantly to youth, and you will most certainly succeed.

HONOR THE GUEST OF HONOR

Something that you must do if you want to survive in the birthday market is give "special recognition" to the birthday child. Your performance must actively involve him in front of all his friends, and it must have a happy ending. Little gag props may amuse and get laughs along the way, but in the end, little Donnie must shine like the star he is on his birthday.

The guest of honor is frequently incorporated into the last trick or routine scheduled on the program. In a magic show it may be the climax with the production of a live bunny, the making of a miniature birthday cake, the presentation of a small magical present to the birthday child from the magician, or perhaps a large silk with "happy birthday" printed on it in hot dayglo colors.

In my own show, the birthday boy and I produce Fuzz-Face, the magical birthday rabbit out of a balloon-to-bunny box. The production is preceded by inflating a long white balloon, drawing a face with whiskers on it in black magic marker, placing it in the "empty" box, and waving several magic wands of various lengths, shapes, sizes, and colors. One wand falls apart and goes to pieces. Another wand keeps changing colors. Another wand keeps multiplying. Lots of laughter and yelling the magic words (happy birthday, Donnie!) How can all this craziness be happening, especially on little Donnie's big seventh birthday?

But in the end, Donnie gets the cheers from his friends for successfully producing the birthday bunny. I also present Donnie with a "Magician's Assistant" certificate and a book containing 101 tricks Donnie can do by himself. And there is "big money" for all of Donnie's friends who have helped so much, and provided such great support. And who gets to pass out the big money? Donnie, of course.

This is the time to just ooze sincerity, and show extra kindness, love, and respect for the featured child. Expect cameras flashing in your face at close range during your "special trick" with the birthday boy. You will be blinded and see spots for the next ten minutes, but keep smiling.

Keep the routine funny, but low key and more dignified, like you're giving him the power to perform miracles and trusting him with this big honor. No matter what type of presentation you make, whether you do juggling or puppets, you can invite the birthday child to come up and assist you. Parents want the birthday child to be featured in your show. Dress the child up with funny hats, give him big magic wands, and provide good photo opportunities. Even if he doesn't do much, he does get the opportunity to be with you "on stage." For Donnie and his friends, it really is a big deal.

HOW TO HANDLE TROUBLEMAKERS

You will encounter children who are more difficult to control than the others; they won't stay seated, they enjoy disturbing other children, and shout out, "I've seen that trick before," or "I saw you put it in your pocket," or "Let's do something else!" What do you do about children who won't settle down?

Some kids get overly excited and act up, yelling wisecracks, and disrupting the show. This can be embarrassing and distracting for everyone, performer and audience alike.

If the host or hostess does not take care of the troublemaker, you must deal with him yourself. At times, some kids will be overly active or talkative, yet not outright disruptive. However, they still can cause distractions and be a nuisance.

Most hecklers will make their presence known early in the show. Some may settle down a bit as the show progresses and can be ignored. Others may continue to badger you and make a nuisance of themselves. It's best to take care of them as soon as possible, or they will make the show a chore for you. If you can get a troublemaker to settle down, you will be more comfortable for the rest of the performance.

Paula Biggio, a clown magician from Chicago, tries to eliminate problems before her show begins. When she enters the home, she is on the lookout for potential troublemakers. Before starting the show, she will approach them and invite them to help. She builds up their egos by letting them know how smart they are, telling them that she knows that they know how most of the tricks and gags work and asks if they will be her helper. She then assigns a task for them to do or has them participate in the show. Kids love to be a part of the show and, as co-stars, will channel their energy into making it successful.

Kids that act up aren't normally trying to be mean; they are simply trying to get attention. Unless you can get control of the situation, they will continue to disrupt you as they strive for that recognition. One of the best ways to quiet a loudmouth is to have him help you in one of your routines. He can come up on stage or stay in the audience, just as long as he is able to satisfy his need for attention.

If you invite troublemakers to assist you, usually they will be more than willing to help and will cooperate once they become a part of the show. In this way they receive the attention they wanted, and will return to the audience and remain quiet. They are now a part of the show and, as co-stars, do not want to ruin it.

Asking the heckler a few standard opening questions and having him hold a sign or some other prop as you continue with your planned routine may be all that is needed to satisfy his thirst for attention. "If there is a problem child who never stops interrupting me," says Vinnie (Funnybone) Deseno, "my favorite (response) is to give him or her a sign to hold and let him hold it up when I point to them. The sign may say laugh, clap, etc. This way the child is no longer a threat or a headache, but is either helpful or a short-lived performer."

> What is white outside, green inside, and hops?
> *A frog sandwich.*

Invite the trouble-maker up when you plan to use a volunteer from the audience, or even create a special routine beforehand for just such occasions. Like any other volunteer, do not ridicule him or play a sucker trick on him to get even. He will be more cooperative on stage and back in the audience if you try to become his friend.

What should you do when kids yell out "I know how that is done"? This doesn't bother me. When I hear that phrase, I will assume they may mean that they have seen that trick before. If asked, they may have a theory as to how a trick works (they're usually wrong). If I believe they do know how it is done, I say "Great, if I can't get it right, will you help me?" This makes them feel important, and you've made them want to contribute to the show. Magician Tom Myers responds to the "I know how that's done," with "oh, you're a magician too. I'd love to talk with you after the show." This is not said as a threat or challenge, but with sincere interest. In front of everyone the child is set up as an equal with the magician. Anything the child does now to disrupt the show will only lower his status. The child is then more cooperative, and usually finds he didn't really know how the trick works and starts to enjoy the show.

A smooth running, fast paced show will reduce opportunities for potential troublemakers. "If there is no dead time," says Myers, "and the show is interesting to the kids, they don't have the time or inclination to think about disrupting. They are busy having fun." It's when the show gets slow that kids usually start to look for ways to inject some excitement, and trouble happens. If you present a good show, your discipline problems will be relatively minor.

At times you will encounter unruly children who just won't settle down for anything. Birthday party clown, Irene Doll, tells of an incident where a child snuck up behind her and stole her bag of balloons. She couldn't do anything about it. So, she relied on peer pressure and told all the kids that she wasn't going to be able to make them any balloon animals. All eyes turned toward the problem child. Feeling the pressure from the group, he gave them back and sat down. Reprimanding was avoided, harsh words were avoided, and an ugly confrontation was avoided. Letting everyone know that the troublemaker's actions would hurt them all will keep him in line. Peer pressure can be a valuable force. At times you may have to stop the show and tell the audience that you can only continue if the troublemaker behaves. You only have so much time to spend before you have to leave; if you are forced to waste time waiting for a troublemaker to settle down, you will have to cut the show short or eliminate the prizes at the end.

If you get into a situation where nothing seems to quiet a troublemaker, you may have to step out of character and just say "No" or "stop that!" in your own parenting voice. The shock of the sudden change in your character should be enough to straighten the kid up. If not, tie him up with rope and gag him (just kidding). If I'm with a particularly difficult group, it helps me to remain patient if I remember that in an hour, I get to leave with lots of money in my pocket.

At times adults can be a problem too. When the show is about to begin, I invite the parents to join the show. If they are a talkative group, I suggest that those who would rather converse with friends go into another room so as not to distract the children. Some people never grow up. Adults who are misbehaving, heckling, or talking too loudly are the ones I bring up as volunteers. The other parents love to see them in silly hats or making weird noises as part of the magic act, and they will settle down when their peers are on stage. The message sent is if you don't behave, you too will be asked to help. Many adults will feel embarrassed when asked to participate in a kiddie show and will simply refuse your invitation and move into another room where they will no longer be a distraction. Others will love the idea and come up to help. Like the problem child, this will satisfy their thrist for attention and they will return to the audience better behaved.

If I sense that the adults will be particularly noisy or if it is a large party, I always use my portable sound system, then I know they can't drown out my voice. If you do these things, you will have a better chance of a good show. The parents will perceive you as an entertainer rather than a baby sitter.

It seems that just about every party has at least one rambunctious, overly excited guest. If the child is not properly controlled, he can turn into a real troublemaker. Some kids are troublemakers in almost any situation and are difficult to control no matter what you might do. Fortunately they are few in number, but even a few can be too many. If handled wisely by being kind and giving the difficult child a chance to get attention, at the end you will have had a successful show and you will have made a new friend.

PARTIES FOR VERY YOUNG CHILDREN

Some performers will not do shows for kids under five years of age. They feel it is too difficult to entertain preschool children. Although it takes a different approach, entertaining very young children can be done. And those who pass up these opportunities are missing a huge market, and chances for several repeat bookings.

Occasionally, you will receive requests to entertain for children as young as one or two years of age. Why people want an entertainer (usually a clown) to come and perform for these very young children is hard to understand, but they do. The obvious problem with this age group is their limited ability to understand what you normally do and their short attention span. You cannot perform your normal show for this crowd. What tickles a six-year-old silly may completely go over the head of a toddler. Toddlers can be very independent and vocal—thus the term "terrible twos" is often used to describe their behavior. They can be a challenge for parents at times, but entertaining them can be a delight.

Their exposure to children's entertainers has come mostly from the television set where the people are only a few inches tall. Compared to these television midgets, and the children themselves, you are a giant. Giants are scary. So don't come up to them with a loud voice or wild motions like you might with an older audience, or you'll scare them to death. To help them feel at ease with you, get down to their level and stay there as much as possible. Some entertainers will spend the whole time on their knees or sitting on a prop box.

If you book a party for a child under three, warn the parent that it is typical for this age group (18 months to three years) to be shy or afraid of costumed characters. Usually, this fear is temporary and can be overcome with the entertainer and parents' help.

You might consider modifying your makeup. Instead of plastering greasepaint all over your face and wearing green bushy hair, just wear a false nose or put a dab of paint on the end of your nose. Keep your face clean except for maybe some eye shadow or highlighting on your cheeks. And leave the wig at home. You don't want to walk into a home and have the birthday child scream with fright at your appearance and run away bawling!

To a one- or two-year-old, clowns and other costumed characters are bizarre creatures. Be gentle, talk softly, and above all, smile and be friendly without being overbearing. Don't approach or allow the parents to bring the child to you. Let the child set the pace. Before approaching the child, ask if it is okay. If he's not ready to interact with you yet, respect his wishes and back off.

When you arrive at the party, plan to carry in a stuffed animal or a puppet or even an interesting toy. This can help serve as an ice breaker. If you are playing with an interesting toy the child will be curious and more apt to approach you sooner.

Find an older child who is not afraid to interact with you. When the toddler sees others having fun and laughing, he will realize you are okay. I begin my show with a puppet routine, to soften up the younger children. Hamilton is my dog puppet, who lives in a dog house. He reflects the children's emotions. If they are very shy, then so is he. As they warm up and invite him to come out of his house and wave at them, then he will become bolder. By the time he comes out of the dog house, most of the fearful expressions have been exchanged to smiles or at the least, curiosity. Hamilton will then attempt to sing a happy birthday song, of course he makes a lot of mistakes, which the children point out. Eventually, we all have to assist him by singing "Happy Birthday."

If the parents are not sitting with the group yet, I invite them to join their children. I explain that these children are just learning about birthday parties, and they will respond better if their parents show them how. I also explain that this will reassure them that I am fun.

How do you entertain a toddler? Finding the Ace of Spades in a deck of cards or turning a handkerchief into a magic wand isn't going to thrill them. They don't understand most magic tricks. They have a short attention span so cannot follow long stories or patter. And they don't have the knowledge or language skills to appreciate jokes that would amuse five- and six-year-olds.

The secret to entertaining toddlers and other young children is to relax and be yourself. Children can sense if you are tense, and they will become tense themselves. The way to entertain toddlers and other young children is to do what you would do with your own children at this age—play with them and smile. The smile is very important. A child may not even talk or even speak English, yet he will understand a smile and smiles are contagious! Just smiling at a toddler or even an older baby can generate a spontaneous smile in return. Laughter is the same way. When combined with silly talk and actions, you can have preschoolers shouting for joy at the corniest stunts. Be silly—the kids will love it. A simple action like peak-a-boo is entertaining for these youngsters. At this age children are very active. Involve them in activities that get them to move.

You can entertain this age group with simple activity games, songs, rhymes, and short say-and-do stories. They love animals and puppets. The motion of juggling with brightly colored balls, scarves, or bean bags will attract their attention and curiosity for a while. Simple juggling is all that is needed, complicated tricks do not impress this group. Young children are visual. They are attracted by what they see. Use props, pictures, and body language in your stories and songs. As you sing, use body actions or props. Show pictures, manipulate puppets, or use hand motions when telling a rhyme or story. Have them participate by following your motions or making sound effects.

As a general rule, the attention span of a child is about two minutes for each year of age. So, a one-year-old would have an attention span of two minutes, a two-year-old four minutes. Your activities should be spaced apart by this time span to keep their interest during your entire visit. You can judge when it's time to move on to something else by the way the kids respond. Mix your activities.

Having the children play with items you bring can also entertain them. One of the best "toys" are juggling scarves. After seeing you toss three scarves around, they will thrill to do the same. One scarf each is enough to keep them busy for a few minutes. These scarves are so lightweight that when tossed into the air they float slowly downward, allowing time to catch them before they reach the ground. Even the motion of them falling in slow motion can be entertaining for the kids. Inexpensive scarves can be made very cheaply by cutting a 14 x 14-inch square of nylon netting. This material is available in fabric stores. Older kids like this activity as well. Stuffed toys or paper toys can also be used.

Balloons fascinate toddlers, but don't let young kids have balloons or any toy that might cause injury. At this age everything goes into their mouths. Kids can choke on balloons and small toys.

As you see, entertaining toddlers does not involve performing a "show." You merely play with the kids and lead them in a series of activities. When talking to parents on the phone, let them know that what you do is geared to the age of the children. For very young children your entertainment consists of a series of short activities appropriate to that age group. Some parents may expect you to perform a thrilling magic show for their two-year-old daughter. Let them know your regular magic show is designed for older kids and that younger ones gain more enjoyment with the activities you have designed for this age.

My all-time favorite age group is children around four or five years old. They are old enough to understand comedy magic and not afraid of clowns. Yet they have a spontaneity that is really delightful.

How do you tell which end of a worm is its head?

Tickle its middle and see which end smiles.

At this age they have a better understanding of language and greater reasoning powers, even though they still have short attention spans, can be timid or demanding, and know how far they can go before they get into trouble and how to get their own way. You can do most of the same types of things you would do for the younger kids, but now you can add some variety. These children are still very visual and full of energy so you want to do things using colorful props and activities that involve them. You can make use of language by telling silly stories and simple jokes.

Young children love bright, colorful props, music, puppets, or animals, silly sounds and super silly words, funny clothes, stories, and, most of all, assisting with the show.

Keep your magic routines simple. Don't use subtle moves or tell complicated stories. Lengthy routines that rely on verbal misunderstandings such as the popular "hoe to blow up a balloon," will not be very successful at this age. The children do not have the language skills to really catch on to this fun routine.

When volunteers come up to help, ask their names and have the audience repeat it. They like to hear their names, don't you? Speak to them gently; if they seem shy, use gentle touches to reassure them on their performance. If you usually put a funny hat or similar item on a helper, ask for their permission first. A simple "Can I put his on you?" will do. If a child says no, and sometimes they will, don't make a big deal of it. I will just let them hold the item or even better ask "Who do you think we should get to wear it?" (You might even whisper in their ear, "Pick a grownup.") Never embarrass them.

I like to get all of the children involved, so I bring paper magic wands (they convert to coloring sheets) for everyone. They really enjoy waving these around and tapping the props. All of my routines require assistants from the audience. If I feel the group is getting restless, I will get them on their feet and have them spin around or hop up and down to make the magic work.

I also change the noises we make while waving the wand. We might have to say Hocus Pocus and then make a raspberry (blowing with tongue out) sound, or cluck like a chicken, bark like a duck, whatever is silly.

Be sure to feature the birthday child in a few routines, if she is willing to participate. This will provide photo opportunities for the parents. If a child is very shy, it will help to have both a parent and child as helpers. Or you can include a favorite relative.

Hunny Bunny, my live rabbit, makes his appearance at the end of the show. Usually, the children are very excited by the rabbit. I allow the children to pet the bunny,

under controlled conditions. As soon as bunny shows up, we give a big cheer for the birthday child. I then ask the children to be seated (you may have to get their attention first), so that "Thomas" can show them how to pet a bunny. Explanations then come, "Bunny likes it best, when you pet him very gently behind the ears." I then ask a series of questions to reinforce my instructions:

"Are we going to pick bunny up?"—No!
"Are we going to touch his nose?"—No!
Are we going to touch his eyes?"—No!
"Where are we going to touch him?"—Behind the ears!

As the children come up to pet bunny, I watch very carefully, to make sure they follow instructions. (Babies always go for the eyes). A few comments such as, "Wow, did you see how gently Brittney was when she touched bunny" or "Hunny Bunny's favorite spot is here," and I point to a place on her back, will help assure the bunny is not abused.

A note of warning, if you make an animal disappear, whether real or drawn on a prop, be sure to have an explanation of where it went. Children in this age bracket will worry. I make it a standard practice to build an explanation into all my routines for children. I do Supreme's Vanishing Elephant, and when we discover the elephant is gone, I will say, "Oh, I forgot to tell you where elephants go when they disappear! Elephants love to take bubble baths, so check your bathtub when you get home. Dimples may be there taking a bath. If you find her, dry her off. Now don't try to keep her, because she eats even more peanut butter than I do."

This explanation will let them know that "Dimples" is okay and gives me a chance for a bit of silly business as well. Often children will say, "But we don't have your phone number," and I will explain that it is inside their magic wands. This lets the other parents find out how to get in touch with me—Sugar Plum—for their child's party; and I don't seem pushy.

I rarely have a problem with children making a nuisance out of calling me. Sometimes they will call, and I talk to them briefly. A few will say "I found the elephant in my bathtub." I will say, "Was she wearing a pink bow between her ears?" If they say yes, I'll say "Well it couldn't be Dimples. Her favorite color is purple." If they say no, my answer is "Well, I don't know who that elephant is, Dimples always wears a bow in her hair." The kids know it's just for fun anyhow.

There are options other than puppets and live animals for entertaining this age bracket. You may be interested in face painting, games, stories, or music. If you have any musical talents, children love to sing familiar songs.

Action songs or stories that include repetition and body movement will work well. Look for these in specialty toy stores, and at teacher supply stores. Your local children's librarian can make good suggestions.

Games for young children should more appropriately be thought of as activities. There should be no competitive games. Gear your activities for fun and participation. Play Kiss the Clown. Draw a clown face with a big mouth on sturdy cardboard. Have children stand close and pitch candy kisses through the mouth. They get to keep the kisses after the game.

Another simple game might be Raining Cats and Dogs. Turn an opened umbrella upside down. The children pitch in novelty cats and dogs. If these are appropriate in size and not expensive, the kids keep them, or you award them another prize just for playing. More games and activities for preschoolers can be found in Chapter 11.

Remember to keep the children safe. Very young children will put virtually anything in their mouths. Giveaways should be large enough so that they cannot be swallowed. Be sure there are no sharp edges or parts that pull off that could be swallowed. For the same reason, do not give balloons to children under three years of age. If the parents ask for balloons for children under three, give the balloon to the parent with instructions to keep it out of the children's mouth. I make them promise to watch the child if they give the balloon to him. If I see a child put a balloon in his mouth and the parent is not keeping their promise, I say "Look, it's in his mouth; keep your promise or I'll have to take it away to keep your child safe."

Some parents are slower than others. At a party I had, one dad with a baby (under one) came up to me just after I gave my safety speech, and said, "At the end of the party could you make several of these for us to take home? We think it would be good for him to bite on because he's teething." I very patiently repeated my safety speech but saw the dad didn't believe me. As this was a guest at the party, I didn't say anything else but "Oops! We ran out of time and I couldn't make his balloons."

SAMPLE PROGRAM
FOR PRESCHOOL CHILDREN

The following are examples of the things I do at parties for younger children. In this example I have six distinct segments. They are briefly described below.

1. I start with a routine using Hamilton my dog puppet. Hamilton will come out of his doghouse only if the children ask him. Have the children yell, "Come out, Hamilton"; when he doesn't come out, ask him why. "Oh, we forgot to say please. Please come out, Hamilton." When he is out, he waves with one paw, then I proceed with the routine. He greets the birthday child and attempts to sing a birthday song. But instead of Happy Birthday he sings another song. When the children correct him, he goofs the song up. Finally, the children all sing "Happy Birthday" with him.

2. In the next segment I use the magic coloring book—a standard magic trick available at most magic shops. You open the book and show uncolored pictures. Close the book and do some magic and when you open it again, all the pictures are filled with color. Instead of using imaginary crayons, I like to use a paint palette. This is a magic prop made of a plastic paint palette with four places to put paint. The paint is actually dry marker ink. I use a one-inch paintbrush. The children come up and pick up paint with the brush, then brush it on the outside of the coloring book. After all the paint is used (with may helpers) we say the magic words and the pictures inside are magically painted. This works well with magical picture frames too.

3. My bunny routine is next. "Have you seen my bunny?" I explain that bunny has disappeared and maybe he showed up at the party before me? When the children say no, I ask if they know what a bunny looks like? Then I proceed into my misidentified bunny bit and ask "What color is a bunny?" Most kids will yell, "white." Then I ask, "Does he have a long or short tail?" Kids say "Short." I might then pull out of my case a white, chicken puppet and say "Oh, here's my bunny." When the children correct me, I will say, "You're right, this must not be a rabbit, it doesn't have ears. Does a bunny have ears?" When they say yes, I'll say "Okay, a bunny is white with a little tail and he has ears, right?" When they say "yes", I'll pull out a white pig puppet. And so it goes, until I decide bunny is not in my case. (This can go as far as you want, because very young children are fascinated with this.) I then decide we will try to make a bunny with magic.

4. The next routine features Super Bunny. This is a magic prop of two bunnies made with rope and a wooden head. One bunny is made with white rope, and the other with blue rope and a red cape (Super Bunny). Also included is a plain white rope. I show the rope and say maybe we can make a bunny with magic. I get the birthday child to swing the rope around and put it into the rabbit hole (change bag). Then as the children are swinging their wands back and forth and yelling "Pink Platypus," the birthday child will hop like a bunny. I produce the all white bunny and laugh and say "Oops!, this looks like a bunny skeleton, he needs to eat more carrots. Maybe

Mary "Sugar Plum" Lostak.

he needs more time in the rabbit hole." The white bunny is placed back in the change bag. I then tell the kids, "What we want is a super, terrific bunny, so we will say, 'Super duper pink platypus.'" When the Super Bunny is produced, I sing the Superman song and make the bunny fly. The kids will all be giggling at this. I say "Well, this is a super silly bunny, but I think we're looking for a real bunny, right?" Maybe we need to make a wish.

5. Next comes the rabbit production. I have several ways to produce a rabbit, but this is my favorite. I use a magic prop, a box with a trick drawer that can be pulled out and shown empty, and the next time it is opened it's filled. I call it the wish box. "Maybe what we need to do is make a wish. When I make a wish, I cross my arms like this, then I close my eyes, squeeze tight, and say I wish the bunny. Let's try the wishing position." I then have them practice. "Now, I think we need the birthday boy to help, and we need another helper." After getting both of them up, I usually have some silly business with

large wands and funny "wishing hats." I then show them the empty drawer and have them stir up the magic particles with their wands. If the party is small, I'll have the other children do this too, perhaps bringing up the boys and girls separately. The drawer is closed, and we all assume the wishing position, and say "I wish for a bunny." We then point our wands at the box and say "pink platypus" and have the two helpers hit the box with their wands. The birthday child gets to open the box, and when he sees rabbit, his face is surprised. I pick the bunny up so all the children can see, because the ones in the front are usually standing by now. I say, "Wow, how did you do that? You really do have birthday magic. Let's give our helpers a big yeah." I then get everyone's attention by blowing my whistle. I settle them down, and have the birthday child show how to pet a bunny.

6. This is when I make balloon animals. I first get everyone seated and make my safety speech to parents. I then make anywhere from three to six sample balloons for the birthday child (it's best to give fewer choices to young children), and then tell the other children they will need to decide if they want a sword, or a dog, or a rabbit. I then have the children who want a rabbit to stand, and all the others will sit until I make their selection.

PARTIES FOR OLDER CHILDREN

Your approach to this age group (ages 6 to 12) must be different. If you attempt to do the same show as for a four-year-old, you will run into problems, especially if you are a clown. Most children above eight begin to be skeptical. They don't believe in magic, Santa Clause, and such. Don't try to fool them. They know that underneath the makeup and funny clothes is a real person. I believe in being honest with children about clowns. Clowns are not fantasy characters but real live people with very special jobs. Absolute honesty about your clown character will defuse a lot of challenges.

If a child says "You're not a real clown, you're wearing a wig." You might say, "Yes and it's my favorite color. Clowns are real people like you, who go to clown school and learn how to be clowns."

They might say, "That's not your real nose!" Comment, "No, but it's my favorite one because it's so____(red, stubby, big, etc.) Some clowns just paint their real noses. You know a famous clown who does that. I'll give you a hint. He really likes hamburgers."

Use the challenging questions to educate these children. You will not lose anything by being honest. By answering their questions, you will free their minds to enjoy your performance.

Parties for older children can be a lot of fun if you have their cooperation. The activities they like are magic, games, balloons, face painting, and stories. If you're doing magic, make sure it is not too simple. This audience appreciates skill and surprises. Children delight in trying to figure out how you do the trick.

Older children love to have their faces painted. You may offer them simple one-item designs or complete faces, depending upon the amount of time you have. If I'm also doing a magic show, I limit their choices to simpler designs; such as rainbows, rabbits, spiders, dragons, or balloons. If the group is small or I have plenty of time, I will do more time consuming designs such as camouflage face, clown face, or an accident victim face with bruised eyes, scars, bloody nose, yuck! (I know it's gruesome, but boys really like it.)

Children in this age bracket are old enough to understand rules and instructions for games. Try to plan games suitable for all levels so that the pressure to win is on the group, not one individual. Relay type games are excellent if there are enough children and suffcient room. If you add funny hats or clothes this can be a lot of fun.

Some examples of the games children enjoy are: Lily Pad, Fried Chicken, Stretch, and Pass the Ring. All these games are described in Chapter 11.

I always have prizes for both teams. I bring two buckets of novelties, one with slightly more expensive items. The winning team chooses from the winner's bucket, the other team from the consolation bucket. If I see one team is winning more than the other, I will rearrange the people on each team.

Games should be fun. If a game or the rules are too difficult, it will not be fun. Feel free to redesign your games to fit a particular group. I have stopped a game and changed the rules, if I see it is needed to make it more enjoyable or more funny.

ADULT PARTIES

Sometimes you will be asked to entertain for a family party where an adult is the guest of honor. Because I am a clown, I will not use risqué humor, dirty jokes, or naughty balloons even at adult only parties.

Usually, this is a birthday party, and I am the surprise. I have done parties for many ages, with the oldest being for a grandfather turning 83. My approach when choosing my program is to let the kid out in the adult. Therefore, I use a lot of the same routines that I use for children's parties.

Most of the time I do a magic show to entertain, although sometimes I am asked to do balloons only. Adults enjoy balloon animals as much as children. Another option is to do balloon hats. You need a large room, however, for this to work without the hats becoming a nuisance.

A little research about the honored guest can help you personalize the show. For a 45th birthday, I will attempt to find out what music, social changes, fashions, television programs, hair styles, etc. were popular during the guest of honor's youth. I set up my show to incorporate something from childhood (like a Davy Crockett coonskin hat), and from the teens (like a favorite musical group), also some event from their 20s or 30s (long hair or high heel disco shoes). By incorporating these items into my show, I provide great photo opportunities and a lot of silliness.

The guests get a big kick out of seeing Tom in a coonskin hat holding a wooden gun singing "Davy Crockett, King of the Wild Frontier," or wearing a long wig and playing his air guitar to a once favorite song.

For an older group, I let them choose what age children they would like to be, from four years on up. This allows them to relive their youth. I handle my magic almost exactly like I would for a children's party. The only exception is that I might have to do a little more warm-up type activities. You will find older adults are a terrific audience and they love to laugh and play. My theory is that they enjoy unloading a lot of their inhibitions, and are not afraid to look silly if they're having fun.

You will need to groom your show for adults. I have found that the magic tricks that require the group to respond in a special way, such as yelling "turn it around," as a children's group might respond (sucker type magic such as Farmyard Frolics or Vanishing Elephant) might not work. The reason is that adults have learned to be polite, and really don't want to make you look stupid or inept, therefore, not knowing you need them to try to expose the trick in order for it to work properly, they will remain quiet.

I have also found that games like those described in Chapter 11 can be a lot of fun for adult parties. You might want to shorten the distance between starting point and end, or change the rules to fit their physical limitations. Have silly prizes for the winners, like fake lips or teeth, and you'll be surprised at how the years fall away from the guests.

How can you tell there's an elephant in the refrigerator?
The door won't shut.

Chapter 4

STORYTELLING

A master storyteller can transport an audience to far-away lands and kingdoms, to feel emotions, and to laugh, all with the mere use of words. By using imagination and fantasy, the storyteller can create a world of enchantment where almost anything is possible. The listeners can experience the past, or the future, take part in an exciting quest, or delight in a silly adventure.

As a birthday party entertainer, storytelling is the most important skill you can learn. Whether you are a clown, magician, puppeteer, or any other type of children's entertainer, you need to learn how to tell stories. Just performing skills like doing magic, making balloon animals, or face painting in themselves is not entertaining. Far from it. A magician can perform marvelous feats of magic, a juggler can demonstrate extraordinary skills at manipulation, a puppeteer can display colorful cute puppets or perform ventriloquism, but if there is no story to accompany the performance, there is no real entertainment. Adult audiences often enjoy and appreciate skilled performers without them speaking, but children quickly get bored. They need to laugh and be pulled into the performance by the performer. This is done through storytelling. To entertain children you need to get them involved and to laugh.

Although children can get some enjoyment from watching a skilled performer, it is the accompanying story that really makes it entertaining and transforms a mere magician or face painter into an "entertainer." All successful performing artists are storytellers at heart. When a magician performs an illusion, the "patter" or story that accompanies the trick amplifies its effect and makes it more entertaining. The movements of a juggler, mime, or clown are also enhanced by the telling of an appropriate story or joke. Can you imagine a puppet show without a story? Storytelling is a key ingredient to creating effective children's entertainment.

All children's entertainment should revolve around stories. The stories may be simple jokes or short skits, or more elaborate tales of adventure or comedy. Some entertainers will use visual aids, such as puppets, pictures, or magic tricks. Some stories have plots, others do not. Some take on the appearance of a casual conversation as the performer talks to the audience and leads them from one trick, gag, or activity to the next. Your entire show is a fantasy adventure created by your patter and presence.

TRAVELING STORYTELLER

My name is Robin Vogel the Traveling Storyteller. In this chapter I will share with you some of my experiences with birthday parties and guide you in the direction towards becoming a successful storyteller yourself.

Traveling Storyteller germinated in a crude form in 1965-66. I was an outgoing, creative, people-pleasing sixth-grader who, rather than jump rope or play ball games, enjoyed gathering crowds of my peers around me on the playground at recess to regale them with stories I made up on the spot.

What especially intrigued my listeners was that I used *them* as characters in my imaginative tales, weaving everyone present into the exciting fabric of the stories. I turned them into flesh and blood parts of the action—castle-hunting ghosts, heroes, murderers (the more violent, the better, which proves kids haven't changed from then to now or vice versa), mustache-twirling villains and feisty princesses—often all mixed haphazardly together in the same intricately plotted, convoluted mystery-romance. The bad guys were always vanquished and the good guys triumphant. Those kids cheered lustily, entreating me for more, feeding my overwhelming need to be the center of attention and bask in a few moments of localized fame among my peers. The stars of my stories rose above the mundane playground arena too, attaining that fleeting moment of fame most of us crave at some point in our lives.

These storytelling sessions became a daily event and extremely popular, with all the kids fighting over the places closest to me on the asphalt. Those seated nearest (mostly because of my nearsightedness), were the heroes and heroines and, being a budding feminist even then, both boys and girls were given equal opportunity to save the day.

What gave me wicked enjoyment was to propel a story right up to its gut-wrenching climax—just as recess was ending. The teachers would order us back into our classrooms and I'd regretfully, dramatically say, "Time's up! We'll have to finish this one tomorrow!"

It gave me a sensational rush of power when my listeners hovered near, begging me even in the classroom to reveal the conclusion of my cliffhanger, but I always firmly insisted, "Sorry—you'll just have to wait 'till after lunch tomorrow to find out if you die or not!"

They waited, but they flocked around me eagerly the following day, elbowing each other out of the way. They listened, became entranced, invited others to join the fun. The groups became too unwieldy to include everyone in the storyline (which is why Traveling Storyteller rarely relates anecdotes to groups larger than 15).

At the age of 12, I was miraculously popular, sought-after, adored; as soon as I entered seventh grade, I was downgraded to "that strange girl who used to tell stories on the playground when we were *children*." No one wanted to listen to me anymore, but in the ensuing years, I replayed in memory the wonderful days when spinning an exciting yarn turned me into the Queen of the Playground. Sigh.

Fate, the Other Mother of Invention

According to the well-known saying, necessity is the mother of invention, and a desperate mother's inventiveness can be a powerful force to reckon with. In my case, personal demands forced me to create a whole new career, and, in turn, an exciting new life.

In January, 1988, my son, Brad, then four, was hospitalized with diabetes mellitus. His doctors told my husband and me that Brad would need extensive blood testing, shots of insulin and a complete dietary overhaul for the rest of his life, difficult changes for an unhappy little boy whose world had been turned upside-down.

Forced to take an increasing number of days off from work, I found myself being ground to bits in the office rumor mill; my job was in jeopardy and everyone was fighting over who would replace me. (Talk about a real-life tale with a terrifying cliffhanger!) One kind supervisor suggested I take a leave of absence, but that would only be a temporary solution to a problem that would never go away. Diabetes is forever.

I felt stressed and torn. We desperately needed my salary, but Brad needed me more, at least until his volatile blood sugar numbers leveled off. His doctors warned me that attaining such stability could take a long time. What was I going to do?

This was my raison d'être for pursuing a freelance career; your reasons don't have to be anywhere near as compelling. The adversity that befell my son merely sped up the inevitable; I'd grown tired of my secretarial job and was anxious to start my own home-based business. I loved to write and had enjoyed moderate success in selling articles and fiction to various publications, but my freelance income hadn't, up to that point, come close to matching the salary and benefits I'd be giving up.

Sometimes, I was to learn, you have to throw yourself wholeheartedly into making a dream come true, even if it means taking a giant step and a terrifying risk.

I Can Do Better Than That!

In the midst of this tumult, I brought Brad to one of the endless string of birthday parties to which he was constantly being invited. A clown was performing magic tricks. This clown apparently had not spent much time perfecting his act. I carefully examined both his amateurish, hackneyed performance and the bored, listless faces of the children. For no reason I could fathom, I started jotting notes, scribbling, "lacks confidence," "can't control the kids," "won't give up on a stunt that's falling flat," "is panicking and the kids can sense it." One little boy kept crowing, "I know how to do *that* trick! See, he's . . ."

Barbara Smith with two of the characters from one of her popular stories.

And he went on to reveal the stunt's secret to the other kids, who laughed and started making fun of the poor guy, flustering him further.

I'd seen similar entertainers, in different costumes (Batman, Ninja Turtles, dinosaurs, whatever the centerpiece of the latest fad). It seemed to me that many of them took little thought of their performance and lacked the precious spark of originality, a must for dealing with today's sophisticated children. One grumpy mother complained, "I paid this guy *a hundred and fifty bucks* and nearly all the kids weren't paying attention! I had to get involved. Why should I hire an entertainer if I end up having to do the work?"

I pondered how I, a freelance writer who adored children (and who was also in dire need of an income that would allow me to spend most of my time with my son), could tap into this rich vein.

When we returned home, I asked Brad, "So, what did you think of that clown?"

"He was yucky," Brad answered in his forthright five-year-old manner. "I saw the same thing at Chris' party last time."

"The same clown?"

"I don't know, maybe. His makeup was different, but he did all the same stuff."

"Brad, what would *you* like to do at parties?"

"I'd like to see a Ninja come in and start chasing everybody!" he chortled, his eyes gleaming.

"Pick something else—something *not* violent," I suggested, laughing.

"I dunno, Ma, maybe a dragon chasing everybody and shooting fire at 'em," he tossed off, and ran to find his coloring book.

Several ideas spun around in my head like billiard balls, clicking audibly, finding winning side pockets in my memories.

I was catapulted into a vivid flashback of my 12-year-old self entertaining friends and friend-hopefuls on the playground. Remembering those days and how much fun I and the other kids had, I decided I would become a traveling storyteller, going from house to house relating tales of adventure, love, death, and triumph to attentive children at parties!

It would, if very successful, serve three purposes: (1) I'd earn enough income to quit my full-time job. (2) I'd be able to take care of Brad, rigorously monitor his diabetes, and be available in case of an emergency. (3) I'd fulfill my lifelong dream to write (or at least be on one of its lunatic fringes) for a living.

Ad-Vice—Display vs Classified

Putting my plan into action proved more difficult than in my rose tinted imagination. I ran a slew of advertisements in local papers (the *Pennysaver*, my town's local tribune, and a publication called *Smart Shopper,* an 8 ½ X 11-inch booklet made up mostly of classified and display ads).

Placing half a dozen ads cost a little more than $100 and, to my horror, didn't elicit even one response. That caused me to panic and doubt my original plan. I nearly gave up right away. I'm one of those impatient people who needs instant, positive reinforcement to feel secure, but so many people encouraged me, saying, "It's such a great idea!" that I pursued it.

Jan, a friend who'd been running a home-based typing business for several years, examined my ad afterwards and told me it wasn't specific enough. "Reading it doesn't really give the reader a clear focus of the unusual service you're providing," she pointed out.

Instead of a small ad, buried amongst dozens of others, she suggested, "A well-placed display ad with appropriate artwork will show exactly what Traveling Storyteller is all about. There's more room for additional words, little pictures that draw attention to your ad. Classifieds, by their very nature of X number of cents or dollars per word, tend to be limiting."

I was embarrassed to admit to Jan, who firmly believes that you have to spend money—sometimes a lot—to make it, that I was hoping I wouldn't have to resort to the more-expensive display ad. At the beginning, I was floundering along, trying to save money by utilizing the cheaper classifieds.

Jan was right, of course. I considered the way I peruse ads, scanning only the display ads—then the individual classifieds later, *if* I have a chance.

Though I haven't found it necessary to run ads of any sort for a long time now, I learned that response to a display ad is much better. If I'd sought and followed my friend's advice before the fact, instead of after, my new career would certainly have blossomed sooner and faster, but this is how a novice learns.

My subsequent display ads tantalized the eye, showing my logo, a smiling fairy godmother brandishing a magic wand, in one corner. It stated, specifically, how I would entertain kids, including the then-unusual idea of child participation. It also incorporated how much I charged and compared my much-more-reasonable fees with those of other local party entertainers.

The response was awe-inspiring, continuing to pull responses long after it stopped running. Why? Because people clipped out the large ad and put it up on their refrigerators with magnets or on bulletin boards in their kitchens. Tiny classifieds can be put up on the fridge, too, but usually end up falling down and disappearing in Limbo Land where small scraps of paper always go.

The moral of this story is, if you have a friend involved in a successful home-based business, shamelessly pick that person's brain for ideas and advice. Remember, you're providing this person with your priceless friendship; the least he or she can do is help you get started in your own enterprise!

However, be sensitive to and be aware of the dangers of competition; if I were starting my own typing company, I'll wager Jan would have deliberately set me on the wrong path (just kidding, Jan, I know you're more noble than that)!

Into the Fray—My First Gig

Getting back to how I finally got my business underway after eliciting absolutely no response to my first ads, I watched, horrified, as my friend's six-year-old birthday boy, followed by nine of his screaming pals (including my own son), raced uncontrollably around a local fast food place.

Inspired as much by sympathy as desperation, I asked my agreeable but not very sanguine buddy if I could try out my gig then and there, gratis (yes, I was shamelessly hitting on friends again). Snatching eagerly at any chance

to calm them down, she said, "Do it! Hurry up! we're gonna get kicked out of here!"

So, unprepared, vulnerable, terrified but eager, I stood before them in my plain old jeans and T-shirt and began to tell a hastily constructed tale.

Dancing, chortling, gesturing, generally making a fool of myself, I performed the rough-around-the-edges, improvisational act in a trembling voice. I knew the birthday boy was a rabid G.I. Joe fan, so he and all his friends went to war and settled the hash of an entire regiment of sadistic villains. Without the name tags I later used, I got some of the kids confused, but they were quick to correct me, and it even added to the fun (a game kids love to play called, "get the grown-up"). Slowly, miraculously, monsters in kids' clothing turned back into ordinary children again—proof of the inherent magic of Traveling Storyteller.

It took a few minutes, but everyone eventually tuned in on my dramatic voice and movements and settled down to listen. I found myself the center of avid, admiring faces raptly watching me, straining to catch every word. By the story's explosive climax, there was applause, cheering, and requests for "More, more!" (A happy blast from my past—and I was 34!)

Several mothers seated on the sidelines listened as enthusiastically as their children, giving me nods and thumbs-up signs. A delicious thrill ricocheted up and down my spine, hailing the first sweet realization that my idea could, if handled carefully and coaxed along properly, be a winner—and lucrative moneymaker.

I was overwhelmed by the response, understanding how an actress feels on opening night when she's given a from-the-gut, award-winning performance and realizes it's only the beginning of an auspicious career.

So it was for me. By the time I left that afternoon, I'd been asked (no, *begged!*) to tell stories at two other parties.

Traveling Storyteller, *my* little business, had taken fragile root!

Traveling Storyteller Takes Off

The best advertising in the world is a satisfied customer, and word-of-mouth proved itself exceptionally kind to me from day one. As I dashed from party to party, always on weekends or week nights because I hadn't yet quit my day job, news of Traveling Storyteller spread around as swiftly as a brush fire, and business grew beyond my wildest expectations.

In 1988, I made between $50 and $60 for a story running anywhere from 30 minutes to an hour. After a few parties for under-three-year-olds that simply didn't come together, I decided the age of my clientele would be no younger than three and no older than ten. Yes, I've bent my own rules, but rarely; inevitably, it doesn't work out. Over tens tend to be too sophisticated to listen to me; they'd rather be skating or playing ball. Under threes don't have the necessary attention span. I found out the hard way that it's difficult to keep the latter absorbed in a story, even with my constantly changing voices and gestures. I'd start a story I was sure they'd find compelling, only to find them growing apathetic and argumentative. How did I handle it, you ask?

Calling upon the adequate skills provided by my once-despised music lessons, I eventually started bringing along my guitar or portable keyboard to parties, composing and singing silly, rhyming verses to enhance the action. Kids adore music, and it can, on occasion, salvage a situation that's going bad. One party comprised of three-year-olds found me abandoning the story altogether and turning it into a familiar song session ("Eensy Weensy Spider," "Rain, Rain Go, Away," "The Wheels on the Bus").

When a story is beginning to flake apart, I might make up dreadful but lively choruses as, "He's way too bad, he makes me mad, I'll find him real soon and send him to the moon!"

I encourage the kids to sing along and yell "Booo!" at the villain or a rousing "Hooray!" for the hero. I play disconcerting chords to make their pulses jump a bit, like background music in old silent horror films. I'll start them on a round similar to "Row Row Row Your Boat," but to a tune of my own devising.

Once I started adding music, giving kids an opportunity to sing, shout or, if they really seem to need it, scream in harmony during the course of the story, it become easier to stretch younger kids' stories to 45 minutes plus—and charge higher rates.

A lot of people believe that being able to play music is necessary to be a successful traveling storyteller, but that's not so. Other sources of music are available besides yourself, as I'll explain later. Heck, you can even go *a cappella*, if your voice is good enough, or you can be silent and have the kids sing en masse. Music is an accompaniment, a back-up, and can take some of the pressure off, but it's not an essential ingredient.

Incidentally, other party entertainers I've spoken with prefer to have the adults leave the room when they perform (they feel silly and self-conscious). Not me! Since I consider myself to be the very best proof of my own talents, I encourage them to stay, silently saying, "Listen up, adults, because when you see what a great job I do,

you'll want me for your other kids' parties and recommend me to friends and relatives."

The Business of Storytelling

I now make anywhere from $100 to $125 per gig, about half of what other party entertainers in my area charge. Some of my fellow party entertainers have expressed displeasure with me because of this, but they calm down when I point out that I don't do shows outside my little community (I want to be nearby in case my son needs me). My cohorts are all willing to go a lot further afield and charge more to compensate for their travel time and for gas and wear and tear on their vehicles.

Because I restrict myself to within a few miles of my home, I have to work a little harder to pull in business than other local party entertainers. I carefully nurture and stroke my local clientele. As a result, I've been blessed with a lot of volume business.

After a half dozen phone calls to fellow entertainers, parents quickly realize I'm giving them a super good deal, so they rarely bother to negotiate for lower fees. "Wow," a lot of parents say upon first contact, "Everyone else wants at least two hundred, and some of them won't stay longer than 45 minutes! One guy I hired to do magic tricks stopped in the middle of a trick and left in such a hurry, he forgot to collect his money—he was late for his next party. I never did pay him, and I guess he saw how angry I was, because he never asked for it."

Even if a story runs longer than planned, I never cut it short; that's a good way to give yourself a bad name and lose future business. Unlike a play, which runs a pre-determined number of minutes, when you're improvising, there are bound to be digressions that change the course of the tale. It might take on another plotline altogether, depending on the kids' reactions! If I have two parties in the same afternoon, I make sure I give myself plenty of time for a story runover/travel time. Inevitably, the tips (and public relations) are better when parents realize I'm not a clock-watcher.

Speaking of tips, most parents tip me generously, so I often collect 10, 20, or even 30 extra dollars. In more well-to-do neighborhoods, I've been handed an additional 50 dollars. If parents have done their homework, they know they're still getting a bargain. I prefer cash payments, but I'll gratefully accept my remuneration in whatever form it's given to me.

I'm *always* asked for my business cards, and I never, ever give out only one! Have plenty handy and never allow yourself to run out. I order a thousand at a clip. Spread them around generously, both at parties and everywhere you meet people. I take shameless advantage of free-for-all bulletin boards in town stores, churches, hospitals, schools, colleges, and libraries, creating empty spaces, if need be, to squeeze in my cards. Be aggressive—if there aren't any extra spaces, make some! Tack up your cards in a stack or tuck them between the cork and wooden border in a neat line so people can help themselves.

If you live in a nice little incorporated village, as I do, all the small shop owners know you, want you to spend the bucks you're making in their stores, and will gladly let you leave a stack of your business cards on their counters or taped in the window. If you have the chutzpah to sit and tell kids a long, complex story, you can surely convince people to help you sell yourself!

I presently average six to eight parties a week, and my overhead—gas for the car, a few strategically placed local ads (rarely necessary anymore, thanks to enthusiastic, complimentary word-of-mouth from satisfied customers and gobs of repeat business), and a bit of polish to keep the tiara sparkling—is negligible.

Be generous with your time in the beginning; do a few shows free at local libraries, hospitals, churches, malls, and schools. Get yourself a big supply of business cards to hand out, stand back, and, if you're good, prepare to be inundated!

I live in a suburban area and rarely have to travel more than 15 miles outside of it. Seventy-five percent of my time is spent within a three-mile radius of my own house! I carry a beeper in case an emergency arises with my son, so I'm always available if needed (which frees my mind for storytelling). Most of my business takes place during weekends, and it isn't unusual for me to race to two or three different parties on a weekend afternoon. During one memorable week, I told a dozen tales to a total of 146 children! (It's a miracle I didn't tell the all-girl Victorian murder mystery to the boys' group panting to be ghost killers, I was so worn out and frazzled!)

My stories are all original, tailored to the individual child, but one woman who adapted my idea haunts garage sales and used bookstores for old volumes of fairy tales and reads those aloud.

"The kids adore the ancient, brooding ghost stories," she says, "and even though the parents ask me to tone down the violence, their kids love 'em as gory and violent as I can tell 'em."

If you choose to go her route, don't expect to get away with reading familiar favorites like Cinderella or Snow White. Even the littlest children have heard those a hundred times: today's kids will only sit still if you tell them stories unfamiliar to them, and without my "hook" of using them as characters in the story, you'd better have exciting, never-before-heard material!

To sum up, what you'll need to be a traveling storyteller is:

- A car (it can even be what ads coyly call a "station car" if you stick close to home).

- An eye-catching costume (not necessarily elaborate, but fun if you're into that).

- A pre-written story (made up or otherwise); or, if you, like me, consider yourself an improvisational storyteller, put together a bare-bones outline and make it up as you go along.

- A love for children (essential—and remember, you cannot kill the ones who give you a hard time!)

- A need to be the center of attention (i.e., frustrated actor/actress).

- A hundred dollars or so for local posters/ads (perhaps your local stores will display them in the windows as a courtesy, as mine do).

- Patience. Patience. Patience.

- Energy and plenty of it!

When I finally felt secure enough to cautiously declare Traveling Storyteller a successful business (which took a full year of mostly weekend parties), I gave notice at my office. My co-workers, who considered me studious and rather boring, were stunned to hear that I'd gone into business for myself, let alone a business like this.

Few women can make a living at something they truly enjoy (and provide their children with quantity and quality time), but "Traveling Storyteller" has proven to be a success story for me—and for minimum effort and outlay, birthday party entertaining can be for you, too!

HOW TO BE A
BIRTHDAY PARTY STORYTELLER
(How I Do What I Do)

As Robin, Traveling Storyteller, I sweep in after the food's been served and everyone's blown off steam for a while, which means the kids are relatively calm and not clamoring for ice cream and cake. I make a grand entrance in one of two billowy gowns (both sumptuous dresses purchased at garage sales for next to nothing), and glittering rhinestone tiara (I splurged—$27).

This diaphanous, floating ensemble brings out the fantasy fairy godmother in my plump self, sets the stage for my unusual entertainment, and makes me feel special. Some people who've followed in my footsteps prefer not to hide behind a costume and take their chances in jeans and sweatshirts. I like the persona I've created, and I think the children do too.

I jot down all the kids' names on gold and silver paper and attach the tags to their clothing with masking tape, a couple of dollars' outlay per party. My memory is borderline at best, and there's no way I can remember who's who on such short acquaintance; use name tags and you won't make a mistake (be sure to stick the tape out of the way of little girls' or boys' long hair).

I sometimes begin the story with the traditional, "Once upon a time," but more often, I'll start out with something that brings us right into the meat of the story: "Sean and his friends were in big trouble; the Tyrannosaurus rex was hungry, he'd broken out of his cage, and to the giant, salivating dinosaur, the screaming kids looked like cookies in a cookie jar, ready for good eating."

Or, "Diane surveyed the dead body for three terrifying seconds, then bolted through the door, where she was met by Megan, who was brandishing a fireplace poker above her head."

Perhaps, "A terrible form of cancer was raging among the residents of Magenta, and Margie, the best of the town's three doctors, was feverishly working to find a cure."

Or, "Glenn was often compared with Ebenezer Scrooge—and Mr. Scrooge was considered the kinder of the two."

It's important not to underestimate the intelligence of your group. If you've got bright kids sitting there, use bigger vocabulary words and more complex plotlines. If they're younger (or older but less mature), go for simpler language, add more songs/music, and don't confound them with a wild, complicated story. You'll lose them early on and run into discipline problems that can easily get out of hand.

After a while, if you're invited to tell stories in the same neighborhoods, as I am, you'll encounter the same kids, pinpoint the troublemakers, and know how to handle them. I usually try to turn the "discipline-challenged" kids into my villains; it's a role they relish, anyway, and they'll almost always listen to the story when they have such an important role—and bully the others into paying attention as well.

I frequently encounter a little boy who suffered head injuries in an accident. His attention span is severely limited, but he's a popular child and has a slew of friends and relatives living locally. He's frequently invited to parties at which I'm entertaining, so if I know ahead of time, I bring along something to keep him occupied, like a simple, quiet game, or a coloring book and crayons.

He's been getting therapy for years, and on those occasions when he seems more alert and expresses interest in being part of the story, I have him sing a chorus all by himself at various intervals (I cue him with a simple gesture). He beams, and I'm rewarded in every way possible for my ingenuity and compassion.

Before I got to know this boy, he disrupted two parties to the point of chaos. His family and friends were grateful that I found a way to include him, and I'm happy I was able to accommodate him. Fate's been unkind enough to this child; families really appreciate it when party entertainers are willing to put themselves out.

I sit before the assembled group, cross-legged and regal on the floor (eye contact is important; sitting in a chair, above them, if you will, gets in the way of the intimacy), and begin my outlined tale, dramatically hamming it up so they'll be drawn in quickly. If my back is bothering me that day, I'll bring a pillow and arrange myself on the sofa with as many kids as possible gathered around me on the same level.

Not everyone can be the star of the story, and if you have a group of 15 kids, you are going to have to relegate at least a third of them to lesser roles. It's important to establish who the birthday child's best (second best, third best) friends are and award the co-starring parts to those children.

Always make sure everyone enjoys a few moments of glory. Get the other kids cheering and clapping for those with even the most minuscule roles—even if you know from the first word that you'll have to waste that handful of second-string friends/despised cousins/kids-Mom-said-I-have-to-invite in a giant anti-matter explosion in your Star Trek-like tale.

The birthday kid and his or her closest friends are going to save the day; that's a given. Why? Because heck, if it were my party, that's the way I'd want it, wouldn't you? You know you would!

First Contact

When you do what I do, you're a great talker. It goes with the territory. The bright, witty voice I inherited from my parents is that of a convincer, a salesperson. Mom was a real estate broker and Dad was a stockbroker, so selling is my heritage. I have one of those dynamic voices people sit up and listen to, and between my rates and my flamboyant promises (which I fulfill), nine times out of ten, I'll win the gig. If I don't, it may be because I'm too enthusiastic (one woman admitted I sounded way too bubbly for that hour of the morning and she couldn't bear my enthusiasm).

My first contact is almost always with the birthday kid's mother. I explain what I do, highlighting the "this is your child's day and your child's story" idea. For the most part, they've heard about me from a friend or contented customer, but in case they haven't, I keep a list of satisfied clients next to the phone who've given me permission to pass along their names and phone numbers as references. If you can do the same it will clinch many of your deals.

Once they commit to a gig, we choose a suitable date. I keep a gigantic write-on calendar tucked into a blotter on my desk and every party is scrupulously annotated there. I'm not well-organized, and if I didn't do it this way, I'd be double-scheduling and completely messing up my life. In addition, I have a calendar program for my computer and note it there, too, so I'm covered twice.

Some party entertainers of my acquaintance require that contracts be signed, but I don't do that. I've only had two parties canceled, both at the last moment because the birthday child got sick, and I secured alternate dates on both occasions. Yes, it's infuriating if someone cancels suddenly and you turned down another opportunity; you do lose out, but maintaining good will is essential, and if someone is forced to cancel on you, take it with good grace, offer another date, and keep your temper in check.

This is a business, and you have to learn to handle yourself professionally. Lose your temper and you've lost the party—probably permanently.

Once it's established that I've been hired to perform my gig, I query the person at length over the phone and fill out a questionnaire I created myself. It asks such pertinent information as:

• Child's name

• Guests' names

• What sport(s) is your child involved in? Which of those is a favorite?

• Does your child have a sports hero? Who?

• Is your child big on TV shows? Which ones? What characters are the child's favorites?

• Does your child have a favorite TV, movie, or sports villain. (I've actually stooped to asking my husband to keep me current on some of these subjects. Yes, sometimes research is necessary, so be prepared to hit the library or ask your husband/wife/kids questions you never thought you'd want to know the answers to!)

• Has your child expressed any special hopes/dreams to you? What, and be very specific, are they? Doctor, lawyer, Indian chief, wild west hero, space shuttle cadet, mall owner, clothing designer, horseback rider?

• Does your child love animals? Which are favorites? Do you feel your child would want that animal included in the story?

• Who is your child's best friend? Which kid is being invited because he or she has to be and your kid doesn't really want there?

• Is there any topic I should steer clear of? What, specifically?

During the course of that first conversation, new questions are constantly being generated, so my

> What happens when you step in front of a car?
> *You get tired.*
> What happens if you step behind a car?
> *You get exhausted.*

questionnaire is merely an outline. It may sound strange to be asking what topics to avoid, but if you start a story about dragons and the birthday child is all dragoned out, they'll be screeching to play "lynch the traveling storyteller," an unpleasant game you won't want to play!

At the suggestion of a friend, I began providing computer-generated invitations and thank you notes. The children aren't being coaxed to come to just any birthday party, they're being invited to a celebration where I, the Traveling Storyteller, am telling a custom-created tale—big stuff. The invitation hangs on refrigerators and subtly reminds Mom and Dad about your unique gifts every time they go for ice cubes or a glass of milk. It's free advertising for you, too.

If you do have a computer, it can be a godsend, keeping track of your obligations, generating invitations, signs, ads, etc. A great many excellent software printing programs are available, so by all means, use 'em if you've got the hardware!

Finally, if someone calls to ask about the nature of your party entertainment, ask where that person heard of you. Keep records of the most successful ads/people/places and keep on using them. If you find yourself too busy to see straight, bless the powers that be and keep polishing that tiara!

Setting Up the Tale

Once I have the facts and come up with a story direction, I put together an outline on my computer, fill in a few sketchy details, and bring it with me. After arriving at the party, I keep the paper close at hand, improvising as I go along, filling in the blanks as I get into the story. Because I have a flair for improvisation, I can get away with this method; I advise most individuals interested in pursuing this particular home-based business to write stories out in their entirety, at least for the first couple of gigs, until they become completely comfortable with the improvisational style. Dead air is not welcome on the radio and even less so in person, when children are listening. Be prepared!

I'm not going to deny that handling a story in this manner can be likened to a high-wire act; it can backfire and you can be left with unhappy, looking-for-trouble, bored kids who refuse to be blasted into the story even with a stick of dynamite!

Fortunately, this hasn't happened to me often, thanks to the careful research I do beforehand, but on the rare occasions it has, I've called upon what I call my "Calming Muses" to help me. What that means is: I force myself to take charge of the situation, change the story in

midstream if I have to, and make it an all-music block if that's what it takes to soothe the savage beasts in my circle. As I mentioned earlier, I found that making the most troublesome children the villains of the piece is an excellent idea. They're already igniting a ruckus, and it delights them to find themselves in the miscreant role in the story and gives them impetus not only to pay attention, but to drag back those kids they've misled in their ill-begotten negative, attention-getting efforts.

When assigning parts other than the starring role of the birthday child, if a kid is acting up, I usually turn to that misbehaving soul with a smile on my face and an upraised warning eyebrow and say, "And you," (fill in difficult child's name) "will be our villain today." I'm not sure about the psychological machinations involved, but whenever I do that, those children whose most gleeful hobby is testing adult limits sense they had better tread carefully. I'm there to entertain; if I have to take time out for discipline, it cuts into storytelling time and that usually brings the wrath of the other kids (and later, his parents) down on the head of the miscreant. Besides, most kids act up because they want to be the center of attention; if I pronounce them my villain, they know they're in for a juicy role and want to hear and be a participant in the story as badly as everyone else.

For instance, I had an ongoing problem with a little boy who enjoyed screaming. He turned up at several parties and just loved the sound of his own shrill voice (preferably raised to glass-breaking decibels). Sizing up his special talent, I turned him into a screaming villain and pointed to him whenever I needed that ear-piercing sound. In that way, I was at least able to control the noise and place it where it was most appropriate in my story. It was still disruptive, but at least it didn't destroy the entire party.

On the rare occasion when a child's conduct is completely unmanageable, I have gone so far as to request that the child leave the room. Since no one wants to miss the fun (or be the target of ridicule from peers), I suddenly find myself with a docile, perfect angel on my hands. Do what you have to do to make it work.

Video and Audio Recordings

I used to get a lot of requests for an audio tape of my storytelling session, so I added ten dollars to my fee, dragged along my cassette recorder, and gave the crowd what they wanted.

These days I'm often asked if I wouldn't mind being taped on a videocamera, which translates into this: I have to suffer with amateur movie-makers flitting all over the room, distracting me and the kids, generally making my life miserable by making me feel self-conscious, causing me to constantly lose the thread of my story. No good!

I settled the problem by contacting some videotaping services in my area. Today, if a parent expresses interest in having a videotape to commemorate the occasion, I add a fee of from 50-75 dollars and utilize one of those services, all of which I investigated for reliability and professionalism beforehand.

Yes, I recommend the video company for other gigs, and if they hear of a kid's party that needs an entertainer, they recommend Traveling Storyteller. It works out beneficially for all concerned.

STORY TOPICS

Stories you tell can range from high-action adventure to silly, humorous animal tales. Be prepared to tell a variety of stories for different age groups and interests. Your stories can be retold from books, modified versions of these stories, or your own original tales.

Personalized Stories

My current stories differ very little from those tales of love/conflict/villains/comeuppance I told on the playground as a child, and the children of today are as enthralled as my peers were. One aspect remains the same—the birthday child, like those seated closest to me on the concrete, is always the star and the story centers around his or her favorite fantasies/activities. If the parents can't give me any clues, I sometimes tell a generic story, especially to younger children, but on the whole, I prefer to utilize my unique hook—a story customized for the birthday child, homing in on whatever is most important to the boy or girl.

I do not differentiate between boy and girl stories—I've had all-girl baseball or soccer teams and boys who asked to be nurses or mommies. I mix and match according to the whims of the child star.

I've told stories involving baseball, basketball, soccer, swimming, volleyball, football, hockey, doctors, nurses, detectives of all kinds in every era, Barbie, G.I. Joe, dinosaurs of all colors, rock stars, television/movie stars, computer whizzes, Batman, Superman (or close facsimiles), lawyers, world-renowned chefs, dress designers, Olympic heroes, circuses, malls, carnivals, platonic romance (ends with a kiss, that's all), cave exploration, race car driving, ad infinitum!

Keep a close watch on currently popular movies and make every effort to go see them, if you can. Each week,

I try to catch at least one current film that might crop up in the requests of my birthday children. Having a ten-year-old of my own helps, because he has his finger on the pulse of what is "in" for children anywhere from five to 12. I also watch a lot of television so I know what programs are popular and who the characters are. This way I keep up to date with the youth and can weave into my stories characters that they can identify with and that appeal to them.

If the birthday boy dreams of becoming a gold medal winner, my story might take place in the swimming pool at the Olympic games set in the near future. Or, depending on what films are popular at the box office, the birthday child might choose to be a cowboy, a dinosaur park ranger, a ghost chaser, a kid left alone with nasty burglars, or a whale-freer out on a sea expedition.

At an all-girl party, depending on the birthday child's preference, everyone gathered might hang out with Barbie and her friends, go back in time to be pioneer women or Victorian do-gooders, or become embroiled in a tough case as youthful Nancy Drew clones in the "Mystery at the Mall."

Sometimes, reflecting our times, the bad guys aren't all black, but have fascinating redeeming qualities. The good guys aren't perfect, either, resorting to childishly trumpeting their victory ("Nyah, nyah, I won, you're bad, you lose, I won, you lost!") Granted, it's not Shakespeare, and the songs are simplistic, but the kids love it and sometimes sing so loud, I can't hear my own voice raised in song!

The possibilities are as endless as the children themselves, and sometimes, as young as they are, their story wishes have stunned me. Expecting the usual request for a breezy mystery or policegirl shoot-'em-up, a grieving father told me that his ten-year-old daughter had expressed a desire to cure cancer (which had taken her mother the previous year). I could barely hold back the tears myself when I transformed her and her friends into hard-working, dedicated young doctors who find a cure for the deadly disease. Or the little boy who, like my son, has diabetes and requested that his story revolve around a day without blood test or shots, and took place in Chocolate Land where he could eat anything he wanted, in any quantity. I had a tough time holding back the tears during that one, too.

Tangents: Risky Business

Sometimes, while I'm telling my story, especially with the younger children, I'll interrupt to ask such thought-provoking questions as, "What would you do about a dragon who acted mean only because he was lonely and needed friends?"

Querying the kids like that requires great flexibility (some would say nerve) on my part. Depending on the answers I receive, the story might take a completely different track than I had planned. For instance, if one of the kids attending Party A says, "Aw, poor dragon—let's show him we're his friends and maybe he'll be friends back," the story will have a different ending than if the more cynical children who've come to Party B insist, "He's only acting mean because he *is* mean! *All* dragons are mean! They don't want friends! Mean is what they do for a living!"

The dragon is showered with love in Party A; wasted in party B. Democracy rules. Incidentally, and unsurprisingly, the mostly boys groups generally opt for the latter conclusion.

So, if I have to sacrifice the dragon for the kids who came to the latter party because that's what the crowd prefers, that's what I do. Like it or not, agree or not, I'm an entertainer and strive to give the assembled group what it wants. If you aren't prepared to have your tale take off on a tangent, don't ask questions; tell it your way and stick to your outline.

On the other hand, if you're feeling just plain contrary that day or don't mind risking raising the ire of the kids (and their parents), don't listen to them at all and end the story exactly as you planned—no matter how they react. I did that only once; the children protested, the disgruntled parent expressed dissatisfaction, never called me back, and didn't tip me.

Now, the customer's always right.

Bailing Out a Sinking Ship

Most of the time everything works out beautifully. When I see the birthday child's face light up with ecstatic surprise at the very personal story I've weaving, I'm inspired and respond by putting everything I have into making it special.

No matter how well prepared you may be, there will be times, however, when the children just do not respond well. In anticipation of the direst emergencies, if my guitar or keyboard fails to appease, I also keep a boom box CD player in my car and bring along several rock, rap, kiddie, and other tapes so I can lead them in a sacrificial Traveling

> What does a chicken say when she goes into a library?
> "Book-book-book-book-booooook!"

Storyteller dance-a-thon—if that's what it takes to get me through that 30-60 seemingly endless minutes when I have bombed miserably. (In one case when this happened, the birthday boy's mom was so mortified at the horrific behavior of Junior and friends, she insisted I take a triple tip and apologized a thousand times as she ushered me out the door). Her responses to the questionnaire were correct at the moment she gave them to me, but by the time I came to do the story, a month later, that fad had faded and this Traveling Storyteller was relating a tale based on a premise that was out, out, out!

Frankly, I'd rather forego the extra tip and just do what I came there to do. Trying to wriggle out from under a story misfire is far too taxing to brain, heart, and nerves.

Party Entertainers, Unite!

I recently started a support/exchange group for party entertainers in my area. We get together once a month to shmooze, exchange horror stories, trade ideas, discuss trends and problems, and give each other suggestions to beef up our gigs.

Thanks to this valuable networking, I received some excellent advice and started using harmless props in the course of my stories—blunt, plastic swords, masks, even pint-sized costumes for the birthday kids. I've picked up a lot of things cheaply at garage sales and thrift shops, altering them to suit my needs by adding sequins, shiny buttons, and appliqués.

If I have a large enough room at my disposal, I'll let the kids stand and act out certain parts of the story. I'll gauge the group, test their temperaments by just talking to them, then decide what direction would be the right way to go. This seems to work better with kids under seven. A quieter, more introspective group of kids will probably want to sit passively and listen. Even if I encounter reluctance at first, by the time the little ones are in costume, holding up magic wands or mighty swords, they usually embrace the format and turn into scene-stealing little hams.

When I told another party entertainer (combination clown/magician/face painter) about a story I'd tried to relate to a group of really young kids who couldn't get into it at all, he gave me a supply of pencil balloons and taught me how to make balloon animals in case I ever got stuck again. Making them is pretty simple once you learn how. The best laid plans are bound to go awry, and the most successful party entertainers are prepared for anything. Although we try not to tread in each other's territory too blatantly, we've borrowed here and there when absolutely necessary.

Party entertainers have suggested other options if my storytelling goes astray and I have to come up with a substitute quickly, including fashion shows, balloon animals, jewelry making, T-shirt/face painting, crystal chart design, visor decorating, petting friendly animals, puppets, dancing, limbo, costume characters, and the ever-popular magic show.

What's important is: each of us maintains his or her own specialty and all of us thrive and provide high-quality entertainment.

STORYTELLING TIPS AND TECHNIQUES

If you don't tell your own personalized adventures, you can, as most storytellers do, borrow tales from books. When selecting stories, don't use familiar ones; find stories that will be new to most of the kids. Children quickly become bored if you start telling an old familiar tale, even if you change some of the details. They already know, or at least think they know, what's going to happen, so the story is less appealing.

Creating your own story or telling an unfamiliar story will keep their interest. For ideas on creating an original tale or to find stories you can adapt to your storytelling, go to your local library and browse under the headings of storytelling, folktales, fairy tales, myths, and humor.

Not all written stories tell well. Some are too complex, descriptive, or lengthy. Choose stories with a simple plot. Avoid stories with unnecessary secondary plots or that require too many characters. These stories become too confusing for listeners. The best stories for oral presentation should involve one central character with a simple plot or theme. In order to keep the plot moving, which is essential for listeners, the descriptive material enjoyed by readers may need to be cut.

You should also avoid stories which use too much dialogue. Dialogue is good in writing, but difficult for telling because it can become confusing to the listener. When listening to someone read a story, it's often difficult to keep track of who is speaking. Readers have a better idea of who is talking because they can see the punctuation and reread as necessary—listeners can't. Using too much dialogue can also slow down the story. Varying the voice can help the storyteller distinguish each character, give the story variety, and make it more interesting.

To hold an audience's attention, a story needs to have conflict or a problem to be solved or overcome, or a goal to reach. Suspense is maintained throughout the story as the main character tries to achieve the goal and encounters trials and roadblocks. As long as the listeners do not know

> Woman: I want to try on the dress in the window.
> Clerk: Sorry, lady, but you'll have to use the dressing room.

how the hero or heroine is going to accomplish the goal, they will remain curious and interested. If they know the outcome of the story or can guess it before the end, the element of suspense is lost and listeners will become bored and impatient. If you can keep the audience guessing, they will be attentive. This is why old stories, even if told differently, are not as enjoyable as new stories; the audience knows what's going to happen. Choose a story where the ending is not obvious, and do not give it away until the last moment.

Look for stories that will fit your personality and method of presentation. If you're a quiet person, you may focus on more easygoing tales and narratives. If you're a high strung extrovert, you may want to choose stories with lots of movement, sound effects, changing characters, and voice changes.

Select stories that you like and that interest you. If you choose a story that you feel parents might like, but you feel is boring, it will probably be boring to your audience as well. Although the story itself may not be bad, your lack of enthusiasm will show and the audience will detect it. Choosing stories that you can put your heart and soul into will make your stories more interesting to your audience, more enjoyable for you, and help you achieve greater success. A key to successful storytelling is enthusiasm. Act excited and it will be contagious. The audience will get excited too.

Look for a variety of stories and choose ones for both younger and older audiences.

Preschoolers like short, rhyming story songs, including group activities, to keep them occupied and interested. Activities serve as an outlet for children with short attention spans and excess energy, and they will pay attention to you longer.

Older audiences can enjoy less physical activities and longer stories. Preteens and older don't like fairy tales as they consider themselves too sophisticated or mature for that.

When you find a suitable story that you like, personalize it. Give the stories new characters (use boys and girls instead of mice, or vise versa) add new twists, simplify it, change the ending, change the time period, eliminate dialogue, eliminate characters, shorten or lengthen it.

Change the names of the characters if you need to. Names can become confusing especially if they sound too much alike. For example, you'll only confuse the listener if your two main characters are named Bob and Bill; Vic and Aaron would be better.

Adopt appropriate language, using slang, accents, metaphors, and similes; paint a picture with your words. However, don't use too much description because it can slow down the action when telling a story. Written stories often use much more description than is necessary or desirable for storytelling.

Be careful about language. It can't be too far removed from that which is familiar to the audience, or else they will become confused and bored.

Use incorrect grammar if it fits into the story and your character, otherwise use proper speech. A storyteller who portrays a rustic or hillbilly type character can use slang and improper grammar, but for a knowledgeable professor or a wizard of words, slang is out of place.

Some storytellers read their stories to the audience. That's okay for libraries and other events, but ordinarily for birthday parties it is best that you don't. Holding a book restricts you from freely expressing yourself and limits your use of visual aids, including natural gestures.

You do not need to memorize a story word-for-word, just know the main points and be able to retell it in your own words. Memorizing a story takes too much time, and forgetting a part can throw you off track, which may cause you to become nervous and forget other parts. Memorizing also makes the story less enjoyable for you to tell, as you may tend to concentrate so hard on remembering the words that you don't put proper feeling into it. However, sometimes key phrases are important, such as the punch line or a repeated phrase; these should be memorized. Some storytellers use cue cards to help them remember the exact wording when it is necessary.

Each storyteller has his or her own style of telling. Yours will develop as you practice and tell. You don't need to try to copy anyone as this will only hold back your own natural instincts and may slow down your progress.

HOW TO TELL A STORY

There is a difference between simply telling a story and entertaining with storytelling. It's not so much *what* you say as *how* you say it. Have you ever heard a joke told by two different people? It's funny from one person, but not the other. They're telling the same joke and saying basically the same thing, but one gets roars of laughter while the other is met with stony-faced silence or perhaps nauseated groans.

The successful storyteller receives a good response because he lifts the listeners out of their present surroundings and places them in his own imaginary world, where they can experience in their minds the smells, tastes, and scenes he describes. They follow the story so intently that when the punch line hits, it's a total surprise and makes them burst out laughing.

If the same joke or story is told in a mundane way, it's boring. Listeners don't relate to it or may figure out the end before it's over. The difference between the two storytellers is basically enthusiasm. One tells the story with excitement and conviction, while the other just repeats something he heard or read, without vocal variations, emotion, or physical expression.

Physical movement and vocal variations can be as important as the words. By using body posture, voice pitch and inflections, a good storyteller can magically transform an ordinary story into an entertaining event. Like an actor preparing for a part in a play, the storyteller must rehearse and study the part. You might try practicing your story in front of a mirror, trying to put yourself in the character's "shoes." Try to feel what they feel and think what they think—really live the part. Several techniques to help you enhance your story and make it come alive for your audience are discussed in the following sections.

Vocal Skills

Nothing will kill your story faster than an audience not being able to hear or understand what you are saying. To tell a story well, you need to speak loud enough so everyone in your audience can clearly hear you. Pronounce your words properly and distinctly so you are understood. Avoid accents or phrases that are unrealistic, sound unnatural, or may be confusing to the listeners.

Don't speak too fast. This is a common nervous habit of which you may not even be aware. A good way to check your speech is to tape record yourself telling a story and play it back. You will be able to listen and evaluate your diction, loudness, clarity, and speed. You can also identify problems, such as words or phrases that you unknowingly overuse.

The storyteller, in a sense, is an actor who plays not only the narrator, but all the characters in the story. To make the story interesting you need to act out each part. When I say act out, I mean to put feeling and emotion into the words, just as an actor would. Emotions and feelings are conveyed by varying the speaking speed, volume, pitch, emphasizing words, using pauses, and adding vocal sounds effects.

The speed or rate of speech conveys mood. When we are excited, we talk faster; when relaxed, we tend to talk more slowly. For example, say the following sentences out loud and at a speed that conveys excitement as if you mean it: "I won the lottery! I won. I won. I won. Now, slow it down and say the following sentences to project the proper meaning: "I'm sooo tired. I don't know if I can get out of bed." The rate of speech can convey different meanings even when the words are the same. Say the following sentence, first with excitement and then slowly with sarcasm: "Oooh thank you, I never knew you cared."

Use a pause to build suspense. For example, pause before announcing the winner of a contest: "And the winner is . . . Justin!" Pause before a character makes a decision or answers a question: "What would I like to eat?. . . I think I'll have . . . ice cream!" Or when something dramatic happens: "The car swerved off the road and rammed headlong into a tree . . . the driver was dazed . . . but unhurt."

The volume of the words shows emotion. The louder, the more emotionally active. Loud speech conveys anger or assertiveness. Soft words imply feelings of meekness, timidness, shyness, embarrassment, or sadness. Say the following sentence once with force to show determination, and again softly to display remorse: "I will *not* go with you."

Inflection or changes in pitch add variety to speech. Raising the pitch can convey doubt, disbelief, or shock. Usually, a higher pitch or rising inflection is used when asking a question: "You mean *our* team won?" Falling inflection usually means determination or certainty: "Listen to me, I *know* how to do it."

Show emphasis by drawing out key words: "Noooo! I won't go."

The speech can become more colorful and realistic with appropriate sounds. For example, if you're crying, sniff as you would if you were really on the verge of tears: "No, sniff, sniff, I want to do it myself." Laugh when the character laughs: "*Ha, ha . . .* you fell for that one!" Make the laugh realistic and not corny. Blow in relief: "Wooh! That was a close call."

Incorporate emotion and feeling into your storytelling using these techniques. If you do so, you will have attentive audiences.

Visual Aids

The primary visual aid you will use is yourself! As a children's entertainer, you are an actor playing the part of a storyteller. As such, the clothes you wear will play

an important part in creating the fantasy of your storytelling. You don't need to wear a costume that depicts the story you are telling, but you should wear something that identifies your storytelling character, something that sets you apart from being just a nice old man or lady off the street. Your character is your symbol or trademark. It is what distinguishes you from all other birthday party storytellers and entertainers. Take care in selecting a wardrobe that is suitable to your personality and storytelling character. Having a defined storytelling character identifies you as a professional.

Your body is a natural visual aid—your clothes, makeup, and body movements. Body language speaks to the audience and adds emphasis. Use natural gestures freely. Movement helps attract attention and, if done naturally, is a great aid in keeping your listener's attention. Move your arms and hands. Shift your weight, move your head and shoulders, make facial expressions, point your finger, shade your eyes as if looking at a distance, hold your nose at a foul smell, and rub a sore arm. However, don't overdo it, becoming so wiggly as to be distractive. Keep the movements natural and spontaneous. If you are uncomfortable with gestures, don't use so much.

A storyteller can enchant and entertain an audience by simply telling a good story. Sometimes, adding prepared visual aids will enhance the story. Most other birthday party entertainers focus their performances on visual aids like puppets, balloons, and magic props and combine them with stories, usually short stories and jokes. The storyteller, on the other hand, focuses on the story and uses props only to aid in the telling of the story. The storyteller should never use props simply to use props, as they can become distracting. However, if the story can be enhanced with the use of props, by all means use them.

There is no limit in the types of props you can use. Like other children's entertainers, you can use hand puppets, magic, balloon animals, etc. Or you may be a little more creative (or different) and use origami, finger puppets (for younger audiences), spring animals, or chapeaugraphy. Chapeaugraphy is the art of using a specially designed hat to depict different characters. The chapeaugraphic brim (a doughnut shaped piece of felt) can be manipulated and formed into a surprisingly wide variety of different shaped hats, imitating characters as diverse as Mickey Mouse or Napoleon.

Younger audiences need visual aids more than older audiences. Showing pictures can draw their attention to the storyteller and story. Although not necessary, pictures help create mental images of the story and keep children entertained. When reading or telling stories from illustrated picture books, show the children the pictures. Or you can prepare some illustrations beforehand to show as you tell the story.

A visual aid that will be of help to you, as the storyteller, is a name tag. People like to hear their names and respond better if their names are used rather than "you," or "hey, you." If you use the children as the characters in your story, use name tags and you won't forget or mix up names. The name tag could be a simple

piece of paper attached with masking tape or you can create special tags that can serve a dual purpose. Prepared name tags can be modified business cards. The cards can have your name and phone number, and perhaps a logo or illustration. Leave enough space for the child's name to be printed in bold letters. Not only will this help you with the kid's names, but it will serve as an advertisement.

Activities

Kids love to participate, especially younger ones. Have them help you tell the story when possible. Have them make the sound effects or recite a phrase that is repeated throughout the story. Have them shout "Boo!" or yell "Yeah!", rub hands together (to sound like walking through tall grass), stomp their feet (like rain), or sing songs.

You can even have them act out parts of the story. If you have helpers, make sure to use as many kids as you can. They don't all have to participate at any one time, but choose different ones throughout the story. Taking part lets kids enjoy some attention and be a part of the fantasy. Make sure the birthday child plays the key roll.

If your audience is getting restless, having them participate in an activity will help "get the wiggles out." For young audiences you can have them each act out the story as you tell it. This is done by leading them with some simple movements that correspond to the story. You, of course, can have the children do any activity, stand up, sit down, wiggle fingers, blink their eyes, etc. to suit your story.

Sound Effects

At times you may want to use sound effects. This can be done using your own voice—growl like a tiger, squeal like a pig, rev up like a car engine, creek like a squeaky door. Some talented people can mimic sounds and it is entertaining just to listen to them. You might also consider using recorded sounds. Record your own sound effects or buy a commercially produced recording and play appropriate sounds as you tell your story. Some cassette players have hand held power switches so they can inconspicuously be turned on or off as you are speaking. A sudden burst of thunder, or the pelting of rain, or the noise of a busy street can easily be added at appropriate times in this way.

Music can be a nice addition to your storytelling. Music can be used in the background to set the mood as is done in all motion pictures and television shows.

It helps create the mood or feeling if properly synchronized with the story. Music can also be used as part of the story. Very young children appreciate listening to music which makes a good accompaniment with story rhymes.

You can play music on an audio cassette or, if you have the skill, play an instrument yourself. A guitar or a portable keyboard works well. You can also create some interesting (and only occasional) sound effects with a kazoo, jaw harp, or percussion instrument. A small drum, for instance, may make a nice addition to a jungle story. Use whatever will enhance the story.

The Beginning, the Middle, and the End

Just as stories themselves have a beginning, a middle, and an end, so should your storytelling. You will want to give an introduction to the story, tell the story, and then finish in a way that lets the audience know the story is over.

When you arrive at a party, you won't immediately gather up everyone to start telling your story. Before you begin with the story portion of your visit, you will need to take some time to get to know the children. Do some simple warm-up activities as discussed in Chapter 3. This will allow the children time to settle down, focus their attention on you, and prepare them to sit and listen quietly to the story.

Warm-up activities will loosen you up and give you an idea of which kids are more energetic than others and which kids you will want to participate and how. Warm-ups also add variety to your visit, are fun, and takes time so you don't force a 45-minute story on kids who will only sit still for 30. You can use this time to make name tags for the children and choose participants.

Before telling the story, you may start with a short introduction. The introduction announces to the kids what you are going to do and gets them in the proper frame of mind to listen to you. You may tell them what type of story it is, why you chose it, why you like it, who wrote it, how it came to be written, etc. Don't tell too much about the story itself or the plot. The introduction should spark their curiosity.

After the introduction you will go into the story. Try to be consistent with your warm-up activities, the introduction, and your story. If you plan on telling an adventure story, but you do a lot of silly things in your warm-up or introduction, the kids will be misled into thinking you will tell a silly story. The switch will confuse them and force them to mentally adjust, causing them to feel cheated or disappointed. Stay in character for all activities you do with the children. You can still do some funny warm-ups, but don't get too silly—unless the story is silly and the character you portray is silly. If your storytelling character is silly, then you will want to tell humorous stories. If you are more reserved, your stories should reflect that, although, for children it is good not to be too serious. Children love to laugh, so make your visit fun for them.

One of the best ways to arouse the interest of an audience and make them want to listen is to personalize the stories. One way to do this, as already explained, is to have the children become the main characters in the story. Another way to personalize stories is to use people and places familiar with the kids. Make the setting the local neighborhood park or school. Use teachers, local sports heroes, and others as characters in the story.

The third part of the story is the conclusion. Sometimes it is obvious when a story is over. Other times it isn't, particularly with nonsense stories. You should do or say something to clearly indicate that you have come to the end of the story. You may say something like "And they lived happily ever after" or "And they never returned to the old house again." You may use body language. For example, when you start your story have your arms folded, open them up as you begin to tell the tale, and as you finish fold your arms again and lean back to indicate the end. Whatever you do, make it clear that you are finished and that you are not just cutting the story off and leaving.

STORY PRACTICE

If you're going to tell a story from a book, read it over several times. Know the plot and sequence of events. Memorize important words and phrases. Study the story and incorporate the techniques discussed in this chapter with emphasis on vocal tone, pitch, pauses, etc. Select one of your favorite stories and use it as a practice exercise, learn it and retell it using vocal fluctuations, sound effects, physical and vocal expression, and body language—put your heart and soul into it and enjoy it! Identify places where an audience can participate. If you can enjoy telling a story, chances are your audience will enjoy listening to it.

For additional information and suggestions on storytelling and how to tell stories, refer to the appendix of this book. The appendix contains both stories and books on how to tell stories. If you are serious about becoming a storyteller or would like to improve your skills in storytelling, I highly recommend reading some of these books.

Chapter 5

BIRTHDAY PARTY MAGIC

A magic act is probably the most popular form of children's party entertainment. Kids naturally jump with excitement at the anticipation of a real live magician coming to entertain them. Even if you are not a magician, you can use magic to enhance and add variety to your show. Many clowns build their shows around comedy magic. Even puppeteers and jugglers use magic effects with success. Any type of entertainer can use simple magic tricks to enhance and add variety to a show.

Being a birthday party magician is easy. All you need is twenty years experience! By that time you think you've seen and been through every possible experience. But even then, you get surprised.

My point is that you're not going to be able to perform a dynamite half hour magic extravaganza after reading this chapter. You will, though, have the benefit of my experiences, thoughts, and suggestions. Only time and experience will show you if you've got what it takes.

A word before we actually begin: if you don't like kids, or don't like entertaining these rambunctious rascals, get out and try some other hobby or form of entertainment. If you're in it for the money, just for the money, you will be disappointed because you will never make much.

But, if you love kids and love entertaining them, you will succeed beyond your wildest expectations and your monetary rewards will both astound, and humble you. You are truly gifted and blessed!

THE MAGIC SHOW BEGINS
THE MOMENT YOU ARRIVE
Make an Impression

If you could really do magic, would you expect to look like a normal, everyday person? Of course not! People expect a bang for their buck, and first impressions are very important. Most magicians wear a tux. Some soften it with a flower in the lapel or snaz it up with a glittery bow tie and matching cummerbund. Kids love things that sparkle and shine.

One of Washington D.C.'s busiest birthday magicians is "Turley the Magician." In real life he is Hugh Turley, a tall, wiry bundle of enthusiasm. He arrives bedecked in a formal tuxedo, complete with black and red cape and crowned by a top hat. Hugh wisely has added round horn-rimmed glasses (looking a bit like silent film comedian, Harold Lloyd) and a carnation on his lapel that instantaneously changes into a huge sunflower four times the size of the original carnation. Wow! Talk about a magical impression!

I invited Hugh to perform with me at the White House last Easter. Willard Scott from television's Today Show was there, saw Hugh, liked his outfit, and went bananas over the flower bit. That very same morning, Willard invited Hugh to be on the Today Show. Man! Did his birthday business boom!

Hugh Turley (Turley the Magician) at the White House with television's Willard Scott.

Mr. Emerald, a popular Maryland magician, dresses in kelley green with turned-up elf shoes. Talk about standing out in a crowd. The minute folks see him, they know who he is. No one has ever confused him with anyone else! How could they? Leprechauns are supposed to be magical, and Mr. Emerald looks the part. Mr. Emerald stays busy and makes "green" throughout the year.

Dynamic Pennsylvania magician, Harry Albacker, dresses as a swami, complete with turban, colorful vest, and balloon-like pants. He looks like he just popped out of the pages of *Aladdin and the Magic Lamp*. As you might suspect, he is a real sight to see coming up the sidewalk to the party. There is no doubt that this man is an entertainer. Harry has entertained literally generations of kids. He's a hard working pro whose show features appearances by several live rabbits of different sizes and colors.

As for me, with a name like Hal Diamond, what would you expect? My outfit is covered with diamonds. Well, actually, rhinestones, but they sparkle and shine like precious gems, and are fascinating to kids. I have a "Jet

Set" backdrop with my name embroidered on it with sequins and I have also stenciled the diamond design on many of my props to gently reinforce the name I want the kids and adults to remember—Mine!

The costume a magician can wear is limited only by imagination and good taste. Just make sure it's clean and looks fresh. Successful magicians don't wear wrinkled clothing. It's hard for kids (and adults paying the bill) to perceive you as magical if you look just like everybody else or, worse, disheveled. Remember, you have magical powers. Be different, be remembered!

Don't Change

Wear your outfit to the party. Don't bring it in a bag and expect to change in your client's home to transform yourself into "Mr. Magic." There is no place in a stranger's house to change clothes. Don't expect to be escorted into their private bedroom and given carte blanche.

Forget the bathroom. It will be inhabited by an endless stream of little tykes, each of whom just can't hold it any longer. If you must use the bathroom, for any reason, lock the door. Little folks never knock, and it's a real blast to hear them announce loudly to everyone at the party that they caught the magician with his pants down! Besides, while you're in the bathroom, the kids that aren't trying to break down the bathroom door and get in will be going through your props and tormenting your rabbit.

If you must use the facilities, for the purposes they were intended, do so before your props are carried in, or after you have them safely in the car.

BE PREPARED
B.Y.O.T (Bring Your Own Table)

Most magicians arrive with a "suitcase table." It's a fold-up table that looks like and functions as a suitcase for carrying props. This easily snaps up and converts into a table on which the show is performed. It looks like a little rolling bar on casters. The back of the table has shelves for setting up equipment and keeping it hidden. The front of the table often comes silk-screened with a picture of a deck of cards, a rabbit coming out of a hat, a clown, or a swami. The enterprising magician will paint

Where does a cow go on Saturday night?
To the moo-vies.

over the store bought design or modify it to include his own name and logo. These handy and functional suitcase tables are available at magic stores everywhere.

Set Up Your Audience

The arrangement of the room is very important for a magician. Unlike clowns, comics, jugglers, and other performers who like children all around them, a magic show must be pretty much a straight on affair. I always try to back up to a wall. This provides security. I have a 5 x 5-foot backdrop with my name sewn on it in sequins (jet sets are available from Abbott's Magic in Colon, Michigan or local magic dealers). It sets up and tears down in two minutes and provides the simple, yet striking backdrop for my show. It makes my act look bigger than it really is, and that's very important. I lay a "control" rope on the floor to define my stage area. Now it's showtime!

CHOOSING THE BEST TRICKS

The best tricks for you to use are those that fit your personality and character, and of course, the type of audience you entertain. Discovering which tricks do this is a matter of trial, error, experience, and common sense. The first magic trick I foolishly purchased was one which climaxed by removing (by what appeared to be an accident) the lady volunteer's brassier! It sounded good to me. It promised fun, excitement, magic, and laughs! What more could an eleven-year-old boy ask for?

Don't buy a trick just to see how it works. That's expensive, and the discovery is almost always disappointing. Instead, find out. No, the dealer usually isn't going to tell you, especially a mail-order house. Go to the library, ask another magician, or think about it long enough and the modus operandi will become apparent.

After all, there are only so many ways of doing something. After a couple of years doing magic, reading magic, watching magic, and sleeping magic, you'll get to the point where you can figure out how everything works. Yes. Even tricks you've never seen before, like the newest ones on David Copperfield's latest special. You will enjoy magic even more because you will stop asking how is it done and, instead, marvel at the presentation, and that's where the real magic is!

Here are some important questions to consider before blowing your wad of money at the magic shop. These suggestions will save you money and may prevent you from buying something that you will never use—like that brassier trick!

MAGICIAN'S GUIDELINES

Here are some basic rules or guidelines that most magicians try to live by.

Keep it secret. Magic is supposed to be mysterious and unexplainable, so don't give away the secret of any trick. If everyone knew how the tricks were done, magic would lose its appeal.

Do a trick only once. A good magician never performs the same trick twice for the same audience. Unless you use a different method to do the trick, the audience will be prepared for it the second time and your element of surprise will be gone.

Know your angles. Be constantly aware of the angles of vision of the audience. What may be hidden from someone directly in front of you may be visible to someone sitting off to the side.

Be an actor. Good magicians are good actors. Your movements should appear totally natural and innocent. Convince the audience that you really did pick up the coin or that you're reaching into your pocket to get some pixie dust, and not depositing a sponge ball which is supposed to vanish.

Practice. Practice each trick until you can perform it perfectly, then practice it some more before showing it to an audience. Use a mirror to see if you can detect anything unnatural or if anything is showing. Kids can be unmerciful if they spot a flaw.

Be original. Never copy another performer's routine word for word. Sure you can use the same tricks and same ideas, but change the act by adding your own patter and style.

ENTERTAINING KIDS

Children will not sit still for anything that does not interest them. They will get antsy and talkative very quickly. They will find ways of amusing themselves like yelling, "This is so boring!" or pinching the kid sitting in front of them, thereby setting off World War III. All this, just as you are about to magically show that 43 and 57 don't add up to 846.

Tricks with playing cards generally frustrate kids. Avoid using cards. If you must, try a deck of jumbo cards or alphabet cards, or a deck of old maid cards, or cards with big circles of color on them instead of faces.

Can it Be Seen by Everyone?

If it can't be seen, it can't be appreciated. If it's too small to be seen, your audience will leap out of their seats and rush forward to see what happened. You will be trampled. Keep them in their seats—use props big enough to be seen.

Is it Too Long or Complicated?

Kids enjoy stories, but not long stories. It is better to do ten three-minute tricks in your show than three ten-minute tricks. Keep everything simple. Mental effects dumbfound and bore kids. Adding up columns of numbers or remembering four chosen cards is not fun for kids. Think short and snappy.

Could This Offend or Embarrass?

"Common sense ain't so common" goes an old saying, and nowhere is it more evident than in some magician's patter. I will never forget cringing at a local magician's presentation of the multiplying rabbits, a cute little trick in which sponge rabbits placed in a spectator's hand keep multiplying. Just before the climax of the trick, he screamed. "What do mama rabbit and daddy rabbit do in bed in the dark?" (Really!) The kids had no idea what he was talking about and said nothing. There was also dead silence from the adults because they couldn't believe what they had heard! In desperation, he belted out, "Make babies!" The reaction from adults after the show was not favorable. Avoid profanity, racial and ethnic slurs, and stereotypes. It's amazing the "entertainers" who subject their young audiences to a rash of insults and cheap cut downs. Ray-Mond, from Westminster, Maryland, a veteran of over 50 years of performing, has told me that he never knew of a performer who was hired because he had blue material, but he knew of several who were fired because they did. Wise words from a sage in magic.

Is This Really Dangerous or Does it Appear So?

You wouldn't believe the number of magicians who show up at a happy birthday party with a guillotine or a disecto limb chopper tucked under their arms! These tricks should be used with great discretion. They frighten the little tykes. "Please stop crying. It's only a trick. Your brother Johnny really won't need a hook to replace the hand he is going to lose!" These amputation effects can be great fun with the older crowd, but handle the little folks with kid gloves.

Needless to point out, tricks with pins, needles, razor blades, and knives are also taboo. I will be the first to agree that there are many great, really great tricks done with the aid of these items, but not at little kids' birthday parties. The one exception may be the "needle (it's really a knitting needle) through the balloon" trick. It doesn't look like a needle at all, and it fascinates, as well as baffles, children of all ages.

Likewise, tricks involving fire or lighter fluids need very special handling and presentation if they are to be used at children's parties. One of the best effects is baking a birthday cake by magic, using a dove pan. But even this trick can be accomplished without fire and still be effective.

Will This Cause A Stampede or Riot?

When I was young and inexperienced and just starting to do children's parties, I thought it would be a great idea to end a show by producing a bowl of candy and then tossing it out for the kids to catch. I told them I was going to do this at the end of the show in honor of Vicki, the birthday girl . . . . Everybody liked that!

I made the bowl of candy magically appear. That was easy . . . . Everybody liked that!

I said that I was about to toss it out for them to catch . . . . Everybody liked that part.

I gently tossed all the candy into a big pile in the middle of the room, right into the lap of the birthday girl, Vicki, and all at once everybody dove onto Vicki with a vengeance! Grabbing hands and kicking feet were all I could see! It looked like a loose ball at the football game. After the smoke cleared and the twisted, clawing bodies were pulled off each other, the kids that got no candy were mad and crying. The kids that got some candy were complaining they didn't get as much as the others. The big fat kid that got most of the candy was complaining that I didn't throw more. The disheveled birthday girl was near hysteria . . . . Nobody liked that!

That was the last show at which I ever threw anything out for my audience to catch.

> "Tomorrow is my father's birthday."
> "What are you going to give him?"
> "Something better than last year."
> "What did you give him last year?"
> "Chicken Pox."

BUILDING TRICKS INTO ROUTINES

I feel that the best magic sequences are ones that combine a lot of smaller tricks and gags along the way to the climax.

Example: it's wonderful to blow up a white balloon, shove it in a box, say the magic word, and pow! The magic rabbit appears. But, imagine how much stronger this effect would be if along the way you dress up your volunteer with a "magician's" cape, place the "official" top hat on his head, bedeck him in a pair of giant oversized clown sunglasses (so he won't be blinded by the dazzle of his own powers!), and entrust him with the magic wand—which promptly falls apart! . . . Or changes color! . . . or multiplies to five! Perhaps instead of conjuring up a rabbit . . . it's a skunk! . . . Or a rubber chicken!

Build your single tricks that take a minute to perform into routines that provide five minutes of laughter and enjoyment. Both you and your audiences will have more fun, and your show won't turn into a game of "I know how he did it" or "I've seen that trick before!"

Proven Add-Ons

Here are some of the most popular and time tested add-on items and what they do. Kids find all of these items very funny.

The breakaway wand is one of the best. It stays rigid for the magician, but falls to pieces when held by the volunteer. You can "reset" it immediately, so it's always ready for another laugh.

Oversized items are funny with undersized bodies. Try an extra large top hat, or the big sunglasses, or comb the apprentice magician's hair with a two-foot long comb!

Things that multiply, change color, or get bigger fascinate kids. The nest of wands keeps multiplying, a similar set not only multiplies, but changes color. The bongo hat starts as a very tiny hat, that kids laugh at because it looks so ridiculously small on the kid's head. But the bongo hat keeps getting bigger and bigger as it is unfolded. Soon it becomes a monstrous hat covering the boy's entire head! When the giant hat is turned around, the laughs really climax because there is a picture of a goofy looking giant's face.

The "bang" gun and the snake gun are sure laugh getters. The first one, when the trigger is pulled, has a sign that pops out and reads, "BANG!" The second shoots one or more four-foot spring snakes. It's screams of fun!

Watching the magician go into a mystic incantation and then produce the wrong item is also fair game for hilarity. Try a fake raccoon, a skunk, a bunch of grapes, an oversized dog bone, or a hot water bottle.

Magician Doc Dougherty.

Some gags can be repeated throughout the show, or used for continuity. The zipper banana keeps getting funnier each time it is removed from the magician's vest pocket, unzipped, a bite taken, and then zipped up and placed back in the magician's pocket. The electric bow tie and the pop-up tie are also good if not played to death. Another excellent running gag is the tape measure wrist watch. Periodically the magician checks the time. "Looks like about 16 inches past the hour."

Other favorites include: the boy-to-rabbit wand, the fall-apart fan, the no-cut scissors, the wilting flower, and the phony telephone that rings occasionally through your act. "It's the president of the United States! He wanted to say happy birthday to Jimmy! . . . This time, it's Bart Simpson! He says have a cowabunga birthday, Dude!"

Doc Dougherty's Mad Hattery or, In Search of the Perfect Birthday Hat

I saw Washington, D.C. pro, Doc Dougherty, get miles of smiles and loads of laughter out of just trying a bunch of different hats on the birthday child. He was in search of "the perfect birthday party hat."

Some hats he pulled out of his magic bag were too small, like the loony blue beanie with a propeller on it. Another was a man's-sized Indiana Jones hat. It was so large it fell over the kid's eyes! Another hat was a clown's bald cap with orange Bozo hair sticking out!

Doc had about a dozen hats and changed them on the kid's head about every ten to fifteen seconds. The modeling of each was met by uproarious laughter from adults, children, and the birthday boy as the magician tried to find the ultimate birthday hat.

As a magical finish to this mad hattery, Doc performed the birthday party hat paper tear, in which two pieces of tissue paper are torn to shreds and, with a wave of Doc's magic wand, magically transformed into the sought after "perfect birthday party hat."

Of course, the child gets to keep the hat as a souvenir of his special birthday and was the star of the magic show with magician Doc Dougherty.

Is this routine funny? Yes! Is it magical? Yes! Is the birthday child the center of attention? Yes! Is it entertainment? Oh, yes indeed!

MAKING YOUR OWN MAGIC

It's easy to go out to a magic shop and buy tricks. But there is also the pleasure and satisfaction of making some of your own equipment. Whichever course you choose to follow, be sure to "personalize" your magic.

Choose a specific color scheme or design and follow it throughout your show. Mine is a series of three interlocking diamonds. (Get it? Hal Diamond.) This will make your act unique, set you apart from the crowd, and reduce the number of times you'll hear some kid yell, "I've seen that trick before!"

Here are several tricks that you can make and perform. Most can be made with items found around your home and at minimal cost.

The Square Circle

Without question, this is one of the best production items ever created. It's been around for a long, long time and it's still amazing.

Effect: A bright yellow cylinder with no top or bottom is shown completely empty. It is placed in a box with no top or bottom. Because of the open lattice work front of the box we can see the tube just placed inside. The box is now lifted up and displayed absolutely empty. After the magic words and byplay, an enormous quantity of silks, ribbons, flowers, party favors, or even a live rabbit is produced!

Method: Both the cylinder and the box are quite innocent. The trickery involves a second tube slightly smaller than the first which holds your "load." This secret tube is covered in black velvet or felt. The inside of the box is also covered with the same black material.

You'll find that a wonderfully deceptive illusion presents itself; when the bright yellow tube is lifted and

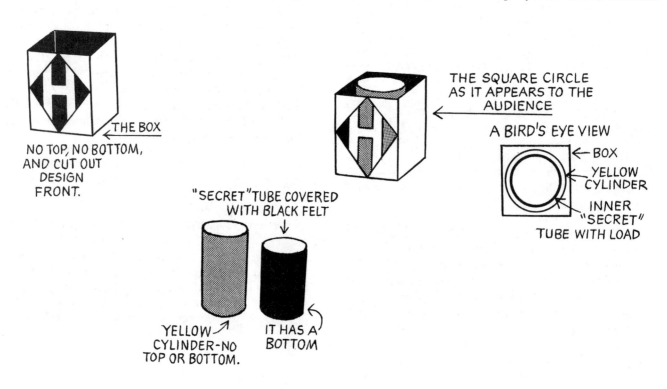

THE BOX
NO TOP, NO BOTTOM, AND CUT OUT DESIGN FRONT.

"SECRET" TUBE COVERED WITH BLACK FELT

YELLOW CYLINDER-NO TOP OR BOTTOM.

IT HAS A BOTTOM

THE SQUARE CIRCLE AS IT APPEARS TO THE AUDIENCE

A BIRD'S EYE VIEW

BOX
YELLOW CYLINDER
INNER "SECRET" TUBE WITH LOAD

removed from the box, the remaining black tube is quite invisible because it blends into the black background of the box. You'll strain your eyes looking through the front of the box and you just can't see the secret tube.

Make the box and tube(s) any size you like, but remember you must be able to easily pack and move this thing if you want to get much use out of it. So don't build one big enough to produce the living room sofa! I would suggest the box be about 14 inches square and about 18 inches in height. The tubes could be about 10 inches and 9 inches in diameter respectively. Paint the larger tube, the only one the audience is aware of, a bright yellow, or cover it with a flashy pattern of contact paper. The outside of the box should be painted or covered in a bright and complementary color or pattern. Make the cut out design on the front whatever will suit your show. Mine has a diamond design. Cover the inside of both tubes and the box in black felt.

When you have your square circle finished, practice before a mirror. Feel how easily you can show the yellow tube and the box empty. Placing in the yellow tube and lifting up the box and showing it empty should be one fluid motion. There are no angles to worry about, but you can't have people looking down at you. Be even or above their sight line. At birthday parties this is no problem, because most the kids will be sitting in chairs or on the floor.

With a little experimentation, you'll discover how useful the square circle really is. It's great for producing larger items, like animals or pumpkins or Christmas balls. And, by dividing your secret load chamber in half with a partition, you can exchange and change your props.

Three knotted silks, a red, a white, and a blue, placed inside, become an American flag! A handful of tinsel confetti sprinkled like magic glitter into the yellow tube becomes a 30-foot Christmas garland! Some cotton, two buttons, and some pink ribbon magically transform themselves into an adorable little stuffed animal bear, complete with a pink bow for the birthday girl. What you can produce, vanish, exchange, and transform is limited only by your imagination.

The Devil's Handkerchief

Effect: An innocent appearing handkerchief is gathered up by its four corners and held in one hand. Small items, like rings are placed inside, but vanish when the handkerchief is allowed to fall open. Of course, when the four corners are gathered up again, the missing items reappear faster than you can say, "Happy birthday, Houdini."

SEW AROUND ALL EDGES EXCEPT FOR FOUR INCH OPENING!

SECRET OPENING

HANDKERCHIEF HELD BY THE 4 CORNERS

Method: Actually you use two handkerchiefs sewn together around all the edges except for a four-inch opening. The handkerchief forms a giant pocket or flat pillowcase shape. The borrowed items are placed inside this large pocket.

You can whip this one out on a sewing machine in no time flat. I use two blue denim handkerchiefs because they conceal the "vanished" item hidden inside more effectively than the standard white ones.

Once you've made it, play with it. Experiment. A shiny quarter placed inside the folds of this handkerchief disappears with a shake. (Don't use two coins; they'll clink together!) Better yet, before the show lay the handkerchief out flat. Place two tablespoons of large silver glitter in the center. Fold the handkerchief in quarters. Vanish the quarter like you did before, but now when you allow the handkerchief to fall open, it appears the quarter had disintegrated into silver magic dust.

The Amazing Magic Wand Through the Balloon

Effect: A metal cylinder is shown with a magic wand running through two holes in the center of it. The cylinder is spun on the wand to prove that the cylinder is empty. The wand is removed from the cylinder. A bright red balloon is inflated and completely fills the chamber of the metal tube and protrudes out at the top and bottom. The magician announces that he will push his magic wand

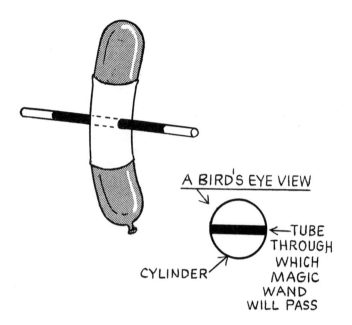

A BIRD'S EYE VIEW

CYLINDER

←TUBE THROUGH WHICH MAGIC WAND WILL PASS

though the center of the cylinder without harming the balloon. The magician does just that!

Method: The can has a permanent tube tunneling through its center. It is painted and appears to be part of the wand.

Make your own from a large empty soup can. Take off the top and bottom and the label. Drill two holes opposite each other in the center. Get a short piece of tubing just large enough to allow your wand to fit through it. Glue or solder it in place. Paint it black to match your magic wand. (No wand? Make one out of a dowel.) Paint the inside and the outside of the can as you wish. Bright colors are best. Get some balloons and you're ready to amaze.

The slower you push the wand through the balloon, the more magical the trick appears. The wand actually looks like it melts right through the balloon. To finish, pop the balloon with the wand through the center. This shows the wand has "really penetrated right through the center of the balloon," and hides your method.

The Endless Egg Production

Here's an easy trick to make that can also be very baffling. Don't underestimate it's entertainment value. It plays big.

Effect: A top hat is displayed and placed on the performing table. The magician reaches in and takes out a handkerchief. He unfolds it and shows both sides. He then folds it in half and holding two corners in each hand says the magic words, "Handkerchief, if you were a

chicken, show us what you might do when the boys and girls say cock-a-doodle-doo!" Immediately, an egg rolls out of the fold of the handkerchief and into the hat.

The magician unfolds the handkerchief, shows it absolutely empty and then repeats the process producing a second egg, and a third, and a fourth, and a fifth. "Five eggs for Johnny's fifth birthday. That's enough!"

The magician places the handkerchief aside, and picks up the hat containing the five eggs. With a wave of his wand, or by saying, "cock-a-doodle-doo backwards" five times, the hat is turned over and all the eggs have disappeared.

Method: All you need is a handkerchief, a rubber or plastic egg, and a short length of thin monofilament fishing line or "invisible" thread. The line and egg are attached to the center of the bottom hem of the handkerchief. Get a hat and you're ready to practice.

Start by having the handkerchief with the egg attached in the hat. Bring out the hat. Reach in and take out the handkerchief leaving the egg concealed in the hat. Hold the handkerchief up by the two corners on the top (A and B). The egg with its line attached to the bottom of the handkerchief remains hidden in the hat. Show the front and back of the handkerchief. Lay the handkerchief spread out on the top of the hat. This time, pick up sides C and D. You'll find the egg pulled by its line is raised out of the hat and comes to about the center of the back of the handkerchief. (Remember you can see the egg

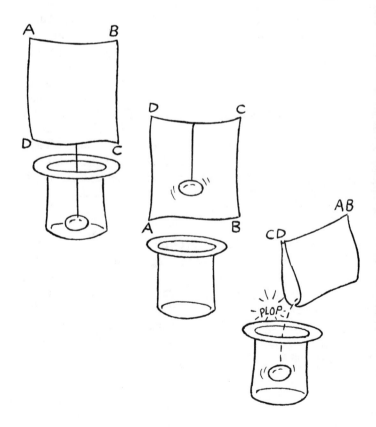

because it's on the back side of the handkerchief, but your audience has no idea it's there.) All you have to do is fold the handkerchief in half lengthwise. (Bring C and D together in your left hand and A and B together in your right hand) move the C and D side of the handkerchief toward the hat and let it rest on the brim. Slowly raise and gently shake side A and B. You see the egg rolls right out of the handkerchief into the hat neat as can be.

Immediately, drop sides C and D, and open up the handkerchief by holding sides A & B in each hand and you're ready to repeat the process and begin producing eggs all over again. When you finish producing your "last" egg, remove the handkerchief and the attached egg hidden in the folds, and place it in your pocket or behind your table out of view.

Practice till you can do it without even looking. It's an amusing trick for kids. They like to yell the words and are amazed when each egg rolls out.

After playing with this for a while, try attaching something else instead of the egg. Try a plastic golf ball, or a Nurff ball, a Christmas tree ball, or perhaps a giant eyeball!

The Surprise Happy Birthday Banner

A surprise banner is an excellent way to start your birthday party magic show or it may be used as a classy finish the birthday child will remember for a long time to come.

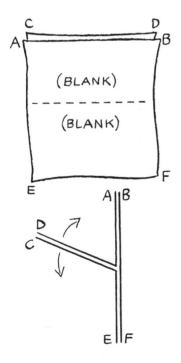

Effect: A large square (approximately 30" x 30") of red velvet material is shown front and back. It is folded in half, two corners held in each hand.

A bag of large colored sequins is shown, then opened, and several spoonfuls are placed in the fold of the handkerchief by the birthday child. After saying the magic words, "Happy birthday, Clint Reed!" the magician allows the square of red velvet to fall open and there, sewn on the red velvet in bright sequins are the words, "Happy Birthday, Clint Reed!"

Method: The red velvet square actually has a secret flap of red velvet half the size of the square. It is sewn horizontally across the center of the red square.

When the flap is held up at the start of the trick, (your right hand holds A and C together as one, your left hand holds B and D together as one.) The red material looks empty. When the flap (C and D) is allowed to drop, (joining E and F at the bottom) the magic writing is revealed.

Try it. It works like magic. Don't be concerned that your audience will notice the flap when its hanging down at the end of the trick, their eyes will be riveted to the written message. I use the brightest color sequins I can find for maximum contrast and impact.

What grows between you nose and chin?
Tulips.

A small amount of sequins, which the child put in, will fall to the floor. I like this glittery effect. If you don't, sew in a little secret pocket at the top into which the child can place the sequins.

I've seen performers use cotton balls instead of sequins. It looks like mini snowballs spelling out the message. You could also use pom pom balls found at most fabric stores. Personalizing your banner for each show (changing the name) does take a little time, but I feel is worth the effort. If you do many shows, you may opt for a generic message like, "Happy Birthday."

The More You Read,
The More Tricks You Can Make

Read as many books on magic as you can get your hands on. As you read and dream, you'll discover additional tricks that catch your eye and you know you can make. You'll feel the great satisfaction that comes from building your own props and using them to delight a roomful of youngsters.

The More You Make,
the More Tricks You Can Buy

In time you will have a repertoire of several dozen "bulletproof" tricks you can use at parties and larger events. As your performing experience and performing income grow, you'll be able to reinvest your earnings in more expensive tricks.

My Favorite Birthday Party Tricks

All entertainers have their own list of 'academy award winning" birthday tricks, the ones they perform best and their audiences enjoy the most. In presenting my list, I caution you that the trick by itself is nothing, and that your routine, your humorous patter, your own personality and presentation of the effect are everything!

Best trick to start a show award: the surprise happy birthday banner.

Best trick to mystify: needle through the balloon.

Best trick to end the show: balloon to bunny box (it's a live rabbit).

Best sucker trick (use with discretion): the fraidy cat rabbit.

Best trick to amuse the little ones: puppet rabbit in the hat.

Best trick to spell the birthday child's name: Joanna the card duck.

Best classic of magic: the linking rings.

Best trick for screams of laughter: Houdini outstripped! (use with discretion).

Best routine for do as I do: birthday party hat tear.

Best trick to get laughter: the bongo hat.

Best running gag: the tape measure watch and the zipper banana (a tie).

Best sight gag: the infamous rubber chicken.

Best move to cause a riot: throwing candy into the audience!

Chapter 6

PUPPETRY

PUPPETS AND PARTIES

Puppets are great entertainment for children's birthday parties. Kids love puppets! This is evident with the popularity of television shows such as Sesame Street, the Muppets, Fraggle Rock, and Barney the dinosaur.

As a puppeteer I have found that most of my parties are for young children, ages 3-7; occasionally I get a party for a child as old as 10, but rarely older than that. The real young children (ages 3-5) really do not understand or appreciate skills like magic or juggling; they just want to be entertained. Puppets work really well with this age group. The older children (ages 5-10) enjoy magic and balloon modeling as well as puppets if they are handled well and are entertaining.

"Entertaining" is the key word here. Keep in mind that children do not care how much practice you put into your show or how much skill you use in making the puppets work properly, they want to be entertained and they want to laugh. If you can make them laugh, hold their interest and have fun with them, then you will succeed. If you incorporate a magic trick and you fool them that's fine, but it is more important to entertain them than to fool them.

I do a routine with a rabbit puppet in which the rabbit's job is to bring me a magic wand. Instead, he brings me a whole collection of odd objects: a fish, a carrot, a string of hot dogs. I, of course, have something to say about each item and become more and more frustrated, which the children love. Kids love to see the adult (puppeteer, magician, etc.) get in trouble. The rabbit finally brings me a wand, but it's a break-away wand. It breaks in my hand, not the puppet's. He brings me a nest of wands, so that each time I take one, he still has a wand. The children love it when the puppet outsmarts me every time. He finally brings out a giant wand and hits me over the head with it. I end up by trying unsuccessfully to make him disappear using the giant wand. I never perform any magic but I do perform about ten minutes of continuous fun, and the kids love every minute of it.

TYPES OF PUPPETS

Puppets, like cartoon characters, come in many different shapes and sizes. There are hand puppets, finger puppets, rod puppets, mouth puppets, marionettes, novelty puppets, and combinations of all of these. For most birthday party situations, both the puppet and puppeteer are in view of the audience. You do not have a big stage to hide behind.

You do not need a puppet stage for birthday parties. At a home party you want to travel light, carry everything in one trip, be able to set up and perform in just a few minutes time in a limited amount of space, and be able

83

to pack up and leave without a hassle. For these reasons, I shy away from using marionettes. Setting up a rack to hang the puppets on, unpacking, and worrying about them becoming tangled or being touched by one of the children is more than I care to deal with. I want to concentrate on entertaining my audience, not worry about someone knocking over the marionettes.

Hand Puppets

Hand puppets are worked on your hand, using your fingers to manipulate the arms and head of the puppet. The hand puppet is made up of a body and a head with an unmoveable mouth. The puppeteer operates the puppet with two fingers (the second and third) in the head, the thumb in one of the puppet's arms, and the fourth and little finger in the puppet's other arm.

Smaller *finger puppets* can be operated with a single finger moving the puppet's head and each arm. These are great for preschoolers.

Hand puppets can be worked over the lid of an open suitcase or can have their own house; a rabbit can come out of a top hat, a puppy can come out of his dog house, a monkey can live in a barrel—use your imagination. A hand puppet can handle props; it can wave a magic wand, be your assistant, perform with a change bag, hand you props, or squirt you with a water gun.

I have performed over the years with just about every type of puppet imaginable and a few that only I would think of, but for the birthday party audience I prefer the simple hand puppet. This type of puppet is easy to operate, packs small with little care, and can handle props. At a birthday party you will be working in tight quarters with little if any set-up time and even less time to pack up, so keep it simple.

Mouth Puppets

Mouth puppets are really hand puppets which have a large moving mouth (like the Muppets), and sometimes rods to control the arms. Because the mouth is its prominent feature, a mouth puppet should be able to speak. What is said could be just simple noises or more fluent dialogue. Dialogue works best if you know how to do ventriloquism. Ventriloquism really isn't hard to learn, but

> What is black and yellow and goes "Zzub, zzub"?
> *A bee flying backwards.*

Mouth puppets.

it does take some practice. I'll talk more about ventriloquism a little later in this chapter.

Rod Puppets

Rod puppets have a rod which runs through the chest cavity to support the puppet and control the head. Some also have two smaller rods which control the arms. Rod puppets work well in dramatic presentations such as plays.

Traditional ventriloquial figures also use rods. We are all familiar with the classical wooden dummy. The rod operates the figure's mouth and head. Some also have movable eyes, eyelids, and arms. These figures often represent humans such as little boys and old men, but the popularity of Sesame Street and the Muppets has led to the production of a wide variety of animal figures ranging from turkeys to alligators.

Marionettes

Marionettes are full-figured puppets with legs and feet that are controlled from above with strings. The body parts are attached with flexible joints and strung to a control rod. A skilled puppeteer can manipulate the marionette so that it moves and reacts with life-like precision. The artistic designs of these puppets and the ability to move them about, seemingly on their own, create the illusion of life and are favored by many puppeteers.

Marionettes, although they are my favorite type of puppet, really do not lend themselves to the birthday party setting. You need a good deal of care in transporting them so you don't tangle the strings. You need somewhere to hang them, and without a stage they must perform on the floor with limited sight lines. Some people, like John Shirley in the Chicago area, have used marionettes very successfully at parties, but personally I find them too much trouble for this type of show.

Spring Animals

Kids really get excited over this puppet. Spring animals are dynamic—about the most life-like puppets made and, unlike more complex puppets such as marionettes, are relatively easy to manipulate. These unique puppets contain a spring covered in fur which make them look like real raccoons, rabbits, and little foxes. The movement of the spring creates the illusion of life. The movements of the spring animal appear to be beyond the control of the puppeteer. The animal can be shown up close and the puppeteer can have it scamper from arm to arm, up the shoulder, or into his pocket at will. In the hands of a skilled puppeteer the internal spring allows the puppet to move back and forth and travel across his body.

These puppets are so realistic that many children will actually believe they're alive! They provide excellent props for magic tricks, because they can be concealed in a pocket or other tight space and magically appear or disappear.

Larry Mahan with skunk spring animal.

Novelty Puppets

There are other types of puppets you can use which I would classify as novelty figures. Although in a strict classification, many of these could be grouped with those already mentioned.

Figures do not have to be human or animal. A shoe, for example, could make an interesting companion. Other figures that have been used include such things as talking socks (the original mouth puppet), gloves, boxes, paper bags, walking sticks, balls, paintings, hats, and paper plates. Anything is possible.

For short routines or gags, puppets can be made out of balloon figures and paper creations. Many of these are easy to make and inexpensive, so they provide an ideal give-away item. Kids will enjoy creating the figures themselves and making them talk.

Most any object, whether it has a moveable mouth or not, can be used like a puppet. You can be creative and different by using a variety of props as puppets. A book, for example, can be rigged so the cover opens and closes like a mouth.

Bob Conrad with an assortment of hand, rod and mouth puppets.

Bob Conrad with one of his novelty hand puppets.

A book entitled *Jokes for All Occasions* could be the performer's tormentor, delivering clever one-liners at appropriate times. A radio is another object that can be used. It doesn't need a moveable mouth, but can have a small light which flicks on and off as it speaks, the light being operated by the puppeteer. When the light flashes and the audience hears the voice, it will appear as if the radio is talking. This idea can be used with other electrical devices such as CD players and computers.

Prop makers have created a variety of talking puppets. The Magic Drawing Board is one of the most creative props I've seen on the market. It consists of a blank drawing board with a light blue grid covered with plastic. Pictures can be drawn on the board with an ordinary marker and then erased with a cloth. The unique feature about this board is that while a face is being drawn, the eyes and the mouth can move. Right before everyone's eyes the picture comes to life and starts to talk. The eyes move from side to side and the mouth opens and closes, all under the artist's complete control. After talking with the animated drawing, it can be completely erased—even while it's moving! A mind-boggling effect!

PUPPET CHARACTERIZATION

The puppet you use can assume any identity you want, which is one of the great features about puppets. A puppet can be a king, a robot, a space creature, an animal, anything. Keep in mind that children love animals, so a rabbit, a mouse, a puppy, or a teddy bear work very well.

My choice for a birthday party is an animal puppet. Kids love animals, and the animal puppet is much more believable than a tiny little man. You can get away with a clown puppet because children don't think of clowns as being real; they are make-believe and so are puppets. Keep it simple; the more elaborate the puppet, the less life-like it will appear. Look at the Muppets—they look like nothing you have ever seen, totally unrealistic in design, but they look alive and are completely believable.

An important thing to remember is to be yourself, be different. Many magicians, for example, perform the same children's magic and use the same routines—the routines that came packaged with the tricks they use. This is why you hear those cries of "I know this one."

The nice part about puppets is they don't come with a routine. You have to do a little thinking yourself; you have to be creative. This lets you be you and you can be different. Maybe you can have a puppet help with a magic trick but give it a different twist. Dare to be different. The secret to humor is surprise; the unexpected is funny. If your audience knows the punchline or what is going to happen, it will not be funny. So don't copy another performer's routine, don't try to copy the Muppets, you can only pale by comparison. Be yourself, not a second-rate copy of someone else. Surprise your audience, be different. It works for me!

Treat the puppet as a real live partner, not a doll or puppet. If you believe in your puppet, the audience will believe. The magic of the puppet is the illusion of life. The puppet can be shy or brash, timid or daring, silly or smart or, like a real person, he can be a combination of these. Give the puppet a personality, let him live.

HOW TO TALK WITH A PUPPET

The most realistic and versatile way to communicate with puppets is through ventriloquism. With ventriloquism you can give the puppet a distinct and separate voice from your own that appears to come only from the puppet. This helps to create the illusion of life and gives your show that element of fantasy or make-believe that children enjoy. Ventriloquism, however, is certainly not a requirement in order to perform with puppets. Your partner can communicate with you and the audience in many different ways.

Magic of Motion

To effectively create the illusion that a puppet is real and can talk, movements are added. Movement is important whether the puppet speaks or not. Intelligent living creatures don't sit stone still and lifeless. Even when just sitting quietly they move a bit, even if it is simply breathing or looking about. If you are to create the illusion of life in your puppets, you must also give them movement even when they aren't actively communicating. The subtle movements of the puppet show the audience that it is a living creature.

Movement is a key ingredient to creating the illusion of life in puppets and indicates when the puppet is speaking rather than the puppeteer. Our eyes are naturally drawn toward movement. If you were looking at a stage where several actors were standing and one begins to talk, your eyes will unconsciously be attracted toward the person who is moving. Likewise, if the actors are basically motionless, our eyes will focus on the one who is moving his mouth and talking. Often he will accentuate his speech with his body. The same thing happens with puppets. When a puppet moves its mouth, the audience's eyes will focus on the movement. At the same time, if the audience hears a voice talking, they will mentally connect the sound as coming from the puppet's mouth. One of the reasons mouth puppets have such large mouths is to take full advantage of this effect.

Focusing on movement is such a strong unconscious action that if the puppeteer remains still, the audience will automatically focus on the puppet as it begins moving its mouth. The puppeteer can then speak in the puppet's voice without detection, even if he does not use ventriloquism. However, some kids will purposely look at the puppeteer's lips just to see if the voice is really coming from him. Younger children will not notice or even care if your lips move. They are too enchanted by the puppets and your dialogue to care about such things. Older kids tend to be

more critical. Some of them may shout "I can see you lips move." But if your presentation is entertaining, they will be more interested in your show than in looking at your lips.

I have seen performers that have no ability in ventriloquism give a puppet a voice and make it talk. The audience can see the performer's mouth move when the puppet speaks. Jim Henson never tried to be a ventriloquist, but when he performed with Kermit the effect was magic.

To make the illusion believable, the movement of the puppet's lips must be in synchronization with the words. Each syllable must be synchronized with the opening and closing of the puppet's mouth. Open and close the mouth once for each syllable at the exact time it is spoken. Practice this until you get the rhythm down to perfection. It is the most important movement your puppet will make.

Another trick used in theater is for the actor to look in the direction in which he wants the audience to look. When the puppeteer wants the audience to focus on the puppet, he will look at it. The movement of the puppet's mouth or other body parts will help in drawing the audience's attention. Likewise, the puppet should always be looking where it should. When it talks or listens to the puppeteer, it should be looking at him. A common problem with beginners is not paying attention to the direction of the puppet's face and eyes. If its eyes or head is allowed to sag, it looks unnatural and destroys the illusion you are trying to create.

When the puppeteer is speaking, the puppet should be looking at him, yet make subtle movements as any living creature would. Movements should be slight in most cases so as not to attract too much attention and look as natural as possible. Sometimes the puppet may be doing something sneaky while the puppeteer is speaking to the audience. In this case it can move with more motion to allow the audience to clearly detect its actions.

Body Language

When people speak, they often use body language—actions or physical expressions to emphasize their words. We all understand the meaning of nodding the head for yes, or shaking it for no. A shrug of the shoulders indicates apathy or lack of knowledge. When we are excited, we talk and move about faster. Conversely, when we are sad or tired are motions are much slower. When we want to emphasize something, we pound our fist or point to the object in question. Puppets, whether they can speak or not, can and should use body language to facilitate communication.

Body language is most important for puppets which do not have moveable mouths or that do not speak. A hand puppet which does not have a moveable mouth can draw the audience's attention simply by movement. As the puppeteer speaks in the puppet's voice, the puppet moves about acting out emotions and ideas. This body language keeps the audience's eyes on the puppet and indicates that the voice is that of the puppet.

Puppets don't have to talk. With practice, your puppet can communicate with actions. It can be happy, sad, frightened, or silly without saying a word. There are several ways to accomplish this. For instance, you can be its translator. The puppet can whisper into your ear and you can tell the children what the puppet says. This works very well and will even help to keep the audience quiet and attentive.

You could also use a squeaker, bird warbler, or some other noise-making device in place of the voice. The different sounds produced by pitch, tempo, volume, and repetition from these objects combined with body language and your commentary can provide all the communication necessary. This technique can produce many amusing situations. The puppet can point to what it wants and act things out as you coax it along until everyone understands what it is trying to say. Harpo Marx, the silent member of the Marx Brothers comedy team, was a master at this.

Ventriloquism

With ventriloquism you can create a totally separate voice that appears to come from the puppet. This is the best method to use to make your partner a believable living personality. A two-way conversation allows for versatility in entertainment.

If you can do ventriloquism, by all means make your puppet talk. I use simple mouth puppets that I make from everyday objects (a sock, a hat, a paper plate and cups, etc.) right before the eyes of my audience. I start by teaching the children how to make a puppet and then bring it to life. The puppet can lead the children in singing "Happy Birthday."

Develop a different voice for the puppet, a voice that contrasts with your voice. If your voice is high, give the puppet a low voice. Make the puppet's voice as different from yours as possible.

When performing ventriloquism remember that young children really don't understand most jokes. They react best to the puppet saying things wrong, mispronouncing words, making mistakes. They love it when the puppet outsmarts you or makes fun of you or your clothes. They like it when the puppet sings or fractures a story or nursery rhyme. They have a very limited frame of reference, so the more clever you are, the less they understand. Keep it simple.

Ventriloquism is basically the ability to talk without moving your lips. You don't need to be an expert at ventriloquism to give your puppet a voice. With a little practice you can do it well enough for children's parties. The children may see your lips move at times, but that is okay; through experience and practice your skills will improve.

To get you started, let me give you a quickie course in ventriloquism. First off you don't have to have any special gift to learn ventriloquism, and "no" you don't throw your voice. Anyone with practice can learn ventriloquism, of course it will be easier for some people than others. As for throwing the voice, this is an illusion. When you go to the movies, the speakers are located all around the theater, but when an actor on the screen speaks, the sound appears to come from his mouth. This is because although we hear with our ears, we locate the source of the sound with our eyes. When we are driving in a car and hear a siren, we look around to see the fire truck, not sure if it is in front or in the back of us until we see the truck. What this means is that our ears are easily fooled. When our puppet moves his mouth and you don't, our eyes tell us the sound is coming from the puppet. Thus the illusion of a voice being "thrown."

Now go to a mirror. With your lips slightly parted, tongue tip curled back slightly behind your upper teeth, and without moving your lips say loud and clearly: "I can talk like this all day." You should have had little trouble saying this sentence without moving your lips. Most words can be spoken without the lips having to move.

Look in the mirror again. Now, without moving your lips say the following: "I can talk like this all day, therefore I must be a ventriloquist." This sentence was much harder. In fact, unless you know ventriloquism you would not have been able to say it without moving your lips.

Try it again. This time, recite the alphabet with as little lip movement as possible.

You will notice that most of the letters can be pronounced without much noticeable lip movement. Several of the letters which require movement in normal speech can be pronounced with the aid of the tongue, without using the lips. Some (B, F, M, P, V, and W) need lip movement for clear pronunciation. In fact, they seem to

---

How do you talk to giants?
Use BIG WORDS!

What do you do when a elephant sneezes?
Get out of the way!

be impossible to say without moving the lips. These six letters are the labial consonants. The letter W can be ignored because it is never pronounced as "double-u" in speech. You will notice that all of the following words can be said without moving the lips even though they contain a W: water, wash, window, where.

The only words you will have any problem with are those that contain the other five labial consonants. You can get around this problem by using only words that do not contain these letters. Substitute words with a similar meaning. For example, instead of using the word "prison" which has the labial P, use the word "jail" instead. This is one trick which is frequently used.

You can create a lot of dialogue by carefully choosing your words. You can get by with just this knowledge of ventriloquism and limit yourself to occasionally moving your lips to pronounce the more difficult words. However, it is difficult to speak like this all the time, especially if you do any ad-libbing. For the most part infrequent lip movement will go unnoticed. You can help to make sure lip movement is less noticeable by leading the audiences' attention away from you as you speak difficult words. Use the magic of motion explained earlier. You have learned that movement attracts the eye. When you say a word with a labial, have the puppet make a clearly distinct movement to attract everyone's attention. Keep the movement natural and you will be able to fool most of the people most of the time.

Another method to mask slight lip movement is to turn your head sideways so the audience can't see your lips clearly. This way you can move the lips slightly on the audience's blind side to make difficult pronunciations. Many years ago, Stan Freberg performed on just about every major television variety show with a space creature named Orville. Orville came out of a flying saucer that stood on a stand and spoke to Freberg. Freberg was a great wit who had provided cartoon voices over the years for Warner Brothers' cartoons, but he was not a ventriloquist. Freberg solved the problem by simply turning his head. He would stand slightly up-stage of Orville and face the audience when he spoke. When Orville spoke, he would turn his attention to the puppet and the audience would see the back of his head while Orville spoke. The puppet was so life-like and funny that no one ever noticed or cared whether he was a ventriloquist or not.

Young children will not care if your lips move a bit.

They are enthralled with the fantasy of the puppet. If you perform for older children or adults, some will watch your lips at the beginning just to see how skilled you are as a ventriloquist. Once their curiosity is satisfied, they will turn their attention to the performance. For this reason you may want to avoid labials when you first start your show. This way the audience will see that your lips do not move, and will concentrate on enjoying the show rather than looking at your lips.

The simple form of ventriloquism which I have described here is easy enough for anyone to learn. If you can devise some way to make your puppet talk without the audience seeing your lips move you will create the appearance of being a seasoned ventriloquist. Being a master ventriloquist, however, is not necessary in order to entertain children. Even if the children do see your lips move, they will not care if your show is entertaining. Some puppeteers use this form of ventriloquism without even bothering to hide slight lip movement, and have success. However, I personally feel that to let the audience see your lips moving while the puppet speaks takes away from the illusion.

Because so many words incorporate labials, it is difficult, if not impossible, to eliminate them all from your speech. Therefore, rather than trying to avoid difficult words, ventriloquists learn how to deal with them. This is accomplished by either using substitute sounds for the labial consonants, or by positioning the tongue inside the mouth to mimic the sounds the lips make. Making this substitution is the hardest part about learning true ventriloquism. Learning true ventriloquism isn't really difficult, but it does take a bit of practice. For a more detailed course in ventriloquism I recommend you read *Ventriloquism Made Easy* by Paul Stadelman.

PUPPET SHOWS

Although many performers may disagree with me, I would say you don't need to put on a regular puppet show. A full-scale puppet show with lighting and sound works very well at schools, libraries, camps—any place where you are in a controlled situation with someone to help maintain control. A home party is much more informal. When you are in someone's home or yard, behavior is quite different than in a school or library group. You are not on a stage, you are in their living room. When you step out of sight behind the puppet stage, you lose eye contact, and in many cases control over your audience. There are a great many distractions to deal with at a home party that we never encounter in a more formal setting. These include:

1. Late arrivals; there is always someone who shows up in the middle of your show. All the children jump up to greet the new arrival, and the birthday child wants her gift. If you are behind the puppet stage when this happens, it can be a disaster.

2. Mom decides to serve food. Things are going much too smoothly, so mom brings out a big bowl of popcorn right at the climax of your show. All the kids run to get some popcorn. You are behind the stage and don't even realize your audience isn't watching.

3. Grandma or grandpa want to take pictures. Not of the show, but of the children watching the show. Flash bulbs blind your audience. Grandpa is standing alongside you or your stage telling the children to smile and look at him. You can completely lose your audience's attention.

4. The list is endless; problems can be created by well-meaning people who just don't think.

When you are standing behind the puppet stage, multiply these problems by ten. I try to always have eye contact with the children, which makes audience control so much easier. Plus you can see what the problem or distraction is; sometimes you can even postpone it; "Mom, please don't serve the popcorn until after the show," or "Everyone stay in you seat, and we will wait for this newcomer to be seated."

A two-person team, one behind the stage and one in front of the stage, will work out fine, but in most cases it is economically unsound in the birthday party situation.

FINDING THE RIGHT PUPPET

Let's start by telling you where not to get a puppet: the toy store. Most commercial toy puppets are made to fit a child's hand, and most of them really don't work. You wouldn't try to play music on a toy piano, so don't try to perform with a toy puppet.

A number of professional puppets are available at your local magic store, or from one of several mail order suppliers. Most professional puppets cost about $35 and up. Unfortunately, because of the success of the Muppets, most of the puppets available are mouth puppets. These are perfect for ventriloquism or lip-syncing recordings, but not much help if you want your puppet to handle props and help you perform a magic trick.

What should you say when you meet a monster with two heads?
"Hello, hello!"

Your best bet is to make your own puppet. It will cost you a lot less and will be an original. It is really not very hard to do, and a large number of books are available on the various methods of making puppets. Check your local library. Most libraries have a very good selection of books on puppetry.

Just a few words about how to take care of your puppet. All of my puppets (I have about 300) have packing bags. A simple cloth bag that the puppet is put into when not in use protects the paint and keeps the costume clean. I only handle my puppets from the inside; I try not to touch the outside of the puppet with my hands, as this will only get them dirty. I have puppets that are over 20 years old and still look fresh and new. Because I handle them carefully and pack them carefully, they stay like new.

PUTTING LIFE INTO YOUR PUPPET

Puppeteers, like magicians, create an illusion—the illusion of life. A puppet in the hands of a skilled manipulator is alive. We never think of Kermit the frog as a puppet, he is a television star. He is alive. To make a puppet seem alive, you must believe in it. Treat the puppet as if it were alive. Make it think and react.

Be aware of the puppet's eyes. Just like you, the puppet should see with its eyes. Make sure the puppet is looking where it should be looking.

A hand puppet should bend at the waist, not at the ankles.

Look in your library for a book entitled *Making Puppets Come Alive* by Larry Engler and Carol Fijan. Practice in front of a mirror and try for different emotions: happy, sad, excited, bored, frightened, or nervous. Think of your puppet as a member of the cast of your show; treat the puppet as your assistant, and treat it with respect. Get to know your puppet, learn all about it. In time your puppet may become the most important part of your show.

Most important, give the puppet something to do. Don't simply have it wave good-bye or hello. Work out a routine for the puppet and practice in front of a mirror. You would never buy a new magic trick and take it to a show and perform it without first practicing all the moves and learning all the sleights. The same is true with the puppet. There is no such thing as an instant puppeteer. It takes years of practice. The business that the puppet does must be thought out and perfected as carefully as the moves of a magic trick, or playing a musical instrument. A great puppeteer/ventriloquist may seem to be working off the top of his head, ad-libbing the whole show, but takes years of practice to make it look so easy and unrehearsed.

There is no magic formula to writing a good puppet routine; you have to start with an idea and work from there. Start with a problem and work to a solution. Build one idea on top of the other until you have a complete routine. Like a play, your routine should have a beginning, a middle, and an end. Something should happen, something should be accomplished. Please don't use the puppet to just wave and shake hands, or even worse, bite the children's fingers. My puppets never bite people's fingers. When little children try to stick their hands into a puppet's mouth I ask them not to do that, as they wouldn't like someone sticking their fingers in their mouths. Remember, the puppet is "real," so it should be treated that way.

IDEAS FOR PUPPET ROUTINES

The hardest part of working with puppets is coming up with your own ideas for routines. Puppets don't come with a suggested routine the way magic tricks do. We have to think for ourselves. Once you get into the habit of creating your own routines you will find it is really not that hard. Here are a few examples:

They See It, You Don't

I call this, "They see it, you don't" type of routine. I work this with a hand puppet over the opened lid of a suitcase which is resting on a waiter's tray stand with the back of the lid facing the audience. I introduce the puppet, when he doesn't come out I explain that he was here a minute ago and I don't know where he went. I look into the case and act puzzled. I explain that he usually comes out right here, pointing to the top of the suitcase lid. As I look directly at the audience the puppet appears, the kids will yell and tell me he is there (in the rare case when they don't yell, you can act puzzled and say, "What's the matter, what's wrong?" This will usually start them yelling that the puppet is there. You look where they are pointing and of course he is gone. "I don't see him," I say.

Once again the puppet appears, the kids yell, but you don't see him. "Where was he? Over here? I'll look in the case," as I lean into the case the puppet appears around the far side of the lid. I look directly at the audience and say, "I didn't see him. Where did you see him?" They will point to the side of the lid. "Over there? He's not supposed to be over there, he's supposed to be right here," I say as I point to the top of the lid while looking straight at the audience.

Again the puppet appears right where I am pointing, but I don't see him, and when I finally look, he is gone.

"I don't see him," I say rather confused.

The puppet appears around the side of the lid again. The kids go wild screaming that he is there; of course when I look he is gone. "Where did you see him? Over there (pointing to the far side of the lid). Let me look." I sneak around in front of the suitcase and peak at the far edge of the suitcase lid, keeping one arm behind the case, and the puppet appears over the top of the lid while I am looking at the side and don't see him. The kids go wild.

I look straight at the audience and say, "I don't know what you are talking about; I don't see anything." The puppet appears on top of the lid, I turn and look at him, look back at the audience, then do a double take. The puppet waves to me. I act totally disgusted and say, "Where have you been?"

You can play this type of routine for as long as you can milk it, the kids love it.

The Over-Sized Prop

Clowns have used over-sized props for laughs for years. Putting these over-sized props in the hands of a small puppet makes them even more out of proportion, and even funnier.

You introduce your puppet to the audience, he looks back and forth and then whispers in your ear. You translate what he said, "What's that, there are lots of pretty girls out there? Yes, there are."

He whispers again, "What? You want to throw the pretty girls a kiss? Okay, do it and get it over with." Puppet throws kisses back and forth over and over again. "How many kisses are you going to throw?" Puppet whispers. "One for each little girl and two for the mommies!—You're a flirt!" Puppet laughs.

You ask, "Are you going to help me with the next trick?" Puppet nods yes. "Okay, get me the magic wand." Puppet brings up a pair of giant sun-glasses and puts them on you. You look at the audience puzzled, take off the glasses and ask, "What is this?" Puppet whispers. "Sun-glasses. I can see that. Whose sun-glasses are they?" Puppet whispers. "Michael Jackson's! Well give them back to Michael Jackson, I don't want them. I hate it when he messes up my hair. Stop that. What do you think you are doing?" Puppet whispers. "You're getting into my hair? Well cut it out!" Puppet comes out with a pair of giant scissors and tries to cut my hair. "What are you doing?" Puppet whispers. "You want to give me a hair cut? I don't need a hair cut. What kind of hair cut would you give me?" Puppet whispers. "A Mohawk? I don't want a Mohawk. Now put those scissors away." Look at the

audience while shaking your head. "What a hot dog." Puppet comes out with a string of foam rubber hot dogs waving them around. When you look at him he wraps them around your neck like a necklace and pulls you into the trunk with him.

You can see that this routine can go on and on using, a rubber fish, spring snake, giant fly swatter, etc. Eventually, the puppet might actually bring out a giant magic wand and help you with a trick, or maybe hit you over the head with it. This type of routine is the magician-in-trouble syndrome; kids love to see the magician or puppeteer in trouble. The puppet can be the ultimate heckler; he can drive you crazy, and the kids will love every minute of it.

The Wrap-Around Monkey Puppet

Although I have said that mouth puppets really don't lend themselves to the birthday party setting, here is an idea using a wrap-around mouth puppet that works. For those of you who do not know what a wrap-around puppet is, it is a mouth puppet (a puppet where your hand inside opens and closes the mouth) with long arms and legs. Small patches of Velcro on the hands and feet allow the legs to be locked around your waist and the arms around your neck. The effect is that of a monkey hanging on to you. These puppets are available in novelty shops or from mail order puppet dealers.

Mouth puppets have to speak, so for starters, you can rely on the techniques I supplied you in the instant ventriloquist course given a few pages back.

Now stand in front of a mirror, mouth in a relaxed smile, teeth slightly parted and say "ooo-ooo" the type of sound made by a monkey. You will find that you can do this without moving your lips. The late Burr Tilstrum of Kukla, Fran, and Ollie fame had a puppet named Cecil Bill who only said "toi-toi," yet by changing the inflection of the sound, we understood what he was saying. Let's use this idea on our monkey.

Walk out with monkey and introduce the monkey to the audience. The monkey shudders, cringes, and begins to shake. You say, "You're not afraid are you?" Monkey shakes head yes and says, "ooo-ooo" sheepishly, then hides his head. You say, "You don't have to be afraid, they won't hurt you." The monkey slowly looks at the audience panning from one side to the other cautiously, then shakes his head no and says, "ooo-ooo" questioningly. You say, "Of course they won't hurt you. See how they are all looking at you?" The monkey shakes his head yes and says "ooo-ooo" cautiously. "See that pretty girl looking at you?" Monkey does a double take and stares at pretty girl in front row and say, "ooo-ooo" appreciatively. "Would you like to meet her?" Monkey nods his head yes and says, "ooo-ooo" excitedly.

You can take it from here, the idea is that an interesting, funny, entertaining routine can be worked up, using only the sounds "ooo-ooo." Now, saying ooo-ooo without moving your lips doesn't make you a ventriloquist, but you never said you were. You're something more important, your an entertainer!

Polly: What are you writing?
Molly: I'm writing a letter to myself.
Polly: What does it say?
Molly: How do I know—I won't get it until tomorrow.

Chapter 7

CLOWNING

What is a clown? That may sound like an easy question; after all, we all know what clowns are don't we? Clowns are people dressed up in funny clothes, do silly stunts, and tell jokes. Anybody can act like a clown, right? If that's your idea of a clown, you're wrong.

Dressing up in mismatched, odd-fitting clothes, telling a few canned jokes, and handing out balloons doesn't make a good clown. Many people are hired to dress up like clowns to stand on street corners and hand out balloons or wave at kids to attract customers to businesses, but these individuals are not real clowns. They are only people dressed up like clowns. Often their makeup and costume are horribly amateurish, and they have no real experience or skill as clowns. A real clown is an effective entertainer.

To be successful, a clown must possess certain skills, just as a magician, puppeteer, storyteller, or any other entertainer does. Wearing a colorful costume or using clownish props does not make a person a clown any more than wearing a white jacket would make someone a doctor. At times children may ask, "Are you a real clown?" or more bluntly say, "You're not a clown, you're just a man dressed up."

Performing as a clown may appear to be simple, and it can be, but you must be prepared just as a magician or puppeteer is prepared. The last thing you want to do is go to a party and just goof around with the children; telling a few jokes or showing a few simple magic tricks and gags isn't entertainment. The children will be disappointed and the parents will be upset. As a children's entertainer, you are paid to entertain. You need to come prepared to take control of the children and present a full 20 to 30-minute show that will keep them enthralled with your presence.

Clowns are lucky; unlike magicians, puppeteers, storytellers and other children's entertainers, they can do just about anything in the way of entertainment including magic, puppetry, storytelling, as well as making balloon animals, face painting, juggling, and other forms of entertainment. You don't have to be an expert in all of these skills. You don't have to be an expert in any of these skills. What you do have to be, in order to be a successful clown, is funny. Some of my funniest skits and routines involve performing these skills without having to master much in the way of technical difficulty. One of my most successful juggling skits requires absolutely no juggling; I fake it with invisible props. Because clowns are silly, I can get away with doing ventriloquism without having to actually do ventriloquism. The kids don't care if they see my mouth move, the jokes and silly actions keep them entertained. I'm not saying it is not important to learn skills; what I am saying is that it is the presentation that is the most important and not the skill.

A juggling clown, for instance, can be an expert juggler yet a poor clown because he lacks the ability to make people laugh. An effective clown can make the act

Evelyn "Berries" Tucker and Janet "Fud E. Dud" Tucker clown around.

come alive for the audience and induce spontaneous laughter. The audience must leave knowing they had a good time.

The successful entertainer receives a good response because he lifts the listeners out of their present surroundings and places them in his own imaginary world where they can experience in their minds the smells, tastes, and scenes he describes. He is animated, he is enthused, he displays emotion, and combines it with physical gestures. The listeners are following the story so intently that when the punch line hits, it's a total surprise and makes them burst out laughing.

Lead the audience into an imaginary world of your own creation, using vocal fluctuations, emotions, and physical movement. Avoid simply repeating jokes borrowed from someone else.

A clown's purpose is to entertain others, and emphasis should be directed toward this goal. For instance, if the clown comes up to someone and begins to joke around, he should not try to embarrass or offend just to get a laugh. Spectators should never be the butt of any joke! The clown is the silly character—it is he, not the audience, who should look like the fool.

Much of the joy in clowning is experienced by the performer himself. To evoke laughter in a child brings a sense of joy obtainable in few other ways. To have children giggle, laugh, and shout with excitement is immensely satisfying. In so doing, they are telling you that you're funny and appreciated. On occasions, after a show, a child has come up to me, given me a hug, and said, "I love you." Sincere appreciation—what better reward could a clown receive?

CLOWN CHARACTER

Not all clowns are alike, nor should they be. That's what sets them apart from each other. One clown can be shy, another boisterous; one clumsy and another skilled; one can wear bright, colorful clothes and another tattered attire without color or glitter. Each one should look and act distinctively different. Although it is easy to spot a clown because of the characteristic costume and makeup, each clown should have his or her own character or personality.

Too often novice clowns don't pay enough attention to their makeup; they put a dab of eye shadow here, some lipstick there and presto, they call themselves clowns. But a poor makeup job easily identifies a novice as an impostor—a person dressed up as a clown—not a REAL clown.

Makeup and costuming are extremely important parts of clowning. Often, it is the unique clown attire and makeup that sets clowns apart from other children's entertainers. To be a real clown you must look the part.

Although makeup alone doesn't make the whole clown, and a clown's performing ability shouldn't be judged solely by what he or she wears, makeup is a highly visible part of the clown costume. Through it the audience gets a feeling for who the clown is, what he or she is like, and what to expect. If you want to be accepted as a real clown, you're going to have to look like a real clown.

One of the most important aspects of the makeup and costume is that it determines, in part, the clown's character. In general, the more outlandish the makeup and costume, the more outlandish the clown's actions and character. Character traits have evolved over the years and have become standard, not just among clowns but even spectators. When they see a clown dressed as a buffoon, they expect him to act the part. When they see a clown dressed in a more pleasant, yet still clownish attire, they expect a more skillful, intelligent character. It is important that you choose the makeup and costume that fits your style. Dressing like a skillful intelligent clown and then acting like a clumsy bumpkin is out of character, confusing, and distracting to the audience. They have been conditioned to expect a certain type of character with a certain type of appearance.

Clown characters are divided into categories which correspond with their makeup designs and wardrobe. Ideally, you will decide on your clown's personality and then design makeup to fit it. This is called developing a character from the inside out. If you are having trouble finding your character, you might pick a makeup style which appeals to you and experiment with the character type corresponding to it.

The three basic clown types are defined primarily by the makeup design. Each is discussed below.

Whiteface

There are two categories of whiteface, the neat whiteface and the comedy whiteface.

Neat Whiteface. The neat whiteface is the most elegant and most simplistic of the clown facial designs. The primary color is white, which covers the entire face. Simple thin features, usually in either red or black, are added to emphasize the mouth and eyes. Few, if any other markings are present. The facial design of mimes are typical examples of this type of makeup.

The whiteface costume has traditionally been a one-piece jumpsuit or a two-piece loose fitting pajama-type garment. The outfit is usually highlighted with a ruff around the neck and large pompoms on the front. The neat whiteface costume is usually elegant, and color combinations are simple. At times the whiteface may even wear a tuxedo: it fits well, although it may have short sleeves and legs.

Because the appearance is more elegant than funny, the neat whiteface clown projects an appearance of skill and intelligence.

Comedy Whiteface. The other type of whiteface is called a comedy or grotesque whiteface. This clown uses the same colors in the same areas of the face as the neat whiteface, but applies greasepaint more boldly so the mouth and eyebrows become a large splash of color, and the nose often puffs into a large bulb. These clowns may wear skullcaps, or more commonly, wigs. They can wear a one-piece jumpsuit, a two-piece pajama-like costume, or an oversized or ill-fitting business suit. Colors and patterns are bright and cheery.

The comedy whiteface does not look like his more elegant cousin, the neat whiteface. His appearance is more outlandish and comical so, likewise, his character is also more foolish and less skillful. He may actually be silly or stupid.

Elizabeth Ann Griffin's character "Sunshine" is a whiteface clown.

The Auguste Clown

The auguste (pronounced "aw-goost") portrays a character that is less skillful and less intelligent than the whiteface.

The auguste's costume reflects his character. A traditional auguste costume is an oversized plaid suit. Some performers desiring a youthful appearance wear a striped T-shirt, solid colored pants with contrasting cuffs, suspenders, and sometimes a vest.

Instead of using white for the base color as the whiteface does, the auguste uses some other light color such as pink, orange, yellow, light brown, or even light blue. White is used only around the eyes and mouth, and other features are generally red or black. Facial features are often bold and outlandish, depicting this clown's zany character.

Auguste (left) and tramp (right) costumes and makeup are shown here modeled by Dan Foy.

The Tramp Clown

The third type of clown is referred to as the character clown. The character clown can have a variety of makeup styles and costumes, depicting a certain type of person like a policeman, fireman, cowboy, or hobo. By far the most popular character clown is the hobo or tramp.

The tramp is often dressed in a tattered dark colored business suit. Although the variations on the business suit are most common, he may wear almost anything that a real hobo might find cast aside by a previous owner. It is important to keep in mind that although the tramp depicts a character who is down and out and wears old ragged clothes, his wardrobe is a costume. As such, it should be clean, nice looking, and fresh smelling.

Makeup has a flesh-colored or pinkish base, depicting a well-tanned skin. Black or gray is used to simulate several days worth of whisker growth on the face. Eyes and mouth are often outlined in white. The tramp's makeup is more like that of the auguste than the whiteface. Likewise, the tramp's character is usually similar to that of the auguste, but may also be skillful like the whiteface. The tramp is often aloft or in a dream world. He can be down trodden and sad or carefree and whimsical—the difference between the sad tramp and the happy hobo.

DESIGNING A CLOWN FACE

Designing a professional-looking clown face and applying makeup correctly are basic skills that all serious clowns must learn.

Which Face Are You?

The first step toward creating your own clown face will be to decide which of the three clown types you want to be: whiteface, auguste, or tramp. Keep in mind that the clown face you choose must be consistent with the character you portray. Is your character wacky and clumsy like a tramp or auguste, or smart and skillful like a whiteface? If you choose whiteface, do you want it to be a skilled neat whiteface or a more clumsy comedy whiteface?

A great deal of the clown's personality is displayed through the facial features. The large exaggerated nose, mouth, and eyes of the auguste and the comedy whiteface clowns depict a zany character. In general, the less bizarre the facial features, the more intelligent and graceful the clown becomes. Your first step in designing a clown face is deciding which type of clown you want to be.

Make the Face You

Every clown face should be unique—just as your own natural face is. A clown face is a type of trademark, and nobody should copy the face of another clown. Many of the same features or markings can be used, of course, but each face should be original.

Start by looking at pictures of other clowns. Visit a local magic shop or costume store or go to the library and look through the books with clown pictures. How do these clowns wear their makeup? What type of markings do they use? Examine the different ways that have been used to outline the mouth and eyes. These pictures will give you the background information you need to create your own face.

After deciding on the general type of face you want and before you even touch any makeup, sit down in front of a mirror and examine your face. Is your face long or short? Round or thin? Do you have a long nose? A dimple on your chin? Is your chin round or square?

Examine all your natural lines and wrinkles. Make faces—smile, frown, look surprised, laugh. What lines or folds in your face are most distinguishable? These folds will be used as guidelines for designing your clown face.

One of the biggest mistakes that new clowns make is to wear makeup as a mask. For best results, makeup should enhance, not hide, your natural features.

Take a pencil and paper. Sketch a picture of your head. Put in all the prominent lines that are naturally in your face. Use these lines as a guide in designing a clown face. Outline the mouth and eyes; add any additional markings you desire. Make several different drawings until you have one or two which suit you the most and save as your blueprint.

With your sketch to guide you, take a black lining pencil and outline the features on your face. (Men should be clean shaven before applying any makeup.) Look at yourself in the mirror; how do you look? When you add white and other colors, will they help bring out your expressions or mask them?

These black lines can be removed with baby oil, baby shampoo, or skin cleanser. Apply one of these cleansers to your face, let it soak in a few seconds, and rub it off with a disposable paper towel. Ordinary soap and water will not effectively wash this makeup off.

Take the black liner again and try another face. Does it look better than the first? Keep trying new designs until you have one you're happy with. Now wash your face completely and dry it off.

Applying Makeup

I will now describe how to apply clown makeup. The following procedures apply to any type of clown face you choose to use. The primary differences are your choice of colors and boldness of the features. Keep in mind that it will take some practice to apply the makeup evenly. Design changes will also become necessary to get a look you are completely satisfied with. Don't be afraid to experiment.

In preparing to do anything, it helps to have the right tools. The same applies when you're putting on makeup. Before you start, you will need: (1) a tin of clown white—the greasepaint which you will smooth evenly over your face. The best brands to use are Kryolan, Bob Kelly, Ben Nye, and Mehron because of their smooth and balanced formulas. There are many other brands; some are okay, others are not so good—but these are the brands the professionals use and trust. Make sure you use oil-based "greasepaint" and not a water-based makeup. The water-based makeup is easy to apply and easily comes off with just soap and water (or perspiration), but does not give the professional look you are trying to obtain and need as a professional entertainer.

The other tools are: (2) a shaving type brush or a soft one-inch wide paintbrush; (3) a 100% white cotton sock with baby powder in it (pure baby powder of just talc and fragrance); (4) paper towels; (5) a plastic shower cap; (6) mirror; (7) Q-tips; (8) two or three very thin art brushes (00 or 01 gauge); (9) baby oil or baby shampoo; (10) paint creme liners.

Applying makeup can be a messy procedure. If at all possible, delay putting on your clown outfit until after your makeup is in place. Some pieces of clothing, however, which have to be pulled over the head may smear your makeup, so it is best to put these on beforehand. If you must wear some part of your costume, be sure to use an apron. You will get the greasepaint on your hands, paper towels, and the table. No matter how careful you try to be, some will find its way onto your shirt or pants.

Put on all the other parts of your wardrobe associated with your face and head—such as wig, fake nose, and hat—after your makeup is complete.

Apply the makeup with as much care as you possibly can. A good job will take time, perhaps 40 minutes or more. Don't be in such a hurry that you make your features unsymmetrical or uneven. The smile on the right side of your face should be the same size as the smile on the left side. Any outlining around one eye should be equal

---

Jane: The teacher says we have a test today, rain or shine.
Sue: Then why are you so happy?
Jane: Because it's snowing!

jiggle the sock above the face, letting the powder fall without touching the makeup. Once a thin coat of powder is on the face, the sock or puff can be patted on the face to get an even coat. It is a good idea to avoid breathing the powder. Excessive powder, or any foreign particles, in the lungs can be a health hazard.

in size and shape to that around the other, unless of course your design is intentionally uneven.

Take care to keep outlining as sharp and even as possible. Messy outlining gives an amateurish look. Other problems to avoid are sagging, smearing, greasiness, caking, and skin showing through.

When you begin to apply makeup, put on the lightest color first. Progressively add the darker colors as you go. White or flesh tone is used as the base color which all other colors and markings surround. The base color will cover most of your face and any exposed skin. The base color for whiteface is white. For the auguste it is usually pink, orange, or tan, and for the tramp it is light brown, pink, tan, or some similar color. Put any white you use on first regardless of the type of face you are creating. For a whiteface you would cover the entire face. For the auguste and tramp you would put white only around the eyes and mouth. Spread on the makeup as evenly as you can. Spots that get too much or too little will eventually stick out like a sore thumb.

After each application of a color, you will need to "set" it by powdering the fresh makeup lightly with baby powder. There are several different methods of applying powder to the face. If you use the cotton sock filled with the talcum powder, shake or hit the sock several times before applying it to your face. This will force the powder through the cloth to the outside where it can be lightly patted onto the face. A powder puff may be used instead of the sock if you wish. Use plenty of powder. If the sock or puff doesn't have enough powder, you run the risk of transferring colors and making a mess of your face.

To avoid the problem of smearing the makeup while powdering, some clowns prefer to throw the powder or

After powdering, look in the mirror. If you see any damp or wet spots, put on more powder. Then take a shaving brush or a soft one-inch paintbrush and brush off all excess powder. Brush from the lightest colors to the darkest so that if some areas are still wet, you won't smear the makeup. Repeat the powdering and brushing process as often as necessary to eliminate all wet spots and get an even coating.

The next step is to remove any excess powder. This is done by splashing water onto your face or by taking a wet washcloth and patting with it lightly—do not rub

your face! Without the water treatment, makeup tends to turn gray and colors fade because of the extra powder that was not removed. Use a soft towel to soak the excess water off your face. Powder applied in this way will give you a professional dry look and prevent the makeup from coming off when touched.

Powdering serves three important purposes. First, it sets the greasepaint, keeping it from sagging and smearing. Without powder, makeup tends to sag, especially when the weather is hot. On a warm summer day, the makeup may begin to look more like a Halloween mask than a clown face. Second, powder eliminates the greasy wet look of the makeup. Third, it makes the makeup dry, so it can be touched without smearing or coming off.

A clown's appearance is sharply improved with a fresh dry look that powder gives. On a long hot day the powdered makeup will last several hours; a light powdering in the middle of the day is enough to freshen it until the end of the day. Applying powder is essential to good clown makeup and is commonly one of the major differences between "lipstick clowns" and professional-looking clowns.

If you are making an auguste or tramp face, apply the base color followed by a second powdering. Application of the more delicate features comes next for all three facial types.

After applying the base color and powdering, check your face. If everything is okay, proceed. Outlining features and small designs go on last. These are most commonly black and red. Once these are on, powder as you did before. Don't worry about putting white powder over the colored makeup, it will be absorbed and will take on the color of the makeup. Remove any excess powder with a brush.

With this information you can design your own clown face and apply the makeup. I have kept these instructions brief and simple, yet detailed enough to get

you started. For a more detailed description of how to apply makeup and incorporate accessory features such as nose and wig, I highly recommend the book *Strutter's Complete Guide to Clown Makeup* by Jim "Strutter" Roberts. Amply illustrated, this book contains a wealth of valuable information about the art of designing a face and applying the colors.

CLOWN CLOTHES
Your Clothes Should Be You

Clothes convey character. The clothes people wear and how they wear them are extensions of their personalities. The same is true in clowning. Each piece of clothing you wear tells others something about yourself. Some people are considered "nerds" just because of the way they dress. Punk rockers are easy to identify by their distinctive clothes and hair styles. A proper wardrobe should be chosen with careful planning.

Once you have defined your clown character, you will have to design a costume to accompany it, one which supports your clown personality. There are no hard and fast rules you must follow, but certain guidelines or standards are traditionally recognized and accepted.

In general, the more slapstick or silly your clown character, the more bizarre your makeup and wardrobe. The neat whiteface, being the most intelligent and skillful of the clowns, wears a costume which is color coordinated and pleasing to look at. His facial features are small and more naturally proportioned than most other clowns. The auguste, and the comedy whiteface to some extent, wear a variety of mismatched, odd-sized clothes. Since these clowns portray zany characters, their clothes should match

their personalities. The more outrageous and comical the personality, the more outlandish the costume.

Contrary to popular belief, a good clown costume is not a mixture of mismatched clothes haphazardly thrown together. That makes for an ugly clown. A good costume is a carefully selected arrangement of style, patterns, and colors. Unless you're a tramp clown, your outfit shouldn't be composed of an assortment of old Salvation Army rejects. Most clowns will use bright cheery colors and designs which are not obtainable in second-hand shops. The clothes must also smell fresh and be clean looking and pressed. Even a tramp clown's costume should be clean and neat, although patches or tears may make it look old and worn.

Go to a few large fabric stores and look at what they have. Some even carry patterns to make clown suits. Patterns not specifically designed for clowns can be modified slightly by a tailor to make a pleasing clown outfit. Costume shops and several enterprising individuals sell custom made clown clothes. They often advertise in the newsletters published by the various trade organizations which are listd in the appendix.

A custom made wardrobe is the most suitable. Costume stores sell only a few outfits. These are usually good but generalized, mass produced, and designed for the "average" clown, not for anyone specifically. They might work well with your clown character, but nothing is as eye catching as an original suit.

An outfit designed by you, using your own choice of colors and prints, becomes your trademark. Such an outfit complements your character and is unique.

Character Aids

Character aids are articles of clothing or accessory pieces of the costume or makeup which help define the personality portrayed by the performer.

The nose is an important character aid and considered a part of the makeup design. Large, round, bulbous noses are silly and funny looking; they make the wearer look ridiculous. Auguste clowns usually wear these types of noses; a neat whiteface clown will not use a large fake nose. The shape of the nose can vary. Most noses are of the round bulbous type, but some clowns use putty so they can mold the nose to a desired shape for a specific clown character. The putty is then attached to the nose with spirit gum.

> Ed: How do you make a skeleton laugh?
> Fred: Tickle its funny bone.

A clown's hair is one of the first things that catches the eye of the spectator. This first glance should tell the observer who the entertainer is and basically what type of personality he or she is portraying.

Although the audience will see the entire costume, their eyes will focus mostly on the clown's face. It is the face which communicates most of the clown's feelings and emotions to the audience.

The clown face is incomplete without an appropriate wig, skullcap, or hair style to go with it. The hair is, in fact, a part of this all important clown face.

The style and color of hair (or lack of it) is one of the most important parts of your clown wardrobe. The effect of hair on our appearance can be dramatic. Even for nonclowns, dying or styling the hair can radically change a person's appearance.

Most tramp and other character clowns use their own real hair and just style it for their acts. Whiteface clowns use their own hair, skullcaps, or wigs. Auguste clowns wear wigs or skullcaps.

The best hair colors to use are red, orange, yellow, and blond. These bright, cheery colors match most clown costumes and are closest to natural hair colors. Many clowns, however, choose to use blue, green, purple, and other less natural colors. Whichever color you use, it should match the rest of your outfit. A pink costume combined with green hair is distasteful; it is usually best to avoid color conflicts.

The most universal article of clothing for all types of clowns is a pair of gloves. Most clowns wear gloves as part of their wardrobe, white being preferred. The wearing of gloves is steeped in tradition and has become a standard practice for decades. One of the major reasons gloves are so popular is because they cover the flesh-colored skin of the hands, reinforcing the clown's cartoon-like image.

Some clowns prefer not to wear gloves because they interfere with a particular activity, such as balloon sculpting or juggling. Others have found that if the fingertips are cut off, they can wear gloves and still work effectively at these activities. Most tramp clowns use fingerless gloves because it gives the gloves a well-worn look.

One of the most important features of any clown outfit are the pockets. They can be used to help identify the clown or be simply a place to carry props and giveaways. Whether you use pockets as a character aid or not, you must have pockets—the bigger the better.

It's best to carry both props and giveaways out of sight by placing them in the pockets. In this way you can regulate the giving of gifts. Also pockets keep props handy yet out of reach of curious children.

> What do you call a boomerang that doesn't come back?
> *A stick.*

Pockets can be any shape or in almost any location. Some are sewn onto the outside of the suit and become part of the design of the costume. Others are sewn on the inside and are largely unnoticeable.

Fake pockets—openings which allow the clown to reach through the suit into bags or pockets underneath the costume—are also useful. An apron with large pockets worn underneath the costume can hold much more than ordinary pockets. Another advantage of the fake pocket is that it prevents mischievous hands from grabbing props.

Other articles of clothing include ties, shoes, collars, hats, boutonnieres, etc. When designing your wardrobe, stop and consider each article. Ask yourself these questions:

• What type of character would wear this?
• What personality traits do people associate with it?
• Are these traits consistent with my clown character?
• Will it match the rest of my costume?

Don't stick on or wear something just because it looks cute. Make sure it fits your personality and style or don't wear it at all. Following these principles will make your appearance one that is truly professional.

CLOWN ENTERTAINMENT
Physical Comedy

Having great looking makeup and a dazzling costume are very important to being a professional clown, but unfortunately, it does not make a person a good entertainer. What the clown says and does is what creates the entertainment.

Humor can be separated into two broad categories, verbal and nonverbal. Verbal comedy is relayed by speech through jokes and stories. Nonverbal or physical comedy is expressed by body movement and facial expression.

Clowns rely heavily on physical comedy to express themselves and create laughter. Clowning and physical comedy are, in fact, inseparable; you can't have one without the other. Many clowns use no verbal dialogue at all, but depend totally on pantomime.

To convey emotions, thought, personality, and actions through physical movement alone requires an acute awareness of body language. Clowns are not the bumbling fools they seem to be; they are skilled performing artists. An inexperienced or untrained clown is readily detectable because he lacks the skill to express himself effectively. Conscious awareness of body movements and practice will allow a clown to master the skills of acting like a fool without being one.

Some of the great comedians of the past such as Charlie Chaplin, Red Skelton, and Laurel and Hardy relied heavily on physical comedy. The slapstick nonsense of the Keystone Kops and the Three Stooges was drenched with physical humor.

We are all familiar with the pie in the face or getting a foot stuck in a bucket. We can watch these old gags again and again with as much amusement as when we saw them for the first time. In verbal comedy, a joke gets "old" after a while and loses its humor; it no longer comes as a surprise. It's different with physical actions, however. Because each actor reacts differently, the same situation takes on a newness that makes it funny time and time again.

Kids are very physical or sight oriented. They love sight gags, the reason clowns have become the classic children's entertainers. Humor that may not affect an adult can throw a child into a fit of laughter. Just watch a toddler play with an adult. Peek around a corner and hide. Not very funny, but the toddler may laugh hysterically. Even a silly looking facial expression can get little ones giggling uncontrollably. As we grow older, physical humor becomes less and less funny, but for kids physical comedy is king. The age groups which you entertain at birthday parties are still enthralled with physical comedy.

Speaking with the Body

Communication without words is body language. We wave our hands "good-by," nod our heads "yes," hold our stomach if it's upset, or rub our eyes if we're sleepy. Physical comedy uses body language to communicate humor.

Facial expressions can be a great tool in communicating with the audience. A face with little expression has the same effect on an audience as a speaker talking in a monotone. All great speakers put a lot of expression into their speaking voices, and to be effective at physical comedy, you must use a variety of facial expressions.

The face physically expresses emotions, feelings, and thoughts. It is the single most important means of nonverbal communication. Because of the great importance of facial expressions, every children's entertainer should spend time practicing as many different faces as can be imagined.

Go to a mirror and practice each of the following emotions. Look at yourself from someone else's perspective. Would they be able to readily identify these emotions expressed by you? Happiness, laughter, anger, sadness, fear, pleasure, surprise, remorse, confusion, excitement, pain, and revenge.

All the feelings listed above can be expressed by the face alone, but body movement can enhance or assist in conveying the proper mood. Review the list again, adding movement from the entire body.

Personality and character traits can also be displayed with a proper combination of facial and body movement. Go back to the mirror and practice the following personality traits: stubborn, clumsy, determined, conceited, shy, confident, stylish, sneaky, talkative, snobbish, nervous, and boisterous.

Use your imagination and past experience to act out these traits. Make every movement project a feeling or thought. Let's use a pie fight as an example. Imagine that someone has just smashed a chocolate cream pie onto the top of your head. What is your reaction? How does it feel? Can you feel the cream drip down the side of your face and neck? Is it hot or cold? What does it smell like? Is it sticky or smooth? These are the situations you must consider when acting out a part.

Practice expressing thoughts, feelings, and activities in front of somebody and ask them to try to identify your actions or feelings. Use the following list to get started. This practice will also help develop your mime skills: hot, surprise, eating, sewing, hunger, sleepiness, windiness, running, searching, inspiration, cold, hammering, taking a picture, digging, skating, swimming, driving, fighting, drunkenness, smelling.

Clown Movement

Clowns and comedians, unlike other actors, don't always display normal actions. Clown movements are performed with obvious exaggeration. Much of the humor and the joy of watching a clown is derived from these bigger-than-life actions. A clown must learn to express his emotions, thoughts, actions, reactions, and personality with the entire body.

A clown's expressions and movements are a caricature of normal movements much like that of a cartoon. The clown is, in fact, a living cartoon character. His actions should be like those of Bugs Bunny, Fred Flintstone, or Scooby-Doo.

Ed: How do you make a cow float?
Fred: Use one cow and two scoops of ice cream.

ARE YOU A REAL CLOWN?

Clown, P.J. Parsons, says "When you hear, You're not a real clown,' respond with, 'Then I guess I really don't know how to do magic, paint your face, or make you this balloon hat after all.' Or come back with, 'You're not a real kid, you're just dressed up that way.' The first response will make them think that they might miss out on something and the second brings on some fun conversation."

You will notice that clowns, like cartoon characters, exert a tremendous amount of energy which seems to accomplish very little. In a chase scene, for instance, a cartoon character who begins to run away from something will jump up in the air and pedal his legs before actually taking off. The clown too, may jump and begin moving his legs before starting on a run.

The chase scenes in cartoons are filled with exaggerated, wasted motion. Turning a corner isn't just a simple turn but may involve hopping on one foot as the turn is made. Participants take the most ridiculous routes, run in circles, and bump into each other. The clown chase scene is done the same way. It's silly sure, but that's what clowns do.

Excitement can be expressed by jumping around, clapping your hands, hugging yourself, and showing others what made you feel happy.

Anger can be displayed by flexing the muscles in the face into a tightly contorted frown. Raise your fist and shake it, stomp your feet, show your teeth, jump up and down. Express yourself fully.

If you're tired and worn out, walk very slowly, feet dragging, arms limp, mouth open, tongue hanging out, and shoulders slumping. You may stumble as you walk, stopping periodically to rest and wipe your brow.

To deliver a punch, pull your arm all the way back, maybe even winding it up, and then swing it in a wide arc so as to be seen easily by the entire audience.

Eating can take various forms. Smack your lips and lick them with your tongue. Open your mouth wide to take a big bite. Make chewing obvious, perhaps even sticking your tongue against the inside of your mouth to make it appear to be stuffed with food. Pick up a few crumbs that happen to fall and pop them into your mouth—savor the flavor.

Exaggerate ordinary actions. Go back to the list of emotions, thoughts, personality traits, and actions. Practice each one again, using slow, exaggerated movements. Remember to act as if you were a cartoon character.

When practicing facial expressions in front of a mirror, take some time and make some silly faces. Move your eyeballs and eyebrows, puff out your cheeks, and twist your lips. Find several combinations that you like. If you have the ability to do something unique or unusual, such as wiggling your ears or nose, add that. I have the ability to flex certain muscles in my face which makes my nose wiggle. This simple skill adds another gimmick I can use for creating laughter.

Funny faces can be used whenever other humor doesn't produce a strong enough reaction. Moderately humorous jokes and gags take on new life and become effective with the addition of a goofy looking expression. Use funny faces freely, but don't overuse them. Too much of the same face loses its appeal, so use several different faces for variety.

Clowning Around

A magician does magic, a balloon worker creates balloons, a storyteller tells stories, a puppeteer works with puppets, and a face painter paints faces. What does a clown do? He clowns around. But what is clowning around? Unlike these other entertainers, clowns are not associated exclusively with any particular prop or technique. They have an advantage in that they have no limits. A magician is expected to do and be competent in magic. A storyteller is expected to spin yarns. But a clown can do anything. He can do magic, tell stories, work with puppets, paint faces, create balloon figures, and he doesn't have to be an expert in any of them, although he can. This allows the clown freedom to do most anything to entertain kids. Some clowns specialize in magic or some other skill. Regardless of the props or skills used, all clowns can be identified by their distinctive makeup, costume, and zany, highly physical actions.

All birthday party entertainers must incorporate humor and animation into their routines to be successful with children. Clowns, more than any other type of entertainer, are characterized by the use of physical comedy and exaggerated movements. Clowns can be quite vocal too, but not all clowns talk. Most birthday party clowns talk; there are some who are talented enough to entertain kids for 30 minutes without saying a word, but it is much easier using speech and there is much more you can do.

A clown uses many of the same skills and props as do other entertainers; he just uses them to fit his style and personality.

Besides the skills described in this book, a clown can also do juggling, perform feats of balancing and other forms of physical dexterity, sing or play a musical instrument, and work with live animals. He need not use any of these means, but can rely on simple props or gags and tell amusing stories or get into funny situations. What he does is not important. What is important is that he present an entertaining show for the kids. Use your own skill and imagination in designing a suitable routine. Many books provide ideas. A couple of books with skit ideas that can be adapted to a birthday party situation are *Clown Act Omnibus* by Wes McVicar and *Clown Skits for Everyone* by Happy Jack Feder. If you're serious about becoming a clown, the best resource you can get is *Creative Clowning* written by eight professional children's entertainers. This book describes the business aspects of clowning, how to create and present clown skits, and all aspects of the clowning profession. It is the premiere book on professional clowning and used as the textbook in many clown schools.

Mother: Why are you home from school so late?
Son: I was the only one who could answer a question.
Mother: Really? What was the question?
Son: Who threw the spitball at the principal?

Chapter 8

ENTERTAINING WITH BALLOONS

Kids love balloons! Any type of balloon—round ones, skinny ones, fat ones, wiggly ones. If you want to see a child's eyes light up with delight, give him a balloon. For this reason, balloons have become very popular with children's entertainers. Balloons can be used as props for short gags and magic tricks or given away as party favors. Balloons, used in skits and routines, have intrinsic appeal that can help make the show delightfully entertaining. Clowns and magicians have used balloons for years; storytellers, face painters, and other children's entertainers are now using them. Some party entertainers use them with such success that they build their show and even their careers around them, billing themselves as balloonologists.

Being a balloonologist, I get the opportunity to make many balloon animals and toys, especially at birthday parties. Balloons and parties naturally go together. In my opinion, a party is not complete unless it has balloons, particularly sculptured balloons. These colorful bubbles create a festive atmosphere, provide a fun party activity, and make excellent gifts.

BALLOON BASICS
Balloon Types

Like people, balloons come in all sizes and shapes. Latex round and tubular balloons are the most common and can be found in any store where toys are sold. Most of the special or novelty balloons, like the long skinny type you would use to make balloon animals, are usually sold in novelty and magic shops. You can also get a variety of balloons from mail order dealers.

Most balloons are identified by a code which describes their size when fully inflated. If you understand this code, you will know how to distinguish between the different types of balloons. This is important because a 260 will be used differently than a 245, but they are so similar in appearance you may not be able to tell them apart.

Round balloons have the simplest code numbers. A number 9 balloon, also called a nine-inch, simply signifies a round balloon with a diameter of nine inches when fully inflated. Round balloons typically vary from three inches to 14 inches. You can find balloons up to 48 inches in diameter, but they are not common.

Tubular shaped balloons, such as the type known as *airships* are designated by a number which signifies both length and width. These balloons get their name because of their resemblance to airships or zeppelins used in the early part of the 20th century. On a 321 airship balloon the first number "3" means that its inflated diameter is three inches. The "21" indicates that when fully inflated it will be approximately twenty-one inches long. Airships include, among others, 312, 315, 340, 418, 524 and even 1040 (10" x 40").

To make balloon animals and other figures from a single balloon, you will need special balloons known as *pencil balloons* or *twistys*. The 260 is the most popular

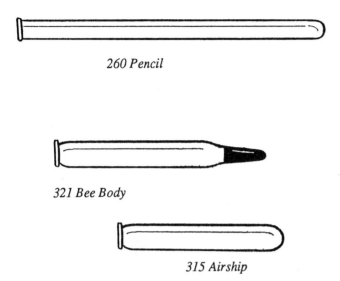

260 Pencil

321 Bee Body

315 Airship

balloon used for this purpose. These skinny balloons (two inches in diameter) grow very long (about 60-inches) when fully inflated, allowing the balloon sculptor to twist them in an endless variety of shapes.

The slightly smaller 245 can be used to make many of the simple balloon figures, like dogs and mice, but is not long enough for more difficult ones such as lions and frogs. The longer 280 allows enough length for the balloon to be twisted in shapes and figures beyond the limits of these other two. Its length, however, is far too long for most common balloon figures.

The 245, 260 and 280 are used when making figures from a single balloon. Multiple-balloon animals and other figures can also be made with the shorter and fatter airship type balloons such as the 321 or 340. These can be twisted together with other types to form large multiple-balloon creations. Because they are large, they are more suitable for stage use than for the birthday party entertainer who is up close to the audience.

Two special airship type balloons often used with balloon sculpting are the *apple* and *bee body* (321). Both of these types of balloons have a colored tip which tapers to a point. This colored portion becomes the apple stem or the bee stinger and adds a colorful touch which helps the finished creation.

Balloon Care

With a little care you can keep your balloons in good working order and avoid unexpected explosions. Being made of latex, balloons deteriorate with age. Heat, sunlight, and air are balloon's worst enemies. How long will

balloons last? If you keep the balloons out of the sunlight in an airtight container, and store them in a cool place, they should easily remain usable for a year or more. However, if you set a new package of balloons down where they are exposed to the sun, such as in your car on a hot summer day, don't expect them to last more than a day or so.

If you buy a quantity of balloons and want to store them for a while, sprinkle a little corn starch or talcum powder on them. This prevents them from becoming sticky with age and prolongs their life.

With proper care and storage, balloons will last a long time. Storing them in a freezer or refrigerator normally isn't necessary.

As you work with balloons you will find, even with a fresh package of balloons, some variation in quality. Every package of balloons has its share of duds—balloons with tiny holes or thin spots that break when inflated. This is to be expected with most any package of balloons you buy, so don't be surprised when you find them.

If your hands are rough and callused, if you have long fingernails, or wear rings you increase your chances of breaking the balloons. Trimming your nails and using hand lotion, especially in winter when dry skin is more of a problem, will help reduce balloon mishaps.

Inflation

If you are new to working with balloons, especially the skinny pencil balloons, you may be surprised at the difficulty of inflating them. Round balloons, and even airships, can be inflated with a little effort. Blowing up pencil balloons, however, takes a good set of lungs.

To soften a pencil balloon and make it easier to inflate, stretch it a few times. But be careful not to overstretch it; a balloon stretched to its elastic limits will develop lumps when inflated. A lumpy balloon will make your finished creation look deformed.

To inflate the balloon, use your cheek muscles to start a bubble. Once a bubble is started, take a deep breath and use your chest and diaphragm muscles to inflate the rest of the balloon with one continuous blow.

Some people like to pull the nipple end of the pencil balloon as they blow. This action tends to encourage the air into the balloon, making inflation somewhat easier. If you try this technique, don't be overzealous. If you pull too much or too fast, you'll make inflation more difficult.

You may experience some dizziness if you have not had much experience inflating balloons. But with a week or two of light practice, your lung strength should increase and you will no longer be troubled with this feeling.

Some people will find that even with stretching,

inflating pencil balloons is not easy. If you still have difficulty, try using a small hand held air pump. Almost any hand pump can be used, as long as the nozzle of the balloon can fit on it. Inexpensive hand pumps can be purchased at sporting goods, novelty, and magic shops. Some small hand pumps are made especially for balloons. In just a few strokes, a long 260 can be fully inflated. T. Myers Magic of Austin, Texas, has designed a balloon pump, called the Pump 1, which is ideal for balloon workers. It stands about three feet tall, but is lightweight and very portable. The real advantage to this pump is that it will inflate a 260 balloon with one easy stroke. In a couple of seconds you can have a fully inflated balloon ready to go to work for you. When you are surrounded by a pack of anxious kids, this time-saving device comes in handy.

Another advantage to using a pump is that you can inflate a limitless number of balloons without killing yourself. For a party entertainer surrounded by a mob of kids anxiously waiting for each creation, a pump comes in mighty handy.

One advantage of not using a pump is that the warm air from the lungs softens the balloon slightly making it more pliable and less likely to break. Pumps fill balloons with cold air which make them more prone to breakage. A good idea when inflating balloons, especially if you use a pump, is to allow a little air to escape after filling it. This will soften the balloon and make it easier to work with. Don't let out too much air, just a little. As you work with balloons, you will be able to judge just how much is best.

Balloon Pouch

A problem with balloons is that if you stuff a bunch into your pocket you can never tell what color, size, or shape you pull out. It is sometimes difficult to pull just one balloon out of a tangled mass of balloons, which will cause you to drop some or have them hang out of your pocket to be quickly snatched by the kids. If you use a bag, the kids are tempted to steal a few or grab the entire bag. Overly excited kids may even reach into your pocket to grab a balloon.

A better solution is to use a balloon pouch. It looks like a nail pouch with a zipper across the top. The pouch has several pockets, each filled with different types of balloons, so you know where each color or size is. The zipper prevents mischievous hands from grabbing the balloons from you.

A pouch is fairly easy to make and can be designed to match your costume or wardrobe so it blends in with your clothes and is inconspicuous. You can also wear it

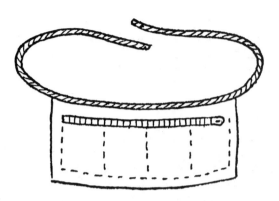

underneath your costume with access to it by way of a fake pocket.

If you use a hand pump, you might even add a loop or a holster on the side to hold the pump when it's not in use.

Keep It Clean

When working with balloons, you will always have defective ones. Some will have holes in them so they won't inflate; others will pop on you, throwing bits of balloon about the room. Parents will not appreciate it if you leave all this debris in their house. Be courteous, and a good example to the children by picking up all balloon fragments and duds and discarding them.

It's a simple matter to store latex fragments in your pocket or some other convenient location and discard them later.

BALLOON FIGURES

I found that kids go wild over balloon animals and other balloon creations. Taking a limp, lifeless balloon and magically transforming it into a lovable bubbly animal fascinates and delights kids, as well as adults. You can make an entire show based on balloons or simply use them as a time filler or party favor.

Balloon animals are much easier to make than you might think. With a few minutes practice you can create a variety of colorful dogs. Kids love balloon dogs. You don't need to know how to sculpt elephants, apes, and aardvarks to please kids. Although many balloon workers can create some imaginative figures, kids seem to enjoy the simple ones the most.

I will show you some simple balloon figures that can be used by any type of birthday party entertainer as a time filler or party favor. You will also learn how to combine clever patter with your creations to make your time entertaining. Party entertainers who want to build their shows around balloons will also find a wealth of valuable information in this chapter.

Bubbles and Twists

Most balloon animals are made using the 260 pencil balloons. You almost never inflate pencil balloons fully when making figures. Usually you will leave an inch or two uninflated at the very end. As you twist off little bubbles and connect them, the air in the balloon will be forced toward the end, gradually inflating the tail. If you don't leave this tail, the end of the balloon will stretch tighter and tighter, making it difficult to twist the bubbles and increasing the chances of popping.

The type of figure you make determines how long this tail should be. A dog, for example, needs only two inches uninflated, while a mouse needs six or seven inches.

Balloon figures are created by twisting off various sized bubbles and arranging them into specific patterns. The bubbles are made by twisting the balloon in opposite directions. Twist each bubble at least two complete revolutions so they won't unravel as you work.

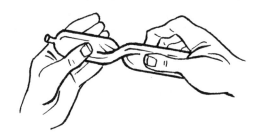

After twisting off each bubble, make sure to continue to hold them, or they will come undone. Only after you have made a connecting twist can you let go. Connecting twists are usually used to connect two or more bubbles. As an example, twist out three two-inch bubbles (1, 2, and 3). The remaining portion of the balloon will be bubble 4.

Make sure you twist each bubble in the same direction or they will untwist in your hand. Connect point A with point B (see illustration). While holding bubbles 4 and 1, twist together bubbles 3 and 2 as shown below.

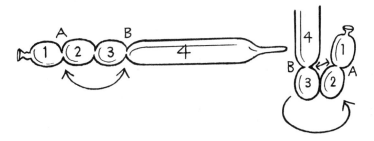

Character Aids

Markings such as mouth and eyes can give your figures a personality, thus making them more realistic. Most all figures you make will take on a more recognizable and lifelike appearance with the addition of these character aids. Certain animals may require distinguishing marks such as whiskers, spots, and stripes to make them recognizable.

Markings can do wonders in bringing your figures to life, but don't over do it! Usually the fewest marks you can make are the best. Too much ink distracts from the balloon itself, and can even look ugly. For most figures just adding eyes and/or a mouth is all that is needed.

Not all pens will write on the latex balloons, and some that do, don't look good. I have discovered the best type of pen is a permanent felt-tip marker such as Sanford's Sharpie. These pens give a nice, solid, black line.

Balloons come in various colors, adding variety to your creations. Even if you can only make two or three different animals, each creation can be unique when you use different colors and make different markings and expressions.

The Dog

The dog is a basic balloon figure. It is easy to make, and is the most requested by children. Many other animals are made in almost the same way. So, once you have learned how to make the dog, making many of the other balloon animals will be easy.

To make the dog, start by inflating a pencil balloon all the way to the end except for about two or three inches. Tie off the nozzle end. Twist off three three-inch bubbles (1, 2, and 3) and twist connect them at points A and B.

Twist off three more bubbles of the same size (4, 5, and 6) and connect points C and D.

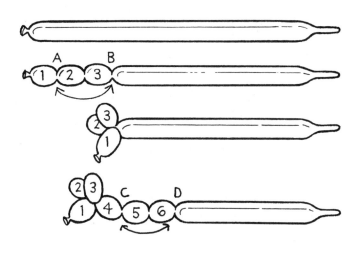

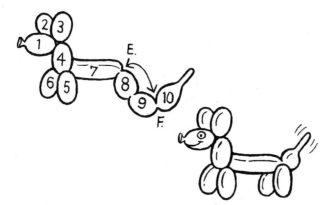

Make an eight-inch bubble (7) for the body and twist off two additional bubbles (8 and 9), the same size as bubbles 5 and 6. You will be left with only a small bubble (10) at the end, to be used as the tail.

Twist connect points E and F. Arrange the bubbles in a realistic position and finish by marking in eyes and mouth.

Your first attempt at making the dog may have resulted in something a little different from the dog pictured here. However, with a little practice your figures will improve.

Variations on the Dog

The steps used to make the dog are basically the same for many other types of animals. By varying the size of the bubbles on the dog's body, you can create other animals. Illustrated here are the dachshund, giraffe, mouse, horse, and aardvark.

Dachshund

Lengthen the body and shorten the legs slightly. Make the same sequence of twists as you do with the dog.

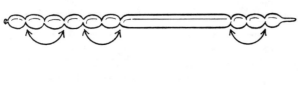

Giraffe

The neck and legs of the dog are lengthened and ears shortened. Add semi-square spots to the neck.

Mouse

All of the bubbles are smaller with a long uninflated portion at the end of the balloon for the mouse's tail. Add whiskers to the face.

Horse

The horse has slightly longer legs and neck but smaller ears.

Aardvark

The major distinguishing feature on the aardvark is its long nose. Make ears and legs very short. When you're finished with the twists, finish by shaping the animal's nose with a downward bend. To do this, grab the end of its nose and bend it over. Hold this position and squeeze the sides of its nose with your other hand.

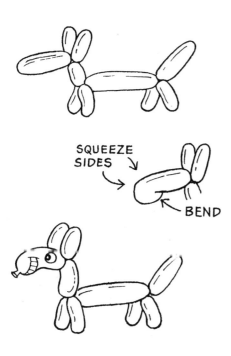

SQUEEZE SIDES

BEND

PARTY FAVORITES

Besides balloon animals, you can use balloons to make other delightful creations. Here are a few examples. For small groups you can make figures using a single balloon as part of your act. In larger groups it is hard for the children to see small balloon figures. Multiballoon figures are better for large groups and even at birthday parties, where audiences tend to be small, larger figures are readily seen. Large multiballoon figures are generally easier to make as well.

Octopus

The octopus requires four 260 balloons and one 9-inch balloon. Inflate the four 260 balloons fully except for about one inch. Bend each balloon in half and twist so that two equal-sized bubbles are formed. Twist connect all four balloons together to form the octopus' eight arms.

Inflate the 9-inch balloon. Attach the round balloon by wrapping its nozzle around the center of the arms several times. Finish by drawing on a face.

Bumblebee

This bumblebee requires two balloons—a bee body (321) and a 260 or 245. Inflate the pencil balloon fully except for about one inch. Twist a small bubble at each end and connect the ends together to make the balloon form a circle. Twist connect the middle to form a figure 8. These are the bee's wings.

Inflate the bee body balloon and leave enough slack to twist it into two bubbles. Make the bumblebee's head by twisting a small bubble at the nozzle end. Connect the wings to the bee's body. You may put eyes and a mouth on if you like. The nipple end of the bee body projects out like the bee's stinger.

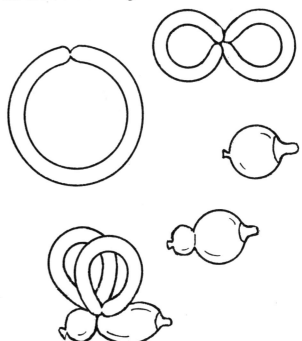

Apple

Apple balloons are much shorter than pencil balloons and a bit wider, so they're easier to inflate. They come in a variety of colors. Their most distinguishing characteristic is the dark green nipple, which forms the stem when making the apple. Another balloon very similar to the apple is the bee body. The difference between the two is that the bee balloon has a longer and more narrow nipple. A balloon apple can be made from either an apple or bee body balloon.

To make a balloon apple, inflate the balloon about halfway. With your finger, push the nozzle into the balloon and all the way into the nipple end. Grab both the nipple and the nozzle with the fingers of your other hand and remove your finger. Now make an apple twist by turning the bubble as you hold the two ends securely. This action will lock the nozzle and nipple together, forming an apple-shaped bubble.

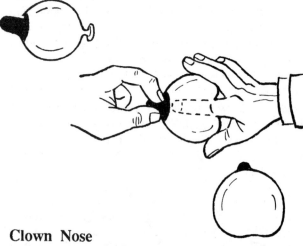

Clown Nose

Using an apple balloon you can make a bulbous clown nose. Inflate the balloon about halfway and twist off two small bubbles, one at each end of the balloon. Pull them together and twist connect them.

Clamp the two small bubbles onto your nose, and presto! You look as goofy as a clown.

Tulip

To make a tulip, inflate a pencil balloon only one inch, just enough to make one medium-sized bubble, and then tie it off.

Take the nozzle and push it with one finger inside the bubble all the way to the uninflated portion. Grab hold of the nozzle with the other hand and twist the bubble a couple of revolutions, locking the nozzle in place.

The tulip is now complete. Using different colored balloons you can make several, put them in a vase and have a bouquet.

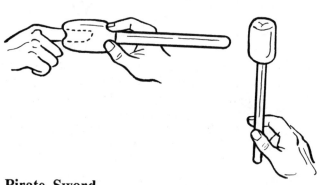

Pirate Sword

Kids love to play with swords. Here is a sword that's fun and safe. Inflate a pencil balloon fully except for about one inch. Twist off one two-inch bubble and one large bubble about 11 inches long. Twist connect points A and B. Bend bubble 3 back and through the loop of bubble 2. Bubble 2 becomes the hand guard and bubble 3 the blade.

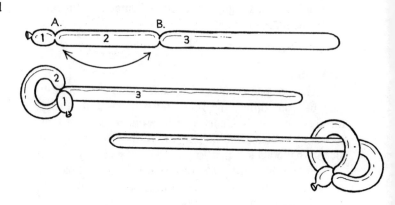

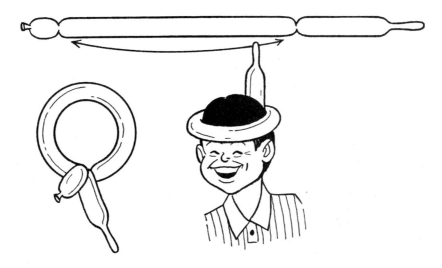

Balloon Hats

Balloon hats are easy to make and popular with kids. I'll describe how to make a basic hat. From that you can create numerous designs of your own.

Inflate a 260 pencil balloon fully except for about two inches. Twist off a two-inch bubble. To determine the size of the next bubble, wrap the rest of the balloon around the head of the intended recipient. Remove the balloon and twist the bubble. Connect points A and B. See the illustration. The basic hat is now complete.

The third bubble will stick up in back, taking on the appearance of a feather in an Indian headband. Turning the Indian hat upside down transforms it into a coonskin balloon cap. Pull the "feather" over the top and connect it to the front of the hat to form a helmet.

These three hats you can make from the basic balloon hat. You can make a variety of others by shaping the "feather" or by attaching additional balloons to it. For example, you can make a dog hat by attaching a balloon dog to the feather or simply molding the feather into the front part of a dog by twisting off a snout and two ears.

BALLOON FUNNIES

At children's parties most entertainers give the children party favors. One of the most popular gifts are balloon animals. Kids expect that an entertainer who specializes in balloons will distribute them before the party is over. This provides you with a relatively inexpensive, yet highly entertaining giveaway.

You should always wait until you are through with the rest of your activities before giving the kids balloons. Balloon giving should be the last thing you do before leaving. Receiving a balloon is one of the highlights of your visit, so it should be saved for last. Also, once kids get hold of a balloon, they will naturally want to play with it. As a consequence, their attention will be divided and you will have trouble controlling them. Balloons are fragile and kids are rough, so some of the bubbly toys will pop or come undone. The kids will insist on a replacement regardless of what else you are doing—which can be very distracting and annoying to both you and the rest of the children. Let the kids enjoy their balloons on their own after you leave.

Creating the balloon animals at the end of your show can be done rather quickly. You can consider this as free time for the kids. Once they have received their balloons they want to play with them, not sit quietly and watch other kids receive theirs. One good way to handle this is to send the children outside after giving them a balloon. You might want to leave a couple of replacements with mom for those that pop.

While you make the children the balloon figures and while they patiently wait, you should use this time as an extension of your show or the party activities. Watching someone create a balloon animal is interesting, for a while, and will interest kids at first, but if you make every kid at a large party a balloon, the ones waiting in line will get restless. Have the making of the balloons be a part of the entertainment. A simple way to do this is to tell jokes and stories while you are making the figures. If you are making a balloon dog, tell a dog joke. If you are making a rabbit, say something related to rabbits. You can tell any kind of joke that relates to what you are making. The stories can last several minutes or be quick one-liners. You can even do stunts or magic tricks involving the creations you make, but don't just hand out balloons like a department store clown. Take the opportunity to entertain with the balloons.

When making balloon figures most people have a tendency to look at their hands and not the audience. If you're talking to the children you should also look at them. This will improve your rapport with the children and help to keep you in control. It also allows them to see your facial expressions. It's okay to glance at your figure now and then, but look up at the audience; they don't want to see the top of your head. If you need to look at your hands for an extended time on a particular figure, hold the balloon up between you and the children so that they can see your face behind the balloon.

I have included some examples of short remarks you can use while making balloon figures for the kids. More ideas can be found in most any joke book.

Have fun with the kids and the creations you make. After making an animal, give it some life by pretending it's alive. Make animal sounds, pet it, and walk the figure to the child.

When making a dog balloon say, "I have a dog that plays classical music on the piano—his Bach is worse than his bite."

When asked if they break a lot, reply, "No, just once."

After making a sad looking bunny say, "Looks like he needs a hoperation."

When making a fish say, "This is a Napoleon fish . . . it's without the bony-part."

When making a skunk (or a dog that looks like a skunk) say, "I made this from in-stink."

"These are my summer balloons . . . some are red, some are blue, some are . . ."

When making a giraffe say, "I crossed a dog with a giraffe. I ended up with a watchdog for the 8th floor."

"I had a dog that didn't have a name. He didn't have any legs and so he wouldn't come if I called him anyway."

If a child asks you what kind of animal are you making, you reply, "A red one."

"My wife bought me a sweater made out of dog hair for my birthday. Only problem is, whenever I pass a fire hydrant my arm flies up!"

"Why did the giraffe cross the road? It was the chicken's day off."

"I went into a restaurant the other day and asked the waitress if she had frog legs. She said, yes, so I asked her to hop into the kitchen and get me a hamburger."

"This is a very lucky bunny. He has FOUR rabbits' feet."

A swan went into a store to buy chapstick. The clerk said, "Cash or check?" The bird replied: "Put it on my bill."

When making an animal and the balloon pops, offer it to a child and say, "Would you like half a dog?" Let the child know you are only joking and quickly make another.

If a balloon pops while you are blowing it up with your mouth, act surprised. Fold your lips under your teeth like you lost your dentures and say, "I blew off my lips!"

If a balloon pops, hand it to a child and say, "Here, this is a worm."

"Do you know what happened to the frog that double-parked? He got toad!"

When asked how come you can twist the balloons so fast, tell them, "I follow the dotted lines."

"What do you get when you cross a cocker spaniel, a poodle, and a rooster? . . . You get a cockerpoodledoo!"

When making a dog, ask the child if he has a dog. If he answers yes, say, "Is it green like this one?"

"Which side of the swan has the most feathers?

. . . The outside!"

"What's the difference between frogs and broccoli? . . . You can't eat broccoli!"

Ask a girl her name. She tells her name (such as Amy). You say, "Amy is an easy name for me to remember because when I was a little girl my name was Amy." This is funny if you are male. Of course, if you are female ask a boy his name and use that.

After inflating a pencil balloon, balance it on your nose.

After making an Indian hat with a feather, tell the children, "This is my Indian hat, it keeps my wig-wam."

Ask the children, "Would you like me to make a dog or a cow?" Wait for response. "I think I will make the dog. The cow is too difficult. Its head is easy to make. It's the udder part that's hard."

Giving names to the animals as you hand them out adds to the fun and makes them more like animated characters rather than just twisted balloons. Think up silly names like: Elmer the Elephant, Jerry Giraffe, Harpo the Hippo, Noodle the French Poodle, Ruby the Rabbit, etc.

BALLOON TRICKS AND ROUTINES

Handing out balloon figures is one thing you may do at a birthday party, but it isn't the only thing. You should also prepare a show or have other activities for the kids involving balloons. You can entertain with balloons in a variety of ways. Tell amusing stories involving balloons, do balloon magic tricks, make balloon puppets and perform a silly skit, have volunteers help you create interesting or unusual figures, show the kids how to make a simple balloon dog or hat, or play balloon games.

The following short skits and gags are samples of what you can do to entertain children using balloons. Several of these can be combined to form a fun and entertaining show. I have purposely selected routines that require very simple balloon creations to illustrate how to use balloons without burdening you with complicated balloon figures. Use these to get started and then work on creating your own clever routines.

Don't give any of your balloon creations to the children until you are finished with your presentation. You may want to bring a large black garbage bag with you to hold your creations while you continue with your show. When you are ready to give out balloons before you leave, you can give these balloons away.

Snap Happy

This is a silly stunt but kids always get a kick out of it. Before inflating a balloon, tell the kids that you need to stretch it a little to loosen it up. Start to stretch the balloon and "accidentally" let one end slip out of your hand snapping the other hand. Yell and jump up and down with pain.

Begin stretching it again. This time let it slip out of the other hand, snapping the opposite hand. Follow this with the same reaction as before.

Now begin to blow up the balloon, holding the nozzle to your lips with one hand and pulling on the nipple end with the other. Release the end of the balloon allowing the balloon to snap your hand—not your face. Pretend that the balloon hit you in the kisser. Holler in pain and make funny faces. Look at the audience with your lips tucked under your teeth as if you lost your dentures and say, "It knocked my lips off!"

When the kids laugh, frown at them. Take the balloon and stretch it like you are aiming to snap one of the kids who is laughing the hardest. "Oh, so you think that was funny eh? Well see if you think this is funny, Mr. Giggles." Aim the stretched balloon at the giggling kid as if to shoot him, but let go of the end in the extended hand. The balloon springs back and snaps you instead. You ham it up as you dance around in pain.

Stand Up

During your performance, blow up a 260 pencil balloon and ask the children if they have ever seen the Egyptian Balloon Trick. Tell them that the last time you did it you were in Egypt and they were laughing so hard that they were rolling in the Nile. Explain to them that all they have to do is to yell "Stand up!" and the balloon will stand up all by itself. Grasp the balloon by each end with two hands, hold it vertically in front of you to make it "stand up" and tell the kids to yell. Release the top end and the balloon falls limp. Repeat again. After failing a second time, tell the kids that manners always work and they should use the word "Please." The third time the kids yell release the bottom of the balloon so it appears to be standing up. It is a simple trick, but it is still great for all ages.

Whiting Tulip

A tulip can be used as a fun game with kids. Tell everyone that the flower you created is magic, and can "smell." Its sense of smell is so good that it can identify those who ate fish-flavored Jell-O for lunch.

Hold the tulip with the thumb and first finger. Ask someone to blow on the flower. As he does so, pinch the stem lightly and push the thumb gently upward, making the movement as inconspicuous as possible. When you do this the flower will drop over, as if dead. Claim that the person must have eaten fish-flavored Jell-O for lunch.

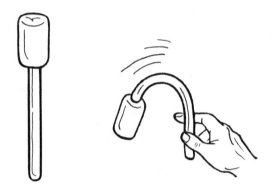

To "revive" the tulip, fan it with your free hand to give it fresh air. Release your grip on the stem slightly and shift the thumb down, allowing the flower to pop back up.

You can end this gag by blowing on it yourself with the tulip dropping over dead. Exclaim, "I don't understand it? I had a peanut butter and jelly sandwich for lunch. Say, come to think of it, the sandwich did taste a little peculiar. Maybe it was the jelly I used. It was a new flavor—the label on the jar said jelly-fish."

Karate Balloon Trick

The birthday mom is a great one for this balloon skit. Have the mom come up to the performing area and show the children her big arm muscles. This is great because she is about to become a "Magical Karate Wizard." Produce a 260 pencil balloon and do some fun bits with the stretching. When it is fully inflated, inform the audience that mom, using her magical karate powers, will karate chop the balloon in half! While the children are laughing, simply twist the inflated balloon several times in the middle and conceal the twist with one of your hands. At the count of three mom karate chops the twist between your fingers of each hand. As her hand comes

down pull sharply on the twist and the balloon will part into two separate balloons that you are now pinching off. This is real magic. Congratulate mom and hand her both balloons. As you do, release the ends and both balloons take off as the children squeal with delight.

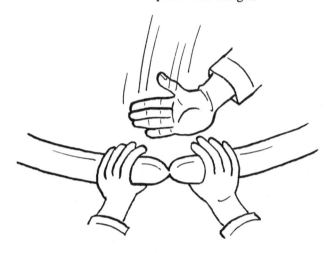

Missing Doggy

Several balloon favorites that I have come across utilize a magic change bag. The unsuspecting participant is promised a dog as you search through the colorful change bag. In one compartment an empty leash is found, in another a collar, and another a doggie toy. The last compartment has a balloon with the tip removed. Of course this causes a laughter riot as the performer attempts to inflate it. Failing in his endeavor, the performer removes another balloon from a pocket, inflates it, and makes a balloon dog.

Balloon Production

This stunt requires a double loaded dove or chick pan—a standard magic trick sold at novelty shops. After the hidden load is produced, the performer repeats the effect and out comes an assortment of colorful worms that can now be inflated and twisted into animal requests from the children.

Appearing Dog

Tell the children you can make a dog, bird, or some other animal magically appear from under a handkerchief. Reach into your pocket and pull out the hanky. As you do also grab an uninflated balloon and conceal it in your hand. Lay the handkerchief out in front of you, secretly over the balloon. Say the magic words and tell the kids the dog is now under the hanky. Since the hanky is lying flat they don't believe you. You prove it by removing the hanky revealing the uninflated balloon.

"See" you say, "I told you I would make a dog appear." They argue saying it's not a dog, its a balloon. You disagree and tell them it is a dog, they just don't recognize it. In order for them to see the dog they must say the magic word. Have them repeat a multi-syllable nonsense word after you, syllable by syllable as you transform the balloon into the dog.

Bouquet of Balloons

This routine creates a nice giveaway item for the birthday child or the hostesses. The idea is to create a bouquet of small flowers in many assorted colors. The bouquet is made from two dozen pencil balloons of assorted colors. Sculpt these balloons into tulips using the directions described earlier. Make 24 more of these simple little flowers in assorted colors to create a dazzling bouquet of balloons. Tie the group together with an uninflated balloon and insert the stems through a hole cut in a small paper dolly to create the appearance of a bouquet of flowers.

Belly Button

One of the funniest effects that you can make is to make a tulip balloon and present it to one of the your audience members. Ask them if they know what it is. Most of the time, the response will be a flower or candy apple. You then say, "Yes, it does look like a flower, but it is really a belly button on a stick." If anyone asks, you can tell them it is an inzee.

Knighthood

This is a short comical routine that involves the performer, a child, and several pencil balloons. From the beginning, you can have a contest to see if your little helper can inflate a balloon faster than you can. If your helper can't, make an extra balloon for the brave lad. Inflate both balloons, leaving a three-inch nipple on each balloon, then twist both into swords. Have your helper kneel so that you can dub him "Sir Lumpy Head" or something to that effect. In return, the helper can dub you the same way. After he dubs you, then you can turn the ceremony into a comical fencing match with many wild possibilities. When finished, use your sword to make a sword belt for the winner. Place the sword into it and send him off stage with applause.

Well Armed

There is probably nothing funnier than watching a birthday child attempt to hold and control eight fully inflated pencil balloons. A great skit for audience participation is to inflate eight balloons and have the child hold several under each arm, some under the chin, some with each hand and several held between the knees , , . what a riot, a great time for pictures! I introduce the child to the audience as the first "Rainbow Brite Cactus." As you remove all eight of the balloons, form them into an octopus and give it to the child. Ask him if they know what an octopus says . . . "I want to hold your hand, your hand, your hand . . ."

Whistling Rocket

Here is a simple activity that lets the balloon fly around the room. Everyone will want to fly these balloons. It makes a fun activity.

Cut a piece of stiff cardboard about $1/2$ x $3/4$". After inflating the balloon, insert the cardboard into the mouthpiece. Release the balloon and let it fly. The balloon will give off a loud whistle as it shoots around the room.

Balloon Assistants

Invite a few of the kids to help you create a balloon figure such as the octopus. Give each of your helpers an uninflated 260 pencil balloon and tell them to blow it up. They try but can't. Ask why they can't do it. They will say it's too hard. Explain to them there is a trick to blowing up balloons. If they stretch the balloon a couple of times first, they will loosen the balloon and make it easier to inflate. Demonstrate by stretching a balloon. As you do this "accidentally" let one end slip and pretend to snap yourself in the face or hand. Yell, "Ouch!" and act out being hurt. Warn your assistants not to let go of the balloon or stretch it too far otherwise it might snap back and hurt someone.

Now, have them stretch their balloons and try inflating them again. They, of course, are still unsuccessful. Tell them there is a second trick that will help them inflate the balloons. The trick is to fill the mouth with air first and, using the cheek muscles force the air into the balloons. Have them all try it. Still they are unsuccessful.

Tell them there is yet another trick. While they are blowing, it is helpful if they pull the end of the balloon out a little to lead the air inside. Have them try that. Again they have no success.

Finally, say that there is one last trick they can do, but if that doesn't work they're out of luck. You then pull out a balloon pump and inflate one of the children's balloons. Hand the inflated balloon back to the child but let go of the nozzle and let it fly. Time it so that just as the assistant is about to grab it, you let it go.

Turn away to get another balloon and blow it up. Start to give it to the second assistant and notice the first doesn't have an inflated balloon. Look puzzled, "I thought I just gave you a balloon. Here take this one." Hand him the balloon without tying it off. As he reaches for it let it go and turn away to get another balloon. After blowing up a third balloon, reach out to give it to the second child and notice the first doesn't have an inflated balloon. Disgusted ask, "What do you keep doing with those balloons?" Look in his hands, under his feet, in his ear, etc. Give him your balloon, again letting it fly away.

Make a fourth balloon and start to give it to the second assistant. Give the kids a funny look. "Are you doing this on purpose?" Realize that you did not tie off the balloon. "Oh, I see the problem. I need to tie the end first." You tie it off. Show everyone it is safe now. This time before handing the first assistant the balloon, push one of your fingers deep into the end of the balloon. As he reaches for it, let the balloon spring from your hand. The pressure of the inserted finger will cause the balloon to take off. Turn and inflate another balloon as if nothing happened.

When you turn around again, he is still without a balloon. "Okay, this time I'll hold it with both hands while you take hold of it." Let your assistant have the balloon.

Inflate everyone's balloon and make the figure. This little bit of business can be very funny if you play along with the kids and act surprised that they cannot blow up the balloons.

They Can Do It

Invite one or two children to help you make a balloon figure. Give them each an uninflated pencil balloon and tell them to blow it up. Wait for them as they struggle. Look at them quizatively and ask, "What's the matter?" They say they can't blow them up. You tell them maybe they got some bad ones and hand them each a new balloon to inflate. They struggle with these without success. "What's the matter?" you ask again. "Are you blowing as hard as you can? Are you using your lips? Are you using your lungs? Are you using your elbows?" "No" they respond. "Well that's the trouble. You have to use elbow grease to blow up these balloons. Here, can you do this?" Move your elbows up and down like a chicken flapping its wings. They follow your actions. "Good, you've got it. Now do that with this." You hand them balloon pumps and have them pump using elbow power.

Once the balloons are inflated, show your volunteers how to make a balloon figure. Select a figure that is easy and that you can do in a matter of seconds. At this stage make yours as quickly as possible. Tell your volunteers to follow along with you as you make the animal. While making the figure, don't look at your assistants. You can continue talking to the audience. Your hands will move so fast that your assistants will not be able to follow you.

When you are finished with your creation, proudly show the audience and turn to the kids and have them show theirs. You look at their balloons, see they haven't done anything, and ask them what's the matter. They will say that you went too fast.

Get another balloon and start over. Your volunteers can use the same balloons. This time make a figure that requires some skill. Make the first bubble slowly and have the volunteers follow. Once the twist is made, hold the bubble with an extended finger but otherwise let go of the bubble. Most people believe that if you twist a bubble it will automatically stay twisted. Holding the balloon this way will make it appear as if it should. Your helpers will find that as they twist the bubble, it just won't stay. After they struggle with this for a moment, continue on.

Show them how to make each twist but go fast enough to keep up the tempo and to keep them puzzled. As the balloons get tighter with each bubble, it is funny to see the expressions of the volunteer's faces as they make the twists. Like all novice balloon sculptors, they will be somewhat apprehensive about the possibility of their balloons popping on them. Their actions can be amusing.

Complete the balloon figure and show yours to the audience. Have your assistants show theirs too. There will be a big difference.

William Tell

Have a volunteer help you with this routine. Make a balloon apple using an apple balloon as described earlier. You will also need a bow and arrow. The bow is made using a 245 balloon or a discarded 260 that can still be inflated most of the way. Inflate the balloon. Tie an uninflated pencil balloon to the ends of the inflated balloon. The bow is finished.

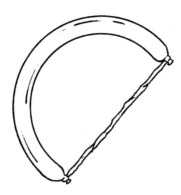

Have your volunteer stand about ten feet away from where you will be standing. Give him the apple and have him balance it on his head. He will have trouble with this because the balloon will tend to fall. Tell him to hold the apple on his head with both hands. You explain to the kids that as he holds the apple you will shoot it off with your bow and arrow.

To make the arrow, inflate a 245 or 260 all the way, but don't tie it off. Place the arrow in the bow and prepare to shoot it at your target. You can play this up. Tell your volunteer there is nothing to be afraid of. You are an expert marksmen and have only killed three of four volunteers in performing this trick.

Have the volunteer close his eyes. Load your arrow and pull back. Count, "Ready, set, go!" Let the arrow fly. The secret to the success of this gag is that the arrow has not been tied off. You do not actually fling the arrow at the volunteer using the bow, but only pretend to. While holding the nozzle on the arrow, pull back the bow, aim, and shoot. When you let go of the nozzle on the arrow, the air in the balloon will project it forward as if it were shot from the bow. But free flying balloons are unpredictable. They whip all around the room in crazy patterns, making the arrow look like a funny trick shot.

Cleo

Make a balloon dog. Give him a name such as Cleo. Tell the audience Cleo is no ordinary balloon dog. He is a highly trained circus dog. The balloon bit is just an act. Cleo will now entertain them with acrobatic skills. Cleo can talk to you silently. The children can't hear his voice but when you hold the dog up to your ear, you can.

"Are you ready to demonstrate your acrobatic skills for the kids Cleo?. . . What's that?" You bring the dog's head toward your ear and listen to what he says. "What do you mean you don't want to? These kids have come a long way to see you perform. You wouldn't want to disappoint them would you?" Cleo whispers in your ear. "I didn't think so. So let's begin." Cleo makes a motion like he is talking. "What's that?" You bring the dog to your ear. "Yes, you have to do ALL your tricks." Continue on with the tricks.

Bend the dog's front legs back to the rear and hold both sets of legs with one hand. Command the dog to "Sit up." As you say this release the front legs and the front half of the dog will spring up as if sitting up. "Good boy, Cleo."

Take a hoop made from a 260 balloon. Bend the dog's front legs back as before. Command Cleo to jump through the hoop. Let go of his front legs and shoot the dog through the hoop. "Excellent job, Cleo."

Bring the dog to the floor and stand him on his legs. Balloon dogs are top heavy and will fall over unless held so continue to hold on until the next command, "Cleo, roll over!" Release your grip and let the dog fall to his side. "That a boy, Cleo."

As the dog is lying on the floor say, "Cleo, play dead!" As you say this stomp on the balloon. The balloon breaks. You remove your foot and look surprised and then remorseful. The kids should be rolling with laughter by this time.

"Cleo, what happened to you?" Pick up the deflated balloon and hold it up by two fingers. Surprised, you look at Cleo and say, "What's that?" Turn to the audience and joyfully announce, "He's still alive!" Speaking to the dog, "Cleo, is there anything I can do for you?" Listen to him. "Oh, you have another trick you want to do? Do you feel up to it? Well, okay." You listen to Cleo's directions repeating them to the audience. "You want me to hold you with both hands." Hold each end of the balloon with different hands. "Pull my hands out . . . like this? Okay, now what?. . . Let got of my left hand." As you say that hold the balloon with your right hand as you release your grip of the left hand. The balloon snaps your hand and you yell with exaggerated pain. Cleo has struck back.

Bumblebee

When making the bumblebee described on page 109, you can have fun with the kids after making the wings. The wings look like a figure 8. Before attaching them to the bee body try to use them in as many different ways as you can think of. For example, put them on your nose as if they were eyeglasses. This is sure to get some chuckles. You can also use them to make a bow tie, ear muffs, angel wings, rabbit ears, a duck's beak, and handcuffs.

Sticky Creatures

After making a few balloon animals, you can give them a charge of static electricity and stick them around the room. You create the static electricity by rubbing a balloon vigorously on your head or a volunteer's head. Now place it on the wall. It will stay put. This works best on fine dry hair.

Before doing this, you might ask the kids if any of them use glue to keep their hair in place. If no one volunteers, select one likely candidate and say, "Your hair is so nicely combed I bet your mother uses glue on it." Ask if you can test your theory. If he or she says yes, then rub a balloon animal in the child's hair and see if it sticks to the wall.

You can also tell the kids that your brain will teach the balloon to stick to the wall. Rub the balloon in your hair and then place it on the wall.

Rub another balloon in your hair and start to place it on the wall. Instead of the balloon clinging to the wall, your head is "pulled" to the wall by static electricity.

The Transformation

Hold up an inflated pencil balloon and tell your audience you will transform this ordinary lifeless balloon into a furry rabbit. Wave a magic wand and then twist the balloon into a dog. Proudly show the dog and say, "A rabbit!" Do a double take. "Wait a minute. This isn't a rabbit. It looks more like a dog!"

Disgusted say, "That's what I get for buying a cheap magic wand. Sometimes I don't get the animal I want. Let me try it again." Wave the wand over another inflated pencil balloon. Prepare the wand so that it has a small pin attached to the end and puncture the balloon with it as you say the magic words.

Continue to hold the balloon by the nozzle and act surprised. "Yakes, a snake! . . . It looks like a baby rattler . . . Ouch! It bit me." Drop the balloon and madly stomp on it.

Flying Elephant

Make a balloon elephant. You can do this by making a dog with a short tail and a long nose. Give the nose a little bit of a curl by bending and shaping it. When you're finished, it will look like an elephant on a diet.

Call your elephant Dumbo. Ask the kids why you named him that. After they respond say, "I call him Dumbo because he is a flying elephant!" As you say that toss the balloon figure in the air and using your balloon pump positioned under the balloon and try to keep the elephant floating as if flying.

Follow this bit by making another animal such as a giraffe or aardvark. When you finish making it, toss it up and pump air under it and say, "Look, it's Dumbo the flying giraffe!"

After pumping furiously to keep the balloon afloat, look hot and tired. You can silently indicate this by sticking out your tongue, panting, and waving your hand near your face to cool you off. Look at the pump, indicate you have an idea. Point the pump at your face and pump cool air at yourself as you breath a sigh of relief.

Comical Balloon Pump

This gag takes a little preparation. Get one of those containers that look like peanut brittle but conceal a spring snake inside. Attach a pump nozzle or funnel to the lid of your snake can, drill a hole in the other end, and mount a fake handle in the hole. Spray paint the entire "pump" like a real one and you are ready to go.

During your show, say you just bought this super powerful pump that inflates an entire balloon in one second and you're anxious to try it. Grab your gimmicked pump and try to inflate a balloon, but the pump does not work. Look confused and exasperated. It must be clogged up. Tell the kids you'll take the top off to see what's clogging it up. As you pull the lid off, the snakes jump out at you. You scream and jump back startled.

Where Did It Go?

Take a balloon and put it on the nozzle of your pump. While you are doing this, don't pay attention to your hands or the pump, but look at the audience and busy yourself talking to them. Get involved in telling them something. As you are talking, nonchalantly drop the balloon on the floor and begin to pump on the handle. Keep looking at the kids and talking, assuming the balloon is being inflated. The kids will tell you there is no balloon on the pump. You ham it up and say of course there is, then look at the pump. Act surprised. "Where did it go?" Look

up and side to side. As you do, step on the balloon to hide it from your view. They will tell you it's on the floor. You look down and don't see it. Look under your arms, up your sleeve, in your pockets. The kids will tell you it's under your foot. You pick up the opposite foot. "It's not there," you say and begin look around again in different places. As you do, step on the balloon with the other foot. All this time the kids have been telling you to look under the "other" foot. Finally, you lift your "other" foot, but it is not there. The kids tell you it's not under that foot, it's under the other foot. You tell them you just lifted the "other" foot and they're just teasing you. Slowly you peek under that foot and you find the balloon. Turning to the audience you say, "Why didn't you tell me it was under my *other* foot?"

You can play this up in a variety of ways. One is to have a fake foot or old shoe with the words "other foot" written on it. When the kids tell you it's under the other foot, pull this foot out and look at the bottom of it. Stuck to the bottom of this foot could be a balloon just like the one you dropped. You looked surprised to find the balloon there and ask the kids how they knew it was under your other foot. They will continue to tell you it's still under your other foot and you can argue with them and tell them you just looked and found it. Finally, lift the correct "other foot" to reveal the original balloon.

Spare Finger

If a balloon pops while you are blowing it up, shake the hand that was holding the balloon and cry in pain. Show the kids your fingers. Bend one finger back to hide it. "I blew off my finger!" Reach into you pocket and pretend to pull out a spare finger. Put it on and your hand is restored. "Balloon workers need lots of spare fingers." Reach into your pocket and pull out a thumb tip (available at any magic shop) and show them that you really do carry spares.

Disappearing Balloon

If part of the balloon figure you're working on pops but leaves some bubbles still intact, hand it to a child and say. "Would you hold this for me?" As you give the balloon to the child, you turn away as if to look for some something to fix the balloon. In the meantime the balloon withers away. You look back at the balloon ready to fix it and say, "Hey what did you do to my balloon?" Grab the balloon and look sad.

If the balloon happened to fly from your helper's hand, you can pretend to look for it. Search behind the child's ears, under his sleeves, etc. The kids will point out to you where it went and you look everywhere to the amusement of the audience until you find it.

Balloon Magic

This is a silly, but fun, stunt. Inflate a balloon and tie it off. Ask the kids if they would like to see you make the balloon disappear. They will say yes. You take out a magic wand and wave it around the balloon while saying some magic words. On the end of the wand you have a tiny pin. Poke the balloon with the pin. Presto! The balloon has disappeared.

It Looks Like A Dog

Make a balloon dog and ask the audience "What's this?" They will say a dog. "Yes, a dog. I can make dozens of different types of animals." Make another dog and ask "What's this?" They will say a dog. You say, "No, it's a cow!" You continue, "I can make dozens of different animals, but they all look like dogs."

Make another dog and ask, "What's this?" They may give several responses. "No, It's an elephant. Do you know how to tell the difference between an elephant and a dog? . . . The elephant has a shorter tail."

"Now do you want to see me make a brontosaurus?" Make another dog. "There, the brontosaurus . . . hey, you have to use some imagination."

Balloon Blowing Contest

Have a contest between one of the bigger kids (or even a parent) and a much smaller one. You could also match a boy against a girl.

Give each of the contestants a balloon and tell them they are going to have a contest to see who has the strongest lungs. The one who can inflate the balloon the fastest is the winner.

Give the underdog a normal balloon. Give the larger contestant a balloon that has a tiny hole. Start the contest. The underdog will inflate the balloon, but his opponent will not be able to accomplish much.

Act surprised that the larger contestant was so unsuccessful. Have them try again with different balloons. Give the bigger kid another balloon with a hole. The results will be the same. The audience will get a kick out of seeing the underdog come out on top.

Conceal a balloon in your hand that matches the one with the hole. To prove to the audience that there is nothing wrong with the larger contestant's balloon say to

him, "Shall I *blow up* your balloon?" Take his balloon and pretend to inflate it. You actually inflate the concealed balloon. As you blow it up, pop it. "Wow! That's what I really call BLOWING UP a balloon!"

Balloon Blow Up

For this routine you need the cardboard core from a empty roll of paper towels. Paint it red and plug up the ends. Stuff string at one end to simulate a fuse. Write the words TNT along the side.

You address the audience, "Would you like me to make you some balloon animals? I'll need to blow up a balloon first, don't I?" Look at the audience and nod your head so they all respond with a "Yes." "Okay in order to blow up a balloon, I need a balloon and . . ." pull out a pencil balloon, "a big stick of dynamite." Pull out the TNT. "How else am I going to blow it up?"

"What's that? Oh I can blow it up with my mouth? Hmm . . . I never thought of that. Okay I'll blow up this balloon with my mouth." Tilt your head back place the balloon on your lips and blow hard enough to project (blow up) the balloon up into the air. "There I BLEW the balloon UP into the air. Oh . . . you want the air inside the balloon? How can I do that? This little opening is too small." Look at the nozzle.

"I know, I need someone with a little mouth to blow the air into it. Do you know anyone with a mouth smaller than mine?" Open mouth wide. "My mouth isn't that big . . . is it?"

Ask someone to come up to help you. "Your mouth looks a lot smaller than mine, would you come up here and help me inflate this balloon?" Have the volunteer attempt to inflate a 260 pencil balloon. These balloons are very difficult to inflate. "I see you're having problems . . . I guess your mouth is too big too. Anybody have a smaller mouth than this volunteer?" Have a second volunteer come up to help you.

"Let's see if you can blow up this balloon." He tries but fails. Thank volunteer and send him back to his seat.

"It looks like everybody's mouth is too big. Now how are we going to get air into it?. . . I know! I'll use a balloon blower upper." Pull out the TNT again. "No, I don't mean this. I mean the sooper-dooper high-tech polymer-coated, nuclear brain powered air injector!" Pull out an ordinary air pump. "Otherwise known as an air pump. With this baby I can blow up anything." Pretend to stick pump into your ear and pump, as you do stick out your tongue and razz.

"This pump has a small enough mouth to fit the balloon and blow it up." You now inflate the balloon until it pops. Jump, "Yaaah! . . . What was that?" Look bewildered. "Oh, I know . . . it BLEW UP! . . . Well, isn't that what you wanted me to do . . . blow up a balloon?

"What? You mean you wanted me to inflate the balloon with air. Well, why didn't you say so in the first place—that's easy!"

The Mugwump

Twist a pencil balloon into a shapeless mass as if trying to create a balloon animal. You can put eyes and mouth on it. "Do you know what this is?" You will get various answers. "Nope! It's a balloon! Ha, ha . . . who said it looked like a dog? I've never seen a dog look this bad."

Untie the balloon and ask, "Now what is it?. . . It's a mess, that's what it is. Or it might be a snake that got run over by a herd of motorcycles."

Start twisting the balloon as you continue to talk. "I will now create for you a very unique animal. Can you guess what it is?" You will get various answers. As you talk twist the balloon into any dog-like figure; the aardvark works well here. "No . . . No . . . You've probably never heard of it because it is very shy around people and always hides. Its called a mugwump. It gets its name from the fact that when it sits on a fence, one of its favorite things to do, it will hang its mug over one side and it's wump over the other."

GAMES AND ACTIVITIES
Animal Sounds

While making balloon animals you may have the children involved in some activity. For each animal you make have the children act out the animal. If you make a dog, for example, have the kids give you their best imitation of dogs. While they are doing this, you can leisurely create your balloon dog.

Here is similar activity. As you make a figure, have the children try to guess what it is. When they think they know they must pantomime that animal until you are finished. Make sure to tell them what it is if they don't all guess right.

Do It Yourself

A fun activity the kids will enjoy is making their own balloon figures. Teach them how to make something simple such as a balloon dog or hat. The kids will love creating their own. The figures may not all turn out like expected but the kids will still enjoy themselves.

After making a figure, boys will often will take the balloons apart and turn them into swords, especially if you made a sword during your visit. They can have a lot of fun with balloon sword fights.

Balloon Puppets

Inflate an apple or bee (321) balloon. Follow the directions on page 110 and make an apple. Draw a face on the balloon. Drape a hanky over your hand and position the apple balloon onto your index finger. Under the hanky your thumb and middle finger become the puppet's arms. Secure the hanky to the hand by putting rubber bands or thimbles on the thumb and middle finger.

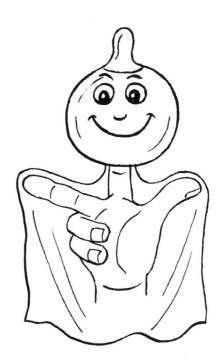

Balloon Juggling

This is a simple fun activity for the kids. Give the kids two or three round balloons and have them juggle them. The older kids may be able to handle three balloons but give the little ones just two. They will not juggle in any particular pattern like in ball juggling, but will simply try to keep the balloons from falling to the ground. This is a good activity especially after you have done some real juggling, although not necessarily with balloons.

Hot Air

Find out who has the most hot air. Invite some of the kids to participate in a hot air contest. Give each contestant a round balloon. Tell them to inflate the balloon as much as they possibly can using just one breath. Once they have inflated their balloons, choose the winner by measuring the circumference of the balloons with a tape measure.

Laughing Balloon

Everybody stands in a circle. You instruct them to start laughing as soon as you toss a balloon into the air. They are to continue laughing until someone catches it. At that moment, they have to be absolutely quiet. The person who catches the balloon tosses it back up. If anyone doesn't laugh when the balloon is in the air, or is caught laughing after the balloon is caught, that person drops out of the circle.

To make the game more interesting, the one who has the balloon can try to fake the others by making some false tosses—swinging the balloon up as if to throw it but holding on. Or when catching the balloon, he can stop before grabbing it. This will fool others into stopping or starting to laugh prematurely.

Balloon Stomp

This is a wild activity the kids will enjoy. You need a playing area large enough for the kids to move around freely. Mark boundaries so that players cannot chase each other down the street. Inflate one round or airship balloon for each contestant. Tie a three-foot piece of string to each balloon and attach the other end of the string to a leg of each child. You're now ready to play.

The object of this contest is for the players to stomp on each others' balloons and try to pop them. The player who keeps his balloon alive the longest is the winner. Breaking can be done only by stomping, no kicking allowed. Stepping on another player's toes is not allowed.

Players cannot go outside the boundary lines. Players cannot grab or hold others. When a player's balloon breaks, he is out of the game and cannot stomp on any more balloons.

If you play this game outside, sharp grass and gravel can easily cause the balloons to burst. To cut down on spontaneous balloon breakage, use large 12- or 14-inch balloons and do not inflate them all the way, which will make them more durable.

Balloon-of-War

Mark a boundary line on the floor with a strip of masking tape. Have two contestants get down on all fours, one player on each side of the boundary line. Hold a round balloon about three feet off the ground directly above the boundary line. Each player positions himself on either side of the balloon and a couple of feet back from the boundary line.

When you drop the balloon, each contestant is to try to get the balloon to land on the opponent's side of the line. The catch is that the contestants can only use lung power to move the balloon. No contact with the body is allowed. Once the balloon hits the ground, the game is over.

Secret Message

The object of this activity is to break a balloon to get a secret message hidden inside and to follow its directions.

On several slips of paper write something for the contestants to do or act out. Examples would be: Act like a monkey eating a banana, Yodel like a Swiss mountain climber, dance like a ballerina, sing Yankee Doodle, roll head-over-heels, tell a joke, make a funny face. Try to get the kids to act as goofy as possible—the goofier the better. You could also put a small piece of candy in some balloons. This game would make a good Halloween "Trick or Treat" game. The contestants would get a treat or do a trick.

You can have the kids break the balloons one at a time in a variety of ways—stomping on them, sitting on them, poking them, etc.

Balloon Squash

This game is a race to pop a balloon. Each contestant is given an uninflated round balloon. When you give the signal, players are to blow up the balloons and then sit on them. The first player to pop his balloon wins. The secret of this game is to put enough air in the balloon to make it pop easily when sat on.

Tug-of-War

Using an inflated 260 balloon, two contestants try to pull each other over a boundary line. Mark the boundary on the floor with masking tape. Have each player step back as far as they can from the boundary line while holding the end of the balloon with one hand. Players must stand on one leg, holding the bent leg with the free hand.

The player to pull his opponent over the boundary line first wins. If a player falls or touches the ground with his bent leg, he is automatically out. If the balloon pops without a clear winner, it's a draw.

Hot Air Balloon

The object of this game is for the players to keep their balloons in the air using their breath. Give each contestant an inflated round balloon. With their heads bent back, have them balance the balloon on their lips. On your signal they will blow the balloons into the air and must keep them afloat. The one who can keep his balloon off the ground the longest is the winner.

To add some excitement, players can blow opponent's balloons away from their owners to make it more difficult for them to keep them afloat. No one is allowed to purposely touch the balloons.

Balloon Toss

Have players sit or stand in a large circle. Have one player in the circle hold an inflated round balloon. Another player will stand in the middle of the circle. This player is blindfolded and given a whistle or other noisemaker. The player in the middle signals when the game is to start or stop by blowing on the noisemaker. When the signal to start is given, the player holding the balloon bats it with his hand to the player on his left. That player catches it and bats it to the player on his left. The balloon is batted around the circle until the player in the middle signals with the noisemaker to stop. The player having the balloon in his position when the whistle is blown drops out of the circle and the game continues. The balloon is considered in the position of a player as soon as his neighbor bats it to him and remains his until he bats it to the next player. It is to the player's advantage to grab and bat the balloon away as fast as possible. The last player remaining in the game is the winner.

RESOURCES

Many books and booklets describe how to make a wide variety of balloon figures. Some of the books are basic and the figures are easy to learn. Others are written for advanced balloonologists and contain a surprisingly creative variety of figures including such figures as the Pink Panther, E.T., Ninja Turtle, unicorn, swan laying an egg, parrot on a perch, dog riding a bicycle, Snoopy on a unicycle. Some of these can be learned with a little patience while others will require some dedicated effort to master. Some of the authors have also included balloon jokes and gags.

Most balloon books are printed in limited quantities and are not available in bookstores or libraries, but can be found in magic shops or mail order catalogs. See the appendix for a list of recommended books.

A WORD OF CAUTION

In this chapter I have explained many of the wonderful aspects of balloons. There is one major problem, however, that you must be aware of if you plan on working with balloons. Never give balloons to children who are younger than three years of age. Young children will stick anything into their mouths, and they have been known to choke and suffocate on balloons. A devastating event for any birthday party!

Be cautious to whom and where you pass out balloons. Give balloons out only when there are no younger children present. Even if you only give balloons to the older children, if younger ones are around, they are at risk. Balloons pop and balloon fragments scatter. These can be picked up by a child and put into the mouth.

Fortunately, this type of accident does not occur often. If it happens to you, however, once is too often and could result in a lawsuit from the parents. If you work with balloons, you should have insurance for your protection. Some entertainers get around possible legal consequences by giving the balloons to the parents and having them take the responsibility of distributing them to the children. This may avoid some of the legal problems, but it still will not make a nasty accident any more unpleasant.

Some parents will want balloons at their party regardless of the apparent risks. If you work with balloons, you should find out if any young children will be present at the party and warn them about the hazards. You might request that the parents limit the party guests by age. Or you can use balloons in your show, but don't give them away. Balloons are great entertainment and make wonderful party favors, but it is best to give them out only when no very young children are present.

Chapter 9

ENTERTAINING WITH FACE PAINTING

Face painting has become a popular form of entertainment at birthday parties. Face painting is my specialty. My name is Marcela Murad and I have been face painting professionally for the past 20 years. My character, "Mama Clown," has entertained at thousands of birthday parties with magic, balloons, puppets, storytelling, and juggling. However, my face painting is what children and adults remember the most and is also my most requested activity.

Face painting is safe, fun, and easy to do. Unlike a few years ago, nowadays there's a great variety of books and videos available on the subject. Some are very simple and practical like my own book, *Put On A Happy Face*, and others are very advanced such as the ones put out by Fardell Paints. If you are artistically inclined, face painting will provide you a way to develop your talents and to create your own unique style. If you aren't, don't worry, you can keep it easy and simple as the kids will enjoy it just the same. The sparkle in their eyes and the expressions in their faces as they see themselves in the mirror will become your reward for a job well done.

In this chapter I will give you guidelines for choosing materials and how to use them. We'll discuss topics such as, preparing the face, sanitation techniques, crowd control, how to make face painting fun and entertaining, and other valuable tips when working birthday parties.

MATERIALS
Paints

The number one rule when choosing paint is: *do not use any kind of paint that is not made specifically for face painting*. Some of the chemicals in those paints are made to be used on other surfaces, not on the delicate skin of a child, and it can cause irritation and allergic reactions.

Due to an increased popularity of this art form, manufacturers of face painting materials have created many different types of water-soluble cosmetic paints, as well as brushes, glitter, and books on the subject. Therefore, there's a large variety of paints available to the face painter today from inexpensive crayons you can purchase at your local drugstore to professional kits designed to fit specific needs. Keep in mind that the highest quality paints produce the best results, last the longest, and are the safest to use.

My kit contains a combination of Kryolan, Snazaroo, Ben Nye, Mehron, and Fardell Paints, all of which have bright colors, do not fade rapidly, dry quickly, and do not smear easily, but most important, they are safe to use.

Some of these paints such as the Kryolan and the Snazaroo have a creamy texture and are easy to work with. The Ben Nye pancake paints, such as the ones in their pallettes, are dry but work well and last longer. Their liquid and glitter paints, as well as the Mehron liquids and Fardell paints require no water, but have a tendency to dry up more rapidly. I like the Mehron Starblend white to cover the entire face.

The paints are all sold in palettes of different sizes or in individual containers. For a person new to face painting, a six- or a twelve-color palette is a good start. For those who consider themselves professional in this field, designing a kit to fit your specific needs will be the most practical and economical way to go.

Basic face painting and makeup supplies are available at most good novelty, toy, and drugstores. You can find an excellent selection at theatrical or dance supply stores. You can also get excellent materials from a number of mail order dealers.

Brushes

A good brush is your most important tool and the one that has the most influence on your results. As with the paints, manufacturers offer a wide range of styles and sizes to choose from. Unfortunately, it is necessary to experiment and to test all of them to discover which ones work the best for you.

A good-quality nylon or sable hair brush is the best choice. Inexpensive craft and hobby brushes, as well as cotton swabs, will make the task more difficult and cumbersome.

The brushes I have chosen for my own use consist of a mixture of brands, styles, and sizes. They consist of three flat and three round brushes in large, medium, and small sizes. I use a very fine brush for detailed work, such as drawing the intricate lines in a tattoo. The medium size is the most practical for the majority of the artwork. Large brushes are best for big bold lines or for covering large areas of skin. A brush called a *scrubber brush* I found at the stencil department of a local craft store, is short, hard, is best for making small dots.

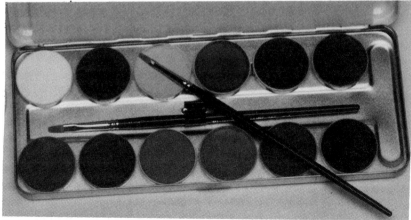

Paint for faces.

I keep my brushes in a pencil box, wrapped in a baby wipe or napkin. I use the same brushes for all colors, rinsing them off with water and wiping them off with a baby wipe. If you are concerned about hygiene as far as using the same brush on or near a child's lips, use a cotton swab when applying paint to this area.

Sponges

Sponges are used when you need to apply a large amount of paint to the face. Some faces, like the clown's, require a coat of white paint over the entire face. A sponge can hold more paint and can spread the paint more evenly over large areas than a brush, producing better results. Use regular cosmetic sponges available at your local drugstore or makeup supplier. As with the brushes, keep a good supply on hand.

I also use a coarse sponge called a stipple sponge for imitating a three-day beard on the pirate and hobo clown. A small piece of paper towel dipped in the paint can be used to create a similar effect.

Cotton pads can also be used to apply large amounts of paint to the face. The advantage of cotton pads is that you can discard the pads after use, which is more sanitary and saves you time in cleanup. The disadvantage is that cotton may leave some fuzz on the child's face. Make sure to use cotton pads and not cotton balls because the balls come apart too easily.

Container of Water

You will need water to moisten your paints and to clean your brushes and sponges. Use a small container of water (a plastic cup works fine) to work with as you paint and a larger container to hold clean water. When the water in the small container becomes murky, dump it out and replace it with clean water. Some painters like to use opaque containers so the murky waste cannot be seen.

Baby Wipes

Baby wipes are used for cleaning brushes, kid's dirty faces, partially painted faces of kids who changed their minds, your hands, mistakes, your working surface, and just about anything that needs a sparkling touch. I never leave home without them and neither should you!

  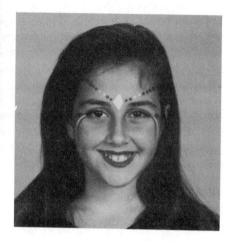

Tiger, space woman, and Indian princess.

Headbands and Hair Clips

Headbands, hair clips, or bobby pins serve to keep hair away from a child's face while it is being painted. They're especially nice outside on windy days when hair is less controllable.

Towel

You may want to put a towel or cape over the children to keep from dripping paint on their clothes. You can use an ordinary towel or a plastic shampoo cape sold at beauty supply stores.

Even though paint will wash out of clothing, the children or their parents may not want them to walk around all day with spotted clothes. If some paint does get on clothes, you can easily wash it off with a paper towel or baby wipe while it's still wet. A small towel on your lap will also prevent your own clothes from getting dirty.

Blushes

I used to use the tip of my finger dipped in red paint as blush for all the designs that required it. Then I discovered that a powder blush was much more effective. I tried some of the commercial brands found at the local drugstore, but none of them seemed as bright or as easy to apply as I wanted them to be. I'm currently using one designed for theatrical use manufactured by Kryolan. The color I use is called Youth Red. Today, all the paint manufacturers offer a variety of shades. If you decide to go with a store brand, choose the brightest red or pink you can find.

Mirror

The biggest satisfaction that comes from face painting is watching the expressions on children's faces as they look at themselves in the mirror. Don't waste this precious moment with a tiny pocket mirror. Use one that is clear and sturdy. Wipe it off as often as needed and, to avoid scratches, make a cover or case to carry it in.

One thing I like to do is glue a picture of a monkey or a funny-looking creature on the back of the mirror. It's fun to ask the children if they'd like to see how they look. Flipping the mirror over, I show them the funny side. It always gets a laugh. Recently, while shopping at a local mall, I found a mirror that already had a built-in frame on the back side. This works even better as I can change the picture from time to time.

When you work a big crowd, a large mirror on a stand or even a table top mirror will add a lot to your face painting experience. Besides the fact that the children truly enjoy looking at themselves, the mirror can serve as an amusement for the other children waiting their turn.

Decorate the back of your mirror using your logo, name, or even your picture. It's important for your client and guests to remember your name.

Carrying Case

You will need a carrying case for all your materials. A decorated lunch box or fishing tackle box works very well. Actually, any brightly decorated box or container big enough to hold all of your supplies will do. I prefer one with a good handle.

Because face painting is a full-time job for me, I have designed a carrying case to fit my specific needs.

My case is red with a yellow handle, which matches my costume, and is made out of heavy plastic. Since I use a large quantity of paints in a short time, I put my paints in 2-ounce containers such as the plastic ones used to hold silver dollars. You may purchase suitable containers from a coin dealer or any art supply store. I refill these containers as they get low and they hold up for a long time. To save my time as I set up and pack up, I label all the container tops with a permanent magic marker. Periodically it is important to give your case an overhaul—clean and arrange everything to make it look neat. The appearance of your equipment is important because it reflects on your character and work.

For a while, I carried the containers of paint loose in the case. This used to annoy me because they would rattle. To solve the problem, I purchased a piece of foam which I cut up to fit the inside of the case. I also cut out enough spaces in the foam to fit each container—plus a place for the sponges and brushes. The mirror, baby towels, and a small terry cloth lay neatly on top of it all.

After many years experimenting with the best way to carry my supplies, I designed a complete kit like the one described above with accessories that could be purchased by other face painters. For further information on these kits, contact Silly Farm Products, a division of Mama Clown and Company, 230 South 14th Ave, Hollywood, FL 33020, telephone (954) 923-6013 or E-mail: Mamaclown2@aol.com.

Extras

To complement my Indian and Indian Princess designs, I carry a bag of feathers and bobby pins to attach to the hair. They make a beautiful finishing touch adding pizzazz to the designs. Feathers can be purchased very inexpensively at local craft stores.

Recently, I began using rhinestones which I apply with a drop of ProFace glue. I use them to make jewelry like necklaces and bracelets, a new trend that has been very well received.

Hair Streak is becoming popular. It's similar to mascara, but comes in a variety of colors including neon. Hair Streak is water soluble and can be applied to the hair to complement the designs. It can also be used as an add-on to your face painting when charging per person as in a fundraiser.

APPLYING PAINT

For best results you should start with a completely clean face. Since face painting is often done at parties and other gatherings, the face you will be painting will often be smudged with candy, food, or dirt. Wipe the face clean with a baby wipe before you apply any paint.

Long hair can get in the way. Because it is bothersome to hold it up out of the way, I use a headband or hair clips to keep hair off the face and away form the paint until the makeup dries.

Full face foundation and heavy shading are best applied with sponges. Lines and fine designs are applied with brushes. Cotton swabs can also be used but the results won't be as smooth and crisp as with a brush. Use a thin brush for fine lines and thicker brushes for coarse lines and markings. Most face designs require the use of some lines.

Paint takes a minute or so to dry on the face. Before it dries it can mix and smear, especially if too much water was used on the brush. Be careful that neither the child, nor you, accidentally touch the face until the paint is dry. Let each color dry before adding another color to avoid unintentionally mixing the colors on the face and producing a third unwanted color.

Thin lines can be applied with a narrow brush. Medium lines require a thicker brush or a Q-tip. Use the thicker brush to color any large area.

Use plenty of paint on the brush but not so much that it becomes messy or drippy. With a good quality paint, such as the ones mentioned, a little goes a long way! It is better to retrieve a little at the time to avoid any waste. Brushes can be washed off in a cup of water. Rinse the paint off the brush before applying another color. Q-tips don't rinse well so use a new one for each color.

For best results when painting lines, use long even strokes rather than short choppy strokes. If you make a mistake, simply wipe off the paint with a wet paper towel and try again.

Kids are naturally wiggly. Encouraging them to hold still will help but won't totally prevent smears from happening. To reduce movement as you paint, place your free hand on top of the child's head or under the chin. You may also steady your painting hand by resting your little finger against the side of the child's head as you paint fine detail.

Be very careful when applying paint around the eyes. When you paint people's faces, be sure to tell them to hold still. As a precaution when you paint near the eyes, have the children keep their eyes closed.

A sudden twist of a child's head can cause you to put paint where it wasn't intended. To avoid getting paint in the eyes or poking someone with the brush, you may want to avoid painting near the eyes. It is also helpful if you hold the child's head steady with your free hand as you apply paint near the eyes.

The skin around the eye is delicate, so apply paint with gentle strokes. Generally, I would recommend that you avoid coloring the eyelids unless you cover them with a sponge when applying a base coat over the entire face.

TATTOOS

A tattoo is a simple drawing such as a small rainbow, flower, butterfly, or unicorn. Tattoos can be painted on the cheeks, the arms, and even the knees and feet. A single tattoo such as a rainbow or flower on the cheek serves as a quick and easy face painting design. Some people use tattoos as their sole avenue for face painting, however, a full simple face is faster and more practical as it doesn't contain the small details. If you are good with a small brush and with details, tattoos alone are a lot of fun and kids love them just as much. Once I painted happy faces on the big toes of some kids at a party and they went crazy making their toes talk to each other.

Tattoos are good for children who do not want to have their faces painted. Assure them that you will never do anything they don't want you to do. Offer to paint something on their hands. By seeing a small design on their hands first, they will usually lose their fear of having their faces painted. Some children may be afraid that the paint will not come off. Draw a small design on your own hand then remove it with a baby wipe to show them how easy it comes off and that there's absolutely nothing to worry about. When they realize that there's nothing to fear the majority of them will let you paint their faces.

A tattoo can be just about anything you can draw. The simplest are shapes such as hearts, stars, or rainbows. Except for snakes, animals are a little bit more difficult and so are superheroes and cartoons.

Look in the children's section of the local book store for instructional books that teach drawing on a child's level, as they are the easiest to learn. Some craft stores also offer a great variety of books and videos to learn how to draw cartoons.

SANITATION

Since you will paint several faces at a single sitting, you should keep your equipment as sanitary as possible. Always wash your brushes and sponges before you use them. Dishwashing liquid works well. And always rinse your brushes and sponges thoroughly after painting each face.

As an extra precaution, I would recommend that you use at least two sets of brushes and sponges. After using one set of brushes, rinse them off thoroughly and then soak them in a small container with a 50-50 mixture of

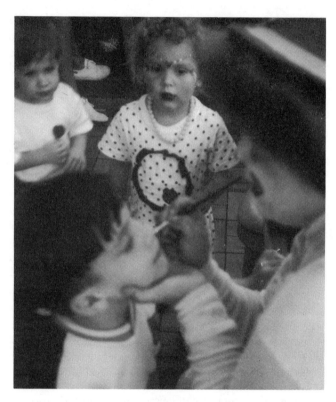

water and rubbing alcohol. This will help keep the brushes sterile. While one set of brushes is soaking, use the other set. Alternate brushes for each face you paint. After the brushes have soaked, rinse the alcohol mixture off them with clean water before dipping them back into the paint.

The most sanitary method would be to use cotton swabs and cotton pads in place of brushes and sponges. Once they have been used, they are discarded so that each face begins with unused materials. Also, cleanup is easier since you don't have to wash out any brushes. Cotton swabs, however, can't produce fine even lines like a brush can. So, you may consider using a combination of alcohol, brushes, sponges, and cotton swabs and pads.

REMOVING PAINT

Removing water-soluble paint is easy, just use ordinary soap and water.

If the paint gets on your clothes, wash it with laundry detergent along with your regular wash. Some colors may be a little stubborn so it is advisable to wipe off as much spilled paint as possible from the clothes before it dries.

Be sure to tell the children and their parents that the paint will wash off with soap and water. (Sometimes, as a joke, I tell them that it comes off with spaghetti and meatballs!) Many parents may assume that the paint, like theatrical and cosmetic makeup, will need to be removed with cold cream or other makeup removers. Explaining to parents that the paints you use are water-soluble and will easily wash off will relieve their apprehensions.

Some children are reluctant to be painted thinking that the paint, like house paint, will not come off. You can show them how easily the paint washes off by applying some to your own skin and washing it off.

PAINTING FACES AT BIRTHDAY PARTIES

Because of the rapidly growing popularity of face painting, family entertainers such as clowns, storytellers, and magicians are adding face painting to their skills. As an entertainer, I get a great deal of personal enjoyment and satisfaction from face painting. After reading this book, you may also be interested in entertaining and earning extra money face painting.

Your first step is to practice creating your favorite designs. Look through some of the many books on face painting. Gather a few of your youngest relatives together. If you don't have any available, borrow your little neighbors and friends. When it comes to face painting, kids are easy to please. Even if your first clown face looks more like Dracula, they will love it. The only way to acquire the feeling, speed, experience, and confidence to master the art is to do it. Practice makes perfect.

Wardrobe

What type of clothing should you wear when you face paint? If you are a clown or family entertainer desiring to add face painting to your repertoire, just wear your normal performing outfit. If you are strictly a face painter, any comfortable and colorful outfit will do.

A unisex outfit may consist of a pair of comfortable pants, a smock with a design that resembles splashed paint, and maybe a painter's hat with your name on it. A friend of mine dresses herself up as a fairy princess and the children love her.

During special holidays you may want to dress up for the occasion. For Christmas you could dress up like Santa, Mrs. Santa, or an elf. For other holidays, use your imagination. The only rule to remember is do not wear any scary costumes or masks. You want to entertain kids, not frighten them.

> Mother: Bobby's teacher says he ought to have an encyclopedia.
> Father: Let him walk to school like I had to.

Setting Up

All you will need is your painting supplies, a table, a chair, and a mirror. Don't forget the mirror. After you've completed painting the face, the child will want to experience the thrill of seeing it for himself. If he can't see what he looks like, he cannot fully appreciate or enjoy it.

When I set up, I place my materials on the left end of a table and the chair on the right. This makes it easier for me to reach them. (If you are left handed, reverse the order.) I sit on the chair and the children will sit or kneel in front of me. I found that if the children are sitting on a chair, I have to bend over too much to reach them and after a while this becomes very tiresome. Because I'm a clown, if I have the child kneel, I ask him or her to do so on the tips of my big clown shoes so the child's knees have a little cushion. You may want to bring a small towel or cushion for this purpose if you do not use clown shoes. Sometimes, if the majority of the children are tall, I take turns sitting and standing up. I will seat the taller teenagers and adults on a chair and stand up to paint their faces.

While the child is kneeling or standing in front of you, hold his face gently by the chin to keep it from moving. Once in a while, you will come across children whom I call "wigglers" or "squinters." They wiggle or squint their eyes shut, making face painting very difficult. When you spot these types, try to talk them into choosing a quick and simple design or a tattoo on the cheek because, no matter what you do, they will move or squint. If you try to do a Batman, which requires a lot of paint around the eye, for example, on a squinter, no matter how good you are, it will probably look as if someone punched him in the eye. If the child absolutely insists on a difficult design, just do the outline and don't color it in.

You might display photographs of each of the faces you offer. Keep in mind that it takes more time and effort to do a full face than simpler faces and tattoos. Children can then look at what you do and choose the design they like best. This also prevents people from requesting designs you can't or don't want to do.

Consider having a Polaroid camera available. The paint will eventually be washed away but a picture will provide a lasting record of the event. Make sure to add a sticker with your name and phone number to the back of each photo.

Crowd Control

At some parties with lots of over-active children, you may feel like you're surrounded by a gaggle of playful geese. It can become a very hectic affair! It is important to maintain order to avoid confusion and hurt feelings. One way to handle this is to have the children form a line and take turns.

Kids can get tired if they have to wait for a long time in line. One of your goals should be to keep the waiting line as short as possible. To conserve time, you should learn the various faces you offer well enough that you can automatically do them without referring back to a book or a photo. As a beginner, however, you may need to refer back occasionally.

You will discover that certain faces become popular, usually depending on which ones you paint first. If you paint a couple of butterflies early, everyone will want butterflies. This is a time consuming face for me to make because I have to cover the entire face.

Unless you have the time to do the more involved designs, it is best to start with simpler faces. With time and practice you will learn how to paint faces more quickly, and may eventually be able to handle the more time consuming faces in larger crowds.

Face Painting Etiquette

Once you have gathered the children and are ready to paint their faces you must set up some rules to ensure that your work will run smoothly and that it will be an enjoyable experience for all who participate.

At a birthday party, the birthday child always goes first, unless he or she personally wants to forfeit this privilege. If it is the child's choice to wait, he or she should have the privilege of cutting in at any time. If the birthday child has any brothers or sisters in attendance, they should be allowed to go to the head of the line. The parents of the birthday child are the ones who are paying for your services so it is important that you please them and give them their money's worth. After the birthday child and his or her siblings have been painted, go to the next in line. A good idea is to paint a number on each child's hand explaining with a smile that you will paint each child according to the number on their hands and have them sit down around you as they wait. This way the children aren't restricted to standing in a line but can gather around you as if watching a performance. Background music, preferably tunes that are familiar and appropriate for the age group, will get them singing and dancing, creating a party atmosphere.

Make sure that whoever is last gets acknowledged and complimented for his or her patience. If possible, I give them a "thank you for waiting so patiently" hug.

Your ability to keep the children entertained will make the time seem shorter and they will enjoy themselves more. In the following sections I will show you some techniques that will help you make your face painting fun for everyone.

MAKE IT FUN

The art of face painting was originally developed and is carried on primarily by professional and amateur clowns and other family entertainers. Why is face painting so popular? Because it's entertaining and allows kids to enter a world of make-believe where they can be animals, superheroes, and other characters. Face painting, therefore, is a form of entertainment. As such, the face painter will become more popular if he or she can make the process as enjoyable and entertaining as possible.

When "on stage," wear a smile. Be cheerful and enthusiastic about painting faces. Face painters who aren't enjoying themselves are easy to spot. It's like being entertained by a performer who doesn't care about the performance and only halfheartedly goes through the motions. Face painters with light hearts and cheery smiles will make the experience a pleasant one for the child.

Part of the reason for children getting their faces painted, particularly if you are dressed up like a clown or are in some other costume, is your interaction with them. Entertain them and keep them occupied by talking to them. This may also help to keep them still as you paint and will greatly increase the joy they experience in getting their faces painted.

What do you talk about? You can explain what you are doing. Describe the colors you are putting on and what features you are creating. Kids are curious and want to know. This will help relieve both curiosity and apprehension and keep them occupied as you work. Be friendly.

The best way to talk to the kids, many of whom may be too shy to talk on their own, is to ask them questions. You can begin with general questions such as:

What's your name?

How old are you?

Do you have any brothers or sisters? What are their names? Ages?

What school do you go to?

What grade are you in?

What's your teacher's name?

Do you like school? Why?

What subjects do you like best? Least? Why?

Do you have any hobbies?

Do you have any pets?

Conversation helps to make children feel more at ease and gain greater enjoyment from the experience. You become more than just a person painting faces, you become a new friend, and they will be more likely to tell others about you. They will also appreciate your finished

Ed: How do you make a strawberry shake?
Fred: Sneak up on it and say "boo!"

design more since it was created by a "friend."

If there is a long line waiting to be painted, talk loud enough for everyone to hear so that those in line don't become bored or discouraged by the wait. Use a lot of stories and jokes.

SILLY TALK

One of the most effective tools you can use when working with kids to get their attention, relieve apprehension, and entertain is to use silly talk. This means saying off-the-wall things and giving ridiculous explanations or answers to questions.

If you have a quick wit, this should be relatively easy for you—just say whatever pops into your head during your normal conversation. Most of us, however, even though we may have a good sense of humor, can't always come up with funny tidbits. That's okay, with a little preparation you can be amazingly entertaining. For example, while you are asking the child routine questions, throw in a few silly ones. Her are some examples:

Are you married?

What do you do for a living?

How may kids do you have?

Is that your wife/husband over there? (point to one of the parents or another child.)

Are you my 5th grade teacher? You look like her.

I bet I can guess your age. Are you 39? (Act surprised when they say no.)

I bet I can guess your name. Is your name Rumpelstiltskin? (Use ridiculous names or names of famous people.)

I bet I know what your favorite dessert is. Is it liver flavored Jell-O? Broccoli ice cream? Spinach pie? . . . Don't you like anything?

These questions are silly, but kids love them.

Besides asking silly questions, you can tell silly jokes, or riddles, sing songs, or pull off some gags. You don't need to be a stand-up comedian, continually throwing out clever one-liners. Simply talk, ask questions, and throw in a joke or gag now and then, but most important learn to have fun. If you are having a great time, your audience will too.

When I paint faces, I always use silly talk that relates to the type of face I'm painting. It doesn't have to be hilariously funny; any silly comments will work. For example, while I'm painting a cat, I may sing a little tune

saying only "meow, meow, meow, . . ." or any other sound except that made by a kitty. Here are a few more examples.

Rabbit. You could sing "Here comes Peter Cotton Tail hopping down the bunny trail. . . ." Change Peter for the kid's name.

Butterfly. Tell the child that she is becoming a beautiful "flutterby." The kids will correct you. At the end, show her the mirror saying, "Fly away, beautiful flutterby, the butterfly!"

Indian Princess. "Now you are the beautiful princess, Standing Cow. When you grow up, I bet you will marry Sitting Bull!"

Princess. "I want you to look in the mirror and say, 'I'm beautiful.'" Their eyes will light up because they truly are beautiful!

Mermaid. "Do you live on the bottom of the sea inside a giant clam? Do you eat fish and sea snails for dinner?"

Clown. If you are a clown face painter, many times the children will tell you that they want to be exactly like you. To this I respond: "Clowns are not allowed to be copycats. If you are a copycat clown the clown police will come and take you to copycat jail. There they will hang you upside down from the ceiling and spin you around. When you get real dizzy, they'll tickle you till you promise not to copycat again. I don't want that to happen to you, so I'll make you into a special clown, okay?" Then, before showing the children their reflection in the mirror, ask for their names. Use the name to create a new clown name. For example: Jolly Johnny the Clown, Silly Sandy the Clown, Wacky Willie, Patty Pepperoni, etc.

Movie and Television Characters. Watch the cartoons often so that you can be "hip" as to what's going on and what makes these shows so popular. Children love it when you get mixed up or confused. For the Ninja Turtles call Donatello, Marshmallow; Michaelangelo, Mary Angelo, etc. Ask them as you paint, "Do you know what happened to Batman when he got run over by the train?" To answer, sing the theme song, "nah, nah, nah, nah, nah, FLATMAN!" Then ask them if they know what happened when he ate too much candy—FATMAN.

Children also love it when I confuse the genders. For example, I may ask a boy if his name is Mary or a girl if her name is George. Also, if the child's mom is present, I may ask if she is his wife. Calling a child something funny as by accident and then correcting yourself is also funny. Example: "How are you sweaty . . . I mean sweetie?"

Confusing the animals and their sounds gets a lot of laughs too. If I see a dog near by, I will tell the child that I like his elephant. The child will respond, "That's not an elephant, it's a dog!" "I know that!" I say, "I have a doggy at home and my doggy always barks like this 'meow, meow . . . .'" Kids love it when you mix things up like this and it keeps them amused.

If you know some good jokes, share them with the kids as you paint their faces. You can even ask them to tell you a joke. Kids love this because it gives them a chance to make *you* laugh. Kids are always telling jokes and most kids have heard a joke they can tell. This is a good way for you to learn new jokes and helps you learn what kids think is funny.

Kids also like it when you tell them stories. Short amusing stories relating to the particular type of face you are creating are very effective. A good idea is to find or make up one of two stories for each of the types of faces you create. When you are asked to paint a face, use one of your preplanned stories. Suitable short stories can be found in any number of children's books from the library or bookstore.

You may have 10 or more kids waiting in line at a busy event and silly talk helps keep them entertained. It also maintains enthusiasm for your services. Learn to silly talk while you work. Be creative, ad-lib, and have fun. If you have fun, the kids will too.

ON THE SPOT

Face painting designs can be divided into many different categories such as fantasy art, animals, and heroes. I have another category that I call "on the spot" which deals with the fact that you will never know what will come out of the mouth of children. Let me illustrate. One day I was at a party, face painting about twenty children. All of them knew the choices and, by the time it was their turn, they knew exactly what they wanted to be. One little boy, however, decided that he wanted to be a rabbi and his mind was so set on it, that as much as I tried, I could not get him to change his mind. Being put "on the spot," I drew a mustache and darkened his eyebrows, and he went happily on his way.

Sometimes you will be asked to make someone into a dinosaur, a horse, an elephant, or a bird which, because of their features (beaks and trunks), are too difficult to design. Rather than do a poor job, I choose to keep these types of designs off my list of choices. If I cannot get a child to change his mind, then I suggest drawing the child's request on the cheek or hand. This is a time when tattoos come in very handy.

Another way to handle this situation without a harsh "no" and without disappointing the child is to tell a story and suggest another similar type of face you can do. For example, when you are asked to do a dinosaur, you can relate this frightening experience. "Once upon a time I ran into what I thought was a big dinosaur laying in the middle of the road sleeping. He woke up with a big yawn, fire came out of his mouth, and he almost burned my brand new hat! It scared me. You know why he did that? Because he was a dragon, not a dinosaur! Now I'm scared of dinosaurs and dragons, so you are going to have to be something else. How about a mean, scary tiger with big tiger teeth so you can chase after the girls?" Act it out to the best of your ability. Children love stories and fantasy and they will usually go along with your suggestion. With time, you will learn to act and talk silly—learning how to say "no" in a fun way.

Most of the time, children can easily be convinced to be something else. If not, have fun with them. For instance, when you are trying to convince a small child to change his mind, you could say something like this: When asked for a Superman, whisper in the child's ear, "Let me tell you a secret. Superman is really Clark Kent and neither one wears any makeup. Shh . . . don't tell anybody. Instead, why don't you be Batman, Spiderman, or Robin?"

Another time when you will be put on the spot is when a parent brings a child to you to be painted and the child is frightened and doesn't want his or her face painted. Don't paint a child's face if the child does not want it painted. When I encounter a pushy parent with a screaming child I look at them straight in the eyes to let them know I mean it and say to them, "I will paint him only if he wants to." Immediately I turn to the child and turning all my attention to him I ask him, "Do you want to have your face painted?" As the child continues to cry I look back at the parents and say, "He said no. Next!" Most of the time this will do the trick.

Sometimes the children are shy and they are afraid of you because you are a stranger to them. Stoop down so that you are looking at them from their level. This alone will do a lot to relieve fears. Be friendly and talk briefly to them. You may suggest a simple tattoo rather than a full face.

If after showing them that the paint is washable, and talking with them for a minute, they still don't want their faces painted, tell them that it's okay. If they don't want to be painted, don't do it.

On the other hand, the day you encounter a child who is letting you paint him for the first time, that will become a happy memory for both of you, and one of the many rewards of practicing the wonderful art of face painting.

Chapter 10

FOOD, FUN AND FROLIC

In this chapter we will cover some ideas you can use to make your birthday party business unique, more fun, more marketable, and more profitable. You may not want to use all of these ideas all the time; some may not appeal to you or fit your style, others may be what you need to set you apart from other birthday party businesses. Perhaps you won't use any of the information in this chapter, but hopefully it will inspire you to think and come up with unique and beneficial ideas of your own.

CATERING

A primary function of most birthday party businesses is to provide entertainment and activities. Another service that can be offered is catering food and decorations. This can be in addition to entertainment or in some cases, it can be the entire service. If you have neither the skill nor the interest of being an entertainer, but still want to share in the benefits of operating a birthday party business, you can focus your attention on providing catering and leave the entertaining to those who enjoy that type of work.

If you concentrate on catering, you will frequently be asked to provide entertainment as well or recommend someone. You could earn extra money by hiring an entertainer. Charge the client for both your services. This fee would include enough to cover expenses and your time in contacting the entertainer.

Ideally, you should check out local party entertainers who would be willing to work with you. Some may even offer to provide their services at a slight discount since you would be taking care of booking the party (much like an entertainment agency would, and they get a 15 percent commission). The client pays you for the entire party, including the entertainment. You in turn pay the entertainer.

Credit card payments are the most convenient and highly recommended. This way you are covered in case of problems. Most large caterers have contracts and require a 20 to 50 percent prepayment. Smaller caterers usually don't bother with contracts. I feel at least a partial payment in advance is necessary. The reason is that after you go to the expense and labor of baking and decorating a cake, you can't afford a cancellation. If you have not been paid in advance, it may be difficult to collect. Credit cards help eliminate this problem. You could use a contract similar to the letter of agreement on page 36 and itemize everything you are providing.

Some services collect payment by check or credit card when they deliver the goods and before the entertainer arrives. Always call the entertainer before each party to make sure he remembers the time and date and address. If the entertainer fails to show up or comes late, it reflects on you. Be very careful with whom you work. Pick reliable people who conduct their business in a professional manner. Many businesses work in a partnership—one taking care of catering and the other entertainment. Since both share in the profit and loss of the business, they both have an active interest in making the business successful and will be very conscientious in making clients happy and satisfied.

Call the parents the day before the party to make sure everything is still on and that last minute changes have not occurred that would cancel or delay the party. Busy parents may forget to call and cancel.

Getting Started

One of the high points of any children's birthday party is the presentation and eating of the cake. The birthday cake, decorated and adorned with candles representing the age of the guest of honor, serves as the centerpiece for the festivities. When the cake is presented, the birthday child is treated with a chorus of "Happy Birthday" and given all of the attention of royalty. Everyone sits in silence as the guest of honor makes a wish and blows out the candles. After that, all share in the joy of eating the cake.

Celebrating a birthday with cake is a tradition. Whether the party is a simple family affair or a full-blown extravaganza, it always has the birthday cake celebration. For this reason, the cake is a very important part of the birthday party.

Having a specially made cake with the words "Happy Birthday" followed by the child's name is a thrill and an honor. A uniquely decorated, custom-made cake is the greatest thrill of all. Many parents lacking the skill or time to make the cake themselves will gladly hire a caterer.

You can make the cake from a mix or from scratch. Making a cake from scratch is definitely the cheapest, but is not as convenient as a prepared mix. You must decide if the extra work is worth the few extra dollars you would save by making it from scratch. You may offer your clients a variety of flavors and decorative designs. These details should be discussed over the phone when the party is booked.

The cake must be decorated and include the birthday child's name, "Happy Birthday Ryan." This will require some cake decorating materials, and if you've never done it before, some practice along with a book on cake decorating. Some areas offer inexpensive adult education classes in cake decorating.

A novel approach to entice customers is to offer a cake and decorations to fit a particular theme or to match the birthday child's interests. If the birthday child likes sports, perhaps the cake can have a picture of a baseball or some other athletic equipment. This added touch makes the food more individual and your services more marketable.

Besides the cake, you may also offer drinks (punch or soda pop), party favors, decorations, paper plates, napkins, cups, forks, snacks, and helium balloons. More and more people nowadays are becoming health conscious. As a unique twist you may offer healthy refreshments as alternatives to the typical sugary fare, such as reduced sugar, low fat cake and snacks.

Party Packages

You might offer package deals or customized services. You can have a set price for certain packages. For example, the basic package (package 1) may be a custom decorated cake, paper plates, cups, napkins, forks, and punch.

Package 2. Could be a decorated cake, punch, paper products, plus snacks.

Package 3. Can be all of the above plus helium balloons, party streamers, and party favors.

Package 4. Can include package 1 or 2 along with games.

Package 5. Can include package 1 or 2 plus entertainment.

Package 6. Can be the whole works.

Of course, the games, entertainment, party favors, snacks, and decorations could each be added separately to the custom decorated cake. You could still offer a theme party package.

Prices are based on the package chosen and number of kids attending. Your basic price may cover a minimum number of guests, such as a dozen, and add x amount for each additional guest. Or your prices may be based on a range, for example, up to 12 guests would be your basic price, 13-18 guests you cost a little more, 19-24 guests still more, and so on. The latter method is a little easier to work with because you don't have to keep an accurate count on guests and as every party giver knows, the number of guests invited isn't always the number that shows. If the parent indicates up to 24 guests, then you bring enough for 24 guests and that is the amount you charge for, regardless of how many actually show up.

Pricing Your Services

In establishing prices for your catering services, you need to take into account the cost of ingredients and the nonfood items you use as well as your time, and still make a reasonable profit. If all you offer is a birthday cake, it's simple. But you may also offer a full meal which could include hot dogs and garnishments, pizza, chicken, punch, or other kid pleasing foods.

At first, you may have a tendency to figure the cost of ingredients as the main factor and underprice your labor and overhead expenses (electricity, utilities, taxes, stationery, wear and tear on kitchen equipment, and the like). You must price your services within the limits which your area can bear. Also, you want to avoid underpricing or you won't realize a worthwhile profit.

Do some research. Call caterers in your area and see what they would charge for the same food and party items. Prices will vary depending on geographic location and the type of people the businesses cater to. A full-service caterer, who offers a wide variety of foods and services, may charge more for a decorated birthday cake than a smaller no-service caterer, which may specialize in only a few items, and has lower overhead expenses.

Your next consideration is for the cost of the food. Make a list of ingredients and quantities needed. Then research the prices of all items at the grocery store. By totaling the cost of all the ingredients for a meal/event, you have the total cost to you. Divide that number by the number of people to be served to arrive at a per-person cost.

Determining the cost of the major ingredients is simple enough. If you use a pound of flour to make a cake, you can be fairly exact, but if you use only a tablespoon of vanilla or a half teaspoon of salt, figuring the cost requires some estimating.

Your overhead is difficult to determine since you cannot easily establish how much electricity was used. Yet such expenses must be covered in the final price.

Most caterers use a system called *factoring* to figure their prices, which involves taking the cost of the ingredients of a meal and multiplying by three to determine the overall cost. The resulting price should cover your labor and material cost, plus overhead, and leave a reasonable profit. To find the per-head cost, divide the sum by the number of guests. These figures are for the food and preparation only and do not include any extras such as the cost of extra help, decorations, or entertainment.

This formula is used by caterers when preparing a full meal. If all you make is a simple birthday cake that cost you $4 to make, three times that would only amount to $12. Your time in shopping, preparing, and baking the cake is worth far more than that. Realistically, you can charge anywhere from $15 to $20 an hour for your labor. Total cost for preparing the cake can range from about $20 on up, depending on the cost of ingredients and time spent. An elaborately decorated cake may take a couple of hours to prepare and, consequently, cost considerably more.

Delivery time is also a consideration. Some caterers deliver all their food, while others allow customers to pick it up (sometimes offering a reduction in the price). A fee to cover the expense of delivery should be included. If you are selling a party package that includes entertainment, and the entertainer picks up and delivers the cake, a delivery charge may not be necessary. If you contract with an entertainer not under your employ, you may have to handle the delivery yourself.

You must keep your prices reasonable in order to remain competitive. But if you underprice your goods and services, you will run the risk of losing money.

If you specialize in preparing a limited number of items, you can calculate a standard price per-person in advance. This way, you can give a quote to a potential customer over the phone rather than having to call back, and you will save time calculating a price for a customer who eventually will not use your services. Keep your fare simple. You are specializing in birthday parties not business lunches and tea parties. As your business grows and you gain experience, you may consider expanding your menu or services. Have a set menu with options the customer can choose from.

Keeping it Legal

Food preparation industries are carefully monitored by the government to keep people safe from contamination. For this reason, you may be required to register your catering business with the local health department, and in some cities, you need to obtain a permit.

The laws on food preparation vary greatly from area to area. Some places have regulations requiring that all food for sale be cooked in a commercial kitchen, while some cities will allow you to cook food at home and sell it in another jurisdiction, but not in your own town. Others allow you to cater in your town but not in a neighboring one. Some cities prohibit preparation of food in a client's home for pay.

Most catering businesses in operation today started out as home-based enterprises and moved to commercial kitchens as their businesses became established. Some remained in the home in violation of local laws, primarily out of ignorance. Some had no intention of going into business full-time. They started making baked items to sell here and there and before they knew it, they were in full-fledged business. Most health codes require certain things in a commercial kitchen. If your kitchen at home does not meet these standards, you will not be legally permitted to prepare food for sale. Check with your local Board of Health for information on the regulations in your area.

If you find that you cannot use you own kitchen, an alternative is to rent a kitchen that you can use. You can rent inexpensive kitchen space at a church, school, or civic club. People in charge of these facilities are often seeking fundraising activities, and renting kitchen space would be a good way for them to earn money with little effort. You could also have the food prepared by an established business and serve merely as an agent and delivery service. This would free you of the time and responsibility of preparing the food. You would mark up the price to cover your services and still make a profit. An alternative, where the law allows, is for you have the bulk of the food prepared at a commercial kitchen and then bring it home for the final touches. A basic cake, for example, could be purchased then brought home and custom decorated.

If your kitchen meets local health regulations, you will be required to have your kitchen inspected by an inspector from the health department. They are mostly concerned with the safety and cleanliness of the premises and of those who work there. Their concerns are sensible for a sanitary environment. They inspect proper lighting, appliance, plumbing and sewage disposal, washing facilities, garbage disposal, and ventilation. If your kitchen doesn't meet all the standards, it can be possible to correct the matter with modest expense. Some of the typical requirements are that all food be stored off the floor, that there be separate facilities (sink and chopping boards) for preparing food and cleaning dishes, that the facilities for disposing of garbage be adequate, that there be enough light for people to work easily and without strain, and that there be adequate refrigerator space to cool and preserve perishable foods.

Speaking of legal issues, it should be mentioned that liability insurance should be seriously considered. When you are serving food, the possibility exists that someone may get sick from something you make.

For more information about catering services, check out the resources in the appendix.

THEME PARTIES

Another type of party package you could offer customers is a theme party. This would work well for an entertainer, but is especially suitable for a catering service that can provide food, decorations, and entertainment. You would have several prepared themes for the client to choose from. Have supplies in stock, or know where to get them easily. You would bake a cake and decorate it

> Mother: Bobby, have you given the goldfish fresh water today?
> Bobby: No, they haven't finished what I gave them yesterday.

in accordance with the theme. Bring decorations that depict the theme. Have activities or games centered around the theme and even present entertainment reflecting the theme.

If all you do is provide food, paper goods, and decorations, you could deliver them before the party starts. If you are also supervising games or activities or are giving a show, you can bring them by just before the party starts. If you are working with an entertainer, you can bring the goods by before hand and let the entertainer show up after the kids have arrived. You wouldn't necessarily want to make two trips if you were handling both functions. You supply decorations but let your client put them up.

The themes you choose can be applicable to any children's birthday party at any time of the year. You could get extra bookings if you prepare some special themes for holidays like Christmas and Easter. The following are samples of themes you could use and the types of things you can do.

Balloon Party

A balloon party would be built around games, activities, and entertainment using balloons. Kids love balloons—helium balloons, animal balloons, and balloons just to play with. Use round balloons for games, pencil balloons for making animals and toys, and novelty balloons like rockets and spinners. Tell balloon jokes and gags. Do a balloon show.

Magic Party

For this type of party you will center your games and activities around magic. Come dressed as a magician, wizard, magic genie, or even a magical clown. Perform a magic show for the entertainment. Teach the kids some simple magic tricks. Give them inexpensive tricks as party favors. If you are a magician or magic clown, you could perform your regular party show.

Circus Party

This type of party is excellent for clowns, although other entertainers can also work this theme successfully. Dress as a clown or other circus performer. Have all the kids become stars of the Big Top by having them participate in circus games and activities. Have a show with wild animals (hand puppets), or have volunteers act out the parts of ferocious beasts (add face paint to make them look real); present a juggling or magic act, or perform a clown skit. Have the kids act out some of the parts.

Animal Party

This could also be called a Zoo Party or even a Puppet Party. Your show and activities can revolve around puppets, balloon animals, or even live animals, such as doves and rabbits. Kids will have fun with hand puppets. A fun craft activity would be for the kids to make their own sock puppet or paper bag puppet. You could also teach them how to make a couple of simple balloon animals.

Intergalactic Space Party

You could also call this a Science Fiction Party. Electronic brains, robots, space creatures, intergalactic storm troopers are some of the things you can use in creating fun activities and games for the kids. Storytelling, magic, puppet, and clown shows with a space theme can round out the party.

Undersea Party

Join the fun with stories and activities about fish, mermaids, desert islands, sunken treasure, ships, sharks, and other creatures of the deep. Eat saltwater taffy, hunt for jellyfish balloons, seek a fortune in hidden pearls or sunken treasure. Eat fish treats like goldfish crackers and gummy worms. Bubble blowing and bubble games are also fun. Blow bubbles under the sea using liquid soap (dishwashing detergent such as Dawn or Joy) and pipe cleaners. Have children try to catch your bubbles with their wands. See who can make the most bubbles, the biggest bubbles, and longest lasting bubbles.

Goblins and Ghosts Party

Have kids come to the party dressed up in costumes. A spooky magic show would fit here.

Dungeons and Dragons Party

You will center your theme for this party around castles, knights, princesses, dragons, and wizards. Adapts well for storytelling, puppetry, and magic shows.

Dinosaur Party

Dinosaurs are popular with kids. Build activities and a show around dinosaurs. For the younger kids Barney the Dinosaur is popular. Bring coloring sheets of Barney. The Flintstones will appeal to older kids. Dinosaur puppets and balloon animals work well.

Mystery Party

This is a great party in which to solve puzzles, mazes, and riddles. As a game or an audience participation activity, have the children solve a mystery. Give them the clues and let them be the detectives. This theme is great for magicians and storytellers. Clowns and others can also build a show around this theme using magic, stories, and jokes. Instead of your normal attire, dress as Sherlock Homes.

Backwards Party

Another name for a Backwards Party could be a Crazy Party. This type of party can be really fun. Everything you do is backwards or upside down. Wear part of your clothing backward. Have the food served and eaten backwards. Put placemats on the floor and have the kids eat under the table. Serve them the cake first and then the hamburgers or hot dogs. Eat weird looking food like green-colored caramel popcorn. Drinks can be a combination of several different types of juices, punches, or sodas—a ghastly mixture the kids will be sure to enjoy. (Taste it first to make sure it is drinkable.) Spell "Happy Birthday" on the cake backwards. Write kid's names backwards on the placemats (using construction paper). Have everyone try to say tongue twisters and silly rhymes. Do everything backwards or in an illogical manner.

Pirate Party

Dress as a sailor or buccaneer. Spin tales of pirate treasure and high seas adventure. Let all the kids play as if they were pirates and have them hunt for hidden treasure. Lead them in games like Walk the Plank described on page 152. Change the names of games and, if need be, some of the equipment to fit the theme.

Pig Out Party

Center all the games and activities around food and eating. Have eating contests. See who can eat a pie the fastest or drink a drink the fastest (this can be funny if the drink is a somewhat unpleasant vegetable juice). Have a contest to see who can eat apples hanging from a string the fastest. Try grabbing an apple with your teeth while it is floating in a tub of water. For many of these activities it may be best to do them outside so as not to mess the floor.

Music Party

Sing songs, play musical instruments, bring kazoos, spoons, drums, and other fun instruments the kids can play. Have them make their own flutes (or noise makers) out of straw. Have all the kids play their instruments and record it on a tape recorder. If you play a musical instrument, have them accompany you with their music or singing. Lead them in songs. Sing funny songs. Follow the examples of the musical comedians like Spike Jones, Ray Stevens, and Allen Sherman. Barry Polsar has written some wonderfully silly children's songs such as: "Never Cook Your Sister in A Frying Pan," "One Day My Best Friend Barbara Turned into A Frog," "I'm A Three-Toed, Triple-Eyed, Double-Jointed Dinosaur," and "My Brother Thinks He's A Banana." For a catalog of books and tapes by Barry Polsar contact Rainbow Morning Music, 2121 Fairland Rd, Silver Spring, MD 20904.

THEME PARTY FUN
Ingredients of a Theme Party

Theme parties consist of a combination of food, gifts, games, activities, and entertainment. What you do is entirely up to you and will depend on what you like to do and what you are best suited for. If you are a magician, you may want to include a magic show (a magic show can fit with several different themes). In that case the other activities you do should not take more than a half hour or so.

You don't need to provide a formal show, however. At a theme party there are plenty of other things you could do to keep the children entertained for an hour. You might spend the majority of your time playing games or doing other theme related activities. Shari Ann Pence has achieved success with her business, Adventures in Partyland, which specializes in party games. She doesn't present a show like most other birthday party businesses. She comes into the home and supervises the kids in an array of original fun-packed games. She emphasizes that the games are all original so everything they do at the party is a new experience for the kids. Many parents find this idea appealing. It also provides an alternative to the typical children's show.

In the following sections we have listed many examples to give you ideas of the type of things you can do. You would not use all of these ideas at a single party—there isn't enough time. Pick and choose the ones most suitable for you. You will find many additional ideas in books on crafts, games, and parties.

Food (Cake)

The most important part of the birthday party celebration is the cake. With a theme party the cake serves as both a decoration and a treat. It should be decorated to depict the theme. For an Intergalactic Space Party the cake could have a design of a space ship or flying saucer soaring among stars and planets. For a Magic Party the cake might illustrate a magician's top hat with a rabbit poking his head out holding a magic wand. Complement the cake with small pieces of candy, red hots, candy corn, gum drops, etc. This makes the cake look special and kids love to get the pieces of candy in their slice.

Other food items you could supply are punch, popcorn, chips, pretzels, cookies, etc. Make the treats match the theme as much as possible.

Decorations

Along with food you could supply decorations to match the theme to help you create the right atmosphere. Crepe paper streamers, balloons, placemats, and wall hangings are some of the most common types of decorations. Strips of crepe paper can be taped across the tops of doorways and entryways and along the wall. Balloons can be placed about the house to complement the streamers. Placemats made of construction paper could have appropriate designs drawn on them. Wall hangings made of shapes cut out of paper are hung on various lengths of string (see illustration on next page).

Have plates and napkins with appropriate designs printed on them. Most decorations you will leave with the parents; they will be included in the price of the party. You may bring in some special decorations which you will keep. An example would be a backdrop or mural decorated to match the theme. If you do any entertainment or group activities, a lightweight backdrop can add a great deal of atmosphere to your presentation. A backdrop can be made out of panels of sturdy corrugated cardboard which are taped together and painted with appropriate designs. Corrugated cardboard from large furniture or refrigerator boxes is a good size. If you can't find a large cardboard box, you can get panels cut to size at a box or container company. The backdrop could have your stage name written it. Have kids get their pictures taken individually with you in front of the backdrop.

For a dinosaur party, have the mural depict dinosaurs. For a space party, show stars and planets. A Dungeons and Dragons party would have a castle, knights, and dragon. For Goblins and Ghosts, have an old haunted mansion with ghosts, and witches flying about. You get the idea, adapt the backdrop to fit your theme.

Some of these decorations can be made by the kids as part of a birthday party activity. You can lead them in coloring their own placemats on construction paper. Have them draw pictures that fit the party's theme.

It is an easy task for children to decorate balloons using a felt-tip marking pen and paper. For an Undersea Party, for example, a cute jellyfish can be made from a balloon and a few strips of crepe paper. A couple of big eyes and a mouth can be drawn on the balloon. Add several strips of crepe paper for the tentacles around the lower half of the balloon and you have a jellyfish. Make planets from round balloons for your Intergalactic Space Party by coloring craters on a balloon. You could make one look like Saturn by adding a paper ring (such as the rim of a paper plate) on the outside of the balloon. Artistic children can draw the earth with all the continents and oceans. Hang these up around the house when they are completed.

The kids can color and cut out shapes for the wall hangings. For a Magic Party cut out paper magical designs

such as top hats, magic wands, stars and such and punch a hole in the top of the cutout. Tie varying lengths of string on the cutouts and hang them from the ceiling. These could be prepared beforehand from photocopies of pictures, similar to those you might find in coloring books, or just use colored construction paper and draw your own designs. You might use glue stick to add glitter to the decorations to give them sparkle.

Gifts and Treats

You may want to have party favors and treats for the kids. You definitely want to send each child home with some type of promotional item, this is discussed further in Chapter 13. You may want to have other gifts available for the kids. Simple toys and treats can be handed out as rewards throughout the party. You could give them as awards for winning or playing the games. You might use them as incentives to help rowdy children follow directions and behave. In the end, though, all the children should be given the gifts so no one feels slighted.

Inserting a small toy inside a balloon makes a clever gift idea. Stretch the mouth of the balloon open and drop the toy inside. Inflate the balloon and knot the end. Tie string or ribbon to the balloon and hang it as a decoration during the party and give them to the children as party favors.

Mr. Sonshine (Larry Mahan) using a portable backdrop at a birthday party.

If you do a lot of games and give out lots of treats, you may also provide loot bags for the kids to hold the stuff they get. Examples of the type of stuff you can give include magic tricks, novelty toys, playing cards, puzzles, small magic or joke books, and candy. If you give candy, check with parents first as some parents will not want their kids to have it. See page 33 for address to Oriental Trading and Tipp Novelty Company which sell inexpensive toys.

Activities

Special activities you do with the kids can be lots of fun and can even be the main event. These supervised group activities can include crafts, games, songs, or any other fun things kids like to do. The activity could be as simple as a stunt or challenge, or as complex as an unrehearsed theatrical-like play complete with costumes and scenery.

Gags and Giggles. A fun activity is to challenge kids to do stunts, gags, brain teasers, and silly tricks. The following are examples of the types of things you can say and do.

Demonstrate a spectacular feat of mind reading. Get someone to write down any word on a piece of paper. You claim that you will write the very same word on another piece of paper, even though it is impossible for you to have seen what your helper wrote. You may even write on the paper first!

After both of you have written something, have your helper tell everyone what he wrote. Then show him your piece of paper and say, "Will you please confirm that even though I didn't see what you had written, I have written the very same word!"

Your helper reads what is on the paper and agrees that your statement is correct.

How do you do it? simple. All you need to write is: "The very same word."

Let everyone in on the trick so they can try it on their friends.

Here is a silly little gag you can play on the whole group or a selected party guest which goes well at an Animal Party, but can be adapted to any theme.

Tell the kids to think of an animal that lives in the jungle.

When they have all chosen one, tell them, "Now, close your eyes."

After they close their eyes say, "Dark, isn't it?"

> "Doctor, I keep thinking I'm a goat."
> "How long have you had this feeling?"
> "Ever since I was a kid."

This stunt is good for a Goblins and Ghosts or even a Magic Party. Tell the guests that you believe there is a ghost in the house. This is a playful ghost that likes to lift people's arms and legs. You believe the ghost is hiding inside the wall. To have the ghost show his presence, tell the kids to stand with their sides next to a wall. Have them press their arms hard against the wall with the back of their hands. While they are doing that, have them say, "Oh, silly ghost who lives in the wall, come on out and show us all." Have them repeat this saying for at least 60 seconds while they are pushing against the wall. After 60 seconds, tell them to stand away from the wall, close their eyes, and relax completely. As they stand relaxed, their arms will rise as if by magic.

There is no real ghost. Their arm muscles are just reacting to the pressure they exerted against the wall.

Show the kids how to make a magic floating finger appear between their fingers.

Have them hold their two index fingers tip-to-tip several inches in front of their eyes. If they look past them at the wall, a little finger, with a nail on each end, will appear between the tips of their fingers. If they pull their fingers apart just a little bit, the magic finger will float in midair—a mysterious optical illusion..

Children's practical joke, riddle, magic, and game books contain lots of entertaining material which you can use. Go to your library or bookstore and have fun collecting funny bits for your parties.

Special Names. Another simple activity is to give each of the guests special names. Give each child a name and write the name on a peal and stick address label and have them wear it. Names for a Magic Party, for example, could be: Marcia the Magician, The Amazing Roger, and Super Dan. Other superlatives you can add to a name include: clever, charming, surprising, wonder, marvelous, gifted, skilled, expert, master, wizard, conjurer, mystical, enchanter, trickster, great, impressive. Announce each name with fanfare. Kids will get a kick out of the recognition they receive on being called these names and they will all want to get their special names and name tags.

For a backwards party proudly announce (with fanfare) each child's name, giving the last name first and the first name last. You can write the names backwards or upside down on name tags and stick one on each child.

Party Decorations. Making party decorations can be a fun activity. A simple activity would be coloring their own placemats. Wall hangings can also be an easy decoration. Cut out shapes from construction paper and color them. Hang the shapes on a string.

For a backwards party have kids use crayons to draw pictures or color in pictures, but they must use their nondominate hands or even their toes! You may even make a mural and tape all the kids' pictures together and hang it on the wall.

Paper Tricks and Toys. There are many simple paper toys that the kids will have fun making and playing with. Things you can make with paper include: party hats, magic tricks, noisemakers, puppets, paper plate masks, and animals. For an Intergalactic Space Party you could make paper rocket ships (airplanes) and fly them around. Have contests see who can fly theirs the farthest or the longest, or see who can make the craziest flight pattern. Have a contest for accuracy, instead of a bean bag toss, fly a rocket ship into a hanger (a hole in an illustrated backboard). There are several books in print on paper toys which you could use as resources.

Photo Session. An excellent activity you can do with the children is to have a photo session. This, however, isn't like getting a family portrait, but is a fun and silly experience. The children get their pictures taken while participating in the make-believe world you create. To accomplish this you must provide a backdrop with a hole in it big enough for a child's face. On the front of the backdrop you will have an illustration. The traditional illustration is that of muscle man, with a hole where the face goes. The child steps behind the backdrop and puts his face in the hole. It looks like he has suddenly become a bodybuilder.

Have the children place their faces into the hole one at a time. Take a picture of each one with a Polaroid camera. They can make goofy faces or act serious, let them have fun. For a Magic Party the illustration could be that of a magician, the child's face being the magician's. You could also have a drawing of a magician pulling a rabbit out of a hat, and the child's face is that of the rabbit. For a Pirate Party the children can be pirates, or the parrot on a pirate's shoulder. A knight for a Dungeons and Dragons Party. A storm trooper for an Intergalactic Space Party. You can have fun with a space party and have a picture of a weird looking space creature with pot belly and antenna. For a Backwards Party have a picture of a person standing on his hands. Kids must get down on their hands and knees to poke their face through the opening. (Someone will need to hold the backdrop for them.) Offer a variety of backdrops for the kids to choose from. They will love it!

The photo allows you an excellent opportunity to promote yourself and get free publicity. Customize the

backdrop so that it has an identifying mark. This could be your name, picture, or logo. On the back of each photo place a preprinted peel and stick label with your name and phone number, and publicity line. For example: "Marsha Graham, The Best in Theme Party Entertainment, (702) 453-5938." Buy a roll of stickers and keep them in your pocket. The kids will want to keep the photos and take them home to show their parents.

Make the backdrop out of paper or cloth. Cloth will hold up better, last longer, and won't easily tear, or wrinkle. The picture can be drawn on cloth lightly with a pencil at first, then darkened with a felt-tip permanent marking pen. Attach the top and bottom of the sheet to dowels. Have kids (or parents) hold the backdrop from behind as the children stick their faces into the opening. (This is similar to roll-down banners with pictures of rabbits and things, sold at magic shops.) The backdrop can be rolled up when not in use. Cloth construction keeps it relatively wrinkle free. You can add color to it if you like by using colored markers.

The backdrop could also serve double duty as a bean bag game if it is made out of wood or sturdy corrugated cardboard.

Instead of using a backdrop, you could dress each child up in simple costumes. For a Magic Party you could use a top hat, cape, magic wand. Make the outfit look good, not made of paper and plastic, but of cloth. A cape can be easily made from a piece of black cloth with a string sewn in around the collar, or Velcro to attach the cape around the child's neck. You may make some silly magic props to add variety, such as a stuffed rabbit in

a hat. For a Circus Party, dress the kids up in clown costumes. You could use face paints to give them clown faces. If you use a mural or large backdrop (as described in the decorations section), you could take the pictures in front of that.

Face Painting. Have the kids paint each other's faces, arms, hands, and feet. You could bring some designs for them to copy or they can create their own. Use water-soluble face paints and remind them not to paint too close to the eyes or mouth. You may also take pictures of them or have a parent take a picture of you and each child. Don't forget to add your sticker to the back of the photo.

Bubble Blowing Fun. Kids love to blow soap bubbles. Give them each some soap solution and a pipe cleaner twisted into a loop. Have contests to see whose bubble will last the longest, whose is the biggest, or smallest, who can make the most with a single blow, or whose will float the farthest. You might play catch. Have one person blow a bubble and see if a partner can catch it with his pipe cleaner without popping it. This activity can be messy, so you may want to do it outdoors.

Joke Telling Contest. Kids love to tell jokes. Let them all be clowns and give them the chance to share their best jokes by having a joke telling contest. (In a Circus Party you can dress them up as clowns.) Select some volunteers to tell jokes. After they have told their jokes, have the audience vote on the funniest. Do this by holding your hand over each of their heads in turn and listen to the applause. Give the winner a small prize. If everyone wants to tell jokes, split them up into two groups and do this activity twice.

Magic Tricks. Kids love to watch magic and bend their brains trying to figure out how the tricks work. Teach the kids how to do some simple magic tricks. They will get a thrill out of being taught by a real professional magician! You could give each of them inexpensive items or tricks and let them keep them as souvenirs. You could teach them the basics of other skills like making balloon animals or juggling.

The Magician's Apprentice. Dress up the birthday child in a magician's costume and have him help you present a mini-magic show. The birthday child could be the magician who is graduating to full magicianship and you are there to test his skills. Tell him what to do, add patter, have him ad-lib and dramatize his part. Perform self-working tricks that will let him accomplish them without rehearsal, or do the tricks for him. The child may not even know how the tricks work. Give him a magician's certificate or diploma afterwards.

Homemade Stories. Have everyone create a story. This can be a fun activity for any type of theme. As the group leader, you choose the theme and main characters. Describe the characters and perhaps choose a simple plot so the children know where the story is headed. Have everyone sit in a circle. You start the story and have them continue where you leave off. Each child takes a turn adding to the story until the last teller finishes it off. With multiple storytellers the tale can take some unusual and humorous twists and turns. To inspire creativity and spontaneity you may have the storytellers build up to a critical situation and then abruptly stop—maybe right in the middle of a sentence. The next person around the circle must pick up the story where it was left off and continue telling for a few minutes. These stories can be very funny. Once everyone has had a turn, you might have volunteers give their suggested endings.

Audience Participation Skits. Make up a story or find funny stories in books and adapt them into an audience participation skit. You be the narrator (or storyteller) and have the kids act out the parts. Tell them what to say and let them ham it up and ad-lib as they please. As you narrate the story, have the characters perform the actions. Let them have brief speaking parts. Encourage them to play it up.

These types of skits make fun party activities and even entertaining shows. Audience participation skits are like storytelling with the audience taking part in the story. Even those who aren't involved in the roll playing can participate by adding sound effects. Let them hiss, boo, cheer, clap, and make other appropriate noises. You might even add background music on cassette. Provide simple costumes the players can easily slip over their clothes to help make your production more theatrical.

This activity can easily take up 30-40 minutes by itself. You may structure your party around an audience participation skit as your main source of entertainment. Some storytellers use ideas that are very similar to this.

Theme Games

The games you may play at a theme party should relate to the theme. You don't need to play games that were originally designed for a particular topic. All you need to do is adapt games to fit the theme of the party. For some games all you need to do is change the name, or some of the terms used. For others you may need to modify visual parts.

For example, Pin the Tail on the Donkey can be modified to fit almost any type of theme. For a backwards party you could play Pin the Tail on the Donkey, but put up the picture of the donkey upside down and pin the tail on upside down. With a Circus Party you could have Stick the Nose on the Clown. Use a large picture of a clown face without the nose. Give a red foam clown nose to each child with a piece of tape.

Dentist: Please, please stop your howling. I haven't even touched your tooth yet.
Patient: I know, but you're standing on my foot.

For a Puppet Party have a picture of a puppeteer and have the kids put the puppet on his hand. For a Magic Party put a magic wand in the magician's hand or a rabbit in the hat. Use a picture that matches the party's theme and have the kids add an important part of the picture.

The Beanbag toss is another game that can be played with any theme. Using the circus theme the backboard for the beanbag toss could be a picture of a clown. The hole in the picture could be the clown's open mouth. The picture used would correspond with the party's theme. A dinosaur with its mouth wide open (the hole) would fit into a Dinosaur Party. A ghost with a wide open mouth fits a Goblins and Ghosts Party. A cannon with its open barrel pointed outward fits a Pirate Party. For a Backwards Party any picture would work, but have the children toss the beanbags over their shoulders or while facing in the opposite direction. Or to make it easier, use a bucket as the target.

Turn to page 153 and read the directions for playing Tic-Toc Find the Clock. This game can easily be modified to fit a number of themes. It fits well with a Mystery Party. The clock could be part of a time bomb and you, Inspector Gismo, and your detectives must find the bomb before it explodes. The first one to find the clock becomes the criminal and gets to hide it for the next round.

For a Pirate Party, change the name to Tic-Toc Find the Croc. Pretend you are in Never-Never Land with Captain Hook and Peter Pan. Tell them a crocodile has swallowed a clock and you must find the crocodile by the sound of the tic-toc. The crocodile is guarding a buried treasure. The one who finds the crocodile first gets to keep the treasure. The treasure can be a piece of candy or a small toy that is hidden with the clock.

Using this same idea, you could play this game at an Animal Party. You could use most any type of animal. A goat, pig, or other animal may have swallowed the clock. For an Undersea Party, tell the children a shark has swallowed the clock and find the shark.

Read how to play Capture the Balloon on page 152. This game is naturally suited for a Balloon or Circus Party. It also makes a fun game at a Pirate Party. You can change the name to Pirate Raid or something similar. Split the children into two groups of pirates. The line represents the boundary between each pirate ship. Have the balloons be the treasure and each group must attack the other ship and capture the treasure. The group with the most treasure (balloons) at the end of the game wins.

For a Ghosts and Goblins Party the children can become ghost busters and play Capture the Balloon, but call it Capture the Ghost. The balloons become the ghosts each team is to capture.

You now have the idea how to adapt games to fit a theme. Several games are described in Chapter 11. Use and adapt these and others for your party games.

To make the games more exciting, you may offer rewards or prizes to the winners. Give each participant a goody for playing and the winner an extra one as a reward. This way everyone gets a prize whether they win or not, so nobody feels left out.

Entertainment

If you do many of the activities already discussed, you will not have time for a show. Presenting a show is optional. If you normally do shows, then you may want to work it into your theme parties. A magic show would not need to be modified for a Magic Party, but for an Animal Party you would need to incorporate appropriate props or patter.

Since a lot of time is spent with activities and games, less time is necessary for the show. If you would normally give a 40-minute show, at a theme party you may reduce that to 20 minutes, depending on the time you spend on other activities. In some cases, there may be no other activities, so all you do is your regular show.

A simple magic theme party, for example, could consist of a customized cake, magic show, and party favors. A more elaborate party would also include a few magic activities, games, decorations, and loot bags.

"Waiter, there's a dead fly in my soup."
"Yes, sir, I know—it's the heat that kills them."

———

Big Man (in a theater, to a small boy sitting behind him): Can you see, sonny?
Boy: No, sir, not at all.
Big Man: Then just watch me and laugh when I do.

———

Wife: Do you have a good memory for faces?
Husband: Yes—why?
Wife: I just broke your shaving miror.

Chapter 11

PARTY GAMES

Games can be used as an accompaniment to most any type of party or they can be the main event. Some birthday party businesses specialize in supervising games rather than presenting shows. The entertainment is in the playing of the games. The entertainer in this case takes the role of games leader.

Regardless of the type of entertainer you are, many parents will want you to lead the kids in some games. Some children's entertainers refuse to do this; they consider themselves entertainers and don't want to be involved in supervising games. That's okay, you don't have to do games if you don't want to. But games add another dimension to the services you offer and can increase bookings and profits. Any entertainer can offer to do games if he or she desires. The choice is yours.

SUCCESS WITH PARTY GAMES
Game Selection

The games you choose should be suited for the age of the kids and the area in which the games are to be played. Games that can amuse very young children would be boring for older kids and the more complicated games that older kids enjoy can be too confusing for the younger ones. Some games are suited for indoors and others for outdoors. Active games like most relay races are outdoor games. Hot Potato, Musical Chairs, and Pin the Tail On the Donkey are best played inside.

When booking the party with a parent make sure you know the age of the kids and where the party is to take place. If you like to do outdoor games, make sure there is a suitable area available. Often, the weather will not permit outdoor games. It can be wet from rain or snow, too cold, or too hot to play outside. Most games you choose to play should be suitable for indoors. Sometimes you will be asked to lead games at an outdoor or backyard party. In these cases you may want to choose a few activity games to take advantage of the situation. Most of the activities you play inside the home can also be played outside, so you can still play your favorite indoor games.

Some children's entertainers prefer to play games where there is no winner or loser. They feel that those who lose feel bad, and they want everyone to enjoy themselves without feeling disappointed. Others feel that competition makes the games more enjoyable and allows a wider variety of games to choose from. Both are true and probably a mixture of both is the best solution. Generally, for very young children the no-lose games are the best choice. These children are not yet into competition and just the activity of the game is enough to keep them entertained. Older kids can have fun with no-lose games too, but competition provides motivation and excitement that makes many games enjoyable.

Shari Ann Pence, who bases her birthday business around games, says kids and parents get tired of the same old games like Musical Chairs or Hot Potato. Standard

145

party games like these have simply gone stale. Old games are still fun for the younger kids, but once children have played these games at other parties a few times, they lose interest. "Kids are always excited to learn something new." She learned that games could make or break a party. So she decided to make up her own games—games with zany names that focused on fun. After leading games at more than 200 children's parties, and observing games at other events, Pence compiled her most successful games into a book called *Games Galore for Children's Parties and More*. This is an excellent source for new games and clever new twists on old favorites.

Games Leader

At a party where games are to be played, you are the games leader. As the games leader you need to get the kids' attention and keep it. Take control, let the children know you are in charge. You are the judge. You control the awarding of prizes, if any. The prospect of winning and gaining a prize helps many older kids (eight and up) participate without acting up. They know that if they purposely mess up, they lose out, and if they are on a team, the whole team loses. This will help motivate them to play the game without overdue horseplay. Younger kids are less of a problem and no-lose games are very successful.

To take control and keep it, be clearly visible and audible. Don't stand behind the kids, be up front where they can see you at all times. Speak loudly and clearly, especially when explaining the rules to a game. You don't want kids distracting their neighbors asking, "What did he say?"

A vital tool for the game leader to have is a noisemaker, something to signal for everyone to stop and pay attention to you. It can also be used to start or stop an activity as well. Outdoors the usual choice is a loud whistle such as those used in sports. For indoors this is far too loud. A bicycle horn would be more suitable. A noisemaker is better than yelling. It saves your voice and lets you get the children's attention without sounding like a marine drill sergeant; it's more effective as an attention getter; and, in the case of a bicycle horn or other unusual sound maker, adds an element of fun and humor.

When you signal for attention, you need to wait very patiently for the kids to quiet down. If you start giving

> Sally: My uncle swallowed a frog.
> Sue: Goodness, did it make him sick?
> Sally: Sick! He's liable to croak any minute!

instructions before you have everyone's attention, you will find yourself stopping and repeating instructions, or worse, reprimanding an inattentive individual. You don't want to be in that situation.

When you have everyone's attention, make a short introduction to the next game followed by directions on how it's played. Give directions in a friendly manner. Show enthusiasm and smile. Your attitude shows and is contagious. If you are enthusiastic, the children will be also. If you stand around like an army instructor, the kids won't enjoy themselves and you will likely have more discipline problems and more distractions. Some preplanned jokes, stunts, or ad-libs can help to keep the atmosphere friendly and entertaining.

After giving the instructions, ask if there are any questions. It helps if you tell the kids the general objective of the game before explaining the rules to them. You will have fewer questions.

As the games leader you will not normally take part in the games yourself. You are the scorekeeper, judge, and referee. It is your job to keep the action alive and the kids entertained. Don't let a game bog down, especially between games when kids are likely to be standing around without anything to do. Jump from one activity right into the next to keep their attention. If you need time between activities or if there is a lull in the action, have a few jokes or gags ready to keep the fun alive. As you see, even doing a games party can involve your skills as an entertainer.

Some games can be played longer than planned if the kids are enjoying themselves. Others can be cut short if interest wanes. If you play a game where some kids must sit out as the game is played, make sure not to continue on so long that they become bored. If some reorganization of the room is needed, have the kids participate. Try to avoid having guests standing around wondering what they should be doing. Tell them what to do. If a game is in progress, have them go to a certain part of the room or sit down.

When a team or individual wins a game, show some special recognition. Let them bask in their victory, but quickly move along.

Winning

Everyone wants to win. Let all the kids feel like winners sometime during the party. Don't single out anyone for losing or make jokes criticizing the losers. You may change teams around or give the losing team some advantage in the next game so that everyone has the opportunity of being on a winning team. Don't risk hurting

Piano Tuner: I've come to tune your piano.
Lady: But we didn't send for you.
Piano Tuner: No, but your neighbors did.

someone's feeling or causing embarrassment. Definitely avoid any games that may degrade players. Don't let anyone become the butt of a joke or get laughed at, such as having them do embarrassing things. They become the center of attention in a way that doesn't boost their self-esteem.

Prizes can be awarded to the winners. It can be something simple like a tootsie roll or small toy. The losers can also get an award for being good sports, being the most enthusiastic, or whatever. This way everyone wins and gets a prize. Another idea for prizes is the activity prize. Instead of candy or a toy, give the winners a round of applause as praise.

Of course, for no-lose games where there is no loser or winner, everybody wins. These games are played for fun. No prize is necessary. In fact, no prize is necessary for any game. Choose the games that work best for you. Make everyone feel like a winner.

Cooperation and Involvement

You may have parties where a shy child does not want to participate. That's okay, don't force him to join in if he doesn't want to at that time. Tell him it's okay if he doesn't want to play, he can still have fun watching the other kids and if he wants to join in later, he is welcome. After seeing how much fun the others are having he may want to participate. You can ask him as the games progress if he wants to join in.

Sometimes pairing a shy child with a more outgoing child will help him loosen up and get into the mood of the party. Or having the child be your partner as you describe the rules of a game may be enough to break the ice. Go carefully. Shari Ann Pence says "One thing I have found to work with hesitant children is to let them watch the other guests to see exactly how the game is played. Then, if the game allows, I pick it up and take it to where they are seated and ask 'would you like to try from here?' Soon they are lining up with the rest of the guests to join in the fun. If they say no, I quickly move on to the next game. Be sure to include them when it comes to handing out favors for each game, whether or not they participated." Most kids, however, are more than willing to join in any games, they love to have fun.

Shy children are a minor problem. It's the overactive ones that create annoying disturbances. In games where children line up, some may push to get to the front of the line. To avoid conflict you should take charge and announce how the kids are to line up. Since the party is in honor of the birthday child, he or she should be given the privilege of being first in line. If there is a struggle over who will be next in line, then you can pronounce the order, such as: shortest to tallest, alphabetical order, youngest to oldest, etc. Let them know that this will be the order of play for each game. Tell the children to remember who is in front of them and line up behind that person every time.

Some games are so much fun, many of the children will want to play them again. Go ahead and let them. You need to be flexible. They will enjoy it more if they are allowed to play their favorite games more than once. Observe the children's enthusiasm while playing the games. If they seem to really enjoy one, you may ask them if they would like to play it again. Don't play a game more then three times, for the kids will begin to tire of it.

You should have more games planned than you have time for. This way if some games aren't as popular popular with a certain group of kids or something unexpected happens, you will have backups. The kids may enjoy themselves so much that you may be asked to stay longer—in which case you would charge an additional fee. Make this point clear if you are asked to stay longer.

If at all possible, have the hostess save the refreshments until after the games are over. You may be invited to share the treats, but ordinarily you should decline. Once your scheduled time is up, request payment and leave. You do not want to overstay your welcome or impose on the family. Your job is to provide the entertainment; you are not a guest.

Game Selection

What games can you play? I have included several games in this chapter as samples of the types of games you can play at birthday parties. There are scads of books on party games. Visit your local library or bookstore, and you are sure to find many suitable resources. I have included the names of a few good books in the appendix.

Do your research before going to the party. Read several game books. Create a games file by writing in a notebook or on index cards those games that seem most suitable for you. List many more games than you would possibly use at a single party. If you do two parties for the same person, or a party for one of the guests, you should be prepared to have games the children have not played before.

Son: Dad, would you do my arithmetic for me?
Dad: No, son, it wouldn't be right.
Son: Well, at least you could try.

Sometimes a game that sounds good on paper doesn't turn out to be as much fun as anticipated. Or a game may not last long or take longer then expected. For these reasons, you should test all the games you use before introducing them at a scheduled party. You may try them out on your own kids and their friends.

One idea that could also provide you with free advertising while you test your games is to offer to conduct some games for free at a local day care center. The day care people would probably be overjoyed to have an entertainer come by and entertain the kids, especially if their cost is simply allowing you to hand out a brochure or toy (with your advertising on it). You may want to do this whether you are testing new games or not, just to get publicity.

Once you have a set of games that are successful with various age groups, you can introduce one new game at a time during a party. If it doesn't take off like the others, cut it short and move on to one of your tried and proven games. If the kids have fun with it, you can add it to your permanent list of games.

Another publicity idea is to take snapshots of the kids during the party. Bring a Polaroid camera with you and take candid pictures as the kids play the games. These unposed photos add to the fun of the event and make the party more memorable. You may want to add a picture of yourself with the birthday child. To make the pictures work as advertising for you, place a sticker with your name and phone number on the back of each photo. You now have an advertisement that the kids and parents will keep for years. You may also take a photo of the winners of certain games. Their prize is the photograph. You can have several hundred address labels printed with your name, phone number, and perhaps a slogan or some descriptive words for a reasonable price. These stickers can be placed on other giveaways as well.

Games for Preschoolers

The hardest parties to entertain at are those with very young children—the preschoolers. They don't understand magic, balloons are unsafe, and face painting is of little interest. Storytelling and puppets can only be enjoyed if the stories or actions are simple. But little children are full of energy. They have short attention spans. Stories and puppets can keep them entertained for a few minutes, but unless they are allowed to move their bodies or talk, they will get bored fast.

Games allow these youngsters to do what they do best, and that is wiggle, move, and talk. The games preschoolers enjoy are different from those older kids and adults find amusing. Preschoolers gain much of their enjoyment just from physical activity.

Several games are described in this chapter suitable for preschoolers. Although the descriptions of these games sound rather unexciting, they are fun for the little ones. All the games for very young children are noncompetitive. Little children are not yet at an age where they understand or appreciate competition. So these games are all highly active, no winners or losers; the fun is in the doing.

Young children enjoy short follow-along stories or rhymes, using the actions of the fingers and hands. You tell the story and act out parts, using your hands and the children copy your motions. Here are some examples:

Five Little Monkeys
Five little monkeys jumping on the bed,
(Five fingers of right hand jump on left hand.)
One fell off and bumped his head.
(One finger falls off hand. Then hold head with both hands and nod head back and forth.)
Mommy called the doctor, and the doctor said,
(Hold right hand up in cupping shape to ear.)
"That's what you get for jumping on the bed!"
(Point index finger and shake it.)
Four little monkeys . . .
(Repeat for four, three, two, and one monkey. End with the following line.)
No more monkeys jumping on the bed."

Ten Little Fingers
I have ten little fingers,
And they all belong to me.
I can make them do things.
Would you like to see?
(Hold fingers up and wiggle them.)
I can shut them up tight
(Make fist.)
Or open them wide.
(Open them.)
I can put them together
(Put palms together.)
Or make them all hide.
(Hide hands behind the back.)
I can make them jump high
(Raise them above your head.)

Or make them go low.
(Bring them down.)
I can fold them up quietly
And sit just so.
(Fold your hand in your lap.)

The Bunny
Once there was a bunny
(Close fist with first and second fingers up.)
And a green cabbage head.
(Use both hands to make cabbage.)
"I think I'll have some breakfast,"
the little bunny said.
(Close fist with first and second fingers up.)
So he nibbled and he nibbled;
Then he cocked his ears to say,
(Straighten fingers representing ears.)
"I think this is the time I should be hopping on my way."
(Move hand hopping along lap.)

Hands on Shoulders
(Do the actions this rhyme indicates.)
Hands on shoulders, hands on knees,
Hands behind you, if you please.
Touch your shoulders, now your nose,
Now your hair, and now your toes.
Hands up high in the air,
Down at your sides and touch your hair.
Hands up high as before;
Now clap your hands, one, two, three, four.

All of Me
(Touch each part of the body as you name it.)
See my eyes.
See my nose.
See my chin.
See my toes.
See my waist.
See my knee.
Now you have seen all of me!
(Raise arm up and out.)

If I Could
If I could play the piano,
This is the way I would play.
(Move fingers like playing piano.)
If I had a guitar,
I would strum the strings this way.
(Hold guitar and strum.)
If I had a trumpet,
I'd toot to make a tune.

(Blow on a horn and move fingers.)
But, if I played a drum,
I'd go boom, boom, boom!
(Pound a drum.)

The Peanut
Peanut sat on a railroad track,
(Pretend to hold peanut between two fingers.)
His heart was all a-flutter.
(Pat chest.)
Around the bend
(Make circle with arm.)
came Number Ten:
(Show ten fingers.)
Choo-choo
(Pull train whistle.)
—peanut butter!
(Palms downward, move hands sideways.)

Five Little Fishes
(Hold up all five fingers and bend them down, one by
one, starting with the thumb.)
Five little fishes
were swimming near the shore,
One took a dive,
then there were four.
Four little fishes
were swiming out to sea,
One went for food,
then there were three.
Three little fishes said,
"Now what shall we do?"
One swam away,
and then there were two.
Two little fishes
were having great fun,
But one took a plunge,
and then there was one.
One little fish said,
"I like the warm sun."
Away he went,
and then there were none.

Five Little Froggies
(Hold up all five fingers and bend them down, one by
one, starting with the thumb.)
Five little froggies
sat on the shore,
One went for a swim,
then there were four.
Four little froggies

looked out to sea,
One went swimming,
and then there were three.
Three little froggies said,
"What can we do?"
One jumped in the water,
then there were two.
Two little froggies
sat in the sun, One swam off,
and then there was one.
One little froggie said,
This is no fun!"
He dived in the water,
and then there were none.

The Turtle

There was a little turtle,
(Make a fist with thumb poking up like a turtle's head.)
He lived in a box.
(Form box with both hands.)
He swam in a puddle,
(Point finger and make circles on palm of opposite hand.)
He climbed on rocks.
(Claw as if climbing.)
He snapped at a mosquito,
(Snap with fingers and thumb.)
He snapped at a flea,
(Snap with fingers and thumb.)
He snapped at a minnow,
(Snap with fingers and thumb.)
He snapped at me.
(Snap with fingers and thumb at yourself.)
He caught the mosquito,
(Grab the air with your fist.)
He caught the flea,
(Grab the air with your fist.)
He caught the minnow,
(Grab the air with your fist.)
But he didn't catch me.
(Point to yourself and shake head "no".)

The Beehive

Here is a beehive;
(Cup hands together.)
Where are the bees?
Hidden away where nobody sees.
(Peek inside cupped hands.)
Now they come creeping out of the hive—
One, two, three, four, five!
(Hold up fingers, one by one.)
Buzz-z-z-z-z-z-z-z-z!
(Have fingers fly away.)

Can You Hop Like A Rabbit?

(Perform the actions standing.)
Can you hop like a rabbit?
(Put hand to ears and hop.)
Can you jump like a frog?
(Crouch down and jump.)
Can you fly like a bird?
(Flap arms.)
Can you run like a dog?
(Run in place.)
Can you walk like a duck?
(Bend knees, lower waste to sitting position, and waddle.)
Can you swim like a fish?
(Make swimming motion.)
And be still, like a good child—
As still as this?
(Fold hands and stand still.)

Where is Thumbkin?

(This finger play can be sung to the tune of "Frere Jacques".)
Where is Thumbkin,
(Both hands are behind your back.)
Where is Thumbkin?
Here I am,
(Bring out one hand and show thumb.)
Her I am.
(Bring out the other hand and show thumb.)
"How are you today, sir?"
(Wiggle one thumb up and down.)
"Very well, I thank you!"
(Wiggle the other thumb in response.)
Run away,
(Put one hand behind your back.)
Run away.
(Put the other hand behind your back.)
Where is Pointer?. . .
(Repeat rhyme with index finger.)
Where is Tall One?. . .
(Repeat rhyme with middle finger.)
Where is Ring Boy (or Girl)?. . .
(Repeat with ring finger.)
Where is Pinky?. . .
(Repeat with little finger.)

"Why did Buster leave his job?"
"Illness."
"Anything serious?"
"Yes. The boss got sick of him."

Finger puppets can give an added dimension to finger rhymes.

An excellent resource of finger rhymes is *Mitt Magic* by Lynda Roberts, a book which describes how to make finger puppets and use simple rhymes to amuse preschoolers. Another book with an assortment of games for preschoolers is *1• 2 • 3 Games; No-Lose Group Games for Young Children* by Jean Warren. Other excellent books are listed in the appendix.

Musical Games

Games can be an ideal time for music. The beat and rhythm of lively music can get kids moving and dancing spontaneously. Add it to an appropriate game and the fun doubles. Not all games work well with music, but those that do can be immensely enjoyable.

Music can be provided by a cassette or CD player with preselected songs of your choosing. Use a good quality cassette or CD player. Music that is muffled or full of static is not fun to listen to.

Musical games are great for preschoolers. A simple musical game for this age group is to play some lively music and have them all dance. You may want to lead the way by dancing too. They will get a kick out of seeing a grownup do a silly dance.

Many of the hand and action rhymes described in the last section can be performed with music.

Music can involve a great deal of physical activity: jumping, skipping, and clapping. Musical Chairs is an old favorite, though dozens of other games are just as much fun. Musical Freeze is one of these. In this game lively music is played while the kids wiggle and dance. The music is stopped intermittently and each time it does, the kids must stop, as if instantly frozen. This game can be played without any particular winner or loser, or to add competition, those who move are out, and the game continues until only one person remains.

Another variation of this game is to use a leader, either you or one of the children. As the music plays, all the kids must follow the leader and do as he does. Everyone freezes when the music stops.

If you like to sing, you can lead the children in a sing-a-long. Add sound effects, a word, a phrase, clapping of hands, or stomping the feet. The younger kids really enjoy this. Many songs containing nonsense words, animal noises, and unusual sounds work great. Take the classic "Old McDonald's Farm" for instance. Tell the children they're going to help you out with the animal sounds. Have fun practicing sounds such as moo, cock-a-doodle-do, bow-wow, baa baa, and the rest. Sing the song having them insert their part on your signal. The songs you use don't have to be funny, but the kids will have fun. They get a kick out of making the sound effects.

The kids can also participate by using physical movement. As the song is sung, the kids can act out certain parts. Some songs are especially well adapted for audience participation. The children's song "Do As I'm Doing" is an excellent activity song. As you sing, tap your foot, wiggle your chin, move your legs and arms, etc. The children follow along, copying everything you do.

A good source for over 50 different musical games is *Musical Games for Children of All Ages* by Esther L. Nelson.

FUN GAMES FOR CHILDREN

The following games will provide you with some ideas to get you started. Choose the ones that will work best for you. Research other books and add appropriate games to your game file.

Capture the Balloon

Ages: 6 and up.

Materials: Masking tape and round balloons for each player.

Number of players: Two teams with equal numbers.

Object of the game: To capture opponent's balloons.

Play action: Using string or masking tape, mark a line down the middle of the playing area. Divide the children into two groups and put them on opposite sides of the line. Give each child an inflated round balloon to guard. Using only their feet, each team is to try to capture as many of the opponent's balloons as they can during a specified time (about five minutes). The team with the most balloons on their side of the line at the end wins. Stress that players must not use their hands or arms, but can use only their feet, legs, torso, and head.

Hint: You might want to have the children play this game in their bare feet so they don't kick other players too hard in the shins.

Walk the Plank

Ages: 6 and up.

Materials: Board or strip of cloth about 6 inches wide.

Number of players: Three or more.

Object of the game: Successfully walk the plank.

Play action: Place a board (or cloth) on the ground. This is the pirates' plank. The children must walk the plank from one end to the other, and back again, without falling into the water. This sounds easy enough, except the water is full of sharks, crocodiles, and piranha. The other children play the part of the hungry creatures in the deep as the victim walks the plank. The sea creatures are lined up along the plank about three feet away. They can't touch the plank-walker, but are allowed to make growling and biting noises and gestures to scare him into falling off the plank and into the water.

Hint: To make the game more difficult use a narrower board.

> Ed: What happened to the human cannonball at the circus?
> Fred: He got fired.

Rapid-Fire Artists

Ages: 7 and up.

Materials: Paper and pencils.

Number of players: Two or more teams with equal numbers.

Object of the game: Identify drawing.

Play action: Each team sends an "artist" to the leader. The Leader whispers to these representatives some animal or other thing to draw. The representatives race back to their respective groups and begin to draw furiously. As soon as a group recognizes what is being drawn, the members yell it, all together. The artist must not give them any tip except by his drawing. He cannot say anything to team members or use letters or numbers in the drawing. Each time a new artist must be sent to the leader.

What Is It?

Ages: 8 and up.

Materials: None.

Number of players: Three or more.

Object of the game: Successfully guess selected object.

Play action: One player goes out of the room. The others select some article or thing. The player returns and tries to discover by questioning what it is. He is allowed twelve questions. He probably will first try to locate it. "Is it in this room?" "Is it in this town?" When he gets it located, he tries to find out something of its nature. "Is it an animal?" "Is it a vegetable?" "Is it a mineral?" When he thinks he has it, he names it. If he is correct, another player goes out and the game continues. If he is wrong and he has some questions left before he has used his twelve, he proceeds to ask some more questions.

Who's the Leader?

Ages: 6 and up.

Materials: None.

Number of players: Six or more.

Object of the game: Find the leader.

Play action: Players stand or sit in a circle. One player goes out. A leader is appointed. The whole group starts clapping and continues until the player sent out returns and takes the center of the ring. His goal is to discover who is leading the crowd in its actions. The leader changes from clapping, for instance, to patting his head, twirling his thumbs, jumping up and down, etc. All the other players do the same thing immediately. All players should not watch the leader. It's amazing how quickly the action goes around the circle, and how difficult it sometimes is to discover the leader. When finally discovered, the leader goes out and a new leader is selected.

Hint: It adds to the fun if the game is played to music.

Who Am I?

Ages: 6 and up.

Materials: Wand or ruler.

Number of players: Five or more.

Object of the game: Guess identity of the impersonator.

Play action: A blindfolded player holding a wand stands in the center of a circle of players. The circle, hand-in-hand, moves around singing some song such as "She'll Be Comin' 'Round the Mountain." When one verse is finished, they stand still. The blindfolded player now points his wand in the direction of the players in the circle. The player to whom it points must take hold of it and repeat three sounds indicated by the blindfolded player, such as "crow like a rooster," "meow like a cat," "bark like a dog," "call hogs," "laugh out loud," "sneeze," or "cry like a baby." The performer may make every effort to disguise his voice. The blindfolded player tries to identify the noisemaker. If successful, they exchange places.

Ha, Ha

Ages: 6 and up.

Materials: None.

Number of players: Five or more.

Object of the game: Keep from laughing.

Play action: Players are seated in a circle. The first player starts by saying, "Ha." The second player says, "Ha, Ha." The third says, "Ha, Ha, Ha." And so it goes around the circle with each player adding another "Ha." In each case the "Ha's" must be pronounced solemnly. The chances are,

however, that it will not get around the circle before the entire circle is responding with gales of laughter. Challenge players to keep the circle going as long as possible without anybody cracking up.

Do This and More

Ages: 6 and up.

Materials: None.

Number of players: Six or more.

Object of the game: Copy actions of other players and add new actions.

Play action: One player begins the game by doing something, such as putting the thumbs to the ears and wiggling the fingers. He points to another player who must repeat that action and add one of his own, such as putting his hand under his chin and wiggling his fingers. The next player may add sticking out his tongue. Each successive player must repeat, in order, all of the actions of the other players and add another. No player may be called on more than once unless he requests it.

Space Station

Ages: 6 and up.

Materials: Chairs for each player.

Number of players: Six or more.

Object of the game: Players must find chair to sit in.

Play action: Chairs are placed in a circle. This is the space station with each chair being a docking point. One child sits in each chair. One player is selected to be "It" or a new space ship looking for a place to dock. The other children are also space ships, who have found places to dock (the chairs). "It" goes from dock to dock around the space station and says, "Can I dock my ship?" Each ship answers, "No!" "It" goes to another dock, asking the same question and getting the same response. At any time "It" may say, "All ships out!" When this is said, all players must get off their chair and find another dock. As the space ships scramble for a new dock, "It" grabs a dock and sits down. The child left standing becomes "It" and the game continues.

Tic-Toc Find the Clock

Ages: 2-8.

Materials: Kitchen timer.

Number of players: Three or more.

Object of the game: Locate the clock.

Play action: Have the children leave the playing area. Wind up a kitchen timer and hide it in the game area.

If the timer has a loud tic-toc sound, wrap it up in a towel to muffle the sound a bit. Bring the children into the room and have them find the clock. Have them locate the "clock" by the sound of the tic-toc. The children will need to be quiet in order to hear the tic-toc. The first one who finds the timer is the winner. The winner gets to hide the timer for the next round.

Variation: For older children use a timer with a soft tic-toc or wrap it up with a couple of towels to reduce the noise. To add confusion and make the game harder, you may plant a decoy "clock" that also ticks. This timer will be in plain sight and not the hidden clock. It's purpose is to create noise to make it harder to hear the hidden timer.

Blind Man's Bluff

Ages: 7 and up.
Materials: Household items such as books, wastebasket, chairs, etc.
Number of players: Three or more.
Object of the game: Complete the obstacle course blindfolded.
Preparation: Create an obstacle course using pillows, books, wastebasket, or other small items in the party area for the children to walk through, step over or around, and crawl under.
Play action: Choose one person to go through the course blindfolded. Before he does, however, let him see and memorize the course. Let him count off how many steps there are between the items. Now blindfold him. While you do, be sure to talk a lot about what he's going to do, how difficult it will be, etc. While you are distracting him with talk, have others remove all the obstacles. Then start him on his course. Everyone will get a big kick out of seeing him wind his way carefully across an empty floor.
Variation: Split the children into two groups. Have one group walk through the obstacle course. After finishing the course take them into another room where they cannot see or hear anything going on in the obstacle course. Quickly have the ones remaining remove all obstacles from the obstacle course. Now blindfold the first player and take him to the start of the course. Tell him to start the course and caution him about the different objects. Watch the fun as the player wanders around the room stepping over objects that aren't there and wandering in circles. Once the child has figured out the game, take the blindfold off, and bring out the next player. Each player who completes the course can watch the others play the game. Tell the players that if they are about to accidentally hit an object or get hurt if they keep walking in the direction they are going, one of the nonplayers will gently stop them and redirect them. This will keep the player from hurting himself as well as confusing him more because he won't be able to touch any familiar objects that will help him identify his location. Keep the laughter down so the players don't get too suspicious.

Lily Pad

Ages: 5 and up.
Materials: Four lily pads made from Astro Turf-type welcome mats cut into the shape of lily pads. Two baseball caps, preferably green with frog eyes. You can purchase froggy eyes in craft stores around the macramé supplies. Two hula hoops or similar item.
Number of players: Two teams with equal numbers.
Object of the game: Finish first.
Play action: Each team gets two lily pads and one hat. The hula hoop is placed several feet away from the starting point and serves as a destination or turning around point. At the whistle, the starting player on each team places the frog hat on his head. He then lays one lily pad down in front of him close enough to hop on. When he is on the pad, he places the other one and hops, each time leaning down to pick up the pad behind him. His feet should not touch the ground, or he has to start over. When the player reaches the hoop, depending upon your rules, he either takes off the hat and picks up both pads and runs to the next person in line, or he turns and continues all the way back to the starting point. The team finishing first is the winner. You can add even more fun with this game if you have their teammates croak "RIBBIT!" each time a teammate hops.

Fried Chicken

Ages: 5 and up.
Materials: Two soft rubber chickens, two frying pans or something similar, two chef's hats, two oven mitts, two hula hoops or juggling rings.
Number of players: Two or more teams with equal numbers.
Object of the game: Finish first.
Play action: At the destination point, the rings or hoops represent the stove top. Place the frying pan, a rubber chicken, and oven mitt in the ring. Have the chef's hat at the starting point. At the whistle, each contestant puts on the hat and runs to the stove. They put on the oven mitt, place the chicken in the pan, toss him in the air and catch it, and then run back to the line. The winning team

is the one that fries all the chicken quickest. Teammates may make clucking noises. "Buck . . . buck . . .buucck!"

Stretch

Ages: 5 and up.
Materials: 16 loops of elastic, made from about a yard each of dressmaker elastic, ¾-inch width. Tie the ends so you have a loop which should be large enough to stretch over each of the children's bodies, without being too big.
Number of players: Two or more teams with equal numbers.
Object of the game: Finish first.
Play action: Team members stand in a line about an arm width apart. At the whistle the first person in line pulls one loop over his head and body, then steps out of loop and passes it to the next person. He then does the same with each loop consecutively. Only one loop at a time may be on anyone. When the last person in line has completed all the loops, he will bring them to the front. The team who finishes quickest is the winner.

Pass the Ring

Ages: 5 and up.
Materials: A piece of rope 20-30 feet in length depending on the size of your group. One to three round shower curtain rings.
Number of players: Two or more teams with equal numbers.
Object of the game: Finish first.
Preparation: Tie the rope into a big loop. Snap a shower curtain ring onto the line.

Have all players stand outside the ring holding the rope with both hands. The players sing:
Pass, pass, pass the ring.
Pass, pass, pass the ring.
Pass, pass, pass the ring.
Or you will be called out!
This is sung to the tune of "Skip to My Lou." The players sing continuously, while passing the ring. At your whim, blow the whistle. The person touching or closest to the ring is out. They step inside the ring of people and assist in catching the next player holding the ring. To make the game more interesting, add several rings to keep the players on their toes. As your rope holding players dwindle, you may have to use a smaller rope. Eliminate players down to two or three. Be sure you are behind the players so that they cannot anticipate the time you will blow the whistle.

Button, Button

Ages: 5 and up.
Materials: One button.
Number of players: Six or more.
Object of the game: Guess who has the button.
Play action: The players stand facing each other in a circle. A player is chosen to stand in the middle of the circle with his eyes closed and count out loud to fifteen. While he counts, the rest of the players pass the button around the circle. They stop when the counter reaches fifteen. The center player opens his eyes and is allowed three guesses as to who has the button. If he guesses correctly, he changes places with the one who has the button.

Magic Carpet

Ages: 5 and up.
Materials: One hand towel (or piece of paper) for each player.
Number of players: Five or more.
Object of the game: To be the last one standing on a towel.
Play action: Hand towels or sheets of paper are placed on the floor, one for each player. The players skip around the squares. At a signal from the leader, they try to stand on one of the squares. While they have been skipping, the leader has removed one of the squares, so one player will not be able to find a square and must leave the game. After each stop, a square is removed. The game goes on until only one player is left. Music can be used to start and stop movement.

Touch, Touch

Ages: 5 and up.
Materials: None.
Number of players: Three or more.
Object of the game: To remember sequence of items touched.
Play action: The first player selected by the leader leaves his seat, touches an object, and returns to his seat. The second player touches the same object, plus another one. Player number three repeats the process and adds another object. When a player cannot remember all the objects he must touch, the game is over and the leader selects a player to start the next game.

Bandit

Ages: 7 and up.
Materials: None.
Number of players: Six or more.
Object of the game: To be the last one remaining in the game.
Play action: The players sit in a circle. When the leader points to a player in the circle and calls out "Bandit," that player must place both of his hands over his ears immediately. At the same time, each of his two neighbors must place the hand nearest the bandit over his own ear on that side. The last of the three to cover his ears is out of the game and has to stand. The bandit then points and calls the next bandit, and the game goes on.

Chase the Animal

Ages: 7 and up.
Materials: Three beanbags.
Number of players: Seven or more.
Object of the game: To pass beanbags around a circle.
Play action: The players form a circle. One of the beanbags is given the name of an animal and started around the circle. After it goes around once, the leader starts another "animal" around the circle. This animal tries to catch up with the first one. After another time around, a third animal is started on its way. There is no winner or loser in this game.

Beanbag Relay

Ages: 6 and up.
Materials: One beanbag for each team.
Number of players: Two or more teams with equal number of players.
Object of the game: To finish first.

Play action: The players are lined up in single file in teams. All are standing. The first player on each team is given a beanbag. On a signal the player with the beanbag raises it up and drops it over his shoulder. The beanbag falls to the ground behind him. The next player in line bends over and picks up the beanbag and repeats the process. When the last player in the row picks up the beanbag, he holds it up in the air to signify that his row has finished. The team finishing first is the winner.

Twenty Questions

Ages: 8 and up.
Materials: None.
Number of players: Four or more.
Object of the game: To guess a name.
Play action: A player writes the name of a person, place, or thing on a piece of paper. He tells the group if the thing he has named is animal, vegetable, or mineral. The other players may ask a total of twenty questions to find out the subject. The questions must be the kind that can be answered by a yes or no. The first person to guess correctly may then ask the players to identify his subject. If a subject is not guessed in twenty questions, the player gives the correct answer and selects another player to take his place.

Chin-to-Chin

Ages: 5 and up.
Materials: One tennis ball for each team.
Number of players: Two or more teams with equal number of players.
Object of the game: To finish first.
Play action: Each team forms a line. A tennis ball is given to the first player in each line. They tuck the balls under their chins and on your signal pass them on through the line, chin to chin. Use of the hands is not allowed. Players should clasp their hands behind their backs. Should the tennis ball fall, it must be reintroduced back into the line one person back from where it fell.

Limbo Dance

Ages: 6 and up.
Materials: Broomstick.
Number of players: Two or more.
Object of the game: Players try to walk under stick without falling.
Play action: Children line up in single file. Two assistants hold a broomstick at about shoulder level. Music is played. One by one the players must walk (or dance) under the

broomstick without touching it and while standing on their feet. No part of their body other than their feet can touch the floor. After everyone has gone under at one height, the broomstick is dropped down a few inches and they all pass under again. The stick is gradually lowered and the children have a turn passing underneath. If a player touches the stick or the ground (except for the feet), he is out. The player who can pass under the broomstick at it lowest level is the winner.

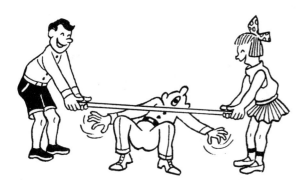

Musical Balloons

Ages: 5 and up.
Materials: Cassette player and music. Balloons for each player.
Number of players: Six or more
Object of the game: To be holding a balloon when the music stops.
Play action: Players stand in a circle. All participants except one are given an inflated balloon. As the music plays, all players pass their balloons in the same direction. When the music stops, the player without a balloon is out. The action is repeated with one less balloon and one less player. Play continues until only one player is remaining. If a balloon pops, any player without a balloon when the music stops is out.
Variation: Instead of using balloons you can use a variety of hats. Each player must put a hat on the head of the person sitting next to him. The hats are passed around the group as the music plays.

Chair Relay

Ages: 7 and up
Materials: Chairs for each player.
Number of players: Two teams with equal numbers.
Object of the game: Win the race around the chairs.
Play action: Players are divided into two teams. Chairs

are lined up in two rows. Each player sits in a chair. The first player rises from his chair and runs around the entire row and sits back in his original chair. As soon as he sits down, player number two gets up and makes the circuit. So it goes until each player has been entirely around. The first team to return to their seats wins.
Variation: As soon as player number one passes number two, that player gets up and follows him. Number three follows two and so on. Each makes the circuit and gets seated.

The Tall Tale

Ages: 8 and up.
Materials: Bag containing several unrelated objects.
Number of players: Four or more.
Object of the game: To create a story using the contents of the bag.
Play action: Game leader pulls an object out of the bag and starts to tell a story using that object. After starting the story, the leader removes another object and one of the players continues with the story started by the game leader. Each player continues the story as new objects are chosen. When the last object is removed, the player must bring the story to an end. Players should restrict their story segments to just a few minutes at most.
Variation: To personalize the story, have players use names of people present or who they all know.

Stiff Upper Lip

Ages: 6 and up.
Materials: One card for each team.
Number of players: Two or more teams with equal numbers.
Object of the game: Finish first.
Play action: Each team forms a line. The players at the head of each line are given a card about 3 x 5-inches in size. The players must hold the card between their upper lip and nose. The card is passed to each player in turn this way. No hands allowed. Only the lips and nose can touch the card. The first team to pass the card to the last team member wins. If the card is dropped, it must be placed back into the line one player behind the one who dropped it.

Patient: I'm always dizzy for half an hour after I get up in the morning.
Doctor: Well, try getting up half an hour later.

Ping Pong Race

Ages: 8 and up.

Materials: A ping pong ball for each team and drinking straws for each player.

Number of players: Two or more teams with equal number of players.

Object of the game: To finish first.

Play action: Team relay. Each team forms a line. A starting line is made using masking tape laid out on the floor. Another strip of masking tape parallel to the first is laid out about 10 feet in front of the starting line. Using only the air they can blow out of the straw, players must push the ping pong ball in front of them, cross over the masking tape marker, reverse direction, and return to their teammates. The next player in line repeats the action. The first team to have its last player blow his ping pong ball back over the finish line (same line as starting line) wins.

Run Run Run

Ages: 5 and up.

Materials: A ball for each player. You can use any type or combination of balls—baseball, tennis ball, football, etc.

Number of players: Six or more.

Object of the game: To grab one ball.

Play action: This is an outdoors game. All players stand behind the starting line. Balls numbering one less than the number of players are tossed out in front of the line. When the games leader gives the signal, all players rush to claim a ball. The player who does not get a ball is out. One ball is removed and the action is repeated. The player to grab the last ball is the winner.

Stone Face

Ages: 6 and up.

Materials: None.

Number of players: Two teams with equal number of players.

Object of the game: Make opposing team members laugh.

Play action: One team is seated in a straight line facing opposing team. The first team does all it can to make the players on the other team laugh. They can use whatever means they can to accomplish this goal without making any physical contact. They can make funny faces, tell jokes, etc. Members of the second must keep a stone face the whole time. If they laugh, giggle, or even smile, they are out. The winner of the first round is the last player to keep a straight face. Players then reverse roles and the laugh makers become the recipients of the opposing players' antics.

Variation: There are many possible variations to this game. One is that all the children can try to keep a stone face while the games leader or another child tries to make the whole group laugh. Players are eliminated as they laugh until only one stony faced contestant is left. A game leader with a good sense of humor can perform a number of ridiculously funny antics to the amusement of the kids.

Simon Says

Ages: 4-8.

Materials: None.

Number of players: Two or more.

Object of the game: Have players do what Simon says.

Play action: Although this is an old game, it is a lot of fun for the younger kids. This game takes on a new dimension when the games leader plays Simon. All players are to follow the actions of Simon when he precedes a command with "Simon says . . ." When he doesn't say "Simon says," all those who follow his actions are out. The novelty of having the games leader be Simon allows for greater variety in actions and trickery.

Run to Mommy

Ages: 2-5.

Materials: None.

Number of players: Two or more.

Object of the game: Children run to their mothers.

Play action: The children line up along a starting line. Their mothers line up about 10 or so feet in front of them. When the signal is given to start, all the children run to their mothers. No winner or loser is identified. The game is played just for the fun of having the kids run to their mothers.

Catch the Clown

Ages: 3-6.
Materials: None.
Number of players: Two or more.
Object of the game: Children try to catch clown.
Play action: Games leader takes on identity of a clown. If not dressed as a clown, you can put on a fake clown nose and/or goofy hat. On the signal, all the kids chase the clown and try to tag him. Play this game as long as the kids remained interested. When interest or energy begins to fade, allow all the kids to catch the clown.

Find the Shoe

Ages: 2-5.
Materials: None.
Number of players: Two or more.
Object of the game: Find hidden shoe.
Play action: Have the children remove one of their shoes and put it in the middle of the room. While the children cover their eyes, hide the shoes in various places around the room. Have the children open their eyes and search for their own shoes and put them back on.

Funny Face

Ages: 2-6.
Materials: None.
Number of players: Three or more.
Object of the game: Make funny faces.
Play action: Line the children up in single file. Have the first child turn around, look at the person behind him, and make a funny face. That person then turns around and tries to imitate the face passing it on to the next child. Let the last child come to the head of the line and make a new face and play the game again.

Copycat

Ages: 2-5.
Materials: None.
Number of players: Three or more.
Object of the game: Copy the actions of the leader.
Play action: The leader stands or sits in a wacky position. When the leader calls out "Copycat," all the children must imitate the leader's position.

Tightrope Walker

Ages: 2-7.
Materials: Masking tape.
Number of players: Three or more.
Object of the game: Walk along imaginary tightrope.
Preparation: Place a strip of masking tape alone the floor to simulate a tightrope.
Play action: Have each player walk along the tightrope without falling. You can make this more interesting by calling out directions such as "Walk the tightrope on your toes! Walk on your knees! Walk using your elbows! Walk using your ear."

Hocus Pocus

Ages: 2-6.
Materials: None.
Number of players: Three or more.
Object of the game: Imitate an animal.
Play action: Players form a circle around the games leader who assumes the character of a magician. Games leader says, "hocus pocus you are turned into _____". (Choose an animal all the kids are familiar with.) They all move about the room pretending to be that animal. The games leader then says the magic word and changes them into another animal. This can continue as long as the children remain interested.
Hint: After a few animals, you may put a little more action into the game by turning them into other animals in rapid succession.

Zoo Animals

Ages: 3-7.
Materials: None.
Number of players: Four or more.
Object of the game: Guess the zoo animal.
Play action: The children sit in a circle to create a zoo cage. One child stands in the center of the cage and pretends to be an animal. The rest of the children try to guess what animal he is portraying. The one who guesses right goes to the center of the cage and becomes the zoo animal for the next round.

Little Seeds

Ages: 2-5.
Materials: None.
Number of players: One or more.
Object of the game: Act out growing like a seedling.
Play action: Tell the children how seeds are planted in the ground and grow. Have them pretend they are little seeds. The children curl into balls on the floor. Then say, "Clouds are coming and the rain is falling. Now the sun is coming out and warming the seeds up. Mr. Sunshine says, 'Wake up little seed, wake up.'" The children open their eyes and slowly start to stretch. Say, "Get up out of the ground, little seed, so you can grow." The children get up and put their arms above their heads. Now say, "Little seed, you have grown into a beautiful flower."

Going to Grandma's House

Ages: 2-5.
Materials: None.
Number of players: One or more.
Object of the game: Act out going to grandma's house.
Play action: Say to the children, "Let's go to grandma's house. First we must put on our coats." Act out putting on a coat. The say, "Let's get in the car." Act out opening the door and riding. Say, "Oh, this road is bumpy." Make the motions of going over bumps. Then say, "Look, let's wave to the policeman." Make waving motions. Now say, "We're almost there. Here comes grandma now. Let's give her a great big hug." Act out giving grandma a hug.

Helping Mother and Father

Ages: 2-5.
Materials: None.
Number of players: One or more.
Object of the game: Act out helping parents.
Play action: Direct the children in doing actions that represent helping their parents. You might say, "Let's help mother sweep the floor." The children act out sweeping the floor. You could continue with making beds, washing windows, dusting, and doing other household chores. Then direct the children in actions that represent helping father such as raking leaves, digging in the garden, or washing the car.

Blowing up a Balloon

Ages: 2-7.
Materials: None.
Number of players: Four or more.
Object of the game: Act out blowing up a balloon.
Play action: The children hold hands in a circle. They blow air out of their mouths as if blowing up a balloon while at the same time making the circle get bigger and bigger. When the games leader says, "Pop," all the children fall down. Before having the balloon "pop," the games leader could let some of the air out of the balloon making the balloon (the circle) get smaller and smaller. The children can move in and out as the balloon expands and contracts.

Patient: I still feel very tired, doctor.
Doctor: Didn't you take those sleeping pills I gave you?
Patient: Well, they looked so peaceful in the little bottle that I didn't want to wake them up.

———

Mother: Donny, it's rude to keep reaching across the table for food. Haven't you got a tongue?
Donny: Yes, but my arm's longer.

Chapter 12

MAKING YOUR BUSINESS A SUCCESS

BUSINESS BASICS

Once you've learned how to do a few magic tricks or make balloon animals, you can't expect to simply go out and start earning money. You must also learn how to stay out of trouble, keep the tax collector happy, and effectively promote and market your business. Success doesn't just happen, you must plan it to happen. In this chapter we will cover the basic information needed to set up a birthday party business—record keeping, taxes, insurance, etc., all the necessary aspects of starting and running a business successfully.

Many people who start out in this business feel they don't need to bother with legal technicalities. At first when they are only working part-time they don't see the need to pay taxes or go through the trouble of registering their business. These are the people who eventually fail to become successful. If you want your birthday party business to be a success and to provide you with the financial rewards you are seeking, you must get into it seriously. You can do it as a hobby, but it will never amount to more than a part-time endeavor. You will have much more success, even if all you want is a part-time operation, if you conform to local laws and regulations and conduct yourself as a legitimate business. You will also reduce your chances of unpleasant encounters with tax collectors and lawyers.

Type of Business

One of the first decisions you must make when you start a business is to determine which of the three basic types of business entities to use—sole proprietorship, partnership, or corporation. Legal and tax considerations will enter into this decision.

A sole proprietorship is the simplest form of business organization and the easiest to operate, especially if you work primarily as a birthday party entertainer. As a sole proprietorship, you *are* the business. You have total control over and responsibility for how your business is financed and operated. All profits you make are yours, but you are also personally responsible for all of your business debts and liabilities. This means that if you cannot pay a debt, the creditor can go after your personal assets to satisfy this debt. One of the nice things about being an independent entertainer is that you have few expenses as compared to most other businesses.

When you figure your taxable income for the year, you must add in any profit, or subtract out any loss, you have from your business. This is reported on a separate Schedule C, *Profit or Loss From Business*, and included with your tax return, Form 1040. Most birthday party entertainers operate as sole proprietors.

A partnership is a relationship between two or more persons who join together to carry on a trade or business.

Each person contributes money, property, labor, or skill, and expects to share in the profits (or losses) of the business. Many birthday party businesses combine the skills and talents of two or more individuals in a partnership that can make them more successful. For example, a person with a computer, accounting skills, and marketing knowledge can be a valuable asset to another person who doesn't know beans about these things, but loves to entertain children. Or one could be responsible for catering and decorations while the other takes care of entertainment. This way each partner can concentrate on his or her area of expertise without having to learn new skills to make the company function. Frequently, both partners will take part in entertaining, as well as doing the office and paperwork. One could specialize in performing magic while the other is primarily a puppeteer. This way their entertainment business will have more to offer and they can refer customers to each other. In a team effort they can share in the expenses and duties and cover for each other when one is sick or on vacation.

Partnerships must file their taxes on Form 1065, *U.S. Partnership Return of Income*. This requires more time and energy to prepare than the form for the sole proprietor. A joint undertaking to share expenses or the mere co-ownership of property that is used in the business is not a partnership. A spouse or children, for example, who help out in the business are not necessarily partners even though they may be compensated for their labors. Although a partnership can be formed with a verbal agreement, it is best to have a formal signed contract. This document specifies what has been invested by each partner and exactly what is expected from each of them.

Corporations are normally owned by a group of people who are called shareholders. The shareholders run the company through a board of directors. Officers and employees in the corporation may also be shareholders or members of the board of directors. Corporations are entitled to special tax deductions not available to sole proprietors or partnerships, but because they are considered separate entities from their owners, the company profits are taxed. Because of this, owners of small corporations could end up paying more taxes than sole proprietors or partnerships. One of the primary advantages of incorporation is that shareholders cannot be held responsible for the company's debts and liabilities. This gives owners some

degree of protection not provided to other types of businesses. Legal judgments against the corporation are limited to the business assets, and lawyers usually cannot go after individual shareholders to satisfy debts. A major disadvantage is that corporations are more closely regulated by the government and the paperwork for starting and maintaining this type of business is an unnecessary burden to party entertainers.

Another type of corporation designed primarily for smaller business is an *S corporation*. This type of corporation allows small business enterprises to benefit from many of the advantages of being incorporated, including protection from liability, without overburdening them with regulations and paperwork. Since this entity was designed for small businesses, the government has put a limit on the maximum number of shareholders or owners an S corporation can have. In many states it is possible for a husband and wife team to satisfy requirements and form an S corporation. However, the amount of work required and the expense of setting up and maintaining the business, which includes many bothersome tax forms and additional taxes that sole proprietors and partnerships don't have to deal with, makes incorporating unattractive to most birthday party entertainers.

If you are running your entertainment business by yourself or with your spouse and family, a sole proprietorship is probably the best type of business for you. Keeping your business simple allows you to devote more of your time to making it successful and less time and frustration with government regulations and paperwork. For more detailed information about the three basic types of businesses and what is required for each, obtain a copy of the IRS publication 334, *Tax Guide for Small Business*. This book is essential for anybody starting up a new business. It describes in detail what records must be kept, what deductions are allowed, and how to fill out the various tax forms, and includes many valuable examples. Reading this book should be one of the first things you do *before* you start up your business. The book is free and you can pick it up at your nearest IRS office, or request one by mail.

Business Name

One of the first things to consider when starting a new business is choosing a name. This can be fun, but you should choose a name with care. I recommend that you pick a name that is simple and easy to pronounce. You don't want people avoiding mentioning you because the name is difficult or uncomfortable to say. You should also choose a name that describes your business and skills

> Judge: Why did you only burglize apartments on the third floor?
> Burgler: Well, Your Honor, that's my story and I'm sticking to it.

> Molly: What's the best way to count cows?
> Polly: On a cow-culator.

so that potential clients and business associates can easily identify what you do.

You can use the name of your performing character as your business name, for example, "Buttons the Clown" or "Alberto the Magician." You may also simply use your own first or last name along with a descriptive term such as "William Gordon, Master Magician" or "Sabrina's Puppets."

Your business name can be different than your real name and your character name, for instance: The Puppet Works, Laughter Unlimited, Rainbow Entertainment, Just for Kidz.

You can tag onto the end of your name words such as entertainment, company, enterprises, etc. Words you should not use are corporation (Corp.), incorporated (Inc.), and limited (Ltd.). These terms all denote a corporation and your business should be legally incorporated before you use them.

Once you have chosen a name, you must go to your local county clerk's office (this is usually in the county courthouse) and register your business name and get a Fictitious Name Statement. This is discussed in more detail in this chapter in the section on licenses and permits.

If you use your own name as a part of your company name, such as "Jan Smith, Balloonologist," in most places you are not required to get a Fictitious Name Statement. Many localities will waive the registration even if only your last name is included in the business name. So "Nelson Entertainment" would not need to be registered. Check with your local county clerk's office to see what the requirements are in your area.

Business Location and Address

Unless you already rent an office outside your home for other purposes, working out of your home is the cheapest and most convenient route you can take. Renting a separate office, especially when you are first starting out and income is at its lowest, is generally an unnecessary luxury and expense.

There is nothing wrong with working out of the home. In some types of businesses home-based workers may not be taken as seriously, or considered as professional or successful as those who can afford an outside office. The great majority of birthday party entertainers, however, work out of their homes, and most clients, realizing this, show no prejudice.

There are many advantages to working out of a home-based office. Convenience is obviously one of the prime benefits. You can spend as much time at the "office" as you need and still enjoy all the conveniences of home. You have constant access to business calls and records. Overhead expenses are lower. You can take time to attend young children or fill other obligations throughout the day. You are also entitled to some important tax deductions. You may be able to deduct a part of your rent and household costs, such as trash removal, gas, and electricity, as business expenses (see *Tax Guide for Small Business* for details).

If you maintain a home-based office, you should be aware of zoning laws. Because of zoning laws, technically it is illegal to operate a business out of the home in many residential areas. The zoning laws were established to protect homeowners from businesses that create a lot of noise, crowd streets and sidewalks with customers/clients, produce offensive odors, and otherwise inconvenience neighbors. Some areas require home-based businesses located in residential zones to acquire "conditional use," or "special-use" permits. Many home-based workers have challenged zoning laws which prohibit or restrict home businesses and, although they have not always been successful, they have usually been allowed to continue to work at home without legal reprisals so long as there are no complaints from area residents. Barbara Brabec in her book *Homemade Money* explains that home-based workers have been able to avoid zoning conflicts by using a post office box or a private postal box as their business address. Since the post office and postal boxes are located in a commercial zone, the business is considered as being located in that zone. But again, there must not be complaints from the neighbors. If you don't disturb your neighbors and no one complains about what you are doing, in most cases you can maintain a home-based office regardless of the zoning laws.

Bank Account

You should open up a separate checking account for your business rather than use your personal account. The reason for keeping your business and personal finances separate is to maintain an accurate record of your business finances. Combining the two will only get you confused later on when you're trying to figure your taxes or assess your business finances.

If you have chosen a business name other than your own name, you will need to add this name to your bank account. This is so you can deposit checks written out to your business and so you can have checks with your business name printed on it. The bank needs to know that you and your business are the same, and they will need to see the Fictitious Name Statement you obtained at the county courthouse for verification.

Some banks will allow self-employed customers to put their business name on their personal checking account. In this case, you can have two personal accounts—one for personal use and one for business. This is the most economical way to go. Other banks may require you to have an actual business account. This is okay, except they usually charge businesses additional or higher processing fees, and minimum balances are usually larger, so it will cost you a little more for a business account. Shop around for a bank that will let you use a personal account for your business or one that has the most economical terms for their business accounts.

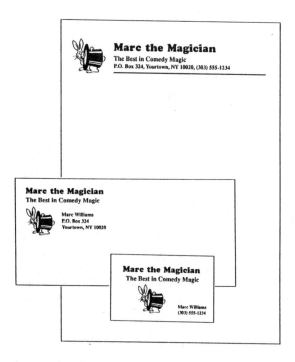

Stationery and Envelopes

An important part of your business success will depend on the image you present. The way you present yourself will influence what people think of you. Even if you are a beginner if you try to look and act like an experienced professional you will be perceived as one. As a professional, you will be able to charge higher rates and interest more people in your services.

One of the best ways to project a positive image is to have professionally designed stationery, matching envelopes, and business cards printed using your business name. I stress "professionally designed" because too many self-employed individuals take little thought in designing a logo or letterhead and their designs shout "amateur!" Have a graphic artist design your logo and letterhead or ask your printer for suggestions.

Printed stationery is important because it conveys the image that you are a successful professional. It is important to present a proper business attitude and appearance. Include your business name, mailing address, and phone number on the stationery.

Telephone

Most home-based businesses use their residential lines for their business. After all, why pay extra for another phone line when one is already available? I don't recommend this. Phone regulations in each state and province vary, and in some places it is illegal to use your personal line in a business. Depending on your local regulations, you may simply be asked to stop, or you may be charged business phone rates, or be hit with a hefty fine. If you print your phone number on your stationery and business cards (as you should), or in advertisements, and answer the phone with a business name, sooner or later you will be discovered. Call your local phone company to find out what the regulations are in your area.

Using your residential phone in your business does not qualify it for a tax deduction. The first phone line in the home cannot be used as a tax deduction. A second line can be fully deductible if it is used primarily for your business. In areas where business can be conducted over a residential line, you can have two personal lines and designate one as your business line. Of course, all long distance business calls are deductible regardless of which phone is used.

The phone you use in business should be answered with the business name and not with a simple "Hello." This is all part of conducting yourself in a businesslike manner and conveying a professional image. If one of your children answers the phone, the caller may think he has the wrong number or doubt you are running a serious business. This may cause a potential client to go elsewhere. You cannot simply tell your family not to answer the phone during certain times. Calls are not restricted to just business hours or on weekdays. Although most business calls will come during normal working hours, you will receive calls at most any hour and on weekends and holidays.

I recommend that you get a separate business line regardless of state regulations. One major advantage of having a business line is that your phone number will be listed in the business section of the phone book. People looking for birthday party entertainers will usually look in the phone book first. Potential clients can also get in touch with you by asking for directory assistance. Not having a business listing is a serious mistake because it will stifle business opportunities and prevent many potential clients from getting in contact with you. The cost of having a business line is well worth it.

You have three options: (1) use a second personal line for business (if state laws permit), (2) add a business line (the best option), or (3) remove your personal line and install a single business line (this reduces the cost of having a second line and gets your company listed in the *Yellow Pages*, but you cannot deduct the basic phone cost for business and you have to constantly regulate who answers the phone).

Another consideration you need to make is using an answering machine or answering service. Having an answering machine is important to a one-person business. You cannot be at home all the time to answer your phone. Potential clients can leave messages with some degree of assurance that their calls will be returned. This prevents them from recalling needlessly or from going elsewhere with their business.

Licenses and Permits

Before you can go into business, you must conform to all government laws and regulations. Most licenses and permits are regulated by local governments: city, county, and state. You can expect to pay something for any licenses and permits you need. Fees can run anywhere from $10 to as much as $100 or more. Some home-based businesses ignore these requirements and get away with it. But I feel it is too much of a risk, and it limits the amount of exposure you can get because if you get too much publicity or too much business, someone is going to find out and you could be hit with a heavy fine or put out of business.

If your business goes by a name other than your own name, you will need to get a fictitious name, also known as DBA, which means "doing business as." If you do business under a fictitious name, you are required to register the name in the county you do business. This prevents other businesses in the county from doing business under the same name.

Before your name can be registered, it must be checked against all the other business names in the county. If the name you have chosen, or a very similar name, is already registered by someone else, you will need to pick another name. If you live in a large metropolitan area it's possible that your first choice is already taken, or there is another business with a name which is very similar. So you might want to have another name selected just in case your first choice is not available. When your business name is cleared and registered, you will receive a Fictitious Name Statement which allows you to do business under that name. In addition to registering your name, you will be required to publish a notice of your business name in a general circulation newspaper. Any advertisement you may plan to run in the paper would satisfy this requirement. But you can fulfill this requirement by placing a small inexpensive classified ad. The county clerk may even provide you with a list of local newspapers which carry such ads. The cheapest papers to advertise in are usually local publications which are devoted almost entirely to classified advertising.

Registration of your trade name is good for five to 10 years (depending on your locality), after which time you will need to renew your registration. If you don't renew your registration, another person can claim your business name and you will have to change your company name. Most county offices do not bother to send renewal notices, so you will have to keep track of when your registration expires. Contact your county clerk's office for details.

Besides the Fictitious Name Statement, most places require businesses to get a local business license. Businesses which use a fictitious name usually must get their Fictitious Name Statement first. All types of businesses are required to get a license. Some occupations such as accountants, lawyers, chiropractors, doctors, and other professionals are expected to have educational qualifications and are required to pass a test before a license is issued. But for most businesses, including entertainers, no special test or certification is required. Business licenses are renewed every year or two.

Every state which has a sales tax issues a sales tax permit. In most states, service sales are not taxable. But if you sell merchandise (e.g., cake, ice cream, decorations) along with your service, you must collect sales tax. If you don't sell any products, you don't have to worry about getting a sales tax permit. For more information on the sales tax requirements in your area, contact your state and city revenue offices.

> Polly: My sister is black and blue, because she puts on face cream, hair cream, and body oil every night.
> Molly: But why does that make her black and blue?
> Polly: She keeps slipping out of bed.

RECORD KEEPING AND TAXES

Bookkeeping is an aspect of business that is often dreaded, but necessary. You must keep accurate records not only for tax purposes, but to help you in the operation of your business. Many business decisions will be based on information from your financial records. The only way you will really know if you're making a profit may be to sum up your profits and subtract your expenses. Paying attention to your business records is particularly important with home-based businesses where personal and business finances can become mixed and confused.

Keeping an accurate financial record is not really difficult. You do not need an accountant to keep your books or produce complicated financial statements. All you need to do is keep a daily record of all your business income and expenses. Buy a couple of ledger books at an office supply store—one to record expenses and the other to record income. Every time you have a business expense or receive a payment, write it down. Write it down that day. Do not wait, or you may forget to enter it. Keeping your books accurate should be a daily practice requiring only a few minutes.

All business transactions should be made through your business checking account. When you receive a payment, deposit it in your account. Pay all your business expenses with a business check. This way your income and expenses are easily recorded and well documented. You may not, however, be able to pay all of your expenses by check. Some payments will have to be in cash. Make sure that these expenses are recorded in your expense ledger and keep your receipts.

Accounting Method

For income tax purposes, you are going to have to choose an accounting method. A method is chosen when you file your first tax return for your business. After that, you must use the same method every year. If you want to change your accounting method, you must first get permission from the IRS. The two primary accounting methods are *cash* and *accrual*.

The cash method of accounting is used by the vast majority of birthday party entertainers. If you sell a product rather than, or in addition to, a service, you are required to use the accrual method.

> Policeman: Why were you driving so fast?
> Motorist: Well, my brakes are no good, and I wanted to get home before I had an accident.

In the cash method of accounting, income is recorded when cash is received, and expenses are recorded when they are paid. Cash is defined as currency, checks, and money orders. All credit purchases and sales are not recorded until payment is received. This is an easy method of accounting, but may not be totally representative of the financial situation of a business because debts or unpaid credit accounts are not taken into consideration.

In the accrual method of accounting, income and expenses are recorded when they are incurred regardless of when they are paid. When a client is billed for services, the sum is recorded in the income ledger as income. When a purchase is made on credit, it is recorded as an expense when the purchase is made and not when it is paid.

As a service business if most all of your income is received on a cash basis, it might be better for you to use the cash method of accounting. If you routinely extend credit or sell merchandise, then you should use the accrual method.

A problem when extending credit to customers is not knowing if payment is going to be on time or even if it is going to be made at all. Once the party is over and the entertainer is gone, it is easy for the client to forget to pay the bill or suddenly become financially strapped. Paying a party debt is given little priority when other bills need to be paid. It is best not to bother with credit or worry about collections. Have clients prepay or pay as soon as you have completed your service.

Deductions

Being self-employed does have some tax advantages. You can deduct on your income tax return any expenses related to creating and selling your services—postage, paper, stationery, costumes, makeup, dry cleaning, recording equipment and computers, travel expenses, gasoline usage, phone, insurance, advertising, bad debts, professional services, taxes, and licenses. Even the cost of food consumed at distances from your home while working is a valid deduction. Any expense related to the operation of your business is legitimate. If you have an office in your home exclusively set aside for your business, you can deduct the rent or part of the mortgage payment for that portion of your home. You may also deduct a portion of your expenses for household utilities (water, electricity, gas). In order to do this, though, the room must be used exclusively for your business and nothing else.

Keep a file and put all of your receipts in it. You must have proof for each expense you claim as a deduction. If you are ever audited, you will be required to produce these receipts. You will need to keep these

Patient: You were right when you said you'd
have me on my feet and walking in no time.
Doctor: That's good; when did you start
walking?
Patient: When I got your bill—I had to sell my
car to pay it.

records for at least three years. Audits can go back that far. Keep a journal and a file. Write down expenses and payments received. Put all of your receipts in the file. Get receipts for everything, including credit card purchases.

Your total business income is figured by subtracting all your business expenses from your business income. One advantage of being self-employed is that a net loss in your business can offset other income. For example, if at year end you had a net loss of $2,000 from your home business, but earned $20,000 as an employee in another business, your total income would be $18,000. To prevent people from claiming business losses every year as a result of an activity that is really a hobby rather than a legitimate business, the IRS has put some limitations on the self-employed. In order to use a net loss to offset other income, a business must keep accurate records, conduct itself in a businesslike manner, and make a profit in at least three out of the preceding five years in which it is in operation.

In spite of some business owner's best efforts, a profit may not be realized in the time specified. For this reason, the IRS has allowed some exceptions to the three-years-of-profit test. The determining factors will be if your activity is carried on in a businesslike manner, you spend adequate time to make it successful, income is used for your livelihood, you have adequate experience in this activity, and you can expect to make a profit in the future.

For further information on business deductions and how to figure your net income or loss, read the IRS publication *Tax Guide for Small Business* (Publication 334) and *Business Use of Your Home* (Publication 587).You need to do this before you start spending money in your business so you will be aware of what you can and what you can't deduct, and what will be expected of you when you figure your income tax return.

Estimated Tax Payments

Because you are self-employed, a portion of your income will not be automatically withheld to pay taxes—a service employers are required to perform. Your tax obligation could be significant, even if you earn a moderate amount. Not only do you have to pay income

tax, but you will also be required to pay self-employment tax (social security tax) which can be twice as much as your income tax. In order to relieve the burden of paying one large sum for taxes at the end of the year, the IRS requires that smaller payments be made quarterly throughout the year. Because of the difficulty of making accurate tax payments during the year, these payments are only estimates. The IRS provides a form (1040ES) with instructions for this purpose. If you don't pay these taxes when they are due, the IRS can charge you interest. They will come after you relentlessly to obtain any payment they feel they are entitled to, so it is best to pay them on a regular basis.

INSURANCE

Insurance? Who needs insurance for entertaining a bunch of kids at a birthday party in the parent's home? What could possibly happen that you might need to be insured?

Let's say while the children are seated on the floor around you and you are moving about in your normal mode amusing the kids, you accidentally step on a child's fingers. Or perhaps while you are juggling hard plastic juggling clubs, you drop one and hit a guest in the face causing an injury. Or during a magic trick something is spilled on the floor discoloring the carpet. Suppose a child had an allergic reaction to a piece of candy you gave out or chokes on a toy or piece of a broken balloon. You are the cause of the mishap, you are responsible for paying for damages and medical expenses, you could also be sued. Insurance is your protection in such situations.

As many entertainers have already learned, liability insurance nowadays is as necessary as props when performing. Gone are the days when you could just walk into a home without thought of insurance coverage. Lawsuit wary businesses which hire entertainers require them to have liability insurance before they'll sign a contract. Even if all you do is birthday parties, you need to seriously consider having insurance coverage.

Some entertainers, to justify their decision for not having insurance, may claim that they have never had a mishap. But even a single accident can be a costly experience for you. You may feel this will never happen to you; you're very careful, you don't use dangerous props or give out party favors that can be eaten or choked on. So why go through the bother and expense of getting insurance? Being careful will reduce your chances of having a mishap, but accidents do happen. Something as innocent as spilling a cup of fruit punch when a child bumps into you, resulting in staining the carpet could be considered your fault. Any number of things could arise that you would not possible anticipate. Having insurance will protect you from these occurrences and give you peace of mind.

In our modern society, lawsuits have become a common occurrence, even for seemingly minor problems and accidents. People want full restitution and even more to pay for psychological trauma and discomfort. Whether they are justified or not, the law allows punitive things for those who feel they have been unjustly injured. Unfortunately, some people look at lawsuits as an easy way to make money and will jump at any chance that may arise.

Because accidents do occur occasionally and because of the possibility of getting sued, you should consider having liability insurance. You need an insurance policy that covers bodily injury to the public as well as property damage. Another area of concern is personal injury. This is often not considered by children's entertainers, but is important. In contrast to bodily injury, personal injury covers injury caused by libel or slander, which might result from frivolous comments. What is an innocent joke to you may be interpreted as an insult to others. At someone else's home, you could also invade someone's privacy by accidentally walking into the wrong room. Personal injury helps to protect you in these situations.

Like auto and homeowner's insurance, a variety of options and deductibles are available. Costs vary. Comprehensive general liability insurance including bodily injury, personal injury, and property damage coverage of $1,000,000 should be adequate for most family entertainers.

You can get insurance coverage for your birthday party business from a local insurance agency. Trade associations such as the World Clown Association, Clowns of America International, Puppeteers of America, The International Juggler's Association, and others offer liability insurance to their members at reduced rates. The World Clown Association, for example offers a comprehensive general liability policy with a $1,000,000 limit and a $250 deductible per occurrence for about $100 a year. To get this low rate the insured must be a member of the World Clown Association and not be involved in performances involving hypnosis, competition racing, pyrotechnics and explosives, throwing objects in and around audiences (juggling is acceptable), production management or promotions management for hire, mechanically operated amusement devices (ferris wheels, merry-go-rounds, and other carnival type rides), or wild animals (pet rabbits and pigeons are acceptable).

Group insurance coverage offered through an association doesn't cover stolen or damaged props or injury to the performer. Also, each person in a team act must buy a separate policy. Acts must be presented under normal, safety-conscious conditions. In the case of a stage show, the policy would cover a volunteer falling off the platform and breaking a leg, but would not cover a volunteer hit with a torch that jugglers were passing around him. The programs are designed to protect entertainers and help them get jobs, while discouraging dangerous acts. Contact these organizations for more details. Their addresses are listed in the appendix.

Al Fellerman Insurance at 1800 Wooddale Dr., Woodbury, Minnesota 55125, offers a similar insurance policy to that of these associations, but is available to any clown or magician (or similar performer) in the United States.

OPERATING A HOME-BASED BUSINESS

Being self-employed requires dedication and self-discipline. When working out of the home it is very easy to be distracted or become involved in non-business activities. You need to spend adequate time promoting your business and developing and improving your skills. Your business will only be as successful as you make it. The amount of time and effort you spend and your enthusiasm will determine the degree of success you achieve.

Besides spending time, you will need to spend some money. It is a general rule that making money requires spending money. Birthday party businesses are no different. Fortunately, a birthday business can be set up with a minimal amount of investment. Since your office is in your home, your overhead expenses are minor. Your initial expenses will be the purchase of business cards, stationery, ledgers for record keeping, and your initial advertising.

Because of start-up costs, inexperience, and time needed to build up a customer base, most small businesses do not make a profit until their second or third year of operation. Although it shouldn't take nearly this long for a birthday party business to be a success, jobs will come slowly at first. If you are dedicated, don't get discouraged, enjoy what you do, and do a good job, your chances of achieving success will be good. One of the challenges

Policeman: I'm going to have to lock you up.
Criminal: What's the charge?
Policeman: No charge—it's all part of the service.

people starting a new business face is staying enthused and optimistic during the first slow months. You may seem to be putting more time and money into the business than it is worth. But this happens to almost all new businesses. So don't get discouraged. It may take you several months to build up your business to the point where you are making a reasonable income. Few businesses are overnight successes, especially home-based businesses, so give yourself time.

Books highly recommended for helping you set up and run a successful home-based business are *Homemade Money* and *Help for Your Growing Homebased Business*, both by Barbara Brabec, and *Small-Time Operator* by Bernard Kamoroff.

SKILLS AND TRAINING

If you are new to the world of children's entertainment, you may ask: Where do I learn how to paint faces, make balloon animals, or do magic? There are no schools for birthday party entertainers. Some colleges and local clown and magic clubs sponsor introductory classes in clowning and magic, but besides that, the only formal training would be acting classes taught in public and private colleges. These classes, although helpful, are not necessary and don't really teach you how to become a good children's entertainer or how to run a birthday party business.

Most children's or family entertainers have a natural sense of humor, enjoy the thrill of being the center of attention, and like to be with kids—the three essential ingredients for success. People with these attributes can learn how to be successful in this business with the aid of books and some practice. This book contains what you need to know in order to start a successful business. There are scores of other books and tapes with ideas which are useful for birthday party entertainers. Visit your local library and novelty/magic shops and look for books on magic, puppetry, skits, and such. Magic shops will usually have the best selection of appropriate materials, as well as have props and costumes you could use.

One of the best books for learning about family entertainment skills and business, is the book *Creative Clowning*. Don't let the title throw you; it isn't just for clowns, but for anyone interested in becoming a children's entertainer. It contains detailed chapters on juggling, magic, music, puppetry, balancing, balloon sculpting, mime, unicycling, stilt walking, skit writing, physical comedy, advertising and promotion, how to work with kids, using props effectively, and costume and character development. Although it does contain a fair amount of jokes, skits, and routines, it is primarily a how-to book, describing how to become a professional children's entertainer. It is even used as a textbook in some colleges and clown schools. If you're serious about becoming a children's entertainer and want to learn how to be funny using a variety of skills, this book is an excellent source.

There are also a variety of newsletters and magazines geared for birthday party and family entertainers. These periodicals are excellent sources for ideas and will keep you abreast of what is happening in the family entertainment business. They provide helpful hits with working with kids, clever party ideas, gags, and routines that you can adapt to your own needs. You also get to know about other party entertainers and the experiences they are having, which will help you be aware of new trends, new laws, concerns, and new ways of doing things that have proven to be successful.

Another way to keep up to date on what's happening and get ideas on improving your skills is to network with other birthday party entertainers. You can do this by joining an established local or national organization or getting together with a small group in your city. Networking with other entertainers can provide you with a great morale boost, a chance to share concerns and problems, and learn how others deal with unusual situations. The appendix lists organizations that would be of interest to you.

I've had a letter from your teacher, Bobby," said his father. "He says you're very careless about your appearance."
"Really, Dad?"
"Yes, You haven't appeared in school for three weeks."

Chapter 13

MARKETING MAGIC

You could be loaded with talent and have a wonderful birthday party extravaganza prepared, but if you don't know how to market yourself, your business will suffer. If you sit back and wait for people to come to you, you won't get many customers. The way you market yourself and your business will determine how many customers you have. Effective marketing requires conscientious planning and effective use of advertising, publicity, and promotion. When you use marketing effectively it can work like magic to bring in new business. That is why I have titled this chapter Marketing Magic.

Marketing your own birthday party business can be fun, exciting, and financially rewarding. It can also be hard work, frustrating, and an endless pit that swallows your money. Be both frugal and highly selective in the promotional items you choose and you will prosper. In this chapter, you will learn some of the most useful secrets of promoting a birthday party business.

MONEY MATTERS

Overpricing or underpricing your services can seriously harm your birthday party business. What you charge for your services and what your services include are important aspect of your marketing.

What you charge may depend on several factors. The primary consideration in pricing is determined by your location and the population base. If you live and work in an affluent, densely populated part of the country, you can charge premium prices. Some areas of the country will pay better than others. Large metropolitan areas pay better than small towns. If you have no idea what the local standard is, call up a few entertainers listed in the phone book and ask them what they charge. Their answers will serve as your yardstick.

You may charge more than one price, depending on what you offer. I charge $100 to appear as a clown for a birthday party. If the customer can't afford this price, I also have a lesser fee of $75. The show is basically the same, but I'm dressed as a magician instead of a clown (it saves me time getting in and out of makeup). Offering two different prices often results in an increased number of bookings.

I feel that it is very important to be versatile, and performing as either a clown or magician gives me freedom when booking performances. I know that I have impressed potential birthday party clients by telling them that I not only perform magic but also do puppetry, ventriloquism, and juggling. These talents seem to go naturally with magic and clowning. Many performers add a variety act to their show in order to increase bookings.

You might consider location in calculating your basic fee. If you live in or around a large city, you could divide the city into three areas and charge a different price for each area. The first area, which is the closest to you, may be any place that you can drive to in under 30 minutes. The second area may require one way travel time of 30 to 60 minutes, and the third area any place beyond that. Your fees may increase by $25, $50, or more to compensate for travel time. In some large metropolitan areas it can easily take a full hour or more to drive from one end of the city to the other. A two-hour round trip drive can take up a big chunk of time, so you are justified in charging extra.

Some customers will do anything to work down the price. If you have a variety of skills, you might consider a show with fewer "bells and whistles." You could offer a less expensive show (with no party favors) or stay for only 30 minutes.

Some entertainers structure their shows to give clients a choice of several options. The price for a basic show might include a 40-minute show plus providing party favors. If the price is too high for the client, the party favors can be eliminated or the length of the show reduced (this would be your low-budget show). You can also use this same idea to increase the price of a show by offering extras. You could offer your clients the choice of two shows—your basic show and your deluxe show (the basic show with add-ons). You could make an additional $20 to $50 per show with add-ons. Examples of add-ons could be making all the kids balloon animals or hats, face painting or body tattooing, supervising games, or even teaching them a few magic tricks. You could offer the client the basic show (at your normal price) or the deluxe show (at a higher fee) that would include your choice of add-ons. This still leaves you the option of offering your budget show to those who can't afford the other two.

When you give a caller your fees, tell her the price of your standard party package and your deluxe package. Hopefully your sales talk will have generated excitement and cushioned any blow for those who expect that your services come virtually free. If she begins to hesitate, you may want to mention that your prices are typical of those charged by other entertainers and are, in fact, cheaper than most because you're not using a theatrical agent or an entertainment service. If she's still reluctant to schedule your service, you can offer her your discount party plan (she may even suggest it). Even if $75 is more than she had expected, it will sound reasonable compared to $100.

> "Every day my dog and I go for a tramp in the woods."
>
> Does the dog enjoy it?"
>
> "Oh, yes—but the tramp is getting a bit fed up."

Emphasize that at the reduced price she will still receive the show, the party favors, and the special recognition for her child.

Some parents want more than just a show, and are willing to pay extra for you to indulge in other activities such as supervising party games. Games are self-entertaining, and if you have a handful of fun games, just being your normal wacky self and goofing around with the kids can be effective. Since you would already be in costume and at the party, it doesn't require much more effort to handle the games or any other add-on. Face painting and body tattooing are also popular add-ons. If you have artistic talent, caricature drawing would make a novel add-on.

Workshops have become popular add-ons with some entertainers. Following the normal show, or a shortened 20- or 30-minute show, the entertainer will spend another 10 to 30 minutes teaching the children some simple magic tricks (or how to make balloon animals, or how to juggle scarves, etc.). Each child will receive a workshop kit or "Bag of Tricks" that contains inexpensive easily learned tricks. Jugglers could hand out sets of juggling scarves, or balloon workers a small bag of balloons (you may need to bring several hand-held air pumps so the children can easily inflate the balloons). Soap bubble blowing, paper toy making, or any type of skill you can perform and teach can be built into a workshop. Workshops at children's parties are becoming increasingly popular. Some entertainers are hired to give just the workshop without the show.

Since you are providing materials for the kids, you will need to price your workshops on attendance. If you plan on doing a workshop for eight kids and 22 show up, a large portion of your profit will be eaten up in workshop kits. You might have a basic price for the first 12 party guests and then add on another $3 or $4 for every additional guest that attends. Confirm the number before the party so you can be properly prepared.

A concern to many established party entertainers are the newcomers who take away business by offering cheaper prices. It is presumed that by offering a lower price not only will the newcomers get most of the business, but customers will come to expect the lower amount as standard and consider higher fees overpriced. All entertainers, it is reasoned, will then be forced to lower their price to compete. The result would be lower income for everyone concerned. Everybody loses. However, a novice entertainer would not expect to charge as much as a polished professional. There is a difference in quality. People are willing to pay for quality. A birthday party entertainer who satisfies his customers will get recommendations and repeat business even if other entertainers are cheaper. Someone who charges a price substantially lower than others will be looked on with suspicion. Generally, the public perceives a high price as indicative of high quality and a low price as low quality. The old saying, "you get what you pay for" applies.

At first, you may charge a lower than average fee. As your experience and confidence increase, raise your prices to the normal market value for professional party entertainment. You should charge what you believe you are worth. As long as your fees are reasonable for your area, even if they are on the high side, you will get bookings if you do a good job and make kids and parents happy.

I strongly recommend that you stick to your price schedule and not make special concessions and lower your price just to pick up a gig. By doing so, you are saying your show wasn't really worth the higher price. Some parents will try to get you to lower your price for them. Unless you have a good reason, such as offering your discount party package, don't do it. You will find that most parents will book you even though you won't lower your price. If you start giving people a break, they will spread the word and others will expect it too. Callers may question why you are charging them more than you charged a neighbor. To them it looks as if you're jacking up the price, and they will resent it. Avoid this problem and stick with your ordinary price schedule. Then, if you're questioned by someone who was referred to you, you have a legitimate reason for the price differences. Explain that prices vary by area and even by which party package they want.

ADVERTISING

Getting your first few bookings will be the hardest. Once you start getting clients, your business will grow through referrals, repeat business, and promotional techniques (all of which will be discussed in this chapter). Your first customers will come from family, friends, and advertising. Family and friends often are willing to help beginning birthday party businesses, especially since they often receive the services free of charge or at a reduced rate. Advertising will be the first step you will take in building up a clientele and get the ball rolling. Once your business has become established, if you do a good job and people are pleased with your services, you will get many referrals and repeat customers. You will then be able to cut down on the amount of paid advertising you do and focus on more economical promotional tactics.

When you give the public notice of your business, you are advertising. Advertising is usually a paid form of publicity in which you have control over the content of your message. This isn't always the case with other forms of publicity. Publicity generated by other means may cost a lot less or even be free, but the message may not cover your business in the detail you would prefer. An example would be a newspaper article which describes you as an entertainer, but makes only passing mention of your birthday party business and gives no clear directions for contacting you. With an advertisement you can give all the information potential customers need to contact you, as well as entice them to use your services. Most forms of advertising will cost you, and advertising can be very expensive. If you are not careful, you could pay a lot of money for worthless advertising.

You can purchase advertisements in newspapers, on billboards, over the radio, and in a myriad of other ways. If you have the money, you could advertise your services on television and radio, publish huge ads in local magazines and newspapers, or other costly avenues. You no doubt will get bookings from these ads. However, when all is said and done, the income you earn as a result of this type of advertising will not pay for your expenses. High cost advertising for a birthday party business is rarely profitable. In the next few pages we will cover the most common and most cost effective forms of advertising for a birthday party business.

The Phone Book is King

Almost all of your business will come via the telephone. People aren't going to write you a letter or drop by your house to inquire about rates for a child's birthday party. Everyone uses the phone.

Most of the people interested in your services will probably learn about you from the phone book. When a mother wants entertainment for her child's birthday, the first place she looks is the phone book. Placing your name in the *Yellow Pages* will bring you a bountiful supply of callers and business. Get listed under both "Entertainers" and whatever your specialty is, such as "Magicians," or "Clowns."

To get your name in the *Yellow Pages*, you need to have a business phone. This will automatically get you listed at no additional charge. If you want more than just your name, address, and phone number, you will be

> Policeman: Your dog keeps chasing a man on a bicycle.
> Man: That's ridiculous, Officer. My dog can't even ride a bicycle.

Ted: My dad's a professional fighter. A featherweight.
Bob: Light, is he?
Ted: No—he tickles his opponens to death.

required to pay extra. A basic listing may be all you need, especially if there are no other entertainers in your area offering the same skills.

Before you place your ad, look at the others. Study them. Which attract your attention first? Which ones can you remember after looking away from the page? Why? Which ads sound more appealing? Why? Follow the lead of those who have been in business for a long time.

If the listings of other entertainers overshadow yours, you may consider using boldface type to help your name stand out. You might consider adding the words "children's parties" to let readers know your specialty. If you don't, you'll get a lot of calls for other types of shows or activities. The cost to add graphics and slogans, however, may be too expensive for your purposes. Begin with a small listing. Give yourself time to grow. Besides, you can always increase the size of your ad, if response warrants it, when the next edition of the phone book comes out. Check with your local phone company for rates.

In most major cities there is what I refer to as the "Yellow Pages War" among magicians and other entertainers. Don't get in the war. Like most wars, everybody loses. In a *Yellow Pages* war, everybody tries to outdo everybody else in the listing. Bigger, they think, means better. The longer, they think, is better. The more colors, they think, the better. After all, the nice man from the phone book company who sold the ad said to go for it. With over two decades of advertising experience, I can tell you they are all wrong. This is only a costly ego trip. The "war" is fostered by the sales rep and fought by the entertainers paying the bill. Don't enlist.

An ad does not have to be large, two color, or boxed to be effective. A simple listing with your name and phone number, plus a "hook" line is fine. What's a hook line? It's a clever little thought to catch the reader's attention and make your ad a little different from the rest of the pack. For example: "Washington's Favorite Birthday Show," "Specializing in Children's Parties," "Featuring Fuzz-Face the Magic Birthday Rabbit," or even, "Making Birthday Memories for Over 10 Years!"

Most people booking an entertainer will run down the listings in the *Yellow Pages*. After casing all of them, they will go for the ads with hook lines because they sound more interesting. Get a hook line.

Phone books usually come out only once a year, so you may have to wait a while before your name appears. Having to wait may be beneficial because it gives beginners a chance to test the water before committing to a listing that will remain in the phone book for an entire year.

Newspaper Advertising

One of the most useful ways businesses make their existence known is through newspaper advertising. Entertainers can also take advantage of this medium. It is often the first type of paid advertising most birthday party businesses make.

There are two types of newspaper ads: display and classified. Display ads usually contain pictures or drawings, and can be very expensive. If you live in area with a large population an ad could cost several hundred dollars for a few inches of space. At these prices display ads often are not cost effective.

Classified ads are composed of straight type with no graphics and little variation in lettering style, but are much less expensive. The biggest drawback with classifieds is that fewer people see them. Usually, people do not even read them unless they're looking for something specific. Most of us think of these ads as a way to sell cars, boats, and real estate, not to find birthday party entertainment. For these reasons advertising in big city newspapers is generally unproductive.

Newspaper advertising is very expensive and it's literally here today and gone tomorrow. Most people discard their newspapers within 24 hours of getting them. Why? There's a new one printed each and every day!

That doesn't mean all newspaper advertising is a waste of money. If you live in a small community, the local paper may be effective. Large cities often have small community papers or shoppers guides which are circulated to only select areas. These may be cost effective for you. Advertising rates in these smaller papers may even be low enough for you to run a display ad, which will be seen by many more people than a classified ad. You may want to try such an ad at least once in your area to see what type of response you get. It may prove an effective means for getting business. Some birthday party entertainers have reported good success with ads in community newspapers that specialize in classified advertising.

Under no circumstances sign a multiple ad agreement which will run for several issues without testing the water. Read that last sentence again. Newspaper ad salespeople will often encourage you to increase your ad size or frequency. They are always friendly, they are always helpful, and they do this because they are all salespeople!

Ignore much of what they say. Survive! See what works best for you. Study what your competition is doing. Start small. You can always take out a larger ad if this method proves beneficial.

Community Bulletin Boards

A 3 x 5-inch card placed on bulletin boards at launderettes, drugstores, beauty shops, restaurants, and other places provides you with an excellent way to advertise at little expense. Except for the cost of the cards, it's essentially free.

It also announces your services to those who are most likely to call you—namely mothers. Women usually do business at places with bulletin boards and will see your notice.

A typical card might read:

PAULINE'S PUPPETS

Make you child's next birthday party special with the magic of Pauline's Puppets

All Ages — Reasonable Prices

Pauline Winston—Puppeteer 321-4567

Your card will be on a bulletin board, possibly lost among a mass of others, each card competing for the readers' attention. If yours isn't noticed, then it's doing no good. If you can design your card so as to grab people's attention, your response rate will soar.

A unique card will stand out, and people will read it first. Many people give bulletin boards only a passing glance, but an eye-catching card will be read and will earn jobs for you. How do you make your ad stand out? You must make it unique. You're an entertainer and that's unique. So let your ad reflect your service. For starters, add color. Bright cheery colors will draw attention. Use colored cards or colored ink on white cards. Add a small drawing or picture. Advertisers know the value of using pictures in their ads. People usually focus on an illustration before reading anything. If you have a picture on your card, people will look at it first. It could be a simple drawing, a cute rubber stamp impression, or even a professionally printed photo or other illustration. Use an illustration which describes what you do.

PAULINE'S PUPPETS

Make you child's next birthday party special with the magic of Pauline's Puppets

All Ages — Reasonable Prices

Pauline Winston—Puppeteer 321-4567

What about the words you use? Keep the heading or title short and to the point. The heading PAULINE'S PUPPETS is a good example. The heading should always be short, descriptive, and interesting. Avoid such sentences as: "If you're looking for entertainment for your child's birthday party, try Pauline's Puppets." This title is far too long. Keep the message short and sweet. Other examples of good headings are: "Liven Up Your Party," "Storyteller," "Crazy Clown," "Balloon Magic."

After the title, briefly describe your services and mention some of the things you do that would entice potential customers to give you a call. You can add other incentives such as reasonable prices, all ages, any location, day or night, special weekend rates.

Using your stage name or company name gives you an identity and tells customers that you're not simply a generic entertainer, but a professional. Instead of just saying PUPPETS, our example gives the company name PAULINE'S PUPPETS. This way the entertainer has identified herself as being unique and different from other puppeteers.

This same approach isn't limited just to cards on bulletin boards, but can be used in newspaper ads, and flyers.

Items on most bulletin boards are usually allowed to remain until the end of the week or month, so replace them periodically. Don't be discouraged if you return in a few days and your card is gone. That's good! Just stick up another and be delighted someone was interested enough to take it.

Better yet, try a notice that has tear off tabs containing your name and phone number. This way several people can benefit from your notice. I put the magic wand on the tear off tab to remind folks that I am a magician. You could add your own simple graphic. Keep your ad simple and this method will serve you well.

Bulletin board card with tear-off tabs.

Flyers

There are many ways you can market your business with flyers. Leave flyers (or business cards) at party stores, kids' clothing stores, day care centers, toy stores, and any other place where kids or parents go. Ask those in charge if you can leave flyers for their customers to pick up. Many store managers will be obliging, especially if you are a regular customer of theirs.

Anytime you have a gathering of kids or parents, you have a potential opportunity to publicize your services, especially if treats or prizes will be passed out. Make up flyers and have them available, or pin one or two on the wall. At parties you can give these out along with a piece of candy as promotional gifts. Of course, all these things will have to be approved by the party organizers. You might even offer a discount coupon on the flyer. A certificate for $5 or $10 dollars off the regular price may motivate parents to give you a call. If you offer to donate something of value, like a discount coupon, party organizers will be more likely to allow you to distribute them. It would also make a nice little gift or party favor that could be given to all the guests.

Use your imagination to find places and means to distribute your flyers. Community and church fairs, and carnivals, are some places to investigate. Zoos and children's museums or any other place where children and parents may visit are other possibilities. Get permission to pass out flyers. You might even sell something like balloon animals, face painting, or character drawing and hand out flyers to all your customers or anyone who shows an interest. Local fairs, schools, church events, or daycare centers may gladly welcome your services. You may even be paid to do it. Especially if you provide a show. Public exposure will help you out greatly, but you need to get that flyer into people's hands. If the event organizers won't allow you to pass out flyers, make sure that you have a sign with your name and number on it so people can contact you.

After a show and while still in costume, some children's entertainers make it a point to visit stores, malls, parking lots and other places where parents might be and hand out business cards or flyers. The added attraction of being in costume attracts attention and instills interest. If you look professional, you will get many bookings from this means. This is an easy marketing technique to do on the way home after a show.

Below is an example of a flyer used by Marcel "Mama Clown" Murad. The front contains an action photo, in eye-catching full color, with the most important information—her stage name and phone number. The saying "a picture speaks a thousands words" is clearly evident in this photo. From this picture, prospective

Flyer used by Mama Clown.

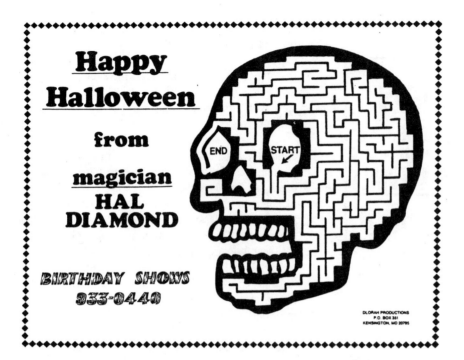

introduce yourself and your business? Have whoever answers the door add a small flyer (see the example) when they drop in the piece of Halloween candy. And do drop in that piece of candy!

The skull maze is best to duplicate on yellow or orange paper. You can easily fit two to a page when you duplicate them. Try running a few hundred copies and giving fifty each to several of your friends. Ask them if they would be kind enough to drop them into the trick or treat bags too. You'll be surprised how well this novel method pays off!

customers can see that Mama Clown is a "professional" by the quality of her costume, makeup, props, and the photo itself. It visually says Mama Clown will bring fun to your birthday party.

On the back she describes her unique quilifications and talents. Since she is bilingual she has them written in both English and Spanish. It reads:

"Twice elected 'Clown of the Year' by the Southeastern Clown Association, Mama Clown is a bilingual performer who has been entertaining children of all ages for the past eight years. Her enthusiasm and cheerful personality are evident in everything she does.

"Whether she is doing magic, face painting, balloon sculpturing, or just clowning around, her audience is always captivated by her talent.

"Mama Clown performs at over 800 birthday parties a year. She also performs at schools, summer camps, malls, department stores, restaurants, and company picnics.

"Mama Clown believes that 'one of the nicest things we can give our children are happy memories.' Her love for children and the art of clowning are some things that anyone who comes in contact with her will remember for a long time. Smiles guaranteed!"

In the United States we have a unique celebration that lends itself well to promoting a children's birthday party business. Every year on Halloween children dress up in costumes and go door to door trick or treating to collect treats. When youngsters in your neighborhood go trick or treating, why not utilize this opportunity to

PUBLICITY AND PROMOTION

Publicity and promotional efforts let the public know about you and your business. These are not always direct sales messages, nor do you always have full control over what is said about you. If you do a good job and customers are pleased with your services, the publicity you receive will generally be favorable and will lead to additional bookings.

Word-of-Mouth

The best type of promotion, and definitely the cheapest, is word-of-mouth. Tell others what you do and ask them to spread the word. If you do a good job for one client, she will tell others and more business will follow. Print up some business cards and pass them out as often as you can.

Some entertainers go a step further and have signs painted on their cars or vans. Wherever you drive, your wheels serve as an advertisement. This is a good way to publicize yourself and get some business, but it has one major drawback. A van with your stage name and number printed on it has a "show biz" appearance. Crooks often equate such advertising with expensive electrical equipment and other things of value, as a result, vans are repeatedly broken into. I have heard this story often from those who use this form of advertising. If you decide to try this, consider yourself forewarned.

MAMA   CLOWN

Sample of some business cards.

Business Cards

It is essential for you to have your own business cards. Every professional performer, full-time or part-time, should have them. You will be asked for them. Get some!

Business cards work in conjunction with word-of-mouth. Whether it's you who tell people about your business, or it's your friends and former clients, potential customers need to have your name and phone number on paper so they can contact you. Business cards act as a gentle reminder to potential clients. They imply, "Make your next birthday party special, give me a call." Be liberal with your use of business cards. Give them out to any prospective customer; hand them out to new clients, give them several so they can spread them around to their associates. Leave several with the hostess after the party so she can pass them out to her friends.

Stop by your local print shop and buy several hundred to start. Keep them simple, avoid useless babble that will clutter them up. Your name, phone number, and what you do are most important. Your address is not necessary. A simple illustration or design, such as a cartoon, adds a great touch. Your printer will have stock art you can pick from.

Conserve cash. After you are established and making big bucks on a regular basis, then go for the foil stock, embossed paper, custom artwork, fluorescent papers, the nifty fold-over business cards or the ones with die cut stars through them.

Don't put anything on the card that could possible date it. For example, don't put a calendar on the back. Many printers will suggest this, but come the end of the year, all your cards will be last year's news, and you will be going back to the printer for more.

If you live in an apartment or move frequently, you may want to write or stamp the phone number on the back rather than having it printed on the front and then having to cross it out and write the current one below it. This gives the impression you aren't stable. Another advantage of writing your phone number on the card is that kids will ask for the card and call you just to chat. By writing the phone number on it you have the choice to disclose your phone number or not. I know several performers who have two business cards, one with the phone number for adults, and one without, for the kids. Both cards list the name and address so if some kids' parents really want to book you, they can easily reach you in the phone book.

I saw a super looking juggler named "Juggling Jimmy" at an outdoor birthday party for a neighbor several years ago. He did a fine show and, from an agent's viewpoint, was very marketable. After the show I approached him. He seemed to be a nice guy. When I asked him for a business card, he said he didn't have any. Instead he quickly scrambled for a pack of matches from

BUBBLEGUM T CLOWN

**BUBBLEGUM'S FUN CLOWN MAGIC
AND BUBBLY FAMILY ENTERTAINMENT
FOR ALL OCCASIONS**

Parties, picnics, grand-openings,
promotions, parades, conventions, etc.

Add a "colorful" and "Bubbly memory"
to your special occasion.

**10423 WEIR STREET
OMAHA, NEBRASKA 68127
(402) 592-1245**

Weber Photo Productions, Box 336, Ft. Collins, CO 80522 (303) 493-6491

PLACE
POST CARD
POSTAGE
HERE

P33353

Post Card

A novel business card is the business post card. The picture on the left is the face of the card and on the right is the reverseside containing the advertising message and contact information. You can get cards made like this from your local printer. The one used in this example was produced by Weber Photo Productions, Box 1929, Ft. Collins, CO 80522.

his pocket and hastily scribbled his name and phone number on the inside cover. "Juggling Jimmy" was an agent's dream, a performer with tons of talent, a strong desire to work, and no idea how to market himself.

Even worse, I met "Davido the Clown" at the Kennedy Center in Washington, D.C., during an open house. His outfit was classy, he performed very well, and he had wonderful rapport with kids and adults. He had a great future and would be perfect for kids' parties. When I asked for a business card, he gave me a rectangle of paper cut from a 3 x 5-inch card with his name and phone number written on it in pencil! How could such a sharp looking performer have no business cards? Incredible!

The most incredible excuse I ever heard for not having a business card was from a mime who will remain nameless (because I never got the name or a card) who said, "I don't give out any business cards because then everybody will want one and I don't have that many. Besides people will start calling me." Amazing. Sad. True!

The Publicity Photo

A publicity photo is a must if you want to be remembered and booked. You will need them for clients, agents, and fans. You should have these reproduced

inexpensively in large numbers and autograph them for the birthday child and his friends. On the border or back of the photo will be your name and phone number.

You will stand out from 90 percent of the other home entertainers running around because they won't have a photo. Use a professional photographer to shoot the picture. Pictures shot at home look like pictures shot at home—they do not convey a professional appearance. A professional photographer will create a picture with the right exposure, lighting, and background. The wrong background can kill an otherwise good photo. You need something that will contrast with your clothes and make you stand out. Expect to pay $50-100 or so. It is money well spent.

Make sure you make eye contact with the camera so you are looking directly at the person who sees the photo. This is a much stronger pose than those that are taken with you looking somewhere else.

Select a pose that gives an indication of what you do. I am a magician and I want to show that in the photo. I don't want to actually show a trick that I may not do in the show which they book.

See Figure 13-1. This is a great photo. It shows action, fun. excitement, but is totally misleading for what type of magic they are going to see at a birthday party

Figure 13-1

Figure 13-2

in their home. If Mrs. Motherokiddies booked this entertainer, she would expect, and rightly so, to see me do what I am doing in the photo. She would expect her lovely daughter, Fatima, and her 14 friends, to see a lady cut in two. She may also expect to see at least two people in the show. Mrs. Motherokiddies would be disappointed.

See Figure 13-2. This is a great all purpose shot good for any type of engagement that I might play. It says magic, but doesn't get into specifics. It also says I am a one man show.

Figure 13-3 is one of my best birthday shots. It's an almost square photo printed on a rectangular 8 x 10-inch sheet. The photo shows the magician and his best magical friend, Blackjack the Magic Rabbit. Yes, Mrs. Motherokiddies and her brood will see both magician and his talented rabbit entertain in their domain. The layout of this photo is also useful because it gives me a nice-sized rectangle of white space at the bottom to autograph or write a special wish or thank you to the birthday child.

Figure 13-3

If you work with an assistant or partner, then by all means include him or her in the photo, but make sure your helper shows up with you or you'll have a showdown with Mrs. Motherokiddies. Choose a pose and setup that fits the venue that you are performing.

Look at Figure 13-4. It's a slick shot of my assistant, Sara, and me. She is attired in earrings, gloves, necklace, and looks ready for an elegant night on the town or perhaps to play a club date, certainly not Bertha's Birthday party held in the basement of their split-level home on Cowlick Lane.

On the other hand, look at Figure 13-5. It shows a more friendly magician and a pretty, as opposed to elegant and formal, assistant. Yes, that's Sara again. This time she has fluffy hair and is wearing a jumpsuit. The photo says we put on a clean "G" rated show, with a surprise

Figure 13-4

Figure 13-5

Figure 13-6

Figure 13-7

Richard Daemer, aka "Mr. Balloonologist," entertains at literally dozens and dozens of parties in the Washington, D.C. area. He enthralls adults and children alike as he inflates balloons of different shapes, sizes, and colors and fashions them into various animals, hats, decorations, and swords. He arrives at the party with his balloon box and pump, and in a half hour or 45 minutes transforms the place into New Year's eve. All ages love watching him blow up the balloons. Sometime they break; kids squeal and love that part. They sit glued to his every move as he sculptures animals, and the children are delighted to take home his creations as souvenirs of the party. He has a good act.

Study his two promo photos. The first one (Figure 13-6) shows him exploding through a barrage of balloons. It promises fun and lots of balloons, but not any specific animal or creation. It also says he is professional. Note the tux; it tells folks they should expect to spend more to obtain his services.

The second photograph (Figure 13-7) shows Mr. Balloonologist with one of his prized creations. It's a stunning shot. It looks like he's about to hand it to you. It's a special creation for the birthday child. For a little larger fee, he'll make one for everyone at the party who wants one. (And everyone always does!) Wouldn't it be nice to have this man entertain at your next party? Yes!

Hugh Turley, one of Washington's busiest professionals had his picture taken with the two seatbelt test crash dummies at the White House one year. They, like Hugh, are very popular in the Nation's capital. He liked the photo, saw the value in making it into a postcard, and uses it as a giant business card. (See Figure 13-8.) It's a great way to say thank you to the birthday child too. Parents like it because it stresses safety.

appearance from a white bunny. And that's exactly what they will get. (Note: because my name is Diamond, I try to plug it into the audience every chance I get. See the interlocking diamond design on the magic box the rabbit is coming out of? That same design appears on much of my equipment. I want my audience to remember the name Diamond so I can be booked again.)

Figure 13-8

An effective way to advertise yourself using your publicity photo is to have it reproduced in color on business cards or postcard-sized cards. Make sure they are in color. Nowadays everybody is used to color in all types of advertising, and children's entertainers are colorful people; black and white won't cut it. Use these as your business cards. Have them printed with your name, phone number, and perhaps ad line such as "The Best In Birthday Party Entertainment" on the front. These are the type of cards people tend to keep and remember. Such cards also show potential customers what you look like and that you are a polished entertainer. Some birthday party entertainers have reported that once they began handing out business cards with their photo, bookings soared and they had to stop handing out so many because they became too busy. Order one to three thousand, it will cost a couple a hundred dollars, and hand them out everywhere. They will bring much more in business than you had to pay out for the printing. One clown handed out about 500 during a parade he participated in. As a result, he reported that his phone rang off the hook for days and six months later he was still receiving calls. One show paid for all the cards he handed out, the rest was money in the bank.

Restaurants

Many restaurants have banquet rooms or side areas for large groups or parties. Contact the owner or manager and interest him in letting you entertain at parties in his restaurant. Such an arrangement will cost him almost nothing and may provide him with additional business.

Parties like this are easy for restaurants because they must be scheduled in advance, giving the cooks and servers plenty of time to prepare. The same food is served to all the guests and is paid on a single tab.

The price the restaurant charges covers the food and your fee, which is added to theirs. Your presence does not cost the owner a cent, but it serves as an incentive for parents to hold a party at his place of business. These advantages have been recognized by many restaurant owners, so inquire about a package deal which would involve your services.

Restaurant work is basically the same as a home party. You can do your normal show as long as there is sufficient room. Depending on the size of the area, you may have to modify some of your regular material.

Sometimes the parents will rent a banquet room at a restaurant and then ask you to come there to entertain. Such an assignment will give you an opportunity to talk to the owner afterward. He has just received some business, highlighted by your performance, and the profits of this party are fresh in his mind. Inquire about setting up a joint agreement for future parties.

Media Coverage

Grab any opportunity you may have for media coverage. It's not as difficult as you may think. I've gotten media coverage from reporters while performing at community and church fairs. A write up in the paper, and even a picture, will put your name in front of the public. This in itself may not get you many bookings, but as people thumb through the telephone listing of entertainers, your name will sound familiar. They may not even remember why they recognize it, but the fact they have seen it before will lead them to consider calling you first. Being mentioned in print is good publicity for you, not only because of the additional bookings you may receive as a direct result, but for the news value. You can use quotations and headlines from newspaper clippings in your marketing efforts, in advertising and sales literature. Use these as third party endorsements. If the media has talked favorably about you, then parents will take notice. They will be thrilled at the opportunity of having such a noteworthy entertainer at Junior's birthday party.

Just going to birthday parties isn't going to expose you to newspaper reporters on the lookout for something interesting to write about. Performing at business and community events is one way to get broader exposure. But still, it's no guarantee of media coverage. Offering to give a show for free at a fundraising event or other good cause is notable and may get you some coverage, *if* the event organizers mention your services in their publicity materials. If you keep your eyes open, you will see entertainers mentioned in newspapers all the time. They may be mentioned because they appear at the county fair, are the featured attraction at a local church carnival, participate in the walk-a-thon to raise money for cancer research, hand out free candy or do face painting at a grand opening, spread goodwill and cheer in a children's hospital or at a seniors center, or give a show at the city's founders day celebration.

Although all of these activities could get you media attention, just participating in them is no guarantee you will get press. If you go about your business simply hoping for a reporter to grab you for an interview, you're in for a letdown. Although this does happen, you can't count on it. You must let the media know about you in order for them to show an interest. How do you do that? You do it with a *news release*.

You can get free publicity for yourself by sending out news releases to your local newspapers, magazines, or television and radio stations. A news release is a brief letter which is written to the media to make a public announcement. This is not an advertisement, but an announcement of something of interest to the community. Although you are not directly selling anything, you are selling yourself and attempting to get valuable publicity and name recognition.

Approximately 25 percent of the news reported in the paper comes from news releases sent in by businesses and organizations. A well written news release may be printed almost verbatim. Most, however, are rewritten. Often, the reporter will call the sender for additional information. Because such a large amount of the news comes from this source, media people welcome news releases. If you're not sending news releases, you are losing out on an opportunity for free publicity.

Any family entertainer can benefit from using releases. In fact, on one occasion I was invited to appear on a radio program to teach the show hosts how to juggle. I spent a half hour with them as a guest while they were on the air doing their regular program. This type of exposure is great publicity and it was the direct result of sending a news release about my "goofy" juggling. I have appeared as a guest on radio talk shows and have files filled with newspaper clippings, all of which were generated by news releases. They can work for any family entertainer.

Sending a news release will not guarantee you media coverage, but it is a step in the right direction. You are guaranteed to have more publicity if you do send out releases, than if you don't. Whenever you have an opportunity to publicize yourself, do it. If you are

participating in any local event, let the media know. If you are doing anything of interest or benefit in the community, let the media know. Often business and event organizers will send out news releases publicizing an event. If you are participating, they may even mention you. Whether they do or not, send your own release anyway.

The secret of making a usable news release is to create a story or news item about yourself that contains news of interest to the publication's readers. That's what editors look for.

What is new with you that might be of interest to people? Have you developed an interesting or novel new act? Do you have a new partner? Do you have an interesting background that contrasts with your birthday party business? Are you donating your time to entertain at a hospital or retirement home or for some charitable cause? Are you doing anything in conjunction with upcoming holidays or special events? (Clowns have National Clown Week in August and magicians have National Magic Day in October.) Are you going to appear at a charity fundraiser, local fair, or some other community event? Have you had an interesting experience involving your party business or stage character? Are you helping out in an election or working for some other worthy cause? This list can go on and on. There are many interesting things you do all the time that you can make into a good usable news release. Some people and businesses send out news releases all the time. As a consequence, they are frequently mentioned in the media.

What are you doing right now that might be of interest? If you are not doing anything particularly newsworthy, then you need to start doing something! You can't sit back and expect reporters to clamor to your door for interviews. You must do something new and interesting. Most entertainers in their normal course of business encounter many situations and events that are newsworthy; unfortunately, most family entertainers never take advantage of them by informing the media.

Not too long ago *The Daily Californian* in El Cajon, California, contained a feature article about a couple, both of whom were clowns, who unknowingly scheduled their wedding on the same day they were to take part in a big parade. In a effort to fill their commitment to participate in the parade and still tie the knot, they combined the two and rode down main street in a golf cart with a sign that said, "Just Married."

The local newspaper thought this wedding would make an excellent story, and a feature article was written about the couple. However, the clowns had not thought to capitalize on the event, and had not informed the media. The newspaper found out from the minister who performed

Barnaby's Puppet Works

432 Main Street, Newbridge, CT 09876

June 10, 19--

<u>FOR IMMEDIATE RELEASE</u>
Contact: Bill Barnaby 555-9876

FIREMAN TURNED COMEDIAN IS NO DUMMY

Long-time fireman Bill Barnaby may be coming to your neighborhood, not to put out fires, but to entertain children as a comic-ventriloquist. He will appear with his cast of five dummies Saturday, June 23, at the Memorial Hospital community fund-raiser.

Barnaby, 40, served as a fireman for 17 years with the Newbridge Fire Department. He recently "retired" from fire fighting to pursue his childhood dream as a professional ventriloquist and children's entertainer.

As a part of the Newbridge Fire Department Safety Program for children, Barnaby has entertained children with Sammy, Lucy, Ralph, and other puppets for over four years. During this time he became a regular visitor to area schools, libraries, and churches.

His grandfather was an accomplish magician and performed professionally for many years. It's from him that Barnaby developed a taste for show business. His first stage appearance was at the age of 12 helping his grandfather in one of his acts. "My grandfather introduced me to the wonderful world of puppetry and magic and I've loved puppetry ever since. Working with the Fire Safety program rekindled that interest and gave me a chance to further develop my performing skills." Barnaby says, without moving his lips.

"Although I worked full-time as a fireman, I goofed off as a comic-ventriloquist in my spare time." Barnaby says. Over the past two years Barnaby has been a highly popular part-time comic-ventriloquist in the Newbridge area, appearing at children's parties, restaurants, and picnics. He also donates his time to charitable causes like this year's Memorial Hospital fund-raiser.

###

A sample news release that could be used by a birthday party entertainer.

the marriage. As a result of this free publicity, both of the clowns had their names advertised, and undoubtedly people looking for clowns will remember their names and contact them. They may also recognize the names while searching through the phone book and contact them first.

Publicity like this can be priceless and can be much more effective than paid advertising. In fact, statistics have shown that articles derived from news releases are generally seven times more effective than paid advertisements.

For a complete description of how to publicize a birthday party business with news releases, I highly recommend the book, *Writing Effective News Releases:*

How to Get Free Publicity for Yourself, Your Business, or Your Organization, by Catherine V. McIntyre. This book describes in detail how to write an attention getting release and how to create ideas that are newsworthy, and provides lots of actual examples used by family and children's entertainers.

Free Shows for Exposure

Offering occasional free shows can be beneficial if you choose them wisely. When you first start out in your new birthday party business, you may offer a few select

—— Writing a News Release ——

A good release can be a gold mine of publicity for you. However, an improperly prepared news release will most likely be trashed. Editors may use only one out of every 10 news releases they receive. Even so, 20 to 25 percent of all the editorial space in newspapers comes from news releases!

"My experience," says Del Hood, associate editor of *The Daily Californian*, "has been that reporters and editors rely on news releases more than they like to admit. They cannot be everywhere and know everything that is going on. News releases frequently are the launching pads for good stories." The media depends on news releases for generating a substantial amount of their news. They need and want news releases.

If news releases are so important, then why are so many releases trashed? The simple reason is because most of the news releases sent to the media are not prepared properly. They are incomplete or lack newsworthy facts or announcements. Many are blatant attempts of self-serving advertising and have no newsworthy content. News releases should announce something of interest to the community that would be of interest to the newspaper's readers or broadcast media's listeners or viewers.

The media does not ignore releases from magicians, clowns, and other family entertainers. They are more than willing to publicize stores about you if you can give them something interesting to write about. The problem is that most family entertainers do not know how to properly prepare a news release and do not know what type of information editors or program directors are interested in and what information a news release should contain. Writing a good news release

is not hard. The following is a basic guideline to help you prepare a winning news release:

1. Use your business letterhead. If you don't have any, simply type your name and address at the top of the sheet.

2. A couple of spaces below the letterhead, type in capital letters: FOR IMMEDIATE RELEASE. This tells the receiver that it is a news release.

3. Below that type the date, your name, and phone number. Editors frequently call for additional information if they are interested.

4. Double-space and type (in all capital letters) a descriptive headline or title.

5. A couple of spaces below the headline, type the body of the release. The body should be double-spaced and limited to one or two pages. One is better. Begin with the most important information, with additional information given in declining order. The information should cover what journalists call "The Five W's:" who, what, when, where, and why. This is the information editors need before they can work with a release. Leaving this information out is one of the major reasons why many news releases are not used. So make the effort to completely answer the Five W's. Avoid sounding like an advertisement; just give the facts. The secret of making a usable news release is to create a story or news item about yourself that contains news of interest to the publication's readers. That's what editors look for.

6. End the release with the symbol "-30-" or "###" which tells the editor there is not another page roaming around somewhere. If you have two pages, they may be stapled together.

friends and relatives a free show just to get the experience and exposure. This will be helpful to you because as a novice the experience will be valuable. You will get a taste of what the business is really like and a better idea how to handle children and present yourself. Another advantage is the exposure you get. Parents will get a chance to see you in action which will, hopefully, lead to additional bookings. Your freebies, however, should generally be limited to just the first few, if any at all. If you give away too many, everybody will expect it, and may even be offended it you insist on charging, since cousin Clare got one free.

Everybody would like to get your services for free and will try if they can. You will get many, many calls and requests to do free shows. Everyone you have ever known or are related to (even distantly) will want your service for free. The person on the phone will tell you it's for a good cause, that they have no money, that it's for people who can't afford a real entertainer, and the biggest line of all—"You'll get lots of great exposure!"

Right! I ask you: "Why on earth would you want to get exposure to a bunch of people who can't afford your act?" Choose your freebies wisely. Learn to say, "No." It's sad news to be locked into doing a freebie when a good paying show wants you for the same date.

Besides, if you do it for free this year, who do you think they will call next year? And how much do you think they'll want to pay you next year? Probably twice as much (2 x $00.00 = $00.00). Say no!

You may be tempted to donate your time and talents on occasion because it's for a good cause and the organization may claim it does not have enough money in its budget to pay for it. I know of entertainers who, out of the goodness of their hearts, have given free shows, only to find out later that the other entertainers at the event were paid. Event organizers will often try to get free entertainment first and then, if more is needed, will pay for it. In fact, they will usually pay for all the entertainment they need if they have to. But why pay for entertainment if someone is gullible enough to give it away?

Once, and I mean once, in a blue moon I still do a freebie, but it must have some value to me beyond the tons of great exposure to people who can't afford me. I do one for my church every other year and one for my brother's church every other year. They give me several dates to choose from and I select the date. You can bet your wallet it won't be in October around Halloween or the week before Christmas, those are the busiest times of the year for me.

I also do freebies for some of the National Football League's Christmas parties, for which I get extensive media coverage. Last year doing the Washington Redskins, I was on three of the main television channels here in Washington, D.C. That kind of freebie really does generate more bookings. Besides it's a real kick to tell Ms. Motherokids that her darling offspring will rate the same entertainer the famous sports teams get.

ENTERTAINMENT AGENCIES

Many independent entertainers increase the number of shows they give by signing on with an entertainment or booking agency. The advantage of an agency is they will promote their business which will benefit all the entertainers they use. They talk to the client, get the booking, and send you out. You are also protected by the agency's contract as well. This eliminates the need for you to worry about collecting the fee. Working with an agency will increase the number of your bookings.

For this service you will be charged a 15 percent commission. This price is usually deducted from the fee you normally charge. The agency charges the client your fee and then deducts their commission. Some agencies, however, will charge the customer an amount 15 percent higher than your normal fee and simply take that as their commission. In the latter case, you end up receiving the same amount you would if you booked the show yourself.

Before an agency will sign you up, you may be asked to audition or show a demo video tape, in addition to submitting a resume. Agencies must protect their reputations and are hesitant to work with beginners unless you can demonstrate a professional quality show. If you are only interested in doing birthday parties and have no interest in business promotions, adult gatherings, company picnics and the like, specify that you only do children's birthday parties. Most agencies prefer to work with entertainers who are versatile and willing to work at any function, not just birthday parties. If you want to limit yourself to birthday parties only, an entertainment agency may not be best for you.

An agency is not likely to keep you as busy as you would like, so you will still need to have a yellow page listing and handle most of your own publicity anyway. As a birthday party entertainer, you can do just as well without an agency. Your own advertising methods (as discussed in this chapter) will bring you plenty of customers and leave you free to schedule your own shows.

GIVEAWAYS

Keep in mind that the more shows you give, the more shows you will give. Repeat bookings and referrals from satisfied customers and guests from your parties will be one of the major sources of business for you. Don't pass by this golden opportunity to publicize your services. Make sure that every party guest carries home a souvenir with your promotional information on it. If you do this and the kids and parents liked you, you will have all the bookings you want.

Giveaways at the conclusion of your act are an excellent way to generate additional bookings. Little Tommy Jones runs home and shows Mom the picture of Mr. Magic and insists that Mr. Magic appear at his next birthday party. Mom looks at the photo and calls the phone number on the back, and Mr. Magic is in action again.

Choose what you give away carefully. Invested wisely, your giveaway dollars will come back to you many times. Here are some tips and ideas.

Gone in a Gulp Stuff

Ignore candy, balloons, and generic stickers such as the ones that read, "I was kissed by a clown" or "IYQ." The only thing they accomplish is to give the entertainer something to do. These are all very short lived items. Most are eaten or destroyed before the little guests get home from the party.

The Assistant's Certificate

All kids like getting awards, and the Assistant's Certificate award or diploma started decades ago and is still the most popular giveaway on earth for the birthday party entertainer.

Although mine is designed as a "Magician's Assistant," yours could be for a "Juggler's Apprentice," "Junior Clown Volunteer," or whatever.

Make sure it has a fancy border and a place for their name, your name, and your advertising copy or slogan. If you're good at computer graphics you can design your own certificate. My certificate was designed by a good friend, Ed Harris. He is a very popular artist well known to magicians and other children's entertainers. His address is 5901 S. Drew Avenue, Minneapolis, Minnesota 55410, USA. Send him four first class stamps and he'll send you his catalog of promotional offerings. All are camera ready. Just add your name, address, and phone number and head to your local quick duplication place.

A piece of red ribbon and a gold seal, sold at most stationery stores, transforms the certificate into a striking looking award that will be taken home, hung up on the refrigerator, and cherished for months to come..

Big Money Giveaway

Everybody likes getting paid and kids are no different. Big money can be given away liberally because it's so inexpensive to produce, or should I say reproduce. Mine came from Ed Harris and is called a "Mystery Dollar." It has my picture and advertising copy on the front and five easy to do tricks on the back. I can duplicate two bills on a standard sized sheet of green paper. Don't pass up big money.

Color by Number Mystery

Here's another great giveaway at birthday parties. It's a simple color by number picture. The completed design shows a magician's top hat, magic wand, and two doves. Design your own to fit your act and copy it onto white paper.

You may want to suggest that the kids have a coloring contest after you leave. Never get caught in the uncomfortable situation of having to judge the pictures and pick only *one* winner; no matter who you pick, *you* will be the loser! "Everybody's picture is wonderful! Michelangelo would be proud of all of you!"

Help the Magician Wordscan

A magician's hat is very magical. Who knows what it might contain! This elementary wordscan invites youngsters to find all the animals listed. And there are some pretty wild ones too! Kids will laugh when they read the list. I'd like to see David Copperfield pull a coyote or a hyena out of a hat! Add your advertising copy in the space at the bottom, and duplicate this great giveaway on bright colored paper stock.

Fun Folders

Another fun giveaway is a customized folder or little booklet containing magic tricks, jokes, puzzles, etc. The folders could be made from 8½ x 11-inch or 8½ x 14-inch sized paper folded acordian style. Each panel could serve as a different page.

You can create these type of folders yourself with ideas from any joke or activity book. Ed Harris has many professionally prepared folders that can be customized with your name and picture.

Customized Magician's Assistant certificate and Mystery Dollar (front and back sides shown).

Color by Number Mystery Picture (left) and Magician's Wordscan (right).

Samples of some fun folders.

FRONT & INSIDE SPREADS

Chapter 14

DIRECT MARKETING

Direct marketing is a form of advertising that deserves special consideration separate from the other forms of marketing discussed in the previous chapter. Direct marketing, or approaching potential customers through the mail, is one of the most cost-effective ways businesses promote and sell products and services. Yes, this is often referred to as junk mail advertising, but it works, otherwise advertisers would not be using it. Wisely used, direct marketing can propel you to immediate success in the birthday party business.

Many service oriented businesses have made fortunes selling through the mail. Surprisingly, very few birthday party entertainers use this powerful technique effectively. Probably the main reason for this lack of interest is that most people don't know how to use direct mail marketing effectively. Many may have tried it without success and given up on it. Direct mail marketing can be the most effective form of advertising you can do—if you do it wisely.

KEEPING TRACK
OF YOUR CUSTOMERS

The hardest part about the birthday party business is finding customers. Without customers you have no business. So your success depends on the number of customers you serve. Marketing can be a time consuming and costly process. For most birthday party entertainers it is also the least enjoyable, they would rather be having fun with the kids and be earning money, not writing advertisements and distributing flyers.

Often, entertainers will work a party, collect their fee, and say good-buy, then never see the customer again. This is a big mistake. Customers are the lifeblood of your business. Once you have found people who have recognized the benefit of your service and have gotten to know you, don't ignore them. They are the most likely people to invite you back either for the same child the following year or for a sibling. It is much easier trying to get a repeat booking from a satisfied customer than it is to try to locate a new one.

For this reason, you should keep a file of all the people who have used your services. They will become your most important customers and provide you with the majority of your future business. They should remain on your customer list until *all* the children in the family become too old for your type of entertainment.

If your customers like you and you showed them a good time, chances are you will be invited back. A brief thank you note sent to the birthday child and the parents lets them know you appreciated being invited to their party. Kids love to get mail, so address the note to the birthday child and remind him to thank his parents for you. This little act of gratitude will make a positive impression and help to get you invited back next year.

189

Marc the Magician

P.O. Box 324
Yourtown, NY 10020

Sample of the front of a postcard (left). Back of card could contain a thank you message (below) or a yearly reminder (bottom of page).

Marc the Magician
The Best in Comedy Magic
(303) 555-1234

Dear Jimmy,
    I would like to thank you and your parents for inviting me to your birthday party last Saturday. It was sooo much fun!
    I really enjoyed meeting all your friends and family. Say hello to them for me would you please?
    Maybe we can do it again sometime.
Sincerely,
Marc

Marc the Magician
The Best in Comedy Magic
(303) 555-1234

Dear Beth,
    Last year I had a great time at your birthday party. If you are planning to have another party this year and would like to see my *new* extra fantastic magic show have your parents give me a call. I would love the opportunity to come to your house again. It will be loads of fun!
Sincerely,

Marc

P.S. Birthday parties are more popular than ever and I am kept pretty busy so to reserve your date call now.

Keep a record of all of the children you do parties for. Record the child's name, birth date, address, and phone number on an information card. File this record by month according to the child's birth date. The following year, about four to six weeks before the child's birthday, send a promotional letter. This will serve as a reminder that you were lots of fun last year, and that you are available again. What you send could be a simple birthday card, a promotional flyer, a personal letter, or a party tip sheet. You may send two or more of these at different times if you don't get a response from the first mailing.

The party tip sheet would consist of some ideas for hosting a birthday party, briefly covering topics on decorations (simple how-to ideas), food (fun recipes), games, and entertainment. Many party books are available from which you can glean useful information to use in a party tip sheet. Your sales pitch should be low key. Use subtle entertainment suggestions to lead them to consider your services. Make sure you include your phone number so they can easily get in contact with you. The primary purpose of this letter is to serve as a reminder that having an entertainer would be fun and to let them know you are available.

Mailings are the most effective way to get repeat business. But you can also pick up new customers using these same or similar materials. Next to the birthday child's family, the best prospects are the party guests. They have seen you in action they know who you are and, more than likely, they would be thrilled to have you come to their house. The giveaways you hand out at the party are one way to entice them to invite you, but once the party is over there is little else you can do to motivate them

to extend you that invitation. If you had the names and addresses of the guests you could send them follow-up sales messages like you do for the birthday child.

Birthday party entertainer John Cooper has devised a clever way to get this information and has had amazing results. He has done this in the form of a fan club. At each party he gives all the children an application to join his fan club. When they fill out the form and send it in, he in return sends them a free membership card, certificate, and prize. Kids love to get things free. The application form asks for the child's name, age, birth date, and address. It is inexpensive, yet colorful and enticing. The names of club members are kept on file and every month he sends out a one page party planner to those who have an approaching birthday. His fan club supplies him with a continual list of names of potential clients and lots of business. John Cooper has written a short booklet describing his birthday party plan in detail, including examples of his party planner, application form, membership card, and certificate. For information on how to get a copy contact him at Smilemakers Entertainment, P.O. Box 911, Forest Park, GA 30051-0911, USA.

Win A Free Magician

Besides party guests, the next group of people you should contact are parents with children of suitable age. How do you locate these people? You can track them down with a special promotion or contest. One such promotion that has proven highly effective is the "Win A Free Magician" contest. The contest could also indicate winning a free clown, puppeteer, etc. It works the same.

What you are doing in this promotion is offering to give away a free birthday party show to the winner of the contest. You won't get paid for this show obviously, but it's the price you pay for the publicity and leads that the contest generates. The bookings you will eventually glean from this contest will more than compensate you for the lost revenue of a single show.

Here's how the contest works. You make a display announcing the "Win A Free Magician" contest. The dispay should contain your publicity photo with your name clearly visible, a box with a slot cut in the top to receive entry forms, and a sign. The sign should read something to the effect of:

Win A Free Magician
for Your Child's Next Birthday Party!
No purchase necessary. One entry per child.
Fill out the entry form and drop it in the box.

Make the display attractive so that it catches the eye of store customers. Since the display can be used over and over again in different stores for a number of years, it would be cost effective to have a graphic artist or professional sign painter design it for you. It will look a lot better if professionally built than if you just slapped something together. A nice looking display also reflects on you and your services. You may also want to make additional signs to hang up in the store window. They can state something like "Win A Free Magician. No Purchase Necessary. Come Inside For Details."

Go to a local store that patronizes kids or parents of young children. Examples would include toy stores, ice cream stores, fast food restaurants, and even clothing and grocery stores. Tell the manager or owner that you have a free promotion that will help bring him more customers. Emphasize that it will cost him nothing. All you want to do is be allowed to set up a display featuring the contest. You may even explain that you will also send local newspapers and radio stations news releases announcing the contest and that their store will be mentioned as the place to pick up entry forms. (See the details on creating news releases in the previous chapter.) Put your display up at one store at a time so that each merchant has an exclusive promotion going, this way they will be more likely to accept your display. You could have more than one display, but the stores should be non-competitive. A toy store and a clothing store would work, for example, but not two toy stores.

Store customers entering the contest fill out an entry form listing their names, address, phone numbers, children's names and birthdates. All of this information is important for you so make sure your entry forms ask for it. Entry forms are dropped into a box. The display is kept up for a minimum of 30 days. At the end of this time you select a winner. Call the winner and schedule your complementary show.

You may get some referrals from this free show, but that is not the reason for the contest. Inside the box along with the name of the winner will be hundreds of other children—all potential customers. You have just created a valuable list of contacts. Send all contestants a letter thanking them for entering the "Win A Magician" contest. Let them know that they didn't win this time and tell them who the winner was. Also tell them about your services. Many of them will contact you for their children's next birthday.

File the list according to birthdate. Thirty days before that date, if they had not responded to your initial mailing send the parent a brochure or other sales material further describing your birthday party show. You can also follow this up with a phone call a week or so after the mailing. Ask them if they are planning on having a party for their child and offer your services. This promotion works wonders for generating new business.

Why did the boy cut a hole in his unbrella?
So he could tell when it stopped raining.

BIRTHDAY PARTY PLANNING GUIDE

One of the best marketing tools you can use is a birthday party planning guide. The planning guide contains helpful information for putting on a successful birthday party. It can include a number of things a parent might find helpful such as ideas for entertainment (that's you), preparing the home for an entertainer, decorations, party favors, food, recipes for cake and fun snacks, party games, and theme party ideas. You can describe your party services as well as provide helpful tips on throwing a memorable party. The planning guide should be useful whether or not your services are used. This way, it not only serves as an advertisement but also a useful guide that the parents would appreciate.

The birthday party planning guide could be sent to anyone who contacts you by phone. Whether they book your services or not, you can get their address and send them this "free" planning guide. People like to receive things for free. You, in turn, have another chance of convincing them to hire you. You also have another address for your mailing list even if they don't use your services this time, you can send them another planning guide or other sales literature next year as the child's birthday approaches. Be sure to send information several weeks in advance so the parents have time to prepare for a party and before they make other plans.

You could also send the planning guide to everyone who schedules a party with you. The information in the guide will help customers prepare for your visit by removing breakable objects and scheduling gift opening and snacks after your show. The tips in the guide may also be useful in making the party better. Recipes, games, decorations, and theme party ideas can save the parents time searching other resources for this type of information, or inspire them to do things that they would not have done, which would make the party more enjoyable for both the parents and the kids.

You can use the birthday party planning guide much like you would a business card. Hand it out to those you meet who show an interest. You may even ask party store or novelty shop owners if you could leave a stack for their customers to take.

Pages 193-196 contain an example of the type of information you can use and how to set up and design an effective planning guide. A 8½ x 14-inch sheet of paper (legal sized) folded into fourths makes a nice size because it can be used as a mailer by typing the recipient's address on one panel and adding a postage stamp. You can expand the information by adding more games, recipes, and party ideas to create a little 5½ x 8½-inch sized booklet. Although not included in the example on the following pages, you could provide information on preparing theme parties and suggest some themes and accompanying activities. Many, or all, of the themes you suggest could include entertainment from you. For example, a balloon theme party would be ideal for an entertainer who specializes in balloons.

HOW TO GAIN MARKET DOMINANCE

Through direct mail marketing you can become the predominant birthday party business in your area and, as a consequence, the most financially successful. As the predominant business you can, and are expected to, charge a premium fee which is in line with your high professional status. People will pay more to get the best or what they perceive to be the best. Even if you are just starting out, if you've got the talent, you can rise to a position of predominance within a few months. Interested? Keep reading.

By far, most of the advertising we are exposed to comes from the media (newspaper, magazine, television, and radio), but are they the most effective for you as a birthday party entertainer? Generally, no. Although some newspaper advertising can pay off, advertising in the media is usually a waste of time and money. This is true for most small enterprises, not just birthday party businesses.

The primary reason large businesses advertise is for name recognition. The more often a store or brand name is shoved in front of someone's face, the more likely they will think of it next time they are shopping. An ad for a new $30,000 Toyota isn't going to motivate you to jump up and run down to your nearest Toyota dealer to buy the car. The purpose of the ad is to plant a seed for the future. It is to let you know Toyota is alive and well and will be there when you are ready to buy. Large companies are successful because they create the image of dominance in the marketplace. The name Xerox has become synonymous with photocopiers. When you think of computers, IBM is usually the first company that comes to mind. With hamburgers it's McDonalds, chicken it's KFC, tacos it's Taco Bell. These are big international corporations who have established their dominance in the marketplace. You no doubt have many local businesses which dominate the market in the area in which you live. When we go shopping the dominant store or product is usually considered first. Becoming the predominant business of its type in an area is a very important marketing strategy.

One of the keys to success even for a small birthday party business is to become the predominate birthday party

The text below is an example of the type of information that can be found in a birthday party planning guide.

DR. DROPO'S BIRTHDAY PARTY PLANNING GUIDE

BIRTHDAY PARTIES ARE SPECIAL

Birthdays are special to children. They are in such a hurry to grow up, they look in anticipation for that magical day when they automatically become another year older. Birthday parties celebrate that event with family and friends, fun activities, and tasty treats. This is their day and, with special planning, can become one of the most memorable events of their lives.

Don't feel you must work for weeks making or buying expensive invitations, party favors, and special treats in order to have a successful party. This planning guide provides ideas that can make your party fun for both you and your children while still saving you time and money. With proper planning, your child and his or her guests will have a delightful time with the least amount of effort possible.

The recommendations in this guide are based on the experience of a birthday party professional. The guide outlines party tips and suggestions that will enhance the fun and enjoyment while reducing the mess and frustration often experienced at unorganized parties.

PLANNING TIPS

How Many Guests Should You Invite?

Some children become so excited about having a birthday party, they may want to invite the entire third grade. A party with 20 or 30 children can become a frenzied affair and can end up as a housekeeper's headache. For example, think long and hard before inviting 25 three-year-olds to drink red punch on your living room carpet! Invite only the number of children you feel is appropriate. Keep in mind the size and nature of the party site. If your party is going to be held in the family room, is it big enough handle the crowd you invite? Most homes can accommodate eight to twelve guests, the typical number at most children's birthday parties.

Invitations may be mailed, hand-delivered, or extended by telephone, but be sure to give your guests ample time to prepare for your party. A week or two notice beforehand is usually enough time. Hand-delivered invitations may be made by your son or daughter when he or she goes to school or you can drop them by your guests' homes.

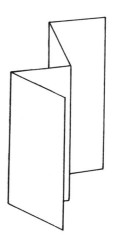

The party planning guide can be written on two sides of a sheet of paper and folded to make a attractive brochure.

Telephone invitations are best extended from parent to parent to ensure accurate communication. Mail is usually the easiest way to announce the upcoming event. Include all the necessary information, such as the occasion, name, time the party starts, time it ends, date, location, and your phone number.

How Long Should the Party Last?

It is important to include on your invitation the time the party is expected to be over. This way parents can promptly pick up their kids. To determine the length of your party, you need to decide what you are going to do. Are you going to invite a children's entertainer, like Dr. Dropo—the mystical wizard of balloons and magic? Are you going to have party games or other activities? Perhaps you may go out somewhere to play miniature golf or go bowling. And don't forget time for refreshments and opening of presents. As with most parties, some guests will arrive after the designated starting time. Allow at least 15 to 20 minutes for latecomers.

The Ideal Party Schedule

The ideal party schedule includes an arrival activity, entertainment, refreshments, gift opening, and a farewell activity. Parties run more smoothly if you follow this order. The highlight of the event for the birthday child is usually the opening of the presents. It should be saved for last, right before the farewell activity and children begin to leave. Refreshments should follow the entertainment portion of the party; this way you don't end up with punch, ice cream, cake, and other assorted treats ground into your carpet, stuck on the walls, and who knows what else. Refreshments are also a distraction, and kids won't pay attention to whatever activity they are involved in. If you paid for an entertainer, the children will enjoy the show much more if they are not competing with each other over popcorn and soda.

If you want your party to last 2 hours, plan on a 15-minute arrival activity, 45 minutes for entertainment, refreshments for 30 minutes, and the gift opening to take 20 minutes. Close the party with a 10-minute farewell activity and you can easily fill a 2-hour period. Following this order of events will make your party run as smoothly as possible.

The Arrival Activity

An arrival activity is recommended to keep the children entertained until all the guests arrive. You want to have all the guests present when the real fun begins. This is a time when shy children can become familiar with you and the new surroundings and when all the children can start interacting with each other in preparation of the good time they are going to have. As the guests arrive, welcome them into your home and let them pay tribute to the guest of honor. A relatively quiet activity works well at this time. Use coloring books and other children's activity books, such as dot-to-dot, puzzles, mazes and other fun activities. You can also get the children to help you decorate the house. Have them blow up balloons and draw pictures to be hung up around the room.

Older siblings sometimes feel left out, especially if they are ignored. You can help them enjoy the party more if you involve them in some way. Have them help you with the decorations and refreshments, supervise arrival activities, set up games and assist the younger children with crafts, and retrieve items tossed in carnival style games. If a relay calls for an even number of players, they can fill the space. Assign them the duty of prize monitor to hand out the prizes and to judge winners of each game. Helping out becomes more fun than a chore. They'll be delighted with the responsibility and feel as though they contributed to the success of the party.

The Entertainment

After the preliminary activities and all of the guests have arrived, the real fun begins. This is the time you bring out the entertainment. The type of entertainment you choose to have can vary greatly. For a simple party you can supervise the playing of games. These can be ordinary party games or you may choose unique games that may follow a certain theme. Often prizes are awarded to the winners of each game. It is a good idea to have a few extra prizes for unanticipated needs such as a surprise guest, broken favors, and tie-breakers. Other activities include packing up all the kids and going to a movie, the zoo, roller skating, an amusement park, or other event. This can be expensive and take a lot of effort on your part.

One of the most enjoyable, and certainly no more expensive, options is to bring the entertainment to your home by inviting Dr. Dropo—The Wizard of magic and balloons—to come to you. Dr. Dropo will keep the children entertained with comedy magic, daring feats of juggling, silly clown gags, and lovable balloon creations. You are free to prepare the refreshments or sit down and relax, letting Dr. Dropo lead the children into his world of fun-filled fantasy. The children will be glued to their seats in amused amazement. The guest of honor usually participates with the Doctor in helping to create the magic and in so doing becomes a part of the show. This participation will make the party a special event for the birthday child. Before leaving, Dr. Dropo makes sure to give each guest a specially made balloon animal. This saves you the trouble and expense of purchasing special party favors for each child, which has become a standard practice at birthday parties. It also eliminates the need for prizes for games since games are not an essential part of this party.

Refreshments

The best time to serve refreshments is when the entertainment is over. Here the children can dig into hot dogs, chips, soda, and of course, ice cream and cake. This is the time where the guest of honor is placed at the head of the table and the guests sing a robust round of "Happy Birthday." A wish is made and the candles are blown out.

Present Opening

To top off the festivities, the birthday child opens the presents last. For the birthday child this is the highlight of the event. Make sure an adult supervises the opening so that each giver may be properly recognized. The process should move quickly so the guests' attention is not lost.

The Farewell Activity

The present opening is soon followed by the farewell activity and the departing of the guests. The farewell activity is something to keep the children entertained as parents gradually arrive to pick up their children. This doesn't necessarily have to be a special event. It could be playing games outside, watching cartoons, coloring pictures, or eating more treats.

By following this outline, you will avoid many potential problems less organized parties create and you are sure to have a memorable event your child will remember for years to come.

LIVE ENTERTAINMENT

Children grow up watching television. The characters portrayed are seven-inch midgets in a fantasy world. They often miss the thrill and excitement of having a living, breathing performer entertain them in person. At a birthday party you can give your child this experience by hiring a children's entertainer.

In preparing for an entertainer, such as Dr. Dropo, to come into you home, you need to designate an area to be used as the stage. The family room is usually the best location. Weather permitting, a lawn or patio can also work well, provided it is not too windy and is not fully exposed to the sun. Neither the children nor the performer will do well with 45 minutes under the glare of the bright sun. If the show is to be held outside, it should be in a shaded area.

Normally indoors is better than outdoors. Indoors distractions are kept to a minimum. The space needed should be at least 6 x 6 feet. In front of the TV or fireplace is usually ideal. Coffee tables, lamps, and other pieces of furniture should be positioned out of the way to allow children to sit on the floor without obstructing their view. With a house full of energetic kids, anything breakable should also be removed temporarily.

The entertainer should arrive at least 15 minutes after the party is scheduled to begin. This allows time for latecomers to get there before the show starts. Arrival activities can keep the children busy until the show goes on. Entertainer's fees are based on the amount of time they spend at the party. Since they often have other engagements afterwards, they cannot be expected to wait for late arrivals.

Food and drink is best saved until after the show is over. During the show the children are encouraged to participate by standing up, waving their arms, and coming up to help as volunteers. If they have refreshments during this time, it is likely to end up on the carpet. Besides, they are so busy having fun they don't have time to eat.

Noise from the radio, TV, or talking can be distracting. The children cannot hear nor enjoy the show if background noise is too loud. Parents and family are invited to sit quietly and listen, but if they want to talk or make noise,

it is best for them to go into another room.

Pick up and remove any toys before the show begins. Toys can also be very distracting. This is one reason why the opening of presents should wait until after the performance. A child may be so wrapped up in playing with a new toy, it is difficult for him or her to sit and watch the show. Some children will insist on squeezing a noisy toy and some may fight or pull toys away from other guests.

Dr. Dropo's magic show and balloon extravaganza lasts for 40 minutes. After the show the Doctor makes all the guests a balloon animal to take home. Other small party favors are also distributed during the festivities.

GAMES

Games are often a favorite party activity. Here are a few suggestions that are variations of some traditional party games. Your local library will have many books on party games from which you can choose. One of my favorites is *Games Galore for Children's Parties and More* by Shari Ann Pence. It contains dozens of original children-tested games for ages 2 through 12.

Pin the Nose On the Clown

This game is played like Pin the Tail On the Donkey except instead of the tail you use a pom pom for the clown's nose. A picture of a clown's face is taped to the wall. Players, in turn, are blindfolded and spun around, then told to put the nose where it belongs on the picture. Preparing this game can make a good arrival activity. You can outline in pencil the clown's face on a large sheet of paper. Have the kids color in the details. Tape can be attached to the pom poms instead of using pins.

Hot Potato

This is a classic favorite. In the original version a potato is passed around by the players. You can add a new twist by using a ball instead of a potato. Have all the players sit in a big circle. Give one player the ball. At your command he quickly rolls the ball to another player. The players try to roll the ball to each other as fast as they can. When you blow the whistle, the one with the ball is out. The player who remains in the game the longest is the winner.

Musical Chairs

This is another classic game that has amused children for generations. Line up enough chairs for each player except one. Arrange the chairs so that every other one faces in the opposite direction. As music is played the players will walk around the chairs. When the music stops, each player is to sit as quickly as possible. The player left standing is out. A chair is removed and the game is repeated until only one chair is left. The player who remains in the game the longest is the winner.

RECIPES

Easy-to-Make Chocolate Cake

With a bunch of excited hungry children almost any cake can be a delight. If time and money are a factor, this simple cake will fit the bill nicely.

$\frac{1}{2}$ cup shortening

$1\frac{3}{4}$ cups sugar

1 teaspoon vanilla

3 eggs

$2\frac{1}{2}$ cups cocoa (regular-type, dry)

$1\frac{1}{2}$ teaspoons soda

1 teaspoon salt

$1\frac{1}{3}$ cups cold water

Cream shortening and 1 cup of the sugar till light. Add vanilla and eggs, one at a time, beating well after each. Sift together dry ingredients; add to creamed mixture alternately with cold water, beating after each addition. Gradually add $\frac{3}{4}$ cup of sugar, beating till stiff peaks form. Bake in greased and lightly floured baking pan at 350 degrees for 30 to 35 minutes.

Butter Frosting

6 tablespoons butter

1 1-pound package confectioners' sugar, sifted (about $4\frac{3}{4}$ cups)

$\frac{1}{4}$ cup light cream

$1\frac{1}{2}$ teaspoons vanilla

Cream butter; gradually add about half the sugar, blending well. Beat in 2 tablespoons cream and vanilla. Gradually blend in remaining sugar. Add enough cream to make spreading consistency.

Popcorn Balls

2 cups granulated sugar

$1\frac{1}{2}$ cups water

$\frac{1}{2}$ teaspoon salt

$\frac{1}{2}$ cup light corn syrup

1 teaspoon vinegar

1 teaspoon vanilla

5 quarts popped corn

Butter sides of saucepan. In it combine sugar, water, salt, syrup, and vinegar. Cook to hard ball stage (250°). Stir in vanilla. Slowly pour over popped corn, stirring just to mix well. Butter hands lightly; shape ball. Makes 15 to 20 balls.

WHO IS DR. DROPO?

Is he a real doctor? He is more of a veterinarian—a balloon animal veterinarian. He works magic, transforming ordinary lifeless balloons into animated bubbly pets. From dogs and frogs to alligators and dinosaurs, he thrills and amuses audiences of all ages. Dr. Dropo has been entertaining children for over fifteen years. He has delighted hundreds of children at birthday parties using juggling, magic, clowning, and, of course, balloon animals. He is a member of the International Juggler's Association, World Clown Association, and The Clowns of America International. He performs over 500 birthday party shows per year and has appeared as a special guest on radio and television shows locally and nationwide. For your next party, invite the wizard of wacky, the one and only Dr. Dropo!

Call (719) 548-1844 to schedule Dr. Dropo for your son or daughter's birthday party. Because of Dr. Dropo's immense popularity at birthday parties, he is in heavy demand. To guarantee his appearance at your party call now. He will help to make your child's birthday a truly memorable experience!

business in your area. When people think of having a birthday party they should automatically think of you first. It is impractical to advertise like big corporations, but you can achieve predominance relatively economically through direct mail marketing.

The three primary factors that affect the success of a direct mail marketing campaign are (1) mailing list, (2) repetition, and (3) sales material. We will look in some detail at each of these.

THE MAILING LIST
Choosing the Right Customers

The ultimate success of any direct mail campaign depends on the choice of people to whom you send your sales literature. Choosing your mailing list wisely can make the difference between whether you end up with a financial windfall or an empty pit.

A vital factor in any successful direct mail campaign is finding the right list of names—your potential customers. You cannot expect to send your sales literature to names on just any list. That would be like using names straight out of a telephone book. Such a list is doomed to failure. Why? Because, percentagewise very few of these people will be interested. How many of the people listed in the phone book have children? How many of these parents have elementary school age children? And of those how many can afford an entertainer? It does no good to solicit people who don't have children of a suitable age or who cannot afford to hire you. Many parents see no need or sense in hiring someone else to entertain their children, they'd rather do it themselves. When you account for all these factors, the response to a general list would be dismal—a total waste of money.

On the other hand, if you could select the perfect customer who would that be? Someone who obviously has children between the ages of 3 and 10 years of age. Someone who has the financial capability to afford hiring you and would be pleased for your help to entertain their children and friends. You *can* have such a list.

Mailing List Companies

Custom made lists are available from mailing list companies and brokers. Look in the *Yellow Pages* of your phone book under the heading of "Mailing List Brokers" or "Mailing Lists." You will find several companies, both national and local. These brokers compile and sell lists of names to businesses for direct mail marketing. They keep names filed under hundreds of categories so that any business can custom design a list for specific products or services. Some of the categories you can choose from include location (city, state, zip code), age, gender, occupation, marital status, children, income level, types of magazines read, hobbies (sport car enthusiasts, book lovers, skiers, etc.), and even their color of hair and eyes. The list can be very specific.

Your list should be comprised of those people who have children of suitable age and an annual household income of about $60,000 or more (the income level will depend on the area in which you live). The higher the income level the stronger will be your response. This is the audience you need to focus on. They are your best customers, and usually the least likely to try to get a reduction in price or complain about the cost. These are the people who will be more likely to give you repeat business and referrals, and the parents of kids invited will likely be of similar social status so bookings from guests will be of similar potential.

A person who uses your services only one time and must save to afford it, is a one time customer. They normally can't afford to have you come back again the following year. Referrals from these customers, while graciously welcomed, are fewer in number and likewise usually one time customers.

About 80 percent of your business will eventually come from repeat customers and referrals. We tend to socialize with those who are of similar economic status. Referrals from parents who have a strong financial background will also likely be of similar status. These are the types of customers who are the most apt to use and reuse your services and tell others about you. Seek after them. If you market to everyone, including those who cannot afford your services, you will occasionally get bookings from mid-income families, but they are almost always one time deals. They won't build up your clientele very fast. So why bother wasting advertising money on them?

You certainly can, and should, encourage any potential customer regardless of economic status, but you will gain far more in the long run by focusing on the higher income group.

There are many mailing list companies who collect and sell lists. Prices range from about $10 per thousand names to $90 per thousand, with the typical price being in the $60-$80 range. Quality of lists varies greatly. The cheaper lists are usually woefully outdated and inaccurate—stay away from them. So be careful about using lists from discount brokers or other questionable sources. The national companies listed in your phone book are probably the best sources.

Some mailing list companies require a minimum order of one to five thousand names. The names usually come on mailing labels, either Cheshire (ungummed) or pressure sensitive (pregummed). The Cheshire labels require a special gumming machine to stick them onto the envelopes, so your best bet is to get the pressure sensitive labels which you peel and stick.

Your Personal List

When you buy a list of names, what you are really buying are the labels themselves and not the names on the labels. In reality, you are only renting the names and can use them only one time. That means you cannot copy the names down and send additional mailings to the same list. In order to reuse the names, you must rent the list again and make another payment.

You may be thinking, how would the list company know if you use the names again? They know because the lists are seeded with dummy names which go back to the list company. If they get an unauthorized mailing, they will bill you again for the use of the list.

You cannot add the names from a rented list to your personal list unless they respond to your mailing. Any person who contacts you, whether he or she books a party or not, can be added to your personal list. So, if you rent a list and receive 25 replies, you can add these people to your own list and mail to them as much as you like.

Bulk Mail

If you send a minimum of 200 letters, you can send them by bulk rate mail, which costs about a third less than first class mail. When you're sending out several hundred letters, this cost savings can be significant. But in order to qualify to send bulk mailings, you must register with the post office and pay an annual fee for a bulk mail permit. If your mailings will be small and you plan on using the permit only a few times, it may not be worth the time and expense. However, if you want to contact several thousand potential customers, bulk mail is one of the cheapest ways to do it. Contact your local post office. They will be more than happy to answer your questions about bulk mailings and will give you a booklet describing this service in detail.

There are some major drawbacks with using bulk mail. One is that you must sort and stack the mail according to postal standards. It's not too hard to do, but does require extra time and effort on your part. Another disadvantage is that bulk mail is slow and frequently gets lost. You can expect about 10 percent of the letters you send by bulk mail to never reach their destination. Why? I don't know, except bulk mail is given low priority by postal workers and is more likely to be lost, damaged, or misdelivered. A more serious problem with letters sent bulk rate is that they are often perceived as "junk" mail. The bulk mail stamp is the dead giveaway. Many people who receive bulk mail simply throw it away without opening it. To overcome this problem, marketing experts suggest foregoing bulk mail and paying for first class postage using a regular postage stamp. This way the letter appears less like an advertisement and is more likely to be opened.

REPETITION
Perseverance Pays Off

Direct mail marketing has been the key to success for numerous companies. Yet, many who have tried it say it didn't work for them. Usually, those who failed tried it once then gave up. You may have tried it yourself, or know of someone who has without achieving success.

The biggest reason for failure with direct marketing is selecting the wrong list of names. This was covered in the preceding section. The second reason why direct mail fails is that it is tried only once. A single mailing to any list of customers, no matter how well chosen, is often *not* very profitable and can be discouraging. If one mailing was a financial failure, logically you might think a second would be just as disastrous if not worse. After all, you might think that those people who were interested responded to the first mailing so a second mailing would be even less productive. This reasoning, however, is inaccurate.

The key to making a good mailing list profitable is to send out several mailings to the same list. The more times you approach the same group of potential customers, the larger your response will be. So, even if the first mailing is not cost effective, follow-up mailings will be. The success of subsequent mailings will make up for a poor response to the first.

Marketing experts advise that to gain a profitable response businesses should send at least three mailings to each potential customer. Some advocate nine or more as optimal. For a birthday party business you may find success sending out regular mailings throughout the year. The more mailings you send, the more your name becomes familiar and the more likely these people will use your service. After several mailings, you become the predominant birthday party business in your area simply from name recognition. As the predominant business, you will be perceived as the best your area has to offer, you will be called more often than your competitors, and you will actually become the dominant birthday party source in your mailing area.

Many people who receive sales literature in the mail say, "Hey, this looks like something I can use." Some of these people will call immediately, especially if a birthday is fast approaching. Most, however, don't act on it immediately but place the information aside where it eventually gets buried, lost, or discarded.

A follow-up letter sent a few weeks later will remind the receiver of the offer and rekindle forgotten interest. This will inspire some to call immediately to make an appointment. Others will again think the offer is good and place it down where it gets lost a second time.

A third mailing will again remind them and they may now act or place it aside. With each mailing the response rate increases. People are reminded that your show will be fun. You begin to become more familiar to them. Many people need repeated exposure to an ad before they are motivated enough to act. Others are hesitant to use the services of a business that is unknown to them, but repeated mailings establish familiarity. Although their only exposure to you may be from your mailings, if you send them often enough the potential customer feels she can trust you; after all, you have established your predominance in her mind.

Some people will hold off calling you because a birthday is still a long way off. Repeated reminders will ensure that the customer does not forget when the birthday does finally draw near.

Determination of Profitability

How many responses do you need to determine if a mailing was profitable or not? A 2 percent response is considered good. A 1 percent response can be profitable and 3 percent or more is excellent. So, if you receive one booking out of 100 letters sent, that's a 1 percent response. Cost for the mailing (e.g., list rental, paper, printing, and postage) may run around $60 for 100 letters. If you charge less than $60 for a show, it appears to be a losing endeavor. If you have a 2 percent response then you earn a total of $120 from two $60 shows. Subtract $60 for the cost of the mailing and you're left with a $60 profit. If this (a 2 percent or less response) were all you received, you may not feel the effort worthwhile.

The secret to success is repetition. One mailing is likely to bring disappointing results. To make direct marketing successful, you *must* send multiple mailings to the *same* people. With each mailing the response rate increases. The second mailing may bring a 3 percent response. A third mailing a 4 percent response, and repeated mailings continue to bring 4 or 5 percent or more—definitely profitable marketing.

Repeated mailings establish your business as the predominant one—the best and the one customers will automatically think of when they need you. If you use a good list to start with, your first response could be 3 percent or better, and higher with each succeeding mailing.

Using our hypothetical $60 cost per 100 names example, if you sent out three mailings, total expense would be $180. You may receive responses of 2, 4, and 6 percent from each one, respectively. That's twelve new customers. Twelve new customers at $60 each or $720, or total profits of $540 (minus $180 mailing costs).

Another point to consider is that your cost per mailing decreases as the number of mailings increase. The price of mailing lists decreases if you rent them more than once because of multiple use discounts. The cost per unit for printing your sales literature also decreases if you print larger quantities at the same time. Instead of $60 per 100 names, for example, the price can drop to $40 or less.

If you charge more then $60 for a show, your profit increases. At $100 per show you would earn $1,020 profit from twelve customers. Keep in mind this is from a list of only 100 people—a very tiny mailing. Normally, mailings are 1000 minimum. With a mailing this size at $100/party, you would receive 120 responses and earn $10,200 profit.

A fee of $100 per show is not outlandish. Many birthday party entertainers charge twice this amount. If you market yourself to a higher income group of customers, you can charge this much and more. In fact, if you are the dominant business, they will expect you to be more expensive than average and be willing to pay for it. Charging too little can actually hurt your business because many of these customers rate quality of the show with the cost. They can afford it and may pass you up for other more expensive performers to get the quality they feel they deserve.

There is an additional benefit you receive for each show you book. Each party is a marketing opportunity in itself that will bring additional bookings from guests and repeat business from satisfied parents. So even a 1 percent response with just 100 names can garner two, three, or more additional bookings. These spin-off bookings are more likely to happen with the higher income customers you are seeking.

Dentist: I'll have to charge you $100 for removing that tooth.
Patient: But you said it would be $25.
Dentist: Yes, but you yelled so much you scared off three other patients.

SALES LITERATURE
Appearance

Your sales literature is the material you send to your prospective customers to announce who your are and to convince them to use your service. It is important that you send material that looks like it came from a successful professional and not a starving performing artist. You must portray success and confidence. Remember, you are trying to become the predominant birthday party entertainer in your area, so you must look the part to achieve the reality.

The goal of your sales literature is to convince the potential customer to consider hiring you and to give you a call. Your telephone conversation and sales pitch will convince the caller you are the person she wants for her child's birthday party.

Writing and designing effective and professional sales materials are important. If you feel you need help, don't hesitate to employ the services of an advertising agency or marketing consultant. Agencies and consultants may charge $200-$800 or more, but the service they give will be worth far more than the fee. Invest your money wisely now and rewards will come—often abundantly.

Millions of people everywhere receive advertisements in their daily mail. A lot of it gets thrown away, but much of it is actually read. One way to attract a reader's attention and entice them to read your material is to use graphics— illustrations and designs. Entertainers are fun people, so show this in your sales literature. Use lots of color and graphics. This is where a graphic artist or advertising agency can be of great help to you. They know how to write and design effective ad literature. It is well worth the investment to have an experienced professional give you some help and not try to cut corners by doing it yourself. Often, self-designed sales literature looks and sounds amateurish. You don't want this—especially if you are trying to establish your business as the best in the area.

Sales Package

The material that comprises your direct mail package may consist of one or more of the following: sales letter, brochure, coupon, flyer.

If you use a formal sales letter, put it on your stationery with your letterhead. This letter would introduce you to the potential client. A flyer would have a graphic design and can accomplish the same goal. A brochure would be a more detailed ad piece much like the Birthday Party Planner described previously. The coupon could be a discount, free gift, or just an attention getter such as "coupon for free laughs for every guest."

You need to create several mailings, each one of them different. You may say the same stuff in all of them but use different graphics, headlines, etc. The first may contain a sales letter, brochure, and coupon. Follow-up mailings may just contain a flyer. Or you may just send flyers each time.

One idea I like to use is "Party Tip" flyers. Each mailing has a different party tip along with my sales information. The tips could be the construction and explanation of simple party games, theme party ideas (which of course would fit your performing character nicely), foods and treats for parties (snow cones, novelty cookies, cakes, caramel corn, fun drinks, etc.), decorating ideas (cake decorating, wall hangings, etc.), or anything a parent might find useful for a children's party. You can find many ideas in a number of books on parties, entertaining, and cooking. If the information is of value, the flyer will be kept for future reference, along with your sales pitch. Because the information is perceived as having some value, your sales message is more readily received and remembered. Make sure you use illustrations. You should include a drawing or photo of your performing character somewhere in your sales literature. This helps to show yourself as a professional entertainer and helps potential customers get to know you. Visual impact is important.

Credentials

In your sales literature you want to convince the customer that you are fun, entertaining, and the best person

ROSCO THE CLOWN
The Best in Birthday Party Entertainment
(303) 555-1234

Hello!

My name is Rosco the Clown. You may have heard of me because I've performed for hundreds of kids all over town doing comedy magic and making balloon animals. I may have been the featured attraction at a birthdy party in your neighborhood recently. If you have a birthday coming up in your family give me a call, I would love to come and show you why Rosco the Clown is known one of the most popular children's entertainers in the city. My schedule fills up quickly so call now.

Sincerely,

Rosco

A simple postcard can be used to introduce yourself to area residents. A postcard is like a mini-flyer.

BIRTHDAY PARTY FUN WITH DR. DROPO

One of the best ways to make your child's birthday a fun-filled memory is to include Dr. Dropo's Birthday Party Package. Dr. Dropo, a professional magician, clown, juggler, and balloonologist will provide loads of humorous entertainment, fun-packed activities, party favors for each of the guests, and special recognition to the birthday child. Dr. Dropo will sweep the children away into a world of make-believe and laughter for a full 40 minutes while parents can relax, knowing the children are well taken care of.

ICE CREAM CLOWN

This a fun and easy party treat that parents and children can make together, well ahead of party time.

1 20-ounce package of Pillsbury's refrigerated chocolate-chip cookie dough.
3 cups any flavor ice cream.
6 sugar cones
Assorted candies—M&Ms, chocolate chips, Red Hots, string licorice.
Frosting, tinted in several colors. Decorating bag and tips (available at cake-decorating stores or grocery stores).

Freeze cookie dough one hour or longer. Heat oven to 350 degrees. Slice six half-inch thick slices from frozen cookie dough; place 2 inches apart on ungreased cookie sheet; bake 10-13 minutes. Cool 2 minutes; remove from cookie sheet and cool completely.

Place one rounded scoop of ice cream in center of each cookie. Press down, and place cone on top of each one. Freeze until firm. Remove from freezer and press candies into the ice cream to form a face. Using tinted frosting, make a collar around the ice cream and decorate the cone tip. Freeze until firm.

Yum
Yum

Dr. Dropo has delighted hundreds of children at birthday parties with his zany juggling, magic, and balloon animals. Call now to schedule Dr. Dropo for your next birthday party, 555-1234.

An example of a party tips flyer. When designing your flyers use a bold headline, picture of yourself, and other graphic designs. Give your qualifications or special skills. Customers don't always remember, even those who have seen you perform, so always mention your special qualities. The main portion of the flyer is the useful information, in this case it's the recipie for the ice cream clown. Always include a call for action at the end of the flyer.

they can have at their child's party. If they are going to pay you, they expect a professional. List everything you can that qualifies you as a professional. Some ideas include: special training (graduate of Ringling Bros., Barnum & Bailey Clown College), number of years experience, membership in professional associations (see appendix), special honors or awards received, news clippings or quotes from media sources about yourself, special accomplishments, special talents or skills, number of children entertained (e.g. ". . . has brought smiles and laughter to over 10,000 children"), and endorsements from past clients or officials (government, school, daycare, etc.).

As a beginner, your qualifications will be few but you can still list several items. Some general all-purpose qualifications or rather claims you might list are: the funniest magician in Chicago, the most enchanting puppeteer in Atlanta, or one of the country's funniest clowns. Expound on the quality of your show. If you have any

Story Theater

with
BARBARA SMITH

STORYTELLING, MUSIC, PUPPET THEATER,
SHADOW THEATER

For schools, libraries, homeschoolers, parties,
organizations, churches

Barbara Smith
P.O. Box 969
West Fork, AR 72774
(501) 839-8022

FEES
$100 for one 60 minute program
$80 for one 45 minute program
$60 for one 30 minute program
*Additional charge for mileage for places more
than fifty miles from Fayetteville, Arkansas*

BARBARA SMITH

Member of...

National Storytelling Association

Arkansas Travelers Storytelling Association

With background as...

Public School Teacher for Eight Years

Director of Children's Programs at Ozarks
Regional Library for Six Years

Storyteller at Workshops, Conferences, School
Programs, Festivals, and Private Organizations.

Comments from audiences:

Children...

"I love your stories and I love your puppets!"

"You're nice and funny. I wish you could
come to the library every day."

"I really like the wise man story."

"I liked the sounds of the music."

"Your stories were really interesting and very
funny."

Adults...

"The stories were entertaining and presented
in a unique way."

"The children in our classes enjoy all that you
do and you add to our curriculum."

"The shadow theater took the story to a new
dimension."

"You were one of the favorites at the
festival."

Barbara Smith's Story Theater

Arkansas children in Washington and Crawford counties sometimes
call Barbara Smith story lady, and sometimes they call her Mother
Goose. A few even call her Mrs. Smith. To quote a writer for the
Northwest Arkansas Times, she is "by any name, as creative."

Barbara performs live and lively story programs for children of all
ages and for adults. Although the children love her puppet skits,
puppet therter plays, and shadow theater presentation of stories, the
stories themselves are the foundation of her programs.

Barbara's story repertoire includes folk tales from many nations and
people; literary stories by some of the world's classic authors (e.g.
Kipling, Thurber, and Saki) and current children's authors; and
legends and sacred stories. She is especially fond of The Jack Tales
and The Grandfater Tales from the Appalachian Mountains and
humorous tales from Africa and British Isles.

Barbara is a musician and actress as well as a storyteller. She weaves
songs, accompanied by autoharp, recorder, or piano, into her
programs. She uses folk music from all over the world and classical
music to add drama and authentic flavor to her storytelling.

Bring the fun of Barbara Smith's Story Theater to your
next event. Call today, (501) 839-8022.

Example of both sides of a 3-fold brochure.

quotes from newspapers or past clients you can use those. Third party endorsements carry a lot of weight. Use them if you have them; if you don't have any, get some. Ask past clients for comments they would allow you to use. These comments can come from paying clients or free shows. Those who receive free shows are especially willing to provide you quotes because they will want to thank you for the show and providing a quote is an easy way to accomplish this. Obviously, the more prominent the person giving the quote, the stronger the influence it will have. If you can get the mayor, the police chief, or local athlete to give you a quotable endorsement, you have a very valuable sales aid.

Headline

One of the most important elements of your sales piece is the headline you use to catch the reader's attention. Make the heading big, bold, and enticing. Use a catchy phrase that fits your character. Examples are:

Make Your Child's Next Birthday Special
with Wanda the Wonderful Storyteller

Brighten Up Your Child's Next Birthday Party
with Wanda the Wonderful Storyteller

Experience the Thrill
of Wanda's Magical Wonderland

Short headlines are usually best because they are easier to read. Examples of short headlines include:

Fun For All
Birthday Party Fun
Traveling Magician
Unique Party Entertainment
The Laughs Never End
Unforgettable Spellbinding Fun
Try Something Different
Your Child Can Be the Star

Make the claim as the best in your specialty. Everyone wants the best—especially the customers you are trying to get, so tell them you are and prove it by becoming the predominant birthday party entertainer in your area.

Call to Action

You want readers to respond to your sales pitch by calling you up to schedule a party. Don't assume readers will be motivated to call, even if they are interested. Many who are interested will delay calling and eventually forget or lose your number. You want them to call you immediately. You need to be bold and make a direct request for the reader to respond by calling you now, not tomorrow, but today, while they are reading the ad, before they put it down and forget about it. This request should be made at the end of your sales pitch so that calling you is the next logical step to take.

Sales flyers that contain useful information are doubly good because they are more frequently kept rather than thrown away, and therefore the request to act is exposed to the customer more often and increases your chance of getting a call.

The following are samples of call to action lines:

"Call now to schedule Dr. Dropo for your next birthday Party, 555-0031"

"Don't delay, call today for a fun-filled party with Dr. Dropo, 555-0031"

"Dr. Dropo's schedule fills up fast, so call now to guarantee his availability for your next birthday party, 555-0031"

"Call now and ask about our birthday party special, 555-0031"

"Surprise your children with Chicago's classiest birthday party clown. Call now 5555-0031"

For more information about direct mail marketing and writing sales materials, I suggest reading some books on advertising or mail-order marketing. There are many popular books available on the subject. The appendix lists several good resources.

What do you call a man who was born in France, raised in South Africa, married in Mexico, and died in Japan?
Dead.

Why was Newton surprised when he was hit on the head by an apple?
He was sitting under a pear tree!

Why isn't your nose 12 inches long?
Then it would be a foot.

RESOURCES

ORGANIZATIONS

The following organizations provide newsletters to their members which carry informative articles on performing techniques, resources, marketing tips, educational opportunities, and other topics of interest to birthday party entertainers. Membership also provides opportunites to attend annual conventions, network with other entertainers, and qualify you for group insurance. It is well worth your time to join one or more of these associations to obtain the many benefits they offer.

Clowns of America International
P.O. Box 570
Lake Jackson, TX 77566

International Brotherhood Of Magicians
P.O. Box 89
Bluffton, OH 45817

National Association of Balloon Artists
P.O. Box 43472
Jacksonville, FL 32204

National Storytelling Association
P.O. Box 309
Jonesborough, TN 37659

North American Association of Ventriloquists
P.O. Box 420
Littleton, CO 80160

Puppeters of America
5 Cricklewood Path
Pasadena, CA 91107

Society of American Magicians
2812 Idaho
Granite City, IL 62040

World Clown Association
P.O. Box 1413
Corona, CA 91718

RECOMMENDED READING

The following resources will provide you with a great deal of information. These books are available at bookstores, mail order catalogs, magic and novelty shops, and libraries. Your local libray is an excellent resource. Here you will find many of the books listed below as well as numerous others. Some excellent resources for birthday party businesses, however, will not be found in your local library, but may be available at your local magic shop or a through a mail order dealer who specializes in family entertainment and children's books.

Balloons
Balloon Sculpting: A Fun and Easy Guide to Making Balloon Animals, Toys, and Games by Bruce Fife;
  Piccadilly Books.
Comedy Magic with Balloons by Norm Barnhart;
  Magical Fun Productions.

Dewey's Amusing Rubber Antics by Ralph Dewey; Dewey's Good News Balloons.

Dewey's Balloon and Clown Notebook by Ralph Dewey; Dewey's Good News Balloons.

Dewey's Bubble Buddies by Ralph Dewey; Dewey's Good News Balloons.

Dewey's Mammoth Multiple Balloons by Ralph Dewey; Dewey's Good News Balloons.

Dewey's Rubber Rascals by Ralph Dewey; Dewey's Good News Balloons.

Dewey's Zany Balloons by Ralph Dewey; Dewey's Good News Balloons.

Entertaing with Balloons by Norm Barnhart; Magical Fun Productions.

Catering

Catering Like a Pro: From Planning to Profit, by Francine Halvorsen; Wiley.

The Complete Caterer: A Practical Guide to the Craft and Business of Catering, by Elizabeth Lawrence; Doubleday.

How to Mangae a Successful Catering Business, by Manfred Ketterer; Van Nostrand Reinhold.

Catering Handbook, by Edith and Hal Weiss; Van Nostrand Reinhold.

Successful Catering, by Bernard Splaver; Van Nostrand Reinhold.

Cash from Your Kitchen, by Catherine Harris; Holt, Rinehart and Winston.

Cater from Your Kitchen: Income from Your Own Home Business, by Marjorie P Blanchard; Bobbs-Merrill Co.

Clowning

Clown Act Omnibus by Wes McVicar; Meriwether Publishing.

Clown Skits for Everyone by Happy Jack Feder; Meriwether Publishing.

Creative Clowning by Bruce Fife, et al.; Piccadilly Books.

Dewey's Clown Gags and Giggles by Ralph Dewey; Dewey's Good News Balloons.

Dewey's Klown Komedy by Ralph Dewey; Dewey's Good News Balloons.

It's Not What You Do But How You Do It! by Don Sminkey; Clown Capers.

Mime Time by Happy Jack Feder; Meriwether Publishing.

Strutter's Complete Guide to Clown Makeup by Jim Roberts; Piccadilly Books.

Face Painting

Face Painting, by the editors of Klutz Press; Klutz Press.

Face Painting, Thomasina Smith; Anness Pub.

Face Painting: Art for Children, by Gill Dickenson; Book Sales Inc.

Make-A-Face, by Sharon McKay and Jane Stevenson; Andrews & McMeel.

Making Faces by Jacqueline Russon; Sterling Publishing.

The Most Excellent Book of Face Painting, by Margaret Lincoln; Millbrook Press.

Put On A Happy Face, by Marcela Murad; Mama Clown Enterprises.

Snazaroo Zoo: Great Faces & Easy Costumes to Bring Out the Animal in You, by Snazaroo Staff; Chilton.

Wild Faces, by Snazaroo Staff; Kingfisher.

Magic

Big Laughs for Little People by Samuel Patrick Smith; SPS Publications.

Bringing Home the Laughs by David Ginn; Scarlett Green.

Children Laugh Louder by David Ginn; Scarlett Green.

Kidbiz by David Ginn; Scarlett Green.

Kiddie Patter and Little Feats: Entertaining Preschoolers with Magic and Funny Stuff by Samuel Patrick Smith; SPS Publications.

Kid Stuff, Vols. 1, 2, 3, 4, 5, 6, by Frances Marshal; Magic, Inc.

Life On the Living Room Circuit by Tom and Merianne Myers; T. Myers Magic.

Professional Magic for Children by David Ginn; Scarlett Green.

Showmanship for Magicians by Dariel Fitzkee; Lee Jacobs.

Marketing/Business

Building Your Mailing Lists by Paul Crown; Oceana Publications.

The Dartnell Direct Mail and Mail-Order Handbook by Richard S. Hodgson; Dartnell Corporation.

Getting Publicity: A Do-it-Yourself Guide for Small Business and Non-Profit Groups, by Tana Fletcher; Self-Counsel Press.

Homemade Money: How to Select, Start, Manage, Market and Multiply the Profits of A Business at Home by Barbara Brabec; Better Way Books.

How Mail-Order Fortunes Are Made by Alfred Stern; Arco Publishing Company.

How to Start and Operate a Mail-Order Business by Julian L. Simon; McGraw-Hill.

How to Become Financially Successful by Owning Your Own Business by Albert J. Lowry; Simon and Schuster.

How to Write A Good Advertisement by Victor O. Schwab; Wilshire Book Co.

Mail-Order Selling by Irving Burstiner; Prentice-Hall.

Small-Time Operator by Bernard Kamoroff; Bell Springs Publishing.

Writing Effective News Releases: How to Get Free Publicity for Yourself, Your Business, or Your Organization, by Catherine V. McIntyre; Piccadilly Books.

Party Games and Activities

Charades & Party Games, by Michael Johnstone; Ward Lock Ltd.

Clap Your Hands: Finger Rhymes, by Sarah Hayes; Lothrop, Lee and Shepard.

Creative Fingerplays and Action Rhymes, by Jeff Defty; Oryx Press.

Finger Frolics: Fingerplays for Young Children, by Liz Cromwell, et al.; Gryhon House.

Finger Rhymes, by Marc Tolon Brown; E.P. Dutton.

Games for the Very Young, by Elizabeth Matterson; American Heritage Press.

Games Galore for Children's Parties and More by Shari Ann Pence; Funcastle Publications.

Great Games for Great Parties, by Andrea Campbell; Sterling Publishng Co.

Great Theme Parties for Children, by Irene N. Watts; Sterling Publishing Co.

Hand Rhymes, by Marc Brown; E.P. Duton.

Hit of the Party: The Complete Planner for Children's Theme Birthday Parties, by Amy Vangsgard; Cool Hand Communications.

More Games to Play with Toddlers, by Jackie Silberg; Gryphon House.

Musical Games for Children of All Ages by Esther L. Nelson; Sterling Publishing Co.

1 • 2 • 3 Games: No-Lose Group Games for Young Children by Jean Warren; Warren Publishing House.

Playfair: Everybody's Guide to Noncompetitive Play, by Matt Weinstein; Impact publishers

Stamp Your Feet: Action Rhymes by Sarah Hayes; Lothrop, Lee and Shepard.

Twiddling Your Thumbs, by Wendy Cope; Faber and Faber.

The World's Best Party Games, by Sheila Anne Barry; Sterling Publishing Co.

Puppetry

Be A Puppet Showman, by Remo Fufano; The Century Co.

The Complete Book of Puppets and Puppeteering by Robert Ten Eyck Hanford; Sterling Publishing Co.

Finger Puppets: Easy to Make, Fun to Use, by Laura Ross; Lothrop, Lee and Shepard.

Finger Puppets and Finger Plays, by Margaret Jean Oldfield; Creative Storytime Press.

Hand Puppets: How to Make and Use Them, by Dorothy Richter; by Frederick Fell.

Making Puppets Come Alive, by Larry Engler and Carol Fijan; David & Charles.

Mitt Magic: Fingerplays for Finger Puppets, by Lynda Roberts; Gryphon House.

Let Your Fingers Do the Talking, by Kathy Overholser; T.S. Denison.

Puppet Plays and Puppet-Making by Burton and Rita Marks; Plays, Inc.

Puppets and Puppetry, by Cyril W. Beaumont; Studio Publications.

Ventriloquism Made Easy by Paul Stadelman and Bruce Fife; Piccadilly Books.

Storytelling

The Art of the Story-Teller, by Marie L. Shedlock; Dover Publications.

Children's Literature Through Storytelling and Drama, by Nancy Briggs and Joseph Wagner; William C Brown Co.

Creative Storytelling: Choosing, Inventing, and Sharing Tales for Children, by Jack Maguire; McGraw-Hill.

Handbook for Storytellers, by Caroline Bauer; American Library Association.

Storytelling: Art and Technique, by Augusta Baker and Ellin Greene; Bowker.

Storytelling: Process and Practice, by Norma Livo and Sandra Rietz; Libraries Unlimited.

Storytelling Step by Step, by Marsh Cassady; Resource Publications.

Storytelling Tips: How to Love, Learn, and Relate A Story, by Duane Hutchinson; Foundation Books.

The Storytime Sourcebook, by Carolyn N. Cullum; Neal-Schuman Publishers.

For a catalog containing several of these and other books write and ask for our free variety arts book catalog. Piccadilly Books, P.O. Box 25203, Colorado Springs, CO 80936.

INDEX